SOUND AND MUSIC FOR THE THEATRE

The Art and Technique of Design

THIRD EDITION

Sound and Music for the Theatre

The Art and Technique of Design

THIRD EDITION

Deene Kaye and James LeBrecht

AMSTERDAM • BOSTON • HEIDELBERG • LONDON
NEW YORK • OXFORD • PARIS • SAN DIEGO
SAN FRANCISCO • SINGAPORE • SYDNEY • TOKYO

ELSEVIER

Focal Press is an imprint of Elsevier

Focal
Press

Focal Press is an imprint of Elsevier
30 Corporate Drive, Suite 400, Burlington, MA 01803, USA
Linacre House, Jordan Hill, Oxford OX2 8DP, UK

Permissions may be sought directly from Elsevier's Science & Technology Rights Department in Oxford, UK: phone: (+44) 1865 843830, fax: (+44) 1865 853333, E-mail: permissions@elsevier.com. You may also complete your request on-line via the Elsevier homepage (http://elsevier.com), by selecting "Support & Contact" then "Copyright and Permission" and then "Obtaining Permissions."

Library of Congress Cataloging-in-Publication Data
Kaye, Deena.
   Sound and music for the theatre : the art & technique of design/Deena Kaye, James LeBrecht.—3rd ed.
       p. cm.
   ISBN 978-0-240-81011-9
   1. Theaters--Sound effects. 2. Music in the theater. I. LeBrecht—James. II. Title.
   PN2091.S6K3 2009
   792.02'4—dc22

                                                                                          2008050055

British Library Cataloguing-in-Publication Data
A catalogue record for this book is available from the British Library.

ISBN: 978-0-240-81011-9

For information on all Focal Press publications
visit our website at www.elsevierdirect.com

09 10 11   5 4 3 2 1

Printed in the United States of America

For my muses—Craig and Miles
—DK

For Sara, my family and friends
—JL

Contents

Foreword by Peter Sellars   viii

Preface to the First Edition   x

Preface to the Second Edition   xii

Preface to the Third Edition   xiii

Introduction to the First and Second Edition by Richard Peaslee   xv

Introduction to the Third Edition by Mark Lamos   xvii

Acknowledgments   xix

The Art of Looking with the Ear by Tazewell Thompson   xxi

1. The Evolution of Sound Design   1
2. The Foundation of Sound Design   12
3. Developing the Concept and Design   40
4. Research, Resources, and Selection   51
5. The Sound Plot   65
6. Working with the Theatre Company   80
7. Preparing to Build the Cues   95
8. Recording, Editing, and Refining Cues   110
9. Rehearsals   118
10. Running the Show   141
11. Approaches and Techniques   167

Feedback: A Directors' and Playwrights' Forum   186

More Feedback: A Sound Designers' and Composers' Forum   223

No More Feedback: A Sound Reinforcement Forum   289

Glossary   307

Index   313

Please visit our Facebook group: Sound and Music for the Theatre

Foreword

We can shut our eyes, but we can still hear. We can shut our ears, but sound is still echoing inside our skulls. We exist in a universe of sound. In the beginning was the Word, and before the Word was written, it was spoken, and its sound keeps speaking in our minds and our hearts, and we can't stop listening.

There are many voices. Mostly we live inside a cacophony, a mélange of whispers and shouts, of traffic congestion and bird song, appliance hum, exhaust fans, television, radio, alarm sirens, and angelic voices speaking softly in our inner ear.

In tandem with the related sense of smell, hearing is that sense that is most deeply associated with memory. Sound evokes place, not space. That is to say, sound is where we locate ourselves, not physically, but mentally and spiritually. Sound exists inside our heads. It is our greatest experience of intimacy. It transports us, it invades us.

When we speak of atmosphere—a productive atmosphere, a peaceful atmosphere—again and again, it turns out that our emotional well-being is attached to a quality of sound. Is it an accident that our sense of balance is located in our ears?

Sound speaks to us of immaterial things: we can't touch it and we can't describe it in words. Sound evokes that part of our lives and that part of our experience that cannot be controlled by or reduced to verbal explanations. Sound evokes that part of our lives that is intuitive, that part of ourselves that can never be compromised, a world of pure feeling, being, and unmediated experience.

Sound is something that we take personally. In recent years, the science of sound has developed a new field called, appropriately enough, psychoacoustics, which operates within the related field of psychophysics. Why does one person speak loudly and another speak softly? We are all differently calibrated. These are not just different levels of experience, different intensities of being. These are not just physical facts; they are character traits that have evolved across lifetimes of moral choices and environmental influences. The sound that we produce, and our responses to the sound around us, operate in a complex equilibrium determined by the ongoing nature of contrast in our lives and what we happen to be going through that day.

Very late in our day, the technology has become available to allow sound to begin to occupy the place in theatre arts that it occupies in our lives. This technology is still evolving, and as it does, the nature of theatre itself will be transformed. This revolution is comparable to the revolution in lighting that transformed theatre in the late-nineteenth century. We are in a position to completely reorient the relationship between performer and audience, to transform a theatrical space, to create distance or sudden proximity, to create a densely populated zone or an endless arid expanse. We are in a position to evoke simultaneous layers of experience: flashbacks, premonitions, visitations, inner voices, the mind wandering or becoming suddenly, unbearably concentrated.

We are beyond the era of sound "effects." Sound is no longer an effect, an extra, a *garni* supplied from time to time to mask a scene change or ease a transition. We are beyond the era of door buzzers and thunderclaps. Or rather, door buzzers and thunderclaps are no longer isolated effects, but part of a total program of sound that speaks to theatre as ontology. Sound is the holistic process and program that binds our multifarious experience of the world. Sound is our own inner continuity track. It is also our primary outward gesture to the world, our first and best chance to communicate with others, to become part of a larger rhythm.

I like to think that the microphone has come to occupy the place in contemporary theatre that the mask occupied in the theatre of ancient Greece. It is a device that creates both intimacy and distance, it conceals and it projects, it acts as a shield and as a medium of relentless exposure. The chosen instrument of politicians and newscasters, it creates power. It fills a vacuum while creating another vacuum: that is to say, it dominates physical and emotional space while at the same time creating a certain inevitable hollowness.

Our tragedy is accompanied by new technology; so, too, will be our salvation. Our last judgment will take place to a different set of trumpets and drums. Like light, sound is frequently used in world religions as a metaphor for salvation. It is time for artists working in sound and in light not to be second-class citizens in the theatre, not to be afterthoughts, not to be utilitarian drudges, but to assume that place of inspiration and centrality that their medium demands. Sound and light are not metaphors for salvation—they are first steps on the pathway to salvation itself, the first glimmers, the first inklings of a new world. The day of judgment comes hourly for each of us. The question for the next generation of theatre artists will be: When that moment comes—as the visible world melts away—what will that trumpet *sound* like?

Peter Sellars
March 1992

ix

Preface to the First Edition

At our first meeting in 1984, both of us felt that we had finally met someone who spoke the same language of sound and music for the stage. Deena was approaching theatre with strengths as a musician, musical director, and composer; Jim had expertise in operating, engineering, and producing the designs and compositions. Although each of us came to the field from different disciplines, we were amazed to find we had so many experiences in common. Our artistic values and attitudes were very similar. Collaborating on our first show (*A Touch of the Poet* at the Berkeley Repertory Theatre), we lamented that there was no resource that offered an aesthetic and practical approach to designing sound and music for the stage. Our collaboration on this book seemed a natural way to remedy this situation.

Collectively, we had much experience in producing effects, training sound operators, and managing limited budgets. We were well-versed in the practical elements needed to design sound for the stage. What we thought was needed was not yet another book about the technical aspects of sound—good books along those lines already existed—but rather a book that would explore the artistic intents, needs, and skills of the sound designer.

This book is for designers who desire both a greater knowledge about the aesthetics of their work as well as a practical approach to the design process. We hope to motivate aspiring designers to new dimensions of their creativity. *Sound and Music for the Theatre* is also for composers who wish to incorporate their expertise and artistry into stage productions; for sound operators and technicians who are asked to be designers; and for community theatres that wish to elevate the quality of their productions by including this long-ignored textural element. Directors or sound technicians looking for methods of organizing and applying sound to a production may also find our experiences useful. However, we are not presenting detailed explanations of electronics or specifics on scoring or composing. We also do not focus on musicals, and for this reason, do not explore sound reinforcement in detail.

The reality of working in the theatre is that one production may make many resources available to the sound designer, while another may provide few or none. Consequently, we have presented ways of working from the most rudimentary, bare-bones situations to the most complex, sophisticated ones. Either way, you'll find that there are techniques to use in any situation to maintain a high level of artistry and assure the integrity of your work.

Ultimately, the stature of the sound designer will be acknowledged to a greater extent by directors, producers, and general managers. Budgetary considerations will not always be an obstacle. We hope that sound design in theatre will continue to develop as an accepted and essential design element.

Deena Kaye
James LeBrecht
April 1992

xi

Preface to the Second Edition

There have been many changes in the world of theatre sound since the publication of *Sound and Music for the Theatre: The Art and Technique of Design*—the most important being the evolution of the use of digital technology and the decline of analogue playback devices. Once out of reach to most sound designers because of cost, MiniDisc and CD players are now commonplace in many theatres. An experience Deena had speaks to the rapid changes that have occurred in the tools we use to produce and perform our work.

In May of 1998, Deena participated in a multicultural event for her son's elementary school in New York City. At the front of the auditorium there was a great deal of confusion prior to one of the school's presentations. The presenters had informed the school that the music that they would be dancing to was on a record, but no one, it seemed had made a record player available for the performance. While teachers and staff scurried to locate a turntable, the announcer stalled for time in front of the increasingly restless 500 children ranging from kindergarten through fifth grade. "So today, children, we will be seeing a dance performed to music that is being played on a record player! How many of you have ever *heard* of a *record player*?!"

Deena was amazed! Less than one-third of the audience raised their hands. Of course, these children were familiar with the latest in computer technology and, in their formative years, will witness the advent of technological advances of such sophistication to rival only the coming of television. Surely some of them had parents (or grandparents?) at home who furtively held on to all their vinyl LPs. But we imagine that by the year 2010, very few children will even know what a cassette is. Or was.

These technological changes and feedback we have received from our readers prompted us to look at our book with fresh eyes. With this edition, we not only bring digital technology into the discussion, but we also invited other voices to share their experiences as working sound designers and composers. We hope to bring our readers new information to fast-forward their sense of sound into the 21st century.

Deena Kaye
James LeBrecht
July 1999

Preface to the Third Edition

When we wrote the updates for the second edition of this book, we thought the technology that sound designers and composers were using had really taken a leap forward since the first edition. If we could have looked ten years into the future, we would have been dumbstruck! For this third edition, we assume that many people will be using some sort of computerized playback system for their cues. However, we'll still give thought to the folks using CD players and simple mixers in our discussions about using technology. We will *also* assume that the once-ubiquitous reel-to-reel tape deck has found its final resting place next to the dodo.

As we reviewed the last edition in an effort to update the text, it's been inspiring to see that the technology available to designers and composers has evolved so greatly. Equally as inspiring is how the art of sound and music for the theatre has received greater recognition and has found its way into so many new frontiers. We are also thrilled that since the last edition, there are now two Tony Awards presented for sound design and that sound design programs are being offered at many colleges and universities.

We consider ourselves very fortunate that in the many years since we first began this exploration of the aesthetic of sound and music in the theatrical world, our colleagues have honored us with their participation in our forums. By offering their experiences and wisdom, our colleagues have given our readers insights that would have been available to them only via a face-to-face meeting. However, sorely lacking from our book and forums was any discussion on sound reinforcement. Our strong desire to acknowledge sound reinforcement designers led us to add a third forum to our book: *No More Feedback: A Sound Reinforcement Forum*. By no means do we consider our coverage to be comprehensive, but perhaps this new section will serve as an interesting basic discussion of this discipline by some of the foremost sound designers currently working in reinforcement.

We welcome the remarkably talented and astute David Budries to our latest literary effort. He has generously and graciously contributed his expert knowledge and experience to this edition.

We hope that our readers find this edition, with its many updates, to be useful and motivating. We are humbled to think that our book has survived close to two decades. If you listen carefully, you can hear us applauding the innovative sound designers and composers entering this still burgeoning and fascinating field.

Deena Kaye
James LeBrecht
December 2009

Introduction to the First and Second Edition

A contemporary definition of music I've always liked is "organized noise." It's often hard to say where one element ends and the other begins, hence such new terms as "sound score" and "soundscape." In this new ball game of hi-tech and hi-fi sound systems, the sound designer—whether working on a play with incidental music and effects on tape or on a full-blown Broadway musical—has become a critical player in the theatre world.

The sound designer has a tremendously creative role to play in any production. The old days of a couple of mono tape decks and two or three speakers are long gone. Audiences now used to rock concerts, discotheques, multitrack cinema sound, and their own stereo systems are too sophisticated to tolerate low-tech sound in the theatre. Directors' ears have also become more acute, and directors will no longer settle for mere "library" effects pulled off the shelf and played on a public address-type system. As for composers, we should be the most demanding of all, but writing the music usually occupies most of our time, leaving little to devote to sound. Also, our technological knowledge may be very limited: sound systems can be real "monsters" these days, with wireless radio microphones for the actors, orchestra amplification, and taped effects all required. Good sound designers will know their system and its capabilities inside out, since part of their task may have been its design.

A large part of the sound designer's creative effort is selecting effects and choosing how they will be played into the house. Take a simple cue like thunder: it can be a muddy rumble or it can be a sharp series of cracks that lift you out of your seat. Good sound designers won't merely dub thunder off an old tape or sound effects record. They may well have their own libraries of material they've recorded themselves—in this case, an actual storm. At least they'll make sure that what they're using is carefully edited and equalized for maximum effect. The sound can then be enhanced greatly by the designer's choice of speakers and by the use of stereo, quad, or panning effects.

Sound designers must be far more than technicians—they should understand how sounds work on the psyche, and not be overly literal. A good painter does not often achieve maximum effect with photorealism. Similarly, a precisely accurate recording of, say, street sounds may not be nearly as convincing as one that's doctored to conform to the reality of perception. Our brains tune out a great deal of sound. It often floats in and out of our consciousness, and a certain sound like a car horn may become obsessive and dominate all others, even to the point of distortion. With this in mind, even after the sound designer has created an effect, where to begin a cue, where to end it, levels, ups and downs, and speaker assignment are all still important choices for him to make.

Innumerable decisions on innumerable cues must be made along the way to opening night. Directors can oversee, but they often won't have the time or the expertise to get exactly what they want. In the case of straight plays, there may be no composer at all, but much existing music and many effects.

The role of sound designer has rapidly come of age, now ranking equal with those of set, costume, and lighting designers. It's fortunate indeed that Deena Kaye and James LeBrecht have given us this excellent, informative new book on the subject.

Richard Peaslee
February 1992

Introduction to the Third Edition

Sound design. The very words sound odd. Who designs sound? And why would you need to? Orators from the past apparently designed it in the way they spoke, or listeners were far keener than they are today: Lincoln delivered the Gettysburg Address to 9000 people. Without a microphone. Outdoors. Long before that there was Epidaurus. Thousands of spectator-listeners listening to, occasionally, whispers from the masked actors. Catharsis ensued, by all accounts.

What has changed? In terms of listening, in terms of hearing—almost everything. We hear differently now. And the sound designer helps us hear the insides of a play, from the way a door is opened offstage to the breeze we hear outside an onstage window. The sound designer focuses our ears on a moment or a place, assisting the rest of the design team. For instance, the set looks like an apartment. The sound designer can let us know if the apartment is in a city; if there are noisy neighbors upstairs or in the hallway; if something is cooking on the stove; or if a bird is singing in its cage. But the design of those rather mundane sounds can key us into the way the playwright and the director want the play to begin psychologically.

We might have a scene set in the outdoors. If we are after a foreboding feel, what sort of birds should we hear? Sparrows? Songbirds? Or... crows? And if it's twittering birds we're after, how can the designer make the audience know that those birds are not stuck in the rafters of the playhouse, but rather in the aural design of the play itself?

We need sound design to focus the ears of the watchers just as acutely as the lighting design focuses their eyes. We need it to enhance not only the volume of a spoken line, but also the sounds around the drama and inside it. Sound design can build suspense, can focus a spoken moment, and can direct the ear to listen with more care. Film has been in the forefront of this technology, and in the last three decades, sound design has entered the live theater with exciting results and some dazzling technology. So now the entire enterprise of presenting and making theater is enriched—indeed enhanced by the subtle psychology that the sound designer invests into the whole matrix of the final grand design of a production. Now sound designers collaborate with the visual designers, and they are also one-on-one with the sound that comes from the actors. Sound design interacts with every single aspect of a production.

The best sound designers I've worked with bring me in touch with whatever show I'm working on in a whole new way; they bring another perspective to my work and literally show me ideas through sound. Ideas I was either unconscious of or that I didn't possess before discussions. Each designer illuminates the play, and the finest collaborators understand in how many infinite ways their contributions intersect and interact. Sound and light work together all through a performance, whether it is something as simple as the music playing as a curtain is going up or as complicated as a wood near Athens infested with fairies on a midsummer's night.

Sound design is one of the richest tools at our disposal for making the piece say what we want it to, both literally and psychologically. From the choice of music to collaboration with a composer, from the sounds that come from the actors to the sounds created to give power and meaning to the play's environment, both its spiritual as well as its geographical one, everything is now impacted, indeed enhanced in all senses, by sound design. It is now, thanks to the work of many, an art form.

I am pleased to introduce you to this new edition of a book that has been used for many years to enlighten sound designers, composers, and directors to the world that I embrace so heartily. Thank you, Deena and James!

Mark Lamos
November 2008

Acknowledgments

We continue to be deeply indebted to Craig Purinton for his indefatigable devotion and tenacious encouragement and to Bill Baynes for his keen and caring editorial input on the first edition. We cherish the memory of Henrietta Yusem, who generously shared her years of experience with us.

We acknowledge the friends, colleagues, mentors, and occasional muses who have shepherded our professional souls. Jim nods to Kimberly Webb, Meryl Shaw, Amarante Lucero, Fred Adams, Deb Dryden, Paul Dixon, Donavan Marley, Des McAnuff, John and Helen Meyer, Tony Howarth, Ken Denison, Carey Perloff, all of the wonderful people who he's worked with at the Berkeley Repertory Theater, and to the memories of Ellen Rush, Dan Dryden, and especially Michael W. Leibert.

Deena acknowledges Phil Lee and Jeff Bush for the safe haven of Full House Productions; directors Tazewell Thompson, Roger Danforth, Richard Termine, and Ron Daley for their creative playgrounds most particularly Doug Kaye the entire population of "Quinnland" David Gaines and Kiki, Jack Scott, and my many students whom I learn from every day, with my special thanks for having tracked my progress and cheered me on throughout this process. This edition is a tribute to the memories of my beloved mother Aïda Kaye, Raymond Marciniak, Frank Wittow, Carl Williams, and Colette Bergé. I am especially grateful to my remarkably talented son, Miles Purinton, who for the past 19 years has shown me how to hear more keenly and creatively.

David acknowledges the incredible patience and support of my family, Karen, Kate, and Meghan and the countless opportunities to develop as a person and designer that were provided by Marvin Ravikoff, Mark Lamos, Mel Marvin, Irene Lewis, Richard Hamburger, Bronnislaw Sammler, my students, Athol Fugard, José Rivera, and all the other playwrights who have provided me with the medium to further explore the human condition.

We appreciate all our kind contributors for their interests, insights, and support, most notably Charles Coes, Eric Dachs, Linda Kalin, Dennis Parichy, April Rodriguez, David Ross for his expert legal advice, and special recognition of Erik Zyman Carrasco for his art and techniques of linguistics. Thank you to Richard Barber for your counsel, and a tip of the hat to Joe Payne, Nick Strong, and Keith Heffner, the technical reviewers who shared their knowledge with us. Their insights from having used our book and reviewed the updates for this edition gave us terrific guidelines.

Our collective gratitude goes out to the amazing staff at Focal Press, a truly wonderful publishing house that unconditionally supports its authors. Lauren Lavery and Tina Adoniou helped make our second edition a reality. And, finally, we offer special thanks to Cara Anderson, Danielle Monroe, Andre Cuello and Diane Heppner who patiently and lovingly helped birth our third edition.

xx

THE ART OF LOOKING WITH THE EAR

The sound designer enters
crawls on all fours from the canyon, the cave, emerges from the shadows
from beyond the back of the house, from the deep background.
She raises her head. She rises. Stands on steady legs. She enters the light.
Outstretched arms have long cleared a central place at the welcoming (tech) table.

He prepares to play a sample of his wares: not from storage or shelves or warehouses

but from a special calling within himself.

Their inner inventory, an eternal work in progress:

the sound of porcelain shattering / door slams, add echoes / bones cracking /
clanging, rattling of old steam radiators / explosion of burst balloons / cannon blasts /
champagne exploding /
rice in a can/pebbles in a can / piñatas bursting / rain beating against a canvas beach
umbrella /
rumble under the floorboards, support with drone / approaching rumble of thunder, on
reverb /
rivets pounded in steel / toad ribbets / the labored breathing of a dying dog /
Marley's clanking chains / creaking of hinges / squeaking rusty pulleys / deep in coal
mines, canaries carol /
a leaden wrecking ball smashing, shattering, demolishing condemned tenements, build
slowly /
a foghorn (like a tuba) bellowing a distress signal / clamorous jackhammers dive into
concrete pavements /
snores like buzz saws / an orchestra tuning / anvils beaten with hammers / crackling fires
snapping dried trees and twigs /
knocks, amplified, more! up a level! more! add broadswords to the knocking! increase!:
"Wake Duncan with thy knocking!" /
an amusement park fun house: bashing bumper cars; piping whistles of a deranged
calliope; bombardment of laughter; screams and cheers and shouts—create pandemonium /

fly buzzes / caged-crazed, shrieking chimpanzees, add maniacal monkeys / raucous
cawing of crows / bleating sheep /
steam train exhaust hisses / wailing cries of cats in heat, layer with snarling cats /
twittering birds chattering wildly /
in the next room: lovers groans & weeping / "tinkling piano in the next apartment"/
roman candles fizzing /
stamping heels of flamenco beats, overlap and mix with rattles and maracas / mirrors
shattering /

scratched long-playing records repeatedly playing the scratched groove, distort further /
horse-drawn carriages over cobblestones / horse-harness sleigh bells, muted / galloping
horses' hoof beats, make thunderous /
clattering of combat-steel-plated shields against shields, decibel raised / fade-out
mournful tolling bells; fade-in joyous jangling bells /

whining violins / whispering conspirators / whimpering wailing babies / distant military
band (Russian & Chekhovian) drums, marching, singing /
restless humid night: crickets or cicadas? /

clocks ticking / birdsongs / birdcalls / catcalls / gurgling pigeons / babbling cauldrons /
sudden sobs / barks / honks / smacks / screams / screeches / sirens / discordant tones /
arpeggios / diminuendos / refrain / slams / neighing / octaves / gushing hydrants and
squealing children.

All this created from observation, imagination, passion.
Sounds that startle, lull, soothe, shock, jolt, astonish.
The audience: one gigantic communal ear, their senses shaken, expanded, extended
(never the same)
evoking: gasps, rapid heartbeats, perspiration, held breaths, hair rising.

Now blast all doors of the audio / visual department!
Smash to smithereens the reel-to-reel Wollensak tape deck,
the rusting razor blades, the splicing tape,
Bury deep in a time capsule.

The sound designer has learned the art of looking with the ear, eyes like tuning forks.
Though the ears are pasted to headsets, the ears are alert, pointed upwards like a cat,
their eardrums vibrate, enlarging, enfolding, conjuring, capturing,
acute to the limitless possibilities on which the curtain has risen.
The worksheet sketched out, plotted.

A lifetime of learning to communicate to the core of listeners,
to the heart of the ear. Confident and attentive to the sounds of silence.

The house lights dim, curtain! Stand by sound cue number one. Sound cue one, go!
And there it is: polished, specific, clarified, captured, diamond-needle sharp, rough,
elegant, transcendent.
The sound designer: alchemist, magician, restless explorer, recorder of the universe, ...
Praise!

Tazewell Thompson
December, 2008

The Evolution of Sound Design

"The trouble with life is that, unlike movies, it doesn't have background music. We never know how we're supposed to feel."

—*Lewis Gardner, 1985*

In a play, not a single word is arbitrary. The director and the actors in a production attribute a value and a reason to every action and every utterance. The set is carefully designed to work within the physical requirements of the script, as well as the specific needs of a particular production. Lights are integrated into the mood of the piece to create a specific atmosphere. To ensure their continuity with the rest of the production, costumes are not created until the director approves the renderings.

Sound design works the same way. The silences—as well as the dog barks and musical underscoring—are determined by specific aesthetic decisions. Meaning and purpose are attached to everything you do as a sound designer. Your talks and listening sessions with the director are your ground plan. Your scratch recordings are your rehearsal props. And your choices for underscoring and ambiance are the "sound scenery" within which the production moves.

As a sound designer, you may encounter the perplexed looks of others as they wonder what exactly sound design is. Tell them that sound design is the creative and technical process resulting in the complete aural environment for live theatre—just like the music and sound accompanying film.

Because sound is among the newest of the theatrical design fields, most audiences are unaware of it as a designed component of a production. Many producers and directors are embracing the wide range of possibilities that sound design can offer. They now readily incorporate the new vocabulary used in the field of sound design when approaching productions.

Most people working in the theatre tend to confuse the duties of a sound designer with those of a recording engineer, a sound supervisor, an audio master, a sound technician, production sound mixer, or a sound operator. It can be confusing because titles and job descriptions in the audio industry vary depending on which medium is being discussed. Within the world of dramatic and musical theatre productions, the job of a recording engineer is to run recording sessions and possibly help manufacture the effects and music cues. A sound supervisor or an audio master oversees the day-to-day operations of a theatre's sound department. A sound engineer (often referred to as an A1) is usually a staff member who implements the tasks set forth by the sound supervisor. A sound technician, or A2, is a crew member who helps with the load-in and installation of the sound equipment, and who may also serve as the sound operator, who runs sound during performances. In some venues, the A2 is an intern. These very necessary positions implement the work of the designer or composer

Be aware that many theatres do not have this kind of full staffing. At times, one person will take on the responsibility for all the jobs. Some theatres will provide a variation of these positions shared between two staff members. At other theatres, you might find that you'll have no help at all. To make your design happen under these conditions, you'll have to be the engineer, installer, and possibly even the operator. Luckily, this is not the case in too many places. Whatever your other duties may be, your primary responsibility as the sound designer is to make the artistic decisions that form the basis for the aural atmosphere of the entire production.

> " 'Art'. . . is being exact about things that do not seem to matter at all."
>
> —*Max Apple*, The Propheteers, *1987*

All choices about aesthetic elements of the theatre boil down to a matter of the individual designer's or director's tastes. Every member of the creative staff has to cultivate a sense of taste in order to trust their own artistic decisions. Some directors and designers develop this quality to a lesser degree than others, as is demonstrated by some productions, which have little sense of style, form, or cohesion.

There are several approaches open to you as you begin the design process. If you're working on a musical, your task may be to provide subtle sound reinforcement of the voices and the musical ensemble, creating a realistic blend that helps to enhance the audience's experience. Some plays may require you to create original abstract environments, or soundscapes. Others might use previously published material and sound effects that are used in whole or cut up, to create new musical ideas from familiar aural cloth, while still other plays might benefit from more traditional original music. You may shape your original music or soundscore to a production by emulating an established, easily recognizable style, or you can create your own sound entirely. Of course, all music can be said to be derivative. Intentionally or unintentionally, you can compose a Mozart-like score or a piece that sounds like a Philip Glass composition. What makes your score unique is your artistic sensibilities and how precisely they fit each theatrical moment.

As a composer involved in creating the underscoring for a play, you can construct your music specifically for the action onstage, as opposed to a musical or a commissioned score for an instrumental ensemble. If you are new to composing for the theatre, you may find the parameters of your composition limited in peculiar ways. A scene change that is too noisy may dictate the need for a boisterous fifteen-second interlude to fill time and cover up the sound of moving furniture. Sometimes you'll have to adapt a lengthy theme so that it resolves within eight seconds to work with the action onstage. Some directors may fit their blocking to your composition, but that is not always the case. Directors who use sound regularly in their productions know that one of the advantages of having original music is that it can be tailored to the moment. The best directors also respect just how much time it takes to do that work.

As a sound designer, you must determine what sounds are essential to represent the reality you want to create onstage. Too many elements in a cue might distract the audience, interfering with their comprehension of the theatrical moment that the sound is meant to support. Whereas overdesigning a show is intrusive, too sparse a design gives the production a feeling of not being fully realized. Your artistry lies in finding the appropriate middle ground—helping the audience's understanding of mood, time, place, or situation without getting in the way. Whether to use two or six phone rings to create tension in a mystery may seem like a minor matter. But your decision one way or the other can ultimately carry as much artistic import as whether you choose Franz Liszt or John Lennon for underscoring. Attention to these details in your sound design has a major impact on a production's viability.

As an exercise, close your eyes and listen to the sounds around you. Distill the more prominent sounds in the foreground that identify your surroundings. Then switch focus and concentrate on the less obvious sounds in the middle ground. Now listen for the more subliminal sounds in the background. Even if you are in a quiet room, there may be a ventilation system or some sort of a mechanical hum. As a sound designer, you need to be aware of the range of sounds at your disposal. If you understand the subtlety and power these textures hold, you will have a command of the full spectrum of sounds from which to choose.

THE DEVELOPMENT OF SOUND DESIGN

Even the earliest reported theatrical "events" used sound effects and underscoring. Primitive ritualistic tribal gatherings for burial ceremonies, rites of spring, or harvest festivals were accompanied by drum playing. Theatre in China and India during the Bronze Age (4000–2000 B.C.) depended little on scenery or props, but was always accompanied and underscored by music and sound.

Medieval drama, which developed over nearly four centuries, served as a proving ground for many of the conventions and devices that became commonplace in the theatre of the Italian and English Renaissance. *Commedia dell'arte* employed abundant musical support of the action, as well as music before and after the plays. It also applied sound effects to the actions, the most recognized being the supplemental sound of the slapstick to heighten the farcical impact of physical blows. For Shakespeare's plays, offstage sound was a necessary element of all productions. According to W. J. Lawrence, "Not all sights seen in the course of the action by the characters were (or could be) shown to the audience, but all the sounds heard by the characters could be, and were, heard by the audience. In other words, sights were sometimes imagined, but sounds, never."[1]

In the Elizabethan theatre, music functioned to create atmosphere and to effect transitions. The dumb show—a common convention of this period that pantomimed action shown later in the play—was always preceded and accompanied by music, often by the same music played before the act. Which instruments were used, and the attitude of the music, did as much to convey the message of the players as did the action.

Most Elizabethan plays included numerous indications for various fanfares and musical calls to accompany a character's approach. The fanfare helps the audience to sense a character's importance. It

4

often has a dramatic effect far greater than that of helping create an air of dignity. "The sennet or a flourish'" was used if he was royalty, a tucket if he was a gentleman, and perhaps the notes of a post horn if he brought an urgent dispatch."[2]

Stage directions in early prompt books sometimes described the tone of the music, calling for composers to make the "recorders doleful," "the bells strange and solemn," or "the pipes sweet."

Production books indicate that many musicians were hired for Elizabethan plays. Other than the obligatory trumpeter, there would always be a drummer, and possibly a consort of recorders and viols. If the playwright wanted a broader variety of music, he could hire additional musicians.

Not only did Elizabethan theatre rely "very largely on musical mood-painting,"[3] but many scripts had indications for offstage sounds or "noises off." Bells, alarms, clocks, whistles, chimes, thunder, storms, gunshots, cannons, wolves, crickets, owls, roosters, the croaking of toads, the baying of hounds, the trampling of horses, the crash of armor, and the clash of swords are but a few of the sounds called for within the plays themselves. For the animal sounds and birdcalls, a talented imitator was usually hired to create these sounds with or without the aid of whistles or pipes.

5

For sounds indicated by the script, sailors with a silver ship's bell, hunters with packs of baying hounds, and soldiers with their own arsenals were hired per performance to supply authentic noises on cue. Many theatres had "thunder runs" built into the ceiling above the audience or stage. These were sloping wooden or iron alleys with shallow steps on which cannonballs would be rolled to produce the rolls and claps of thunder. Several theatres in England have these original troughs intact and use them to this day.

As the Restoration, Neoclassical, and Romantic periods of theatre evolved, emphasis on offstage sound and music went in and out of style. As costumes, sets, props, and lights became more lavish, sound was no longer needed to establish so many of the production elements. With the introduction of gas lighting in 1820, production values changed significantly. Scenery became a "set," elaborately constructed and furnished, with an emphasis on realistic settings and conversational dialogue.

Realism (not to be confused with naturalism, a movement that preceded realistic theatre) presented the play as a scientific document, a slice of life. Nemirovich-Danchenko's and Stanislavsky's 1898 production of Chekhov's *The Seagull* at the People's Art Theatre (later known as the Moscow Art Theatre) challenged the methods of established theatres. What was revolutionary to theatre in this production has become today's standard for the realistic form.

In addition to the visible scenery, this production used a large number of sound and lighting effects. For example, at the beginning of the play: "Darkness, an August evening. The dim light of a lantern on top of a lamp post, distant sounds of a drunkard's song, distant howling of a dog, the croaking of frogs, the crake of a landrail, the slow tolling of a distant church-bell . . . Flashes of lightning, faint rumbling of thunder in the distance."[4]

As realism and, later, expressionism evolved as accepted theatrical styles, the technology for the use of sound also developed. The demands for sound in an expressionist play such as Thornton Wilder's *Our Town* spurred on a new creativity. In a note at the beginning of the script, Wilder states: "The use of many props is indicated in this script, but except for those used by the Stage Manager and for the umbrellas in Act III, it must be understood that all are imagined." For *Our Town*, the challenge of creating a complete environment against the bare walls of a stage relied on the connective tissue of the character of the stage manager, the commitment of the actors to this innovative staging—and sound.

The first production of *Our Town* in 1938 used no recorded sound. It relied on effects created backstage by the actors and stagehands to supplement the onstage action. While live offstage sound was nothing new, Jed Harris, the director of the original production, pioneered a modern theatrical trend by deciding to use live sound to underscore the mimed action.

The simplicity of the show dictated a similar style in producing the effects. Keeping the reality of Grover's Corners contained within its own microcosm was best accomplished by having the sound come from within the stage structure, as opposed to sound coming from above the stage or from house speakers. Live offstage effects were used to produce train and factory whistles, school bells, and church chimes. Attention was given to where these sounds originated, indicating location. Newspapers were thrown offstage in accordance with an onstage actor's movements; grinding coffee in a coffee mill imitated a lawnmower; thunder in the second act was created with a manual thunder drum. All environmental sounds—the rooster, chickens, Bobwhites, crickets, horses—were created vocally by an actor or by a multitalented stagehand.

In the Lincoln Center's 1988 revival of *Our Town*, there was an earnest effort to re-create the original concept for the sound. Most of the same images were reinforced with live sound coming from backstage,

6

sounds almost identical to those used in the original production. Again, because of the nature of the play, live sound proved to be a better choice than taped or recorded effects.

The use of prerecorded sound effects was limited until the mid-1930s, when sound effects recordings for the stage became readily available. Bertolt Brecht incorporated recordings into his productions in the 1930s, but cited Piscator's 1927 production of *Rasputin* as being the first to make use of such recordings (in Piscator's *Rasputin*, a record of the voice of Lenin was played). With the introduction of the long-playing record in 1948, the amount of material that could be stored on a disk was greatly increased and the sound quality vastly improved.

Consider how difficult it must have been to cue double turntables during a performance. Even with records specially pressed with the cues for a production, the timing might be inaccurate. At busy cueing times, it was difficult to do clean starts and fades; if the record were scratched, it would skip. A cue consisting of complex sounds, necessitating the use of two turntables simultaneously, would complicate the process even further.

By 1952, tape recorders had begun to replace turntables for general use in the theatre. However, if the show had many cues, records were still used instead of tape. Renting turntables was more affordable, and there were many more effects available on record than on tape.

In 1956, Garson Kanin directed a charming but short-lived production of *A Small War on Murray Hill* that used recorded sound effects extensively. There was no sound designer to find the effects or to fit them into the production; the stage manager found effects and music, and Kanin approved them. A gifted electrician operated numerous tape decks, playing over three hours of continuous sound—comprising 150 sound cues—during every performance. Kanin used sound on a regular basis, and it was always an important element of his shows.

Many Broadway productions of the 1950s made the attempt to incorporate sound. Directors with Hollywood backgrounds, such as Garson Kanin and Arthur Penn, seemed to be the most innovative. They tried in earnest to emulate the sound of the cinema. But for shows that opened out of town, many of the original cues were cut by the time the shows came to Broadway. Tapes and records were not completely reliable, and the sound quality was often poor. Because sound was generally the last consideration, if a music or sound cue intended to enhance a scene became annoying instead of refining, it was often dropped. There didn't seem to be time during out-of-town runs to work with a cue that needed adjustment, whether live or on tape.

The first time sound was heard was often in the first technical rehearsal. In some cases, those who had creative input never even heard the sound or music until the first public performance, as was the case for the producer for a one-man drama called *The Gospel According to St. Mark*. The subject matter was deeply religious, with a reverence surrounding the piece. Union rules dictate that some houses must hire orchestras, even when there is no music involved. Many producers allow the musicians to "sit one out," but some feel that since they are paid to be there, they should play. For *The Gospel According to St. Mark*, it was agreed that the orchestra would supply intermission and after-show music. On the opening night in Philadelphia, the producer and the audience were appalled to hear the orchestra start their *entr'acte* with a rousing version of the song *Making Whoopee*.

With so many complications, it's understandable that, until recently, producers were reluctant to include more than the required minimum of sound in their productions. They might easily have felt that it was more trouble than it was worth. Fortunately for the state of theatre today, sound reproduction technology has dramatically improved. The sound designer is now better able to correct problems and realize her own creative vision and the director's ideas. In addition, many directors recognize the virtually limitless uses of sound and music and how these elements can enrich their work.

As far as can be determined, the first person to actually be called a sound designer was Dan Dugan, who was producing designs for the American Conservatory Theatre in San Francisco for their 1968–1969 season. That same year, the Broadway production of *Hair* included the credit "Sound by Bob Kernan." In 1971, Abe Jacob was the first to receive sound designer billing on Broadway for his work on *Jesus Christ Superstar*. Once there was an established title descriptive of sound work, more sound designers could be credited as such.

Contemporary styles of theatre, abstract and progressive as they may be, invariably incorporate sound and music. Yet as cutting-edge as these pieces appear, they actually recall the conventions of classical theatre in the use of sound and music.

The equipment of the modern audio industry has given the sound designer a remarkable set of creative tools. With digital audio workstations (DAW), CDs, synthesizers, samplers, computer-assisted playback systems, and high-quality loudspeakers now technologically

8

and economically accessible, the sound designer can provide a higher level of sophistication to the use of music and sound for productions than was ever possible before. Although there are now many choices of how best to execute the design, decisions about what to use are dictated by varying degrees of budget and equipment availability.

A modest but growing amount of technology is developed primarily for use in the theatre. It is generally more lucrative for a company to produce a device or computer program for consumer audio, professional music, recording, or film markets. Designers and technicians for theatre must keep track of the technology being developed for other markets to see what can be applied for use on the stage. That said, the trends in professional theatre and themed entertainment have helped our industry to grow substantially. Individual listeners and audiences alike have increased expectations for high-quality sound delivery systems in every area of sound and music production. This has allowed theatrical sound designers to take advantage of a continuously improving set of creative audio tools.

MIDI (Musical Instrument Digital Interface) technology has revolutionized the way in which music is performed and recorded. It has opened up many ways for controlling both hardware and software versions of synthesizers, drum machines, and samplers. MIDI has been embraced by theatre designers, composers, and technicians seeking new ways of creating sounds, executing cues, and composing music. Lighting boards can have cues triggered by a MIDI message, allowing lighting and sound to be precisely coordinated. Some designers use MIDI triggers to play sounds that have to be synchronized instantaneously with an action. Wireless MIDI devices and ingenious controllers blur the line between sound operator and performer. An actor can trigger a sound with a gesture; operators can interact with greater spontaneity with the action on the stage.

The 1990s saw the reel-to-reel tape deck replaced by compact discs, MiniDiscs, DATs, and samplers as the sound designer's playback device of choice. As the cost of computers and digital sound equipment came down, more and more sound designers gained access to this technology's superior ability to store, manipulate, and reproduce sound and music. Computer-assisted playback systems designed especially for the theatre have become more commonplace, almost as prevalent as those for lighting. Digital audio workstations not only are utilized to manufacture cues, but also have become a staple at almost every tech table. Their use allows designers more flexibility than they have ever had before. Adjustments that once took all night in the studio can now be made in a few minutes during technical rehearsals in the theatre.

Designers can anticipate the cost of equipment continuing to drop while the quality of sound reproduction continues to improve. Designers' ability to create and manipulate sounds will increase as software and computers improve, allowing their imaginations freer reign. They will be able to produce whatever environment the production dictates with the use of pristine, natural sound reproduction and advanced technology allowing them to change the acoustic environment of the performance space.

It's encouraging that at every level of theatre, the incorporation of sound into a production is commonplace. Whether an actor throws a CD or two into a boombox backstage or a sound operator uses a cassette deck to play ambiance through borrowed home-stereo speakers, the attempt to include sound is being made. Wireless microphones attached to sword blades lent a heightened quality to a battle in a contemporary production of *Henry V.* Sound artist Christopher Janney and choreographer Sara Rudner's piece *Heartbeat: mb* utilized medical technology so that Mikhail Baryshnikov could dance to the sounds of his muscles and the rhythm of his heartbeat. Computer-assisted playback systems that move the sound over the audience's heads in *Miss Saigon* boosted the sound of a helicopter's arrival and departure. These are but a few of the more sophisticated examples of sound design in modern theatrical, musical, and dance productions.

With the new advances in technology and the affordability of equipment, theatres are more willing than ever before to incorporate the many benefits offered by using creative sound design. More designers are now using equipment specifically developed for theatre sound. Even the poorest theatres have affordable audio tools that allow for greater expression. With this greater facility comes more aural opportunities and more room to play. As directors become aware of what sound and music can add to a production, it is more likely to be included in all productions. More importantly, the director will be more ambitious every time sound is incorporated into a show. As sound design has become more established as a commonplace design element in all theatrical forms, budget and planning for the sound designer are no longer afterthoughts. Now when productions are planned, more directors demand the same resources and care for designing and staging the sound as they do for the other critical elements of the show.

The expanded use of sound in theatre productions is not limited to sound effects. The same resources and planning are going into the realization of musical scores. The use of live music is regaining prominence at all levels of theatre production. More prevalently, actors are being sought after because of their musical skills. Sound designers and composers work together to create unique performances that use sound and music as a foundational element of the performance. Young directors who have grown up in this age of audio are now being professionally trained to work with music and sound. This advance alone is providing some of the energy that fuels the creative use and development of *Sound and Music for the Theatre*.

REFERENCES

1. W. J. Lawrence, *Pre-Restoration Stage Studies* (Cambridge: Harvard University Press, 1927), p. 200.
2. Francis Ann Shirley, *Shakespeare's Use of Off-Stage Sound* (Lincoln: University of Nebraska Press, 1963), p. 17.
3. Jacob Isaacs, *Production and Stage-Management at the Blackfriars Theatre* (London: Oxford University Press, 1933), p. 6.
4. Raymond Williams, *Drama in Performance* (New York: Basic Books, 1968), p. 2.

The Foundation of Sound Design

One summer I visited the Civil War battleground at Gettysburg. I had been designing sound for a World War I drama and several Shakespeare plays that had called for various sounds of battle and war from several different periods. The battleground had many small hills and distant mountains, high grasses, and stands of trees. Of course, there were also monuments and statues that had not existed back then, but there was a fort and markings of barracks and cannon sites. As I stood in the relative quiet of this historical site, I became very aware of the silence and I started vividly imagining the sound of those past battles. There were many tourists there that day. I couldn't help but wonder if, as they were imagining the history of this battleground, they, too, could hear in their heads the percussives and reports of the past: the cries and shouts, trumpets and drums, how the sounds must have bounced off these various structures and echoed throughout the valley.   —DK

Just as a painter formulates a mental image when facing the canvas so, too, does a sound designer need to have an aural "vision." If you can't hear the sound in your head, you'll have a hard time determining what to create and how to create it. Allowing yourself as an artist to aurally daydream will open your imagination. Imagining sounds in the context of a production is the first step in designing sound for the theatre. You must hear sound not as a single entity, but as an interaction of parts making up a whole. Many individual sounds may comprise one effect; many effects used together constitute a design. The sound designer is asked to produce a whole from the parts, so the separate sounds that make up the whole are the essence of your design.

When your mind wanders to a jungle and you feel the humidity rise, what do you hear? Insects? Birds? Rain? Monkeys? Leaves rustling? The word *jungle* connotes many different sound images to different people. In taking mental inventory, you'll pull up dozens of elements that could be applied to a jungle. Whether your jungle experiences come from a safari you went on or from old Tarzan movies, you'll draw upon *your* aural/sensory memory in choosing elements for your palette. Your artistic judgment and taste will help you decide what is superfluous and what is appropriate for illustrating *jungle* with sound.

Now imagine a soundscape that you've created as it travels through the air and into your ear. Hear the individual aural elements emanating from various locations around you. Imagine the sounds enveloping you, stimulating your senses. This is the act of *auralizing*—of imagining sound in space, over time. Your aural imagination is an essential part of designing sound. If you were to auralize the exiting spirit of an individual who has just passed on, you might imagine the sound emanating from a stage center position, then traveling directly upward into the fly gallery. If you can aurally imagine this gesture, then it becomes relatively easy to develop a delivery system that will realize the particular effect in the theatre.

13

Visual artists in theatre work within the parameters of color and texture. Lighting designers use warm or cool colors. Set designers use textures that are soft or harsh. Costume designers use fabric patterns that are busy or simple. Sound designers have the same options open to them—all of these visual descriptors can apply to sound.

Some sounds have human characteristics. Take the sounds of weather, for instance. Rain or snow can be calm, menacing, inviting, or foreboding. Just as a menacing person presents the threat of attack, an approaching rainstorm with distant thunder poses the threat of a more violent storm to come. And just as a person who is friendly and warm makes you feel relaxed, the tempo, rhythm, and muffled lull of a gentle rain can be soothing and comforting.

Once you determine the specific ambiance, effect, or aural statement you want to create and find its basic building blocks, you then have choices about how you achieve the end result. With just the basic ingredients listed above, a jungle can elicit many sorts of different emotions. By reading the script, meeting with the director, and tapping into your own past experiences, you can gather a list of sounds that make up a total design. But without very specific consideration about the dramatic and emotional impact you want your sound to make, the finished sound design will become chaotic.

THE FUNCTION AND INTENT OF SOUNDS

In dealing with a particular cue, even one as simple as a car horn, you must ascertain many facts about that sound. Ask yourself why the sound is there in the first place. Is it to announce an arrival? To show impatience? To suggest traffic? How specific or arbitrary is the relationship between the sound and the dialogue? Is the sound associated with a character, and if so, does it need to reflect an aspect of the character? You need to know the period of the automobile, the distance that it is coming from, the time of day, the weather conditions, and the locale. To build a sound cue that will be supportive and appropriate to the play, you must glean information from the director, the script, and the production itself.

Beyond mere function, there is a psychological intent behind the use of a particular sound device. This intent derives from the playwright or director and relates to the character affecting that device. An offstage car horn, blown by a character already introduced to the audience, may show that he is angry, impatient, or late for an appointment. If the horn is meant to summon someone, the result may be to annoy a particular character to the point of rage; in this case, the cue's function is not to bring the character outside, but to trigger a reaction. The intent behind a cue, then, has bearing on how you choose to execute it.

There are times when your sound design must create an unseen character interacting with the characters onstage. In this case, you develop an offstage reality that is more completely realized than just the surface effect of a horn. This design choice not only supports but also interacts with the onstage action. With the horn that enrages an onstage character, for instance, you could add (offstage or prerecorded) the extra annoyance of someone in the car yelling for the character to come out.

14

In *Sgt. Ola and His Followers*, there is an unseen character—a pet female pig named Mr. Truman, who belongs to Pioba, one of the onstage characters. The playwright, David Lan, uses the pig as part of the comic relief in the play. Pioba and Mr. Truman have a rather funny conversation in the first act. Mr. Truman is offstage and is stubbornly refusing to get out of the mud puddle in which she is splashing and come home with Pioba. In the production I worked on, the unseen Mr. Truman was attached to the end of a taut rope offstage and was physically, as well as vocally, defying Pioba. The director stated what the eight different retorts from Mr. Truman throughout Pioba's speech might be. A series of pig grunts and squeals were edited down to short and long "comments," with the proper inflections. These pig vocalizations were played over a backdrop of sounds of Mr. Truman playing in a mud puddle. Specific comments from Mr. Truman ("Leave me alone! I don't want to go home!" or "Too bad, old man"—all in pig language) were interjected appropriately in response to Pioba's entreaties. By establishing a unique personality for Mr. Truman, the sound design turned the unseen pig into a character.   —DK

SOUND DESIGN AND ONSTAGE ACTION

A sound design does not exist in a vacuum. It is dependent upon its relationship with the performers, director, stage manager, technicians, designers, and audience to make it meaningful. If an actor is portraying a king, he will never successfully be a king unless the other actors onstage acknowledge him as their ruler. In the same sense, some sound cues need to be acknowledged by the characters. A cue can be brilliantly developed and executed at the perfect time in a scene, but if the actors do not work with it, it will be meaningless and intrusive. Even if the characters do not acknowledge a particular cue, the actors should be aware of it.

15

When the director specifically requests certain music or a sound effect, it is possible—because of other elements of the show demanding attention—that the cue will not be understood or acknowledged by the performers. When it looks as if your intention for a cue is being ignored or misinterpreted, bring this to the attention of the director and the actors and, if necessary, remind the director of what was requested. If the director's intention has changed, you may need to redo the cue. Do not consider your questioning or reminding an imposition; maybe the director forgot what was discussed with you in early meetings. The director has the entire production to consider, but you have to make sure that the dramatic potential of the sound is being fully realized.

The interaction between the sound cues and the actors should be encouraged as early as possible. If the actors can start working with rough cuts of cues during rehearsals, so much the better. If they're hearing some of the cues for the first time in tech, you and the director might want to describe the subtleties of the music or the sound so that they can begin to "play" the cues and integrate aspects of a sound design into their performance. Cues can trigger certain transitions if they occur at appropriate moments. Actors often rely on these occurrences and use them as acting beats. In effect, the sound becomes another character sharing the stage with them. Often, the audience uses these cues as emotional triggers as well.

The context within which a sound effect is heard will help shape its purpose. It's not enough to say that a fast, high-pitched bell is always going to be a happy sound. If the scene involves a wedding, and joyous bells are heard, they will undoubtedly support the moment. But if every time the audience hears this sound a maniacal farmhand appears onstage with a pitchfork in his hand, then bells ringing in the wedding scene might evoke terror and impending doom.

EMOTION AND CONTRAST

Once you can attribute human qualities to the sounds you are creating, you can achieve the texture you need for a particular scene. And once you determine the emotion that you want your effect to illustrate, you can vary the pitch, rhythm, volume, equalization, timing, and tempo of a cue to temper its basic feel—within limits. For instance, in a realistic setting, you cannot alter the pitch or the volume of a door buzzer without destroying the sense of reality. Yet by subtly altering the timing of the rhythm and the length when playing the cue, you can support the emotion of the character ringing the buzzer—anxiety, impatience, reluctance, happy anticipation, or foreboding.

Sound can, on occasion, go beyond the emotional to the physical. A low rumble played through a subwoofer can put a physical presence into a room.

16

For a production of U. S. A. at the Berkeley Repertory Theatre, I created an ominous, very low frequency rumble that rolled through the theatre to close out the first act. During previews, it became apparent that some patrons were perceiving the sound as an approaching earthquake. It was decided that there should be warning signs posted outside the doors leading into the performance space that said to the effect, "There is a moment in the play in which you might sense there is an earthquake. There isn't." —JL

Since the 1990s Russia has had a VLF (very low frequency) modulator under development, operating at frequencies below 20 Hz. At low power, this directable acoustic weapon could induce nausea, vomiting, and abdominal pains. At high power, it could cause a person's bones to resonate, which is apparently quite painful and incapacitating. While this might be a bit of overkill for a theatrical event, it does underline the human body's sensitivity to the visceral effects of sound.[1]

I just did the sound for a movie where I had to create the sound of someone's tooth being pulled out with a pair of pliers. I put the sound of a crunch and a metal click together to represent the tooth being shattered as it was pulled out. Even though I created it, I could not listen to it without feeling sick. It gave me the shivers each time I heard it! After a while, I would put my fingers in my ears and go "La la la, la la la la" out loud whenever we came to that point in the film.   —JL

When creating a drone to underscore the witches' scenes in *Macbeth*, the director's instructions were to "give him a two ton machine turning in Hell." I built a looped sequence of layered low bass tones and polytones, dropped the octaves, and doubled the discordant sounds until I achieved what sounded like, at least in the studio, a very complex and tiered continuous tone with visceral rumbling and movement.

When I took it into the theatre before the first tech, I heard it in its full glory for the first time. There were several people working on the set, hanging lights and painting while the sound operator and I adjusted the levels. The moment the churning started, I was overcome with a wave of nausea. Every person in the theatre had the same reaction. This sound was disgusting, to such an extent that it truly caused physical revulsion. This could have been a weapon! I had to extract a number of layers of this effect to make the sound less nauseating. Actually, it became very useful. For many years, it lived at a sound studio with which I was connected. It was labeled "Deena's drone" and was the foundation of many future designs.   —DK

Having sound or music that contrasts with the emotions of a scene can be a device just as powerful as having sound and music that supports them. The impact of the action can be made all the more potent by introducing an effect that works as an emotional counterpoint to an onstage situation. For example, suppose you're designing sound for *The Haunting of Hill House*, a play somewhat in the tradition of a Gothic horror story. Instead of using music that is conventionally scary, you could juxtapose the obvious element of horror with a piece of music that connotes innocence, perhaps a music box playing a child's nursery rhyme. Because the storyline includes the haunting of the house by a child, you could insert a random line of the nursery rhyme in a child's singsong voice. This could prove frightening in relation to the grotesque sounds of actual hauntings that happen throughout the play (doors and walls being shaken from the foundation, the house seeming to suck the occupants up). The sweet music could be used to foreshadow something evil.

APPROPRIATENESS

With an awareness of the function of the cue, you must ask yourself, what are the era, time, and location for this particular sound cue? Is it noon in present-day Manhattan? Is it breakfast time in rural Georgia, circa 1920?

Suppose you're on the second floor of a large midtown Manhattan office building. You observe a Checker cab stopped at a busy intersection. The driver impatiently leans on the horn while trying to edge out into the traffic. The sound you hear will include screeching tires as the cab nearly collides with another cab. Both cabs blast their horns, and you're aware of the continuing whine of the second car as it recedes into the urban traffic and away from the first cab.

The horn you hear in rural Georgia would sound very different. It might echo throughout the sparsely populated valley. If it's daybreak, you might hear a rooster crow and the distant approach of a Model T jouncing closer, announcing its approach with a distinctive "aooga."

These examples are simplistic, but you can see how much thought needs to be given to the most basic cue. Whether the sound is live or prerecorded, it must be appropriate to the situation, geographically accurate, and not anachronistic. If you're creating a design for a show that takes place in Papua, New Guinea, find out what musical instruments are actually played there and research the sounds indigenous to that area (see Chapter 4 for more on researching sound). You may opt not to include those particular instruments, but at least you'll have a working knowledge of the sounds from that region.

In *Macbeth*, a loud banging on the castle door is called for in the Porter scene (Act II, Sc. 3). You need to consider the time period in which the play is set. If it is in the year 1250 A.D., realize that the door would be made of different materials than if the scene takes place at a rural villa in present-day South Africa.

THEATRICAL FORMS/STYLES OF SOUND DESIGN

When designing sound and music for a production, you must decide whether to lean toward a more *realistic* or more *stylistic* approach. Both of these theatrical forms have their extremes. For a realistic production, a sound design can be involved and cinematic, or it can be selective and representational. With stylization, the sound design can be either abstract, where the designer represents his or her thoughts through impressions of sounds, or absurd, where nonsense seems to prevail.

THE REALISTIC APPROACH

In a realistic approach, the sound effects and music should be true to life, with strong attention paid to factual detail. Music can emanate from practical sources or can be used, without the characters' awareness, as bridges preceding or following the action and dialogue. Should the music or sound originate from a practical source, such as a radio, characters will obviously be aware of it. Incidental music (underscoring) used in this convention usually is nonmotivating to the characters, supporting the action but not influencing it. In other words, the music may manipulate the audience, but it doesn't often outwardly affect the development of the characters.

Consistency is important in this form, but does not always have to be strictly observed. There are times when, because of focus onstage, it is necessary to ignore a prior indication of a sound cue. Let's say you have established that the sound of a toilet being flushed offstage should be heard onstage. Imagine the character that has used the bathroom walking onstage during a passionate love scene—to the sound of the toilet flushing. Unless a comic effect is intended, you may have to sacrifice the sound convention at that point. The sound cues need not be totally comprehensive of all elements that would occur in real life, but should include enough of them to clearly represent reality. When these rules are broken, you create *abstraction*, which we discuss in the following section, "Stylistic Approach."

One variation on pure realism is a *cinematic* form—a design that incorporates a strong sense of ambiance, employing lush and detailed underscoring. Music follows the action more closely, as in film. (Consistency, in this case, is vital: once you've associated particular sounds or music to an action, it's essential to carry through accordingly.) With cinematic form, the sound designer draws together many elements to present a complete wash (or backdrop) of an environment.

19

Two examples of cinematic designs I created were in productions of *A Touch of the Poet* and *Cherokee County*. In both, there were preshows, entr'actes, and incidental music that did not influence the characters. There were also cues for internal music, supposedly from a live source—in the case of *Cherokee County* from a jukebox, and in *A Touch of the Poet*, presumably from a live musician offstage in the bar. Both shows used extensive ambiance to set the scenes. For *Cherokee County*, Act III, it was a summer evening in rural Georgia, complete with crickets, bullfrogs, and distant hound dogs; for *A Touch of the Poet*, there was an ongoing hubbub of bar patrons well into an evening of drinking. Ambiance was continued throughout both of these scenes, with volume adjusted up and down to provide focus.

In the two shows, underscored music led the audience through the scenes, manipulating their reactions and commenting on the situation. In *Cherokee County*, the preshow included music from the 1960s that moved from house loudspeakers to an onstage jukebox from which the characters occasionally made selections. When the records playing weren't specific choices of the characters, I chose music that followed and commented on the development of the scene. At the end of *A Touch of the Poet*, the character Nora sits alone, hearing the merriment coming from the offstage bar. There is a concertina endlessly repeating a happy Irish jig, contrasting with her sense of abandonment and hopelessness.

In both cases, once the precedent of atmosphere through sound was developed, it continued realistically in all similar scenes.   —DK

The *representational* form uses sounds as genuine as those found in cinematic realism, but the overall design is sparser. Music is less incidental and more specific in this form. The cues remain true to life, but occur only when necessary. The artistic challenge here is selecting sounds that will support the action without fleshing out every nuance. It may not be necessary to hear every aspect of a jungle, for example; the voice of a single bird may be sufficient to convey the mood. Working in a representational form, the sound designer tries to find bare elements that will express a broader environment.

Journey into the Whirlwind called for strong but isolated effects and music. This one-character play about a woman arrested and put into a gulag is told by her after the fact. Theatrically, the audience remembers the situation with her. The motivating sound images were percussive: a phone ringing requesting her presence for questioning, a train bringing her to camp, a prison door closing, a proletarian worker singing a Soviet propaganda song about the Fatherland. These were all her memories. Because of the overall sparseness of the production, the play called for me to select simple representational sounds from these incidents.   —DK

You may come across a situation where other design elements are stylized, but the directorial decision is that the sound be realistic. *Our Town*, for example, has detailed, realistic sound without a realistic setting. In this case, the sound design must supply the audience with much of their factual perspective.

In *The Search for Signs of Intelligent Life in the Universe*, first produced on Broadway in 1986, Lily Tomlin portrayed characters fully equipped with costumes that were created only with sound. Otts Munderloh's work was a groundbreaking feat in the field of sound design. Sound effects were implemented to underline a majority of Tomlin's gestures. Her characters included a young punker who prepared to go out for the evening and donned a leather jumpsuit with zippers of all lengths and sizes and a bag lady who wore an umbrella hat and sneakers fastened with Velcro. These "costume changes" were created through judicious choices by the sound designer and performer, and were carried out by the performer and sound operator carefully synchronizing sound to action. In a heavy sound show like this, you would have a good deal of artistic freedom—as well as the responsibility not to confuse your audience or go overboard with unnecessary cues.

THE STYLISTIC APPROACH

The stylized theatrical form distorts reality with qualities such as exaggeration, distortion, or conceptualization. In a scene where a man is about to be executed, the sound designer might use the sound of breathing or a heartbeat to elevate the tension. This is a highly stylized effect and a powerful artistic decision.

Abstract form represents the artist's interpretation of reality, and so is impressionistic or expressionistic. An abstraction of reality alters the basic sound, but doesn't completely disguise it. If you're building a battle in the year 1500, you know that one of the main weapons of that time was the sword. You could distort the sound of the blades cutting through the air by slowing them down and adding reverb to lengthen and highlight their importance in the battle. This method differs from the more stylized technique of miking the weaponry to pick up every clash of metal. The distorted sound may not even be immediately recognizable as blades cutting the air, but you have selected an element from a realistic source upon which to base your interpretation.

In a production of *Conference of the Birds*, I compiled abstract aural images that had the effect of making the sound an extension of the language. There was a core group of actors taking a journey, but they did not use conventional language. Instead, they had melodies written in an eleven-note sequence in a pentatonic scale from which they could choose to "speak." Each bird character used a limited number of vowel and consonant sounds. There were three other characters who spoke English, but their voices were always treated electronically, and the tone of voice as well as the words were altered to create meaning. There was also a narrator whose speech was unembellished, but there were depictions of images through sound as he told the story. There was a moment when the travelers were gathered around a fire and the dialogue described the image of moth and flame. A stylized fluttering was heard—a high, bell-like shimmer—and visual images of the moths were shown before they vanished into smoke. A bell chime reverberating with the help of a digital delay indicated that moment. The only music in the piece was a continuation of the themes written for the "language" of the five core characters. It was played live on a synthesizer, following the flow of the action and staying within the confines of the five different note themes.   —DK

When you conceptualize, you find the idea of the sound that you want to represent and attempt to find another sound that has the same connotation. For the *absurd* form, you can consciously pick sounds that will be ridiculously incongruous and somewhat disorienting. In Joe Orton's *What the Butler Saw*, there is a garden outside of Dr. Prentice's office. Many entrances and exits are made through a door leading from the garden. One way of paralleling and reinforcing the departure from reality that builds throughout the play would be the use of animal sounds coming from the garden. Not only could you increase the amount of wildlife dramatically, you could also use species (such as wildebeest) completely inappropriate for modern-day suburban England. Absurd and surreal elements in the sound design are appropriate for Orton's outrageous comedy.

CONVENTIONS OF MUSIC AND EFFECTS

Music and effects used in a production fall into four categories: framing cues (preshow, entr'acte, and curtain call), underscoring, transitional sounds/music, and specific cues. *Framing cues* act as the bookends of a production. They exist outside the actual action of a play. They can comment on what will be or has been seen, but work independently from the actor's presentation of the play. In musical terminology, the preshow is a prelude, the entr'acte (at intermission) a bridge, and the curtain call a coda.

Underscoring accompanies the action of a scene and is not heard by the characters onstage. Its purpose is to underline the emotions of the moment. To maintain the focus of the scene, it may be helpful to place underscoring upstage of the actors. This forces the audience to listen "through" the actors, and keeps the sound literally in the background.

Transitional sounds or music represent a movement of the action through time or place. They exist outside the action and can link one scene to the next. Placing transitional sound or music cues in loudspeakers away from the stage helps support the idea that the cue exists outside the action of the play.

The characters in a play are, however, aware of *specific cues*. While not at all devoid of emotional appropriateness, specific cues are more informational in purpose than the other forms, and are aural events that form part of the theatrical environment. Location of these cues is dictated by the practical placement onstage of the sources from which they emanate.

Do not feel married to the notion that only music can be used for preshow, entr'acte, and curtain call. Familiar sounds can also serve as lead-ins or bridges. A clip from a television show that is recognizable to the audience, for example, can work as well as music to establish the mood of a production. Hearing Ralph Kramden and Ed Norton along with the laughtrack from *The Honeymooners* will place you in the 1950s as easily as would hearing Fats Domino singing *Blueberry Hill* (assuming that these aural events are part of your prior experience).

Once you set a convention as to how the music is used, be consistent. This is not to say that there won't be situations where you want to break convention for the sake of effect. But in cases where you'll precede the first act with a preshow, bridge scenes with pieces of transition music, and cap the ends of acts with music, stay aware of symmetry. Also, carry through with sound what the director is doing dramatically. If each scene ends with tentativeness and a feeling of anticipation, look for that same quality in the music you select. If it seems that the director is giving finality to a particular scene, let your music or sound have that same sense of completion.

If music is supposed to serve as an outside comment that the characters are not supposed to be aware of, treat it that way throughout. In the same sense, if the music and sound are connected to a character, don't confuse your audience by throwing in commentary sound out of nowhere. *Commentary sounds* are often-clichéd themes and signature music, such as using *The William Tell Overture* (a.k.a. *The Lone Ranger Theme*) for a chase scene. They are best used in broad comedy, melodrama, and stylized productions. On the other hand, don't make your musical puns so obscure that the audience doesn't get the joke.

For simplicity's sake, it's best to keep music within a certain range of instrumentation and styles. But even if the style is intentionally a hodgepodge of different kinds of music, you can still establish that as a convention, so that the audience will not be confused. They will easily accept the variety of the pieces if you are using them as comments or jokes.

FRAMING CUES (PRESHOW, ENTR'ACTE, CURTAIN CALL)

Preshow and entr'acte sound can consist of music, voiceovers, a montage of sounds, or a blend of all of these. Many directors use preshow music to establish a period, location, or mood. Preshow music also helps familiarize the audience with the style of music to be used in the production. You may choose not to use music as a framing cue when the production is a presentation of a total concept, like the broadcast of a radio program or a beauty pageant. Both of these premises might include an abundance of internal music, so preceding the production with music that sets the style is unnecessary. Instead, you could help establish the reality with appropriate announcements or the venue's natural ambiance.

The length of a preshow is an artistic choice. One option could be to have the preshow start at house opening, bringing the audience into the aural environment. You may want to prepare the audience for the show once they have been seated for a certain amount of time. When you have a specific piece of music leading into the opening of the show, you should make this a separate cue, rather than tagging it onto the preshow, to facilitate the cueing. You may opt to go with a short preshow, perhaps because you want to use thematic music to lead directly into the action instead. Rather than using washes of sound to set the mood, you may introduce a more specific theme just before house lights go to half. In these cases, the music acts more like a transitional cue. Sometimes you may decide to have silence before curtain, but then you must also determine how much of a silence you want and what will be the last sound heard before that silence.

The entr'acte may be shorter than the preshow. If there is a ten- or fifteen-minute intermission and you are using music to end the act, you may not want to begin the entr'acte until three minutes or so before the next act is to begin. Should you want to go with a longer entr'acte, some productions call for breathing time after the last cue of the preceding act before beginning the entr'acte music. This allows the members of the audience to absorb what they have just experienced before going on to something else that demands their focus.

Preshow and entr'acte can make a strong impact when crossfaded into the action at the top of the act. Perhaps you're establishing a 1960s ambiance inside a diner. You may wish to have period cuts playing in the house as a preshow and, as the light preset is coming down and into black, crossfade to the stage. When the lights for the scene establish, you can continue the sound from an onstage juke-box. At this point, the preshow music becomes underscoring.

At some theatres, it has become commonplace to hear an announcement just prior to top of the show. Announcements range from asking theatregoers to turn off their cell phones or reminding the audience that photos and recording are prohibited. If you have to include such an announcement in your preshow, try to persuade the producer not to play it immediately before the top of show sequence. After all, your preshow is there to set the appropriate mood for the show and chances are that an announcement will break the mood. If you use a sequence of music for your preshow, try to build it so that one piece ends, the announcement comes on, and then another piece of music begins. Simply fading out your music for the announcement and fading it back in will seem sloppy and will make the announcement even more of an intrusion than it already is.

UNDERSCORING

Underscoring is often referred to as incidental music—with the misleading connotation that such music is superfluous and not well planned. No element of your sound design should ever contain elements that have not been thought out. Because underscoring is not heard by the characters, you have more variety within the design. You are not constrained by the conventions of the play either in style of music or instrumentation. You don't have to mirror the music that has been used as part of the action of the play.

To clarify, you might have decided that all internal cues in a production will be ragtime music, coming from a phonograph or an offstage piano. That is the convention within the play. In using underscoring, though, you may employ a completely different style of music, which may or may not include elements of ragtime. The underscoring can serve as a character theme that the audience hears and that the actor can work with, but of which the character is not aware. With underscoring, you're creating an entirely different dimension through which you can elicit a certain response from the audience.

In a production of *Still Life* from Noel Coward's *Tonight at 8:30*, the director chose to juxtapose the sounds of steam trains arriving at and departing from a train station with segments of a Schubert quintet. The sweet strains of the Schubert and the harsh hissing of the steam engine formed an effective dichotomy. The play deals with a couple's meetings and the progress of their relationship. The movement of the quintet in segments supported this progress, so that its closing phrases coordinated with the end of the play. Effectively, the music became more bittersweet as the couple eventually parted. The constant background reality of the trains would either begin or end the music cues. The convention, although predictable, was never boring, and the music kept the progression fresh. The train cues varied to correspond with express, local, fast, and slow trains.   —DK

TRANSITIONAL SOUNDS OR MUSIC

There are no rules or formulas for how to incorporate transitional music into the production. Many designers and composers use music that is thematic to particular characters—that is, played as signatures for the audience whenever these characters appear onstage. After deciding what the instrumentation and sound will be, you need to address the context in which the music will be heard. You and the director should decide whether the music will cap off a scene or precede the next one, or whether combining two different themes can serve both purposes. By using themes that are easily recognized, you can aid your audience and advance the flow of the show by helping to chronicle the progression of action. Note that you can do the same thing using ambiance or sound effects.

At the ends of scenes or acts, you may want to begin the music under dialogue and let it continue to usher out the ending of the scene. There may be times when you allow transition music to continue into the action (after beginning prescene or preshow) and find a place that it can effectively end within the scene. Underscoring in this way can have a very dramatic effect, but find subtle places to begin and end, or it will sound too melodramatic. However, if you're going for melodrama, the more blatant the placement of a cue, the better it may work.

In *The Merchant of Venice*, the setting alternates between Venice and Belmont. One way to delineate these switches could be composing or compiling separate themes for Portia, Antonio, Shylock, and possibly for Launcelot and Jessica. This would indicate, by character association, where the next scene would be: Portia dwells primarily in Belmont, Shylock in Venice. By identifying the location with music, the audience has an early clue as to locale and to which subplot will be taking place. To make each scene complete, since so much Shakespeare is in French-scene format (whereby scene divisions are marked by character entrances and exits), a theme of one character can be used to begin the scene, and a theme of another can be used to end it, signaling what will follow. Additionally, there are several places in *Merchant* where music is indicated in the script. These cues, where musicians are called to play as part of the action onstage or offstage, are *required music* (see the next section).

A *segue* is a device that takes you from one place in a scene to another. This movement can be a trip through time or a change of location. Transitional sounds or music link one scene with another scene, while the segue leads from one point within a scene to a different point in that same scene.

SPECIFIC CUES

Specific cues fall into five areas: required music, spot effects, ambiance, progression of effects, and voiceovers. All sound cues need to be emotionally correct, but specific cues are primarily informational in nature, supplying of-the-moment data and supporting play development. Omitting these cues would be conspicuous. When characters let the audience know that they hear a marching band, a barking dog, a car horn, or a ringing phone, those cues had better be there. When a specific cue that falls within the realistic realm breaks the convention of that reality, it makes that cue abstract.

Required music is a particular piece of music that is indicated at a certain moment in the script. Sometimes the director has blocked a certain action to support it. In *The Private Ear*, there is a seduction scene that is literally choreographed to the builds in an aria from *Madame Butterfly*. With some required cues, you could substitute one aria for another. But in the case of *The Private Ear*, the timings and actions were worked out by the playwright to this specific composition.

Spot effects are specific sounds such as thunderclaps, dog barks, and explosions. In a loosely adapted production of the melodrama *The Tavern*, the director and sound designer set up a convention that every time someone came in the front door, a crack of thunder sounded and a wind-and-rain track bumped on. When the door closed, the wind and rain stopped and what was left of the thunder rapidly faded. All of these effects were individually cued, and their placement was specific. This obvious technique was not distracting, and even became an in-joke with the audience. Included in this category are source-specific sounds, like a television or telephone.

An *ambiance* can be perceived as a foreground, middleground, or background element, its primary purpose being to provide an atmosphere or a setting, rather than to highlight a specific short duration event as the spot effect does. For this reason it is most often observed as a background element, even if it begins as a foreground event. When spot effects are used in a series and are not individually cued, they take on the properties of an ambiance. Ambiance should become a backdrop in front of which other sounds or the action of the scene may play. Traditional backgrounds are crickets or ocean waves—sounds that can be established and then play without drawing much attention to themselves—but ambient sound can be more complex than this. Ambient sound is longer in length than most cues, but needn't play for an entire scene. The main difference between a spot effect and ambiance is that ambiance blends into the background, whereas a spot effect takes focus. Spot effects are often added to an existing ambient track. For example, what if you wanted to illustrate the sound of a person rowing a boat on a lake on a stage without any real water? You could trigger the sound of an oar hitting the water, being pulled back, exiting the water and re-entering on the next stroke in synch with the actions of the actor. This might sound a bit odd as an isolated sequence, but if you add the background ambiance of gently flowing water and some light forest sounds, those layers will act as a kind of glue, allowing the oar to have spot effects to blend more realistically into the scene.

Spot effects and ambiance can be combined creatively. In essence, ambiance shouldn't have any landmarks in it (loud, attention-getting sounds), because you can't determine where in the action they'll occur. Using a summer-night-in-the-country ambiance as an example, you would use many sounds that could be heard in such a setting: crickets, dog barks, frogs, train whistles, owls, trucks on the highway. Some of these sounds can become obtrusive, and placing them in an ambient sound field could be inappropriate. This doesn't mean that these effects can't be used in a scene—it just means that they have to occur at the proper moments. If inserted wisely, specific cues in an ambiance, such as a dog barking, can play as seamlessly as the ongoing track of crickets and form part of the background. By including these dog barks, you can reinforce the mood that you wanted to achieve with the ambiance, and create something more textured than just a monotonous drone of crickets.

The sounds of a busy setting like a construction site are noisy and complex, but, within a scene, they can provide an atmosphere that recedes into the background—as long as no single sound is over-whelming. In Act II of *A Touch of the Poet*, the offstage bar is full of rowdy drunks. There are many references to the "boys in the back room," so not to hear them would seem odd. While an Irish bar ambiance is not as benign as a field of crickets, it is possible to estab-lish this track without stealing focus.

Some ambient sound fields may be difficult to recognize immedi-ately. Adding in other, more recognizable sounds when the ambiance first establishes can remedy this problem. A soft, lazy summer wind might sound like white noise to some people, but adding in a bit of leaf rustle or a branch creak might just be the extra "spice" needed to say "wind" to the audience. These added elements are sometimes called *identifiers* or *sweeteners*.

Occasionally, the script demands spot effects that seem to come out of nowhere. If you find mention of just one thunderclap in a script, it may be appropriate to set up distant rumbles ahead of it, to suggest a realistic progression of effects. The same holds true with the time after an effect—you may want to have a storm dissipate slowly.

In the script for Tennessee Williams' *The Night of the Iguana*, the playwright indicates only a few specific thunderclaps dur-ing the storm at the end of Act I. It might seem appropriate to add rumbles prior to the first cue mentioned, to form a realistic build. Additionally, you could choose to tie in the storm that ends Act I with the top of Act II, bringing in a simple, distant thunder rumble as an aftermath of the storm.

If your intention is to create a realistic storm, gauging the length of a progression of effects like a thunderstorm is essential. If the scene that holds the storm runs fourteen minutes, you should deter-mine exactly where in the script you first start a distant rumble and how quickly it grows to its peak. You can create a realistic build, whether or not it is an authentic timeframe for a storm. After all, the timeframe is dictated by the theatrical clock of the scene, not real time. As with any sound design, there are no rules to this. Sometimes you want to create a progression, and sometimes having the thunder as a surprise is appropriate.

Voiceovers appear within the action of the play, but are not perceived by the characters. In a voiceover, the audience hears disembodied speech—sometimes embellished with effects—presenting information or thoughts. To heighten the effect of a voiceover, you can play it through loudspeakers not used for realistic effects. Artificial reverberation can be added to voiceovers as an additional means of expressing the stylization. Conversely, presenting a voiceover in a realistic manner can *ground* the effect of the voice, enhancing realism. In the proper context, this might seem very real, or possibly frightening, especially if there is not a person present making the sound.

In *The Private Ear*, the playwright indicated a scene with specific voiceover cues containing dialogue. The actors were to freeze as these taped cues were played. The script also indicated a change in lighting and specific action to bring the actors in and out of this cue. It was stylized to the extent that the tape was supposed to speed up at the end of the voiceover as if a tape recorder were actually put into fast forward.   —DK

CREATING FOCUS WITH CUEING

When you think of the word *focus*, you normally think of a camera. When the lenses inside of that camera are in their proper relationship, the image is in perfect focus: everything you see through the viewfinder is seen clearly. Similarly, careful setting of all the controls you have over a sound will achieve correct focus for your sound design.

A *sound cue* is any introduction of an aural element into a production. *Cueing* refers to the manipulation of that element. That manipulation could be in the timing of its entrance, volume change, addition of signal processing, segue, transition, or exit of that element. The subtleties that you incorporate into your cueing control the focus of that cue.

Some cueing choices may seem obvious. A phone should start ringing before a character says, "I hear the phone." But how far in advance of the line should the ringing start? If there is a chaotic moment onstage, the phone could start to ring in the middle of that moment. Although the audience is immediately aware of its presence, it may take a while before the characters onstage acknowledge it.

This can add to the chaos. On the other hand, if there is a tense confrontation where there is no dialogue, the ring of a telephone may be a jarring interruption to both the audience and the characters onstage. In this case, leaving a space before the ring may help build the tension. There is as much dramatic impact in hesitating with the execution of a sound cue as there is in the pauses an actor takes. If you consider emotional pacing when cueing, the overall sound design starts to develop a character of its own.

THE VOLUME OF A CUE

An established ambiance doesn't have to stay at the same volume for its duration. When the volume is higher, the effect becomes more scenic. When the volume is lowered, the actors' voices become more predominant. The placement of that fade is an artistic choice about where that focus is necessary. One can usually sense—by reading the script, watching rehearsals, or talking to the director—where changes in the scene occur. Lighting cues often happen at these transitions; a good place to adjust the volume of a sound cue is at such a shift of focus. If you sense that the action of the play is switching focus to the environment that surrounds it, then a boost in the volume of the ambiance will help the audience to experience the place along with the characters. Where to start this modification, along with the rate of change and execution of the fade, can make the transition either obvious or imperceptible.

In terms of considering volume as it applies to music, remember that the addition or deletion of volume affects the musical intensity. Of course, layered in these choices are rate, rhythm, tempo, location, and movement of the music. Sound and music can be thought of vertically, with the highs signifying a lightness and the lows demonstrating weight.

It's too simplistic to say that establishing focus is as easy as raising the volume. Levels that are inappropriately high become annoying; sounds played so softly that the audience cannot recognize them become distracting. If the audience has to expend a lot of energy trying to figure out what (*the hell!?*) they're hearing, then their focus on the show is lost. If you feel that the cues must be played so softly that they are inaudible, then they probably have no place in the design.

RATE OF EXECUTING THE CUES

While placement of a cue is crucial to giving the cue its proper focus, equally important is the rate at which the cue is executed. One of the conventional techniques used with ambiance is called *establish and fade*. It isn't always necessary to have a soundtrack running throughout a scene. A constant rain track in the background may become more of a distraction than a support after a while. If the characters are making constant references to the rain and it isn't heard, it will seem odd. But if you are simply establishing a mood and place, you can let the background fade out. The audience will eventually accept sounds that are fairly simple and unobtrusive, since a constant wash of background sound fulfills its purpose within a short period of time. The audience wants to focus on things that are changing and giving them new information. They know there are birds singing in the garden—they don't need the continuous sound of the birds once that has been established.

Depending on the type of ambiance being used, you can either fade out the sound gradually or take it out quickly. Gradually fading out a sound will be less obtrusive than popping it out. The previous example of the rain is a case where it's better to fade the sound gradually. Since the rain is a rather dense background, if it went out quickly the sudden lack of ambiance would be noticeable. However, a sparse track such as a single singing bird is easier to lose rapidly. Since birds naturally pause between calls, an abrupt ending to the soundtrack can seem authentic.

Suppose you have established a jungle ambiance and the lead actress is about to deliver a pivotal speech. If you start to soften the background just prior to that speech, the actress will appear to jump out from the background with much more presence. A lighter ambiance, such as distant ocean waves, must be faded out completely to affect this kind of focusing. Removing it isn't jarring, though, because the cue was already subtle.

Another way to soften an ambiance is to lower the volume or fade out busier elements. Although you might hear a city ambiance playing out of just one pair of loudspeakers, it could comprise many tracks. If the city background is being delivered on a multitrack playback device and you've split the ambiance into three stereo tracks composed of horns, traffic, and urban roar (the hum of the city), you could soften the ambiance by first fading out the horns and then lowering the volume of the traffic. By doing this, you've lowered the overall volume of the cue and made the most distracting sounds less noticeable.

If you've been running a rather obvious background ambiance and you remove it completely, you may draw attention to it. Sometimes that's acceptable—you want the abruptness of a sound going out to make an impact. But if you need to sneak out a sound, do so when there's a distraction, such as talking, laughter, or an entrance.

32

If you're at the end of the play and all the lights are fading down to a pin spot on a character, you may choose to break the realistic convention along with the lighting designer. You have a choice of fading your sound down to complement the lighting or fading the ambiance up to embellish the final tableau. The ending of a cue can also be motivated by a specific action onstage.

In a production of *Savages*, I introduced a subtle high-frequency tone during the interrogation scene. This tone dropped into hearing range from the frequencies beyond those perceptible to humans. As it dropped into audible range, it leveled off to a faint, constant, siren-like squeal and floated in the theatre as a sinister presence. Dumping it just as the man being interrogated delivered a horrible description of the murder of a young girl pulled focus right to that actor and drove his story home. —JL

The effective use of silence in your soundtrack can also improve focus onstage, especially in key moments.

In a production of *Macbeth*, I used a soundscape of strong, grotesque drones, torrential wind and water, and drums of war. There was one scene where Macduff's wife and child are peacefully at home. The director wanted to introduce a very realistic effect of morning birds and sunlight, which would clash with the preceding drear. In the climax of this scene, the wife and child are visited by murderers and brutally slain. At the appearance of the first murderer, the bird track was instantly cut. The silence was deafening. The director might have opted to precede this scene with effects previously introduced to announce any foreboding action. But by introducing this subtle device of obvious silence, it was possible to achieve a very chilling effect. —DK

THE LOCATION AND MOVEMENT OF SOUNDS

The location and movement of a sound are as vital as all your other considerations. In a realistic design, a sound should come from its implied location. Onstage telephones should ring at the source. An outside environment heard from the setting of an interior should be placed so that it seems to emanate from open windows or doors.

Movement is often used to provide greater realism and is often necessary to make an effect seem complete. An airplane that is supposed to fly overhead should have movement. To create such movement, consider the rate of execution in an expanded sense. Its distance, type, and purpose of flight will dictate the speed at which the plane establishes and fades. Faraway planes take a long time to build, close planes zip by, an old single-engine plane doesn't move as fast as a jet, and a plane on a joyride may travel more slowly than a plane carrying a donor heart to the hospital. The rate of the actual movement of the plane from one area of the theatre to another will depend on how close the plane is supposed to be—the closer the plane, the faster the movement.

Movement can also help establish location. If you want to reinforce that a scene takes place outdoors in a valley surrounded by mountains, providing echo to a loud effect such as a shout can work quite well. In *The Night of the Iguana*, Tennessee Williams calls for Maxine to yell "Fred!" and for us to hear her shout echo off the nearby mountains. If the series of fading "Freds" were to move around the theatre, the expanse of the unseen mountains would come alive.

Also consider the freedom of being able to think not just linearly with the placement and movement of sounds, but creating aural illusions and phantom images that can be placed in any location in the theatre. Just as an exact location within the theatre is used for realism, playing your sound out of many speakers at the same time will make its location unspecific. Ghosts and phantom sounds floating and moving unpredictably in the theatre can be quite powerful.

What supports this abstraction is the lack of positional specificity. Sounds do not need to be limited to simply left and right. There are so many more possibilities when you consider adding depth and motion to the cues.

CHARACTERISTICS OF THE SOUND CUE

Not all of the sound or music that you are asked to provide will be prerecorded. Sometimes it's necessary to use live effects (a crash box), musical instruments, or *practicals* (working effects like an onstage doorbell). The immediacy and literal hands-on element of a live, nonrecorded sound adds another level of life to the design. Some cues will be a combination of live and prerecorded sounds.

Volume, quality of tone, and balance are important acoustical characteristics of both live and prerecorded cues. The difference between live and prerecorded sound is the method of adjusting these traits—instead of making adjustments at your mixer, you have to shade live sound acoustically. Some live sounds that you will have to consider are the performers' voices. Simulating the environment from which the voices emanate is something that you can control by the same principles involved in controlling the properties of musical instruments.

Should a crowd scene need to sound larger than it appears, you may wish to supplement the live crowd noises with a recording. Your prerecorded cue should match what has already been established onstage. Consider age range, sex, and general tone of the crowd (happy, angry, accented, foreign language). If there is relocation or dispersal of the crowd, decide if you want to include that detail on tape or have it happen live. Fine-tuning when mixing actors with recordings can be achieved only by rehearsals.

Practicals are used onstage as they would be used in real life. If the sound cue is to be from a radio or television, give qualities to the recording that will maintain the sense of the medium. A speaker in the playing area of the radio or television will help, but also be aware of how much making the sound thin or tinny will add to the realism. Consider the period of the appliance: an old Victrola will sound very different than a state-of-the-art stereo system.

EQUALIZATION AND TIMBRE

Equalization (EQ), a term applied to prerecorded or miked sounds, refers to changing the tone or timbre of a sound, usually to compensate for deficiencies in its reproduction. Adjusting the treble, midrange, or bass frequencies can enhance the sound—making it truer to life. Exaggerated boosting of the low end in a thunderclap will make it more foreboding; boosting the higher frequencies on car horns can make them much more irritating.

Timbre refers to the tonal color of a sound. When trying to adjust volume or timbre, it may be difficult to change these qualities independently. A technique used to lower the volume of an effect will also change its timbre.

In a production of *A Touch of the Poet*, an actor walked through an upstage door that supposedly led into the bar offstage. As he came through the door, the actors offstage started a general barroom hubbub, which continued past the time the door closed. The first time this occurred in tech rehearsal, the reality that existed onstage was lost. Having the door closed did not affect the actors' voices, as they still came through clearly over the tops of the flats. I had the choice of constructing an enclosure around the actors or placing an enclosure around their mouths. The most expedient choice in this case was to cover their mouths. Handheld masks were constructed with sound-absorbent material attached to their interiors. When the actors talked into them, their voices became muffled and lower in volume—closer to the sound that would have occurred if the barroom were really an enclosed room. This was carefully rehearsed to achieve the desired effect. However, the first time the masks were used, the actor portraying the principal character was not told what he would see when he poked his head into the "barroom." It caught him quite by surprise to see ten sets of eyes peering at him from behind these strange devices!   —JL

VOLUME AND THE MIX

One of the easiest controls over a cue is volume, but determining the proper playback volume of a cue is not simple. As mentioned earlier, a cue needs to be established at a level that is in keeping with the amount of focus it requires. A thunderclap that is supposed to scare the daylights out of the characters should have the same effect on the audience. Music that underscores a tender love scene must not overwhelm the moment.

An increase in volume may assist a comic moment by exaggeration. If, in a broad comedy, there is a scene where wasps invade a picnic and the comic action depends on the characters being threatened, then the wasps need to be played larger than life. In a thriller, the wasps may pose a serious threat, and the buzzing might also be played at an unrealistically loud volume.

By burying specific emotional triggers in the mix (like crying, laughing, or screaming), you can insinuate more of an impact into the "face value" of a cue. A buried sound is not perceived as that specific sound, but becomes part of an overall mix. If the emotion-prompting sound were to be recognized, it might be too heavy-handed, but by hiding it in the mix, you can subliminally suggest emotion.

I was having a difficult time trying to find a hook for my design for *Machinal*. The production was stylized, so I couldn't provide purely realistic sound effects and backgrounds. However, I had to be cautious of going overboard. To do so might make the audience think that the central character was crazy, something the director adamantly wanted to avoid.

Driving home from rehearsal one night, I had one of those "Eureka!" moments. I realized that by mixing real sounds with complementary, emotionally evocative sounds, I could subtly stylize the effects without going over the

of creative expression and technical precision—must balance music and effects to the action onstage.

A piece of music inherently contains all of the variables we've discussed in regards to sound effects. But the qualities of rhythm and tempo are usually thought of as just for music. The high-pitched versus the low-pitched instruments are another quality to consider. However, when you start thinking about sounds and ambiance in musical terms—the low brass of the classic foghorn or the fast tempo of a jackhammer—then your sound palette and aural imagination can have greater possibilities.

REFERENCES

1. J. Wiley, E. Larsen, and R. M. Aarts (2002) Reproducing low-pitched signals through small loudspeakers. *J. Audio Eng. Soc.*, 50(3), 147–164.

3

Developing the Concept and Design

While I was resident sound designer for the National Shakespeare Company, I had the opportunity to work with many different directors and their interesting concepts every season. During the first meeting with the array of new directors one year, the discussion turned to our upcoming production of *A Comedy of Errors*. The director said he planned to do it in the style of Italian *commedia dell'arte*. It occurred to me that the musical counterpart of this style might be *opera buffa*, a very broad form of comic opera. I mentioned this to the director and the idea appealed to him immensely. I knew it could sometimes be distracting to have music with lyrics for background underscoring, or even for leading into or out of a scene. However, in this instance, I could isolate some of the sillier sounds and use the voices as though they were the instruments. It was painstaking editing. For example, I had a chase scene accompanied by a frenzied quartet of hysterical sopranos, angst-ridden altos, tedious tenors, and booming, buffoonish baritones. For one specific cue calling for a knock on a door, the director wanted to have a very loud, stylized sound to accompany the action. I found a melodic phrase of an enthusiastic bass joyously proclaiming "Dinga-donga-dinga-dong." This was repeated several times and became a *lazzi* (a set bit of comic business used by *commedia Zanis*). Later, the same character had to ring a doorbell, and the sound that answered him was a distinct, burlesque knock on woodblocks. The actor playing against the cues enjoyed these novelties and wanted as many preposterous effects worked into his bits as possible. —DK

Imagine that you're finally hired to design a show for a theatre at which you've been anxious to work. However, you're quite disappointed when they tell you that you'll be doing their annual production of *A Christmas Carol*. Even though they've done this show every year, they're excited to finally have a sound designer working on the play. At first, you might feel like you're walking into a creative dead end. But just imagine *A Christmas Carol* without sound—what did they do about effects until now? Look at this as an opportunity to make the sound in this production the best that the company has ever experienced, and they'll wonder how they were ever able to do this show *without* a sound designer.

Start work on any show by finding a hook. If the director is undecided about a style of music, or if the script doesn't indicate where to start a design, then suggest a time frame, a composer, an instrument, or a type of music—a starting point for giving the production continuity and focus. Is there something about one of the characters that makes you think of a certain piece of music?

In *Sisterly Feelings*, a broad English farce by Alan Ayckbourn, one of the characters is constantly whistling Mozart melodies off-key. There are lines in the script indicating his sometimes-annoying habit. For our production, we decided to use Mozart's *Ein Musikalischer Spass* (*A Musical Joke*) for framing cues and bridging the scenes. With its whimsical, exaggerated air, this piece reflected the tone of the play very well. The playwright indicated many cues necessary to the action; one included a hapless picnic invaded by bees. Because many character reactions depended on intruding bees, we chose to broadly stylize the buzzing in an almost cartoonish way. The audience heard an annoying, amplified swarm swirling around the stage, dive-bombing the characters until they had no choice but to abandon their plans for a peaceful outing. Both the music and the effects in this production captured the sense of farce and fun that the playwright intended and that the director wished to carry through.   —DK

41

WORKING WITH THE SCRIPT

Actors often begin to work with their scripts by highlighting all of their lines. In early rehearsals, they may mark down their blocking and make notes about motivation or character traits. As a sound designer, you have similar information to retain, and you will often refer to your script when developing your design.

On the first read-through, try to absorb the play without taking too many notes. You could, however, note each occurrence of sound indicated in the script. If you feel ambiance or a sound cue not indicated by the playwright rising out of the pages, pencil notes in the margin or make notes on a separate pad. If you're making a list, write down page numbers and brief comments—just enough to jog your memory. Figuring out exact cue placement is not important now, nor is how or where the cue will begin or end. If you're unfamiliar with the text, the first read-through is the only time the material will be entirely fresh to you, so use this vantage point to put yourself in the position of the audience. Notice what takes you by surprise—could the surprise be supported with sound?

During the second read-through, look at your notes in context. If you were keeping notes during the first read-through, write all of your cueing notes into your script before you start reading it the second time. Try to hear in your head the sounds you want, fleshing out your original notes. Anything that occurs to you at any point in the process is worth exploring or mentioning to the director. If you've marked up your script, clean up your writing so that if you go back to the notes in a few days or weeks, they'll be clear enough to remind you of your original ideas. The margin of your script doesn't allow for much room to write, so keep more detailed notes and ideas separately. Eventually, much of this information might find its way onto your initial sound plot (see Chapter 5). When the playwright has indicated a specific piece of music to be played at a particular time, or has called for a sound to be part of the action, these *indicated* cues should be incorporated into your notes. Always make the director aware of such cues, because as she has worked through the script, sound and music may not have been foremost on her mind. Cues implied by the script may not have registered with her. It's part of your job to make her aware of what is both indicated and suggested in the script.

STAGE DIRECTIONS

Some stage directions will describe actions that will need your attention. If the script has a character going over to a jukebox, making a selection, and playing it, determine what sound is needed to interact realistically with that action. Consider the mechanics of the onstage equipment. Is it an old jukebox or a modern one? If the prop onstage is not practical, does the director want to add some realism by including the sound of the machinery? If so, determine how complex the cue needs to be to support the action onstage.

Perhaps the stage directions indicate "Vera exits stage left to mix cocktails." The questions you must answer as a designer are: Should we hear Vera making the drinks? If so, when do we want to hear her?

What sounds are involved in her actions? Is she making martinis or margaritas? Should these sounds be performed live, or should they be prerecorded? Bear in mind the cue's function and focus when answering these questions.

LINE INDICATIONS

A character's lines may allude to a car approaching, or they may mention that there's a riot going on down the street. These are clues that a sound may be needed, but neither of these situations *demands* that you include a cue. You or the director may decide that the audience doesn't need to hear these actions. Depending on the sound design for the production, it might be enough that the character just mentions the situation.

If the sound design is sparse, only the most essential sounds need to be heard. If, on the other hand, the sound is designed very cinematically, it will be necessary for the audience to hear everything happening outside the house. The car, even if only heard, may be the first introduction of a character and may be representing him before the audience ever sees him. In this case, you can have the sound of the automobile taking on the properties of a character. For example, a revving, menacing, souped-up sports car can be a useful precursor to an evil character's entrance.

43

Hearing a car arriving, idling, and shutting off may build suspense and tension. However, even if you've set up the convention of hearing cars, you might not include this cue because the director wants the audience to concentrate on the action onstage, or because the cue would have to occur at a strategically awkward time in the action (e.g., someone is about to get kissed, killed, or ambushed). If there's no appropriate place for the cue, it may be necessary to forego it.

HIDDEN CLUES

That same approaching car might not even be mentioned in the script. But if a character suddenly appears and announces that he parked his car in the driveway, you might decide that you want to hear the car approach. Depending on the director's decision as to how close the driveway is to the action onstage, you may even want to hear the car door open and close. If the car is directly outside the window, you might hear the motor revved before it is shut off. In most cases, if the character leaves, you must reverse the sequence of these sounds—the car door opens and closes, the car starts up, and it pulls away—unless these cues would intrude on the focus. Another consideration is the urgency or anger of the character, and how those traits would affect the amount of time it takes him to get to the car, how fast the car starts, and how hastily the vehicle pulls away.

Make the director aware of the complexity of these cues—he may not want so much stage time devoted to a cue, and you can save yourself a lot of unnecessary work if you know how intricate the director wants an effect to be. You and the director may decide that all the audience should hear is the car driving away, or you might even decide that the car is too far away to be heard at all.

THE DIRECTOR'S INTERPRETATION OF THE SCRIPT

The director may choose to veto a playwright's indications, eliminating sounds entirely or replacing them with concepts of her own. When the director chooses to ignore the playwright's ideas, find out the reasoning behind her decision. By doing so, you'll obtain useful insight into the director's tastes. This inquiry should never take the form of a challenge. Remember that you are working on the director's interpretation of the play, and any of the playwright's concepts are subject to modification by the director.

44

Before you start researching music for a production, find out what kind of approach the director is taking with the play. Let's say you're doing a production of *Tartuffe*. You may have already started researching the music from the period in which the play is set, which is Paris in the mid-1600s. If the director informs you that this particular production is set in the antebellum South, the music you have researched will be of no use. If it occurs to you that Stephen Foster's music might be appropriate for the pre-Civil War era, mention it early on to your director, because if she's dead set against your idea, it's better to find out before you start designing.

CHOOSING SOUND EFFECTS OR MUSICAL EFFECTS

Sound effects are often regarded as purely informative and music as purely emotional. However, music and effects can have similar attributes. You may be involved with a production where you find that music would be completely inappropriate. For whatever reason, adding even the most minimal of melodic themes to this production would make a dramatic moment melodramatic. If the director wants something to underscore a scene or a transition, remember that you can use sound effects to create a moment just as effectively as if you were underscoring with music. If your idea had been to use music at a certain point and the director feels that music would be intrusive, try to discover a sound effect that embodies some of the feeling you wanted the music to instill. For example, if your instrumentation employed light, fluttery flutes, would birds chirping quietly serve a similar function? Would jackhammers drilling in concrete cause the same dramatic tension as a piece of music utilizing heavy percussion? Depending on what the production calls for, you can evoke the same emotional pitch without music. Conversely, sound effects may be replaced by music. When stylization allows, you can choose to replace foghorns with underscoring on a tuba or a thunderstorm with the theme from *Victory at Sea*. It is your imagination, creativity, and aesthetic sensibilities—as well as the director's—that serve as your guidelines.

CONSIDERING OTHER DESIGN ELEMENTS

The colors on the set, the timing of the lights, and even the textures of the materials used in the costumes are all important for you to take into account as you create sound and music cues. How stylized or realistic other design elements are will certainly affect how you choose to build the sound or utilize the music. You want your design to complement the overall concept that the other designers are expressing.

When a thunderstorm is indicated, confer with the lighting designer before considering how to build the storm or starting to produce cues. You and the lighting designer should discuss every detail about developing the storm. When using real-time thunder, take into consideration the intensity and timing of the lights, because the farther away the lightning strikes, the greater the time between the flash and the thunder. In some instances, the timing of the light cues will depend on the placement of the sound cues. It's always important for you and the lighting designer to work together and respect each other's needs and ideas.

For a production of *Othello*, I had not been given any concrete information from the director about her concept. I found my first hint of what direction to go in when I saw the renderings for the set. The colors of Cyprus were hot and arid in contrast to the cool, aquatic feel of Venice. This suggested to me that I might find a contrast of themes. As the design developed, I employed two distinct styles of music that implied this opposition.   —DK

Some designers will rely upon you for input, so you may have the opportunity to express preferences to the prop department and the set designer. The sounds of elegant, tinkling dinnerware as opposed to more practical plasticware for a Noel Coward play can establish the moment as much as the smartness of the clothes or the sophistication of the set dressing. If the set has practical door chimes, you might even be involved in choosing them.

In *The Man Who Came to Dinner*, there are numerous doorbell rings indicated throughout the play. Each ring of the bell heralds the entrance of one outlandish character after another to interrupt what appears to be an idyllic setting. To enhance the contrast between the peaceful setting and the chaotic antics of Sheridan Whiteside's zany friends, we chose the first seven notes of *Home Sweet Home* recorded on a glockenspiel to use as the doorbell. The tune's simple innocence belied the havoc onstage, particularly at the opening of the play where there was much activity and other bell ringing: front door, phone, and otherwise.   —DK

Whenever the director cannot express his ideas of where a piece is set aurally or what the sounds for the show should be, take clues from the costume style or set design. If the costumes set in the mid-1700s are extremely frilly and ornate, you might look at the composers of the period and choose compositions and instrumentation that match those qualities. If the set has a barren, cold look and is set in ancient Greece, you can try to find instrumentation consistent with that atmosphere.

In the early 1980s, I worked on a production of *Beyond Therapy*. I was having a hard time deciding what kind of music to use for the various scene changes. No through-line was coming to me; there was no style that seemed right. I talked to the director and asked her what clues she had given to the other designers to tell them what she wanted. She said that she had told the set designer that she wanted the show to look high-tech. Bingo! A few months before, I had gone crazy over a band (*Our Daughter's Wedding*) that used no acoustic instruments. I was at a concert where the trio sang and played only synthesizers and a drum machine. The sound was very modern, electronic, and sterile—in my mind, very high-tech. Needless to say, the music worked very well. The most surprising thing was that the director (who was at least twenty-five years older than I was) loved the music.   —JL

Taking inspiration from another design element is a great way to approach your design. If you're able to reflect the visual aspects of a production with sound, you can present your director with tangible choices and illustrations of your design aspect that will clarify for him, through your interpretation, what he was able to express to other designers. If you have the opportunity to work with a director or designers on an ongoing basis, you'll develop a mutual vocabulary that will make it easier to communicate in terms of your mutual needs.

MEETING WITH THE DIRECTOR

You're hired for a production and have thoroughly familiarized yourself with the script. The next step is meeting with the director. If the director has never worked with a sound designer or composer before, you'll have to find a way to draw out her ideas and desires about sound and music. This could be difficult to verbalize for someone who has never had to articulate ideas about music. The problem is that music is often an emotional experience that does not easily lend itself to articulation. If you've never worked with this director before, you will not have developed a mutual vocabulary.

THE FIRST MEETING

Both you and the director must state your expectations and desires for the production. If you've worked with the director before, you've already established some type of working relationship and a way of discussing sound and music. She may even have asked for you for this project. Be prepared to offer examples and suggestions at the first meeting. But for a director with whom you are not familiar, the most important thing to do at the first meeting is listen. Try to get a sense of how she approaches the possibilities of using sound and music. At the same time, don't hold back your ideas until you're asked for them—make suggestions. If you find that the director is unaware of the potential for sound and music, offer several options.

I was involved in a production with William Hurt in which he was debuting as a director. There were only a few practical cues indicated in the script. There was no specific call for music. We decided to use music in preshow and the sounds of an ocean as transitions to set locale and mood. Hurt, a most accomplished actor, was still new to the many technical choices one could make about sound as a director. I must say, I've worked with few directors who have been as enthusiastic about the possibilities of sound design. He was delighted that there were so many choices to be made, such as the differing types of oceans, intensities of waves, length of time between crashes, with or without seagulls, and so on. For all the cues in this production, he treated the sound as if it were another character. —DK

When presenting your ideas, go through the script with the director and discuss each possible cue indicated. If you know from looking at your preliminary sound plot (see Chapter 5) that there are special demands that will require rehearsal time, mention that as well. Arrange, if necessary, special meetings with the director—for auditioning live musicians who may appear onstage, approving instruments that will appear onstage, and so on. As sound designer, you are in charge of all sound elements that are part of the production, and it's your responsibility to anticipate and schedule these additional meetings.

After that first meeting, you will probably have developed a working sound plot to which you and the director can refer for all of the production's sound and music cues. While determining how to accomplish some of your ideas, you may find that building certain cues will eat up all your time and budget. No cue is impossible, but some can be so elaborate that there is simply not enough time and/or money for them. By the time the show actually opens, that chorus of singing alligators accompanied by a thousand kazoos may be only a distant memory. Keep the entire sound design in perspective. Budget your time as well as your funds.

Some directors will want you to develop ideas as the show goes through rehearsals. In this case, the purpose of your early meetings may be only to determine what you both do *not* want. The sound then evolves as part of the rehearsal process, with you working closely with the director to distill the developments that unfold during rehearsals.

SUBSEQUENT MEETINGS WITH THE DIRECTOR

Some directors are so specific at the first meeting that any further discussions consist only of you offering examples from which to choose. What will be needed from you and when it will be needed depend on the director and the production. You can discuss your design in more detail once you've started to search for the sound and music she has requested.

If the director asked you for several rough examples of music for a dozen cues, don't present her with twenty choices for each cue—you'll only confuse the issue. With either music or sound, it's always easier to ask the director to pick from two or three choices than from many (you can still have more ideas waiting in the wings, anyway). With too many selections, the director might put together a hodgepodge of sounds devoid of any artistic cohesiveness. Be prepared to offer your preference when asked. If the director is unfamiliar with making these sorts of design choices, you'll have to guide her along.

Some subsequent meetings are for the director to hear cues that have been built. It is not a good idea for the director to hear cues for the first time at the technical rehearsal. If you have misinterpreted her idea of what a death knell sounds like, it's better to hear about it while there is still the chance to rerecord—rather than having the entire cast and crew wait around while you two debate the finer points of bell ringing. Remember that your time to revise cues is limited during tech. Often, the only time available to remake cues is when you'd rather be eating or sleeping.

A less-than-ideal situation may occur if you've been hired from a distance. You may have met with the director several times and agreed upon materials to be used, but you are not physically with the production until you arrive for tech rehearsals. With this arrangement, it is crucial that the director clearly state his needs in advance. Final timings before you produce your design might be given over the phone. When your recordings are finally in use, you'll be away from your production studio where it's easiest to make changes. In some situations, the lack of access to a studio means that only minor adjustments and edits are possible. But as digital audio workstations have become more affordable and smaller, more designers have the option of taking a portable studio on the road with them. This allows them a familiar workspace when away from home.

BUDGETARY REALITIES

Determining the resources you need to create your design can, at times, be very challenging. While some theatres have a healthy budget for sound, others require you to be more imaginative. If you find that ideas discussed in your preliminary meeting with the director are impossible to achieve (given a tight budget, lack of equipment, or insufficient manpower), let your director or the production manager know as soon as possible. Even if you can't extend the budget, someone else might be able to get the producer to reallocate funds.

If a cue that a director has his heart set on costs extra—for renting additional equipment, hiring musicians, or finding studio space to record specific cues—you should never sacrifice your own fee to accomplish it.

Even if you think that you've accounted for every particular in planning your budget, leave some margin for error. A 10% buffer is a good starting point. If you were hired on a predetermined budget, calculate whether you can do the job within that amount, and if you can't negotiate further fees, consider how important the job is to you. In time, you can learn to make a good case for your design needs based on how this contribution helps the overall production. But for this to work, the director will have to be in your corner because she may have to make a cut in one area of the production in order to support your design idea.

Most producers understand how to budget time and money for the lights, sets, and costumes. But for some, sound is a relatively new design field. Because of that, or just a lack of understanding of what goes into a sound design, your contribution may be a belated consideration and woefully underbudgeted. You or your director may need to explain the significance of the sound and music in this production to the producer. Lay out the scope of what your work entails, and make sure he understands that the compact disc or sound files he receives as a final product of your time and effort represent just as much work as does any other design element.

4

Research, Resources, and Selection

In 2003, Irene Lewis asked me to design a production of Shaw's *Misalliance* at Center Stage. I did not know this particular work at the time, but I loved Shaw and was excited about working on this production. In our early meetings, we determined that it would be wonderful if we could hear G. B. Shaw's voice (knowing that recordings had been made and that Shaw loved to hear himself speak) as a preshow cue. Our intent was to offer the audience a little peek into the character of this great writer and orator. And so I went about an investigation into a source for these recordings. I tried the usual suspects: online music retailers, libraries, and dramaturgical friends, and managed to find some promising clips. The fact that Shaw was born Irish but lived in London most of his life led me to hop onto the Internet and contact folks at the BBC, believing that they would certainly have a number of valuable resources. While that produced good but limited results, I still wanted more depth. Most of what they had was available on commercial recordings. As time passed and I began to get a bit frustrated at my small pile of resources, I kept digging in England. Finally one resource asked, "Did you check the Historical Sound Recordings Library at Yale?" OK; I was embarrassed. I'm a Yale professor and I did not think to check my local resources. So I walked down the street to the Gilmore Music Library to find a wonderful resource in Richard Warren, the curator of that collection. Needless to say, Richard had a wonderful set of offerings that I was able to access for the production. Just recently, I rechecked my usual Internet resources and found a few new reissued recordings, but nothing like what I was able to find just outside my office door.   —DB

Your research for the sound and music of a new project can begin at the moment you've decided to do the show. One of the first steps is thoroughly reading and understanding the script. After initial concept meetings with the director and possibly with the other designers to determine the slant being taken on a particular production, you can start gathering your resources. If music is to be part of the show and you're unfamiliar with the style or period of the script, collect and listen to as much music from that period as possible. Try to gather examples to offer in the first few design meetings. If the production requires an exotic setting, playing a recording at a meeting and presenting authentic music and sounds will be more effective than trying to explain how an instrument sounds.

Sometimes what you bring into early meetings can influence and inspire certain aspects of the production. The dramaturge might show articles and pictures to the cast and production crew to familiarize them with the atmosphere of the production. Your sound and music contributions can be equally useful. Hopefully, your colleagues will start incorporating your ideas into their work as they go along. For example, the style of music you decide to employ could tell the costume designer that the show will be more comical and lighter than he had originally thought, so he might modify some of his costumes and materials accordingly. Having even a sketch of the sound and music can assist the director during preliminary developmental rehearsals. Even if you haven't determined what you are using, or if you yourself are composing or hiring a composer for an original score, try to impart the flavor of the music and sound early in the rehearsal process. If the director has not yet established exactly what she wants for the show in terms of music or sound, and you can present something early in the process, your input will probably have more influence. The earlier you offer your ideas for a sound design, the more likely it is that they will be adopted.

Once you've presented initial information to your director, you may be asked to dig further into a style of music. Your discoveries at every step will supply the director with a myriad of choices and help the cast members to educate themselves about what is appropriate for a particular historical era.

By researching sound and music for a production, you acquire a base of knowledge upon which you will draw throughout your career. The more times you delve into completely unfamiliar territory, the faster and more successfully you'll develop your researching technique. You can become quite well versed in many genres, from Depression-era Southern folk blues to the spiritual music of the Aboriginals to eighteenth-century Spanish boleros to old-skoolhiphop by learning how to research thoroughly.

As you approach a production, consider the alternatives before settling on one specific sound or style of music. Does a certain piece of music have a strong ethnic background? What instruments will you use to represent different characters? Is the play a comedy or a tragedy? Is it period, contemporary, or abstract? Depending on what you and the director have discussed about the characters and the show, you can choose whether you want an ensemble orchestration, a solo instrument, or possibly a combination of two or three instruments employed at different places. You may want a solo instrument with a mournful wail to represent a character who is lonely and brooding. If the play is broad and farcical, a big, bright symphonic sound used as underscoring will not overwhelm the audience the way it might for a more delicate think piece. If you compose, you may find that you can emulate the style of the period and opt to write original music.

Obviously, if your production is a comedy, your sound design or composition will call for more up-tempo and/or quirkier sounds than would be the case with a traditional production of a history or tragedy. For a Shakespearean comedy set in the Elizabethan era, you might need court instrumentation and also a more rustic sound at different times throughout the play. For example, in *A Midsummer Night's Dream*, incidental music can herald the changes in locale for the royalty, the lovers, the mechanicals, and the fairies. At times, interpretations of Shakespeare may be more experimental and more modern, and whenever the show is set more unconventionally— *Macbeth* in 1130 A.D., *Hamlet* in the Victorian era, a 1950s *Twelfth Night*—you should surround the production with the sound of the era that the director is attempting to capture (e.g., for *The Merry Wives of Windsor* set in 1880 New Orleans, try a live zydeco band; for *Julius Caesar* à la *The Matrix*, use modern synthesized, sampled, and processed sound and music).

When beginning a music search, first find which composers fit into the years surrounding the play. A useful tool for researching eras is a timeline. There are many websites and history books that include a timeline linking world events and prominent people within each era. Although there may be no information about music, such a timeline can at least give you a sense of the style of the time. Sometimes symphony orchestras or opera companies distribute a timeline detailing the music and composers represented in their seasons. Although it may be limited in scope, this type of graph can be quite comprehensive for the era that it covers, with a composer's date of birth and death keyed to the artists, writers, and world events of the time. Other timelines categorize composers by periods of music and mention only key historical events corresponding to their

53

works. Any of these versions of a timeline is useful in giving you an overview of a period unfamiliar to you.

Online references, such as Wikipedia, have their information organized in numerous ways. Searching for "Popular Music in 1900" should bring up a fairly organized list of subjects to read.

For shows set in much earlier historical periods, you might also consider composers preceding the era by as much as 50 to 100 years. Writing styles and instrumentation were constantly changing, and in bypassing an earlier era, you might be sacrificing many possibilities. In doing preliminary research for this kind of show, you'll also find mention of which instruments were in use and what developments and trends were taking place in music—for example, the sonata form, counterpoint, or instruments accompanying singers.

For shows set within the last 100 years, you will need to be much more accurate with musical selections meant to represent a specific year. You can be certain that there will be a music historian in the house, a ragtime buff, or a jazz aficionado who'll be irritated once he hears a certain piece of music that he knows hadn't yet been written at the time set for the play. As long as there is someone alive to remember that *Colonel Bogie's March* was written and used during World War II, it's not a good idea to use it for transition music in *Ah, Wilderness!*, which takes place on July 4, 1906. Whether you're researching ancient or modern music, your work must be thorough if you're to avoid anachronisms.

There are many places to locate music and sound effects, but the Internet provides easy access to various music and sound effects libraries. There are numerous websites that allow you to audition, purchase, and download music and sound effects, as you need them.

MUSIC RESOURCES

Throughout your sound search, rely on your artistic imagination to circumvent any limits on resources—there are always options. Music can be either composed or pulled from other sources. You can select music from your own collection of recordings, the collections of friends or colleagues, Internet resources such as iTunes, postproduction houses, or the public library.

Once you've decided to use a certain group of instruments from an established era or a specific locale, your library is a great place to start your search for the right music. See what is available under a particular composer's name, a country, or a title of a certain composition. You can often find everything you need on a subject by looking

54

up music under either country of origin or date. For instance, entries listed under "Music-Italy-Sixteenth Century" will include all instrumentation and artists of the era and will have references to both music and literature on the subject. Look under the instrument, the artist, or the name of a composition. Be inventive. Many libraries have music divisions with librarians who can tell you who wrote music during Moliere's or Ibsen's time—or even who wrote musical settings for their plays. Some of the better-known labels that specialize in period music are Musical Heritage Society (MHS), Deutsche Grammophon, Harmonia Mundi, Allegro, Qualiton, and Nonesuch. Smithsonian Folkways, Putumayo, Arhoolie, and Elipses Art all have comprehensive series of authentic sound recordings that deal with the music indigenous to different cultures and countries.

Reference books are also good starting points. *The New Grove Dictionary of American Music*, *Baker's Biographical Dictionary of Musicians*, *The New Oxford Companion of Music*, *The Oxford Dictionary of Music*, *The New Oxford History of Music*, *The Harvard Dictionary of Music*, *The Music Article Guide*, *The Music Index* (guide to periodicals), and *The Rilm: Abstracts of Music Literature* (a cumulative index) are all publications that can help you delve into different subjects and styles of music.

55

If your public library has recordings that can be checked out, you can "audition" music at home. If the library has listening facilities, you can narrow down your choices before lugging any materials home since you may be limited to the amount of material you are permitted to borrow at any one time. Something with a title that sounds perfect for your needs might turn out to be light-years from the kind of sound you had in mind. Always gather more than you think you might use. This initial screening will go rather quickly. You can probably tell by listening to the first few seconds of each cut if the music has vocals, if it has the type of instrumentation you're looking for, or even if the tempos will work for you. The more you listen, the more your ideas will solidify.

Of course, there are lots of places on the Internet to audition music. Apple's iTunes store gives you a thirty-second excerpt of any song they carry to listen to. However, you can't choose which thirty seconds to listen to, so it's a bit of a crapshoot when researching long classical music pieces because you might not hear a portion that's relative to your needs. Researching music utilizing everything from search engines to the Internet Archive (www.archive.org) is merely a jumping-off point in your quest for knowledge. The library that is the Internet is open 24/7 and has resources from all over the world.

If you're searching for something that your library doesn't carry, you can also use music stores as research venues. Some stores have salespeople who specialize in particular areas of music. You may find stores devoted exclusively to classical, ethnic, or folk music. Look for a music retailer that has listening stations, what was once a commonplace service in the middle of the last century. A small number of stores will allow you to listen to any recording they have in the store on headphones.

If it seems that the type of music you're looking for is so obscure that you can't locate any preexisting recordings, try to find a similar sound. For instance, let's say that you're looking for an instrumental representation of a rustic French bistro. You've read descriptions in books of what might be appropriate. You've even watched (and listened to) some movies that re-create the place and period of your production, but you can't find any recordings that are exactly what you're looking for. You might try the traditional music of either Canada or Louisiana because of their links to French heritage for recordings that suggest the appropriate instrumentation and atmosphere

When choosing the medium of your recording, you have two options to consider: physical media such as DVDs or compact discs or downloaded, compressed digital audio files such as MP3s or AACs. Compared to most downloaded digital audio files, compact discs and DVDs are the best option for higher quality source material because they use uncompressed audio files and are produced at a higher sampling frequency. Compressed audio files can be up to one-tenth the size of their uncompressed equivalents (and therefore quicker to transfer over the Internet). They obtain this smaller size by losing information that the compression software deems unnecessary. An exception to this rule can be found in audio files that use lossless compression. Files that have been compressed using FLAC or ALAC, for example, may be half the size of an uncompressed AIFF or WAV file, but retain all of the information to reproduce the audio just as well as the uncompressed file. Be sure to look in the Glossary for more information about these file formats. Be aware that the lower sample rates and compression of downloaded music mean that they will not sound as good as CDs or DVDs. You should let your ears be the judge as to whether the sound quality of an MP3 or other downloaded file is good enough for your needs. Try to avoid mixing MP3 and CD audio within the same production, as the difference in quality between the two could be obvious and, therefore, a bit distracting. Digital music downloads do have their advantages, however. You often have the choice of downloading just the selection(s) you want as opposed to buying the whole album. These music files are also ready to obtain at any hour and are easy to transport on a hard drive or small jump drive.

Don't underestimate the value of LPs and 78s in providing an option for source material. A scratchy record might be the perfect source given the proper circumstances.

SOUND EFFECTS RESOURCES

Sound effects can be culled from field recordings, from studio recordings, from your own sound collection or that of your theatre, or from purchased or private sound effects libraries. The Internet also offers many opportunities to download sounds for a fee or for free. Two good sources for downloading sound effects are Sounddogs.com and the iTunes store.

Sound effects can be created, but sometimes substituting the sound of a boiling kettle for a steam train simply doesn't cut it. There are occasions when nothing is as viable as an authentic recording.

I once needed a background tape of a lively neighborhood street—the script specified Brooklyn in the summertime. I live in New York City, so one Saturday afternoon I drove to a residential neighborhood in Brooklyn, bringing a picnic lunch and field recording equipment. I parked as inconspicuously as possible (in the middle of the block) and simply dangled the microphone out the window. Not only did I pick up the specific sounds and general ambiance of this neighborhood, but also recorded a raucous marital spat, a drug deal, a three-alarm fire being fought at the house on the corner, three little boys pretending that they were superheroes, and a hot tip for off-track betting that two neighborhood men were discussing for the fifth race at Aqueduct. All of this occurred outside my car window in less than two hours. I then had enough tape of general street noise to work with for this production—and I never found better examples of sirens for another show I did a year later. The little boys' voices were quite useful several months later in yet another show, and I'm sure someday I'll find a use for the other isolated events. (I checked the paper the next day and the horse in the fifth race won at 17 to 1 odds.)   —DK

There are many recordings of the sounds of steam trains, large industrial equipment, junkyards, farms, oceans, railroads, disasters, and other atmospheric settings. Complete sound effects libraries are available from such labels as Sound Ideas, Network, Valentino,

Hollywood Edge, Digi-Effects, and BBC; all of them provide an index listing the effects and their lengths. Sound Ideas provides a stand-alone database application that allows you to search their entire catalog for a sound. The database is modifiable so that you can add your own library of sounds to it and limit the catalog search to just the Sound Ideas libraries you own. The entries for each sound are detailed, so you're not searching just on a file name, but on the description of the sound.

It's good practice to archive your materials when you complete a show. If you have twenty-five minutes of evening ambiance (crickets), fifteen minutes of ocean, or exceptionally fine barking dogs, rest assured that you'll need them in future productions. These sounds are important assets in your own library. There is bound to be a perfect thunderclap you've created that you'll never be able to duplicate. You can always embellish it, double it, or build on it for other productions.

Many designers store their sound effects libraries on a hard drive. As your library grows, it will be impossible to remember every sound you have or where it's stored. Naming and organizing your library carefully will allow you quick access to your sounds.

58

When you store your sounds on a hard drive as sound files, you can maintain your library as a collection of folders organized by category. For instance, you can include a folder full of animal sounds. Within that folder, files can be organized within subfolders by mammal, reptile, or amphibian, and so on. Then you can organize those files in subfolders by species.

A hard drive of sounds might be organized using the following subjects:

- Alarms and sirens (clocks, fire, burglar)
- Ambiance (urban, rural, tropical, office)
- Animals (wild, domestic, mammals, reptiles)
- Cartoon sounds (pop, boing, zip, bonk)
- Created or designed sounds (ascension to heaven, gates of hell, Venusian snowstorm)
- Electricity (buzz, snap, hum)
- Elements (air blast, whoosh, rockslide, fire, water movement)
- Household (shower, toilet, lawnmower, mouse trap)
- Human (scream, chew, snoring, crowd)
- Materials (wood snap, glass crash, metal clang, plastic cup drop)
- Office/industry (copy machine, stapler, cement mixer, jack-hammer)

- Sport/leisure (basketball bounce, baseball catch, merry-go-round, roller coaster)
- Transportation (car horn, truck start and drive away, bus brakes, airplane takeoff)
- Warfare (cannon, rifle, pistol, arrow whooshes)
- Weather (wind, rain, thunder)

As your library grows, you might want to reorganize it. You might have had just a few bird sounds initially, so if you've added a number of specific bird calls, you might want to organize them into folders organized by the specific parts of the world where the birds are found.

Since all computer operating systems and most digital audio workstations have search functions, naming your files comprehensively is important. Develop a naming convention and try to stick to it. For example, a simple naming convention might be a description and source. An ambulance siren that you recorded for a production of *Julius Caesar* might be named "Ambulance Siren 1.JC." A dog bark found on Sound Ideas disk 6001, track 34 might be named "Large dog bark SI6001.34." You could take your naming convention further by ordering the descriptive words by major category and then subcategory, so that the large dog bark might be called "Dog, large, bark SI6001.34."

Organizing and maintaining your library can take a good deal of thought and time. There is no perfect cataloging scheme. Get ten sound designers into a room and ask them how to categorize a library and you'll get at least eleven answers. Where would you file a glass crash? Under glass? Crashes? Fight sounds? Household sounds?

Don't forget that it's good practice to have a backup copy of your library stored in a safe place. If your working copy is damaged or lost, you can easily make another copy of the backup.

OUTSIDE CONTACTS

Maintain a black book, a Rolodex, or a PDA to keep track of the businesses and people whose services you employ. People whom you meet professionally can be an invaluable help. Keep track of resources in many areas including music experts and repair shops. When you're expected to know how to do everything from building cues to maintaining the equipment, it's comforting to know someone who might be able to help. Many people even peripherally connected to the business are great fans of the theatre. Become familiar with your local stereo shops, music stores, and electronic equipment centers. You might find someone there who loves the theatre and would be happy to assist you.

THE LEGALITY OF PULLED MUSIC AND EFFECTS

Your producer should obtain rights clearances on any music or effects that are used, regardless of the level of the production for which you are designing sound. All libraries have a copy of 17USC, the United States copyright laws. Refer to them for the exemptions.

When using a recording of music that is not in the public domain, an attempt should be made to reach the artist directly. Even if the artist approves the use of his material, though, he does not always hold the rights to his own music. Permission to use his material may have to be cleared through his manager, producer, or publishing company—parties that may not be as generous with the material as the artist (they may ask for a royalty or a hefty licensing fee). If you can't get through to the artist, contact performing rights organizations such as ASCAP (the American Society of Composers, Authors and Publishers), BMI (Broadcast Music Incorporated), or a clearinghouse (a company set up to clear musical rights and schedule royalty payments). Composers register their music and receive royalties through these organizations. Stringent laws apply to the use of music through ASCAP and BMI, but such laws are intended more for arenas, exercise studios, nightclubs, stores, and other businesses that use music for background ambiance than they are for theatrical use. Your budget, the size of the theatre, the number of performances, the way the music is used, and many other considerations will determine the fee that you would pay through ASCAP or BMI.

Clearing the use of music may involve a certain amount of red tape. You should not have to obtain permissions yourself, but give all the details to the production office so that they can secure clearances for you. Theoretically, all the producer needs to do is contact the artist (or her estate) directly with information about the production and what material is being used. What an artist will demand for permission to use her composition can vary widely. Sometimes she'll allow a piece to be used gratis, with only a mention in the program; sometimes she'll ask for a royalty, especially when the piece is used for dance. It depends on your production and on the artist.

Licensing of prerecorded sound effects varies from source to source. Some sound collections—such as Sound Ideas, which is a complete library of sound effects—take the purchase price as a buyout. You may use them freely as long as you don't try to sell the effects as your own. However, most of the sound effects recordings purchased at commercial retailers forbid the reproduction of their effects without written permission.

SEGMENTABLE MUSIC

Many compositions are set up thematically with sections (phrases) that you can refer to as A, B, C, D, and so on. A *phrase* is the smallest complete unit of musical thought, and it can be either created as an indivisible whole or structured by combining two or more smaller segments. Often, two parts of a musical phrase can sound almost identical, with the first part having a different resolution that doesn't sound as final as the ending of the second phrase. If two phrases together take twenty seconds and only ten seconds are needed for the cue, using the second phrase alone gives you the same musical statement in a shorter version. In Figure 4.1 one does not need to read music to see the patterns in the formation of the notes. The eight-measure phrases, A and B, can be evenly split in two.

61

FIGURE 4.1 Variation V from Mozart's *Piano Sonata in D Major* (K. 284) excerpt.

If you were to use A and B thematically, you could segment this composition in many ways for different timings and effects. You could:

- Use the sixteen measures of A and B in their entirety
- Repeat the eight-measure section of A and repeat the eight-measure section of B
- Use all of A alone at the top of a scene and repeat A2 at the end of the scene
- Use B2 as a tag that will serve as a musical punctuation at the end of the scene
- Edit A1 and B2 together to recall the beginning and end of the theme only

There are as many permutations of the composition as your needs for different timings. When you've introduced a theme and need to punctuate briefly between scenes, especially for Shakespeare, where the acts are often broken up into many scenes, the abbreviated forms of these themes are very convenient. You can use the entire piece or just the beginning of the two-part phrase at the top of a short scene and use the second phrase to end it. The audience will remember the musical statement, and the scene will be "framed" nicely.

When the director wants themes for certain characters, select instruments and musical strains that are easily extracted from a larger piece of work. Sometimes these themes will run as short as eight or ten seconds. With a piece of music that is sixteen, twenty-four, or thirty-two measures, you can usually find a shorter musical segment that sounds complete. You don't have to be able to read music or have the score in front of you to be able to discover such a segment.

As you listen to a segment, try isolating it from the rest of the piece to see if it can work alone, as a freestanding musical statement. Might it connote a particular feeling appropriate for your production? When listening to a piece of music with the idea of removing a small section—for example, a certain passage of a Brahms *intermezzo* or a certain lyric of a ballad by Jewel—plan how to extract a passage cleanly from the rest of the composition. Listen for "breaths" in the music that allow a clean edit or for small pauses that don't bleed into the next phrase. If none of these exist, your alternative is to do clean fades in and out.

If you have a basic background in music or you're working with a composer or music director who can assist you in determining the key of the music you are using, there are ways to blend the respective pitches of recorded and live music. For example, if you have pre-recorded music for either a preshow or an entr'acte leading into live singing (either *a cappella* or accompanied), you can change the key of the entire composition by adjusting its pitch so that the last note of the prerecorded music will be the same pitch used as a cue for the singers onstage. This technique gives a feeling of continuity to what happens *before* the action onstage, and works especially well when the prerecorded music is instrumental. Virtually all digital audio workstation software can perform a pitch change without changing the speed of the recording. But beware that there are limits to how much you can alter a recording before it sounds unrealistic.

To adjust a musical piece so that it better fits the situation, or for reasons of length, you may sometimes have to tack on different endings or beginnings from other sources. Certain production techniques allow you to take chords or notes directly from the piece itself and lengthen them—isolating the note or chord, looping this small segment, and adding it on to the existing tape. Suppose you have found the perfect piece for a theme, and all that's missing is a fanfare to introduce it. If the only suitable fanfare you can find is neither in the same key nor in a complementary one, you can change its pitch to make it fit the original. If you need to cut a piece short at a breath in the music, try adding some reverb to the end so that there is the appearance of a natural ending, not an abrupt silence.

PRESENTING YOUR CHOICES

If a character would best be represented by a certain selection of instruments and a style of music, try to find three choices for each theme to present to the director—remember not to offer dozens of alternatives (see Chapter 3). If a director is not musically articulate, she may have difficulty expressing what does or does not work for her. If the choices you offer have variety and fit within a certain character perception, the reaction from a director will give you more insight into her ideas so you can better supply what she wants.

For a production of *Much Ado About Nothing*, I had pulled three pieces from different sources to represent the character of Dogberry. He is traditionally played as a pompous buffoon, so I found a tuba solo, a bassoon bass/lute/sackbut trio, and an oboe/cello duet. Each of these selections had a sense of humor—one was more stately, one extremely slow, and one more blatty and silly. I let the director choose from these. If none had fit her idea of Dogberry, it would have been easier for her to articulate what character aspects were missing from my selections than to put into words what she wanted. In this somewhat reverse manner, the characters became more clearly focused. Actually, she loved the tuba solo.   —DK

When working on a show, you cultivate the germ of an idea. However, researching sound and music for a production may lead to materials and resources that modify the initial idea and guide you into new directions of development. Allow for this fluctuation in the process, and trust your artistic judgment as your rudder. As you narrow down the choices, a concise design composition evolves—only its execution remains.

64

5

The Sound Plot

All designers utilize paperwork to help them organize, remember, develop, present, and produce their ideas. Scenic and costume designers think by way of drawing. Lighting designers develop a light plot, which is a scale drawing that shows where all of the lighting instruments are located in the theatre, how they are plugged in, and what color filter is used. Similarly, many sound designers use a *sound plot* to assist them throughout their design process.

The sound plot is a concise table of information detailing the sound and music cues of a production in order of occurrence—in essence, it's a list of the sound cues. In its early stages, the sound plot identifies the cues and indicates their placement in the script. Later, the plot expands and includes more technical information regarding the production of the cues and the complete sound delivery system.

The information listed in the sound plot can be referred to when producing *operator cue sheets* (the instructions the sound operator uses to run the show; see Chapter 10), or when organizing "to do" lists (e.g., for effects sources). Whenever discussing the sound design with the director, you should have the sound plot at hand as a quick reference and a convenient way of seeing the scope of your design. Often a sound designer and a composer will concern themselves with the consistency and symmetry of their design, in which case a concise overview of the cues can be quite useful. Seeing the entire scope of the cueing can help the designer budget the show in terms of time and money.

The sound designer usually revises a sound plot numerous times before the show opens. As the sound design evolves over the entire production period, be sure to keep the sound plot up to date.

THE PRELIMINARY PLOT

The preliminary sound plot may consist of only the information that you gleaned from your first or second read-through of the script. It could also include ideas that have evolved after various meetings. The preliminary sound plot should list how you refer to the cue (its name or description), its page number, and any notes that might be important. At this point, the plot might indicate where in the action of the play the cue happens and might offer a detailed description of the cue.

Figure 5.1 is an excerpt from a preliminary sound plot for a production of *Measure for Measure*. The entries "I, iv" and "Inside a nunnery" indicate which scene the effects are in and where that scene is set. Often—and especially with Shakespeare—a director will refer to sections of the play in terms of act and location ("The prison scene in Act IV"). Having scene and place information in the appropriate location on the sound plot points you to the proper spot in the play. Act and scene are written in Roman numerals to distinguish them from page numbers (in the script). The location information is written in lowercase to differentiate it from other comments or notes. Note the page 67 "FADE OUT BIRD" cue. Fadeouts are just as important as any played cue. It is necessary to define fade information so that you are aware of the flow of the cueing. Knowing the flow of the cueing means that you know what equipment is in use at any moment in the show. Understanding the flow of your design will become important when you start determining the structure of your playback system.

SOUND CUE PLOT FOR MEASURE FOR MEASURE, REVISED 8/4/08   Page 1

ACT/SC	PAGE#	EFFECT	NOTES
I,iv Inside a nunnery			
	66	BELL AND BIRD	
	66	KNOCKS	BACK UP IF THE CUE ISN'T LIVE
	66	KNOCKS	BACK UP IF THE CUE ISN'T LIVE
	67	FADE OUT BIRD	AT THE END OF THE SCENE
II,ii Still at Angelo's			
	85	ANGELO UNDERSCORING	HIGH SEDUCTIVE, VILE SWEETNESS
II,iii Prison			
	86	X TO PRISON- LIGHT BACKGROUND	SLIGHT REVERB & OCCASIONAL SOFT SOUNDS
			ALL SOUNDS COME FROM ONE LOCATION
II,iv Back at Angelo's			
	88	X TO ANGELO UNDERSCORING	

FIGURE 5.1 A preliminary sound plot.

Most sound plots are generated using a computer. Designers use database, spreadsheet, or word processing software for this task. Developing your plot using a database program allows you to make as many layouts for your cue information as necessary. You might make a separate plot for the director and stage manager with just page number, effect, and notes on it. If the director and the stage manager have to wade through too much nonessential information, they may resist referring to your plot during the rehearsal process. Another layout could be used to make cue sheets. When using a database application to make your sound plot, you should assign each cue a number. This will make it possible to sort your cues in order of their occurrence.

Creating your sound plot in a database system allows the designer to track all the cue-running detail on a laptop or desktop computer. Many designers make their own systems for this purpose. Figures 5.2 and 5.3 show some screenshots from a sound plot created in a FileMaker Pro database template.

The term *Src*, or *source*, in Figure 5.2 refers to the source of a sound, whether it's a microphone, CD, MD, deck, synthesizer, sampler, crash box, or computer-assisted playback system. Note that we use Src as a generic term for any source of sound. When filling out your plot, include any source that produces sound (samplers, CD players, cassette decks, and even microphones) under the category Src.

SUBSEQUENT SOUND PLOTS

After you and the director have met and talked through the show, you will undoubtedly make some changes in your approach to the design. Ideally, you and the director will have established a conceptual starting point for the development of the aural elements of the production. Using the notes from this meeting, revise your sound plot to reflect any changes. You might want to distribute this revised plot to the director, since it can serve as a guide to remind him of where you both decided sound might fit into the production. Later plots also contain technical information regarding loudspeakers, sources, track numbers, and, if you haven't already added them, cue numbers.

These additional technical notes aren't as important to others who see your plot (the director or stage manager) as they are to you, but such notes will assist you in manufacturing the cues.

The next item added to your plot would be the loudspeaker assignment for the cue, indicating either a single loudspeaker or a

Rosencrantz and Guildenstern are Dead

Sound Cue Summary **Page: 1**

1/19/2009   Designer/Composer David Budries

Center Stage, Baltimore, Maryland

Cue No.	Page	Src.	Description	Area	Time	Notes:
100	3	Qlab	Curtain Speech	PRESENTATIONAL	0:50	
103	3	Qlab	Music -First Hearing	UPSTAGE RT	1:20	Humorous!
103.9	3	Qlab	Fade Music-First Hearing	UPSTAGE RT		
108	5	Qlab	Music -Second Hearing	UPSTAGE LT	1:20	
108.9	5	Qlab	Fade Music -Second Hearing	UPSTAGE LT		
112	9	Qlab	Music -Third Hearing			
112.9	9	Qlab	Fade Music -Third Hearing			
118	10	Qlab	Music Tragedians Arrive	PRESENTATIONAL		
118.9	10	Qlab	Music Tragedians Arrive	PRESENTATIONAL		
122	12	RF1	Music Tragedians Flourish	PRESENTATIONAL		
125	12	RF1	Player (Larry's) Underscore			
130	14	RF1	Sting			
134	16	RF1	Sabine Fanfare	PRESENTATIONAL		
142	20	RF1	"Calculator"			Thumb Piano
146	24	Qlab	Ophelia Hamlet			
148	24	Qlab	Claudius Gertrude Enter	PRESENTATIONAL		

FIGURE 5.2 An excerpt of a cue summary from a production of *Rosencrantz and Guildenstern Are Dead.*

Stage Mamngers Sound Cue Summary | Rosencrantz and Guildenstern are Dead | 1/19/2009

Cue No.	Page	Src.	Description	Actor	Cue Line
100	3	Qlab	Curtain Speech	w/Lights	Pre Show
103	3	Qlab	Music -First Hearing	Rosencrantz	What Suspense
103.9	3	Qlab	Fade Music-First Hearing	timed	What Suspense
108	5	Qlab	Music -Second Hearing	Guildenstern	Redistribution of Wealth
108.9	5	Qlab	Fade Music -Second Hearing	timed	Redistribution of Wealth
112	9	Qlab	Music -Third Hearing	Guildenstern	... have thought
112.9	9	Qlab	Fade Music -Third Hearing	timed	... have thought
118	10	Qlab	Music Tragedians Arrive	Guildenstern	... for a deer
118.9	10	Qlab	Music Tragedians Arrive	SM	... for a deer
122	12	RF1	Music Tragedians Flourish	Player	Tragedians
125	12	RF1	Player (Larry's) Underscore	Rosencrantz	...suggestive
130	14	RF1	Sting	Player	...about average
134	16	RF1	Sabine Fanfare	Player	...of the Sabine Women
142	20	RF1	"Calculator"	Guildenstern	odd numbers, I lose

FIGURE 5.3 A cue line summary layout from the same production.

69

ACT/SC	Q#	PG#	EFFECT	SRC	SPEAKER	TRX	NOTES
	2	55	TOP OF SHOW MUSIC	A	HOUSE	1 & 2	1) BELLS 2) TICKS (SOFT, DIST. FADE IN)
I,i Duke's Palace							
	3	58	TRANSITION MUSIC	A	HOUSE	1 & 2	1) BELL 2) TICKS (TICKS PLAY FIRST)
I,ii A Street							
	4	64	ORGAN/TIME MUSIC (TRANS.)	A	HOUSE	1 & 2	1) ORGAN 2) REVERB
I,iii A Monastery							
	5	64	ORGAN FADE OUT				
	6	68	TRANSITION MUSIC-ORGAN	A	HOUSE	1 & 2	1) ORGAN 2) REVERB
I,iv Inside a nunnery							
	7	66	NUNS CHANTING	B	HOUSE	1 & 2	
	7.6	70	NUNS FADE UP				
	7.7	66	NUNS FADE OUT				
	8	70	STRICT CLOCK MUSIC (TRANS.)	A	HOUSE	1 & 2	AT THE TRANSITION 1) TICKS 2) BELL
II,i Angelo's							
	10	78	TRANSITION MUSIC-BELL	A	HOTSPOTS	1	TICKS OUT
II,ii Angelo's							
	11	86	PRISON BELL & AREA MIC ON	A	HOUSE & CEILING	1	ADD LIGHT REVERB TO ROOM
II,iii Prison							
	15	88	TRANS. MUSIC/ AREA MIC OUT	A	HOUSE	1	
II,iv Back at Angelo's							
	16	95	FADE IN NUNS	B	UPSTAGE	1 & 2	FOR ISABELLA'S SPEECH
	17	95	PRISON BELL- AREA MIC ON/ NUNS OUT	A	HOUSE	1	MIDDLE LEVEL OF REVERB

FIGURE 5.4 The first sound plot, revised.

group of loudspeakers. A group is sometimes referred to as a distribution area. Information such as which playback source (SRC) is used and what output channels on the device are used may also be determined at this time.

Figure 5.4 is an excerpt from the final sound plot from the production of *Measure for Measure* seen in Figure 5.1. Notice how, over the

70

course of rehearsals, the sound design has developed substantially. Initially, there were no sound cues on the plot until I, iv; now there are five before that point. The page 66 "BELL AND BIRD" sound cue that was to introduce the nunnery was replaced by the sound of nuns chanting. Added to the headings on the plot are columns for cue number, the source (SRC), speaker assignment, and what tracks are being used. The notes column has evolved from jottings about the function or nature of the cue to details that will assist in the building and teching of the show.

In Cue 2, the "1 & 2" under TRX indicates that tracks 1 and 2 are going to be used for this cue. Under notes for Cue 2, "1) BELLS 2) TICKS" tells what effects are going to the first and second tracks in that cue. This needs to be figured out before transferring your cues to the playback device. In this example, "A" and "B" under SRC refer to two CD players. When making your cues, it's easier to consult the sound plot to determine what effects should go on which tracks than to figure it out as you go.

Once the production is in technical rehearsals, the sound plot has all of the basic information about a cue that the designer needs for quick reference. Notes like "SOFT, DIST. FADE IN" remind the designer how a cue should be executed. By having track notes like "1) BELL 2) TICKS" on the sound plot, the designer can tell the operator the proper track to adjust when a change is desired. Many designers keep their own set of cue sheets so that they have complete information about each cue readily available. The sound plot comes in handy because it uses fewer pages to describe the cues since it is less detailed than the cue sheets.

As soon as you've decided where the sound cues will come from (their location in the space), you should consider making a simple sketch of your system in plan view (bird's eye view) and label your individual loudspeakers and loudspeaker areas. Label loudspeaker areas by their function: front fill, high center fill, surrounds, for example. If your console output assignments are fixed, then you can add that to this drawing as well. This (as in lighting design) is often called a magic sheet. For larger systems, these can get quite complex and may have to be expressed on multiple sheets. Once you have this guide, you can easily make your loudspeaker assignments.

Most designers set up their own convention for identifying the loudspeakers. Some refer to the loudspeakers by letters (speaker A, B, C), some by numbers. If you're using a simple four-speaker system—two speakers over the stage, two in the rear of house—you could label them A through D, starting to your left and moving clockwise. With more complicated setups, designers often name the loudspeakers by number and location (upstage left) or by function (kitchen radio). This approach is more precise and less confusing to you, the audio engineer and the operator. If more than one loudspeaker is being used at a time, label them in a way that refers to the function of the grouped loudspeakers (or loudspeaker area). If you're using all of the loudspeakers out in the house, naming this group "house mix" on your plot should indicate to what loudspeakers the cue is sent.

SOURCES OR PLAYBACK DEVICES

Manually operated designs should be constructed with ease of operation in mind. Even a show running on a computer-assisted playback system will benefit from a well-thought-out, organized design. This is not to say that you must avoid tricky cueing sequences—even when manually cued, most sequences can be operated with enough practice. But the fewer changes your sound operator has to make at the mixer, the less chance there is for error.

As you scan the sound plot, you might see cues that are similar. If a script indicates one thunder cue, it will probably need at least five or more. If you are operating manually using a simple system, dedicate a specific playback device and a specific channel to those thunder cues. This will simplify operation by reducing the number of times that the sound operator needs to reassign inputs. If there are different cues in the scene that play out of different loudspeakers, put them on another playback device. If that is impossible and other cues come between the thunder cues, record them on a track that you're not using. Logical planning will cut down on the number of moves the operator has to make. Organizing the effects using various decks is not difficult if you use the sound plot to see the overall picture of the design. Putting similar cues on the same playback device and track can also save you time during the sound level session. The level-setting session (see Chapter 9), which precedes the first technical rehearsal, is where preliminary volumes are set for the cues. The sound designer usually needs double the time that the theatre allows for a level-setting session—in fact, some theatres do not provide for a level session at all. By having similar cues on one deck and track, you can set the level for one transition music cue and thus approximate that level for all of them. Many shows start out with preshow and/or lead-in music, cues that usually come from the house loudspeakers, as opposed to effects speakers or those used for underscoring onstage. There are often other framing cues in the show (see Chapter 2). Once you've set the preshow music, you'll be familiar with its qualities—its loudness, presence, and texture. And chances are that other cues of the same type (intermission music, postshow music) will demand similar presentation. To set the sound level of the intermission music, you can look back at your notes for the preshow and try those settings as a logical starting point. By using one speaker setup and limiting the framing effects to the same playback device, you can cut down on the reassigning that your operator will have to do while establishing a reference point by which you can estimate the settings for the other cues.

TRACKS

In addition to keeping similar cues on the same playback device and track, there are other considerations in choosing a track for recording music or effects. Is the cue going to be presented in mono, stereo, or in a multichannel mix? When a show is operated manually, it is essential to look at the speaker assignments of the playback device channels in preceding cues. Doing so allows you to distribute your cues so that the sound operator doesn't have to reassign inputs on the mixer more than necessary. Is there going to be a crossfade from one loudspeaker (or group of loudspeakers) to another?

In most circumstances, a mono cue should be recorded on one channel. If only one channel is used for a mono cue, the other channel(s) can be preset for cues (except for volume) later in the show. If it means cutting down on the amount of reassigning for the sound operator, then using two channels for mono is acceptable. This situation can occur when a mono cue is sandwiched between two stereo cues. Also, it is usually easier to crossfade between loudspeakers by crossing input faders. Crossfading from a group of house loudspeakers to a set of underscoring speakers upstage is simple whenever two faders have the same program material. Assign one fader to the house speakers and the other to the underscoring speakers. This is easier than trying to move a number of output faders at one time.

CUE NUMBERS AND LETTERS

Cues need to be labeled sequentially so that the designer, sound operator, and stage manager can identify them. Numbering sound cues is the practice of many designers, but some designers and stage managers prefer to label sound cues by letter. They feel this helps separate sound cues from light cues, which seem always to be numbered. When using the lettering system, most designers avoid the letter Q. If the stage manager calls "Cue Q," it sounds like a stutter and can be easily misunderstood. Once you get to Z, go to AA as a cue label.

73

74

Souvenir by Stephen Temperly

Sound Cue Summary   Page: 1

1/19/2009   Designer/Composer David Budries   Westport Country Playhouse - Jason Robards Theatre

Cue No.	Page	Src.	RNo.	Description	Area	Dur.	Notes:
116 Op6	I-30	SFX		Queen of the Night-	Gramophone	01:27	with LX Q40.5
117	I-30	SFX		Needle Lift-Queen of the	Gramophone	0:01	
118 Op2	I-32	SFX		Queen of the Night Excerpt	Gramophone	0:05	
119	I-32	SFX		Needle Lift End Q	Gramophone	0:01	
120	I-32	SFX		Queen of the Night Excerpt	Gramophone	0:13	
121	I-32	SFX		Needle Lift	Gramophone	0:01	
122	I-32	SFX		Queen of the Night Excerpt	Gramophone	0:13	
123	I-32	SFX		Needle Lift End Q	Gramophone	0:01	
135	II-49	SFX		Applause Sustained	Aud Specials	0:22	Then She Enters... With LX Q70
136	II-49	SFX		Applause End Q	Aud Specials	0:10	
137	II-49	SFX		Burst of Applause/Brava P1	Aud Specials	0:24	
138	II-49	SFX		Abstract Clap Ending	Aud Specials	0:12	

FIGURE 5.5 A sound plot or cue summary.

When inserting a cue under this lettering system, the most common approach is to add a number after the letter: a cue inserted between Cue C and Cue D would be called Cue C1. Under the numbering system, an inserted cue will be a point cue (utilizing a decimal point) or will use a letter (starting with A) after it. Thus, a cue added between Cue 4 and 5 will either be Cue 4.5 or Cue 4 A. Letter or number the cues late in the sound design process to keep the number of point or "A" cues to a minimum, since these cues can be cumbersome for the stage manager to call.

While the lettering system can work for smaller, manually operated shows, a numbering system is essential when you create a sound plot using a computer-based system. Additionally, when using a database application for creating your sound plot and other paperwork, a cue number must be entered for each record. Typically, the cue number is the reference used for sorting cues. This technique requires that you leave some space between cues for new ideas (cues) to be inserted. Consider using a different numbers sequence from the lighting designer. If lighting starts with Q1, then you can start with Q100 or 200.

There are no hard and fast rules when it comes to numbering your cues. However, a rule of thumb for me is to use whole numbers for the beginning of any cue sequence, point cues (Q11.2) for internal moves within the cue, and .9's (11.9) to stop or fade out a cue. I skip a few numbers before I label the next cue so that I leave room for cues that may get inserted into the cue sequence at a later time. This way, I shouldn't have to renumber existing cues. There is no perfect system for numerical cueing, but it beats the daylights out of letters when you have a 300-cue show. The stage manager usually gets used to this system very easily. —DB

Some designers choose to include other information on their plots, such as:

- Time, or length of the cue
- Timings of how long the play's action that corresponds to the cue ran in rehearsal
- Count, or rate of execution of the cue (fade up or down, waits, etc.)
- Detailed notes about the construction or mixing of the cue and its options
- Detailed publishing information related to previously published materials used in the play

Stage Managers Cue Summary | Souvenir by Stephen Temperly | 1/19/2009

Cue No.	Page	Src.	Description	Actor	Cue Line
116 Op6	I-30	SFX	Queen of the Night-Transition	FFJ	Lowers the arm onto the gramophone
117	I-30	SFX	Needle Lift-Queen of the Night	FFJ	Lifts the arm from the gramophone
118 Op2	I-32	SFX	Queen of the Night Excerpt P1	FFJ	Lowers the arm onto the gramophone
119	I-32	SFX	Needle Lift End Q	FFJ	Lifts the arm from the gramophone
120	I-32	SFX	Queen of the Night Excerpt 2	FFJ	Lowers the arm onto the gramophone
121	I-32	SFX	Needle Lift	FFJ	Lifts the arm from the gramophone
122	I-32	SFX	Queen of the Night Excerpt 3	FFJ	There There! - GO
123	I-32	SFX	Needle Lift End Q	FFJ	Lifts the arm from the gramophone
135	II-49	SFX	Applause Sustained	Cosme'	Then... she entered - GO
136	II-49	SFX	Applause End Q	FFJ	settles herself to sing - GO
137	II-49	SFX	Burst of Applause/Brava P1	FFJ	Finishes the Aria - GO
138	II-49	SFX	Abstract Clap Ending	FFJ	moves her hand to her heart - GO
140	II-50	SFX	Q140 Serenata	Cosme'	I began the introduction - GO
140.05	II-50	SFX	Medium Cackle 4a	FFJ	wildly shakes her maraca
140.1	II-50	SFX	Small Laughter @ Maraca	FFJ	2x maraca shake
140.2	II-50	SFX	Small Laughter @ Maraca #2	FFJ	2x maraca shake
140.3	II-50	SFX	Small Laughter @ Maraca #3	FFJ	2x maraca shake
140.35	II-50	SFX	Small Laughter @ Shake	FFJ	1x maraca shake
140.4	II-50	SFX	Small Laughter @ Maraca #4	FFJ	2x maraca shake
140.5	II-50	SFX	Small Laughter @ Maraca #5	FFJ	2x maraca shake
141	II-50	SFX	Applause	FFJ	The Song Ends - GO

FIGURE 5.6 Stage manager's cue summary.

- Actor and cue line or action. (this is especially useful for a stage manager's cue summary layout because it's information that you want to share with them)

Figure 5.6 shows a variation of a sound plot, a stage manager's cue summary. Developed using a database program, this summary shows only information that the sound designer believes to be relevant to the stage manager.

THE LOUDSPEAKER PLOT

As sound designers have access to more complex systems for the playback of their work, many find that they need additional paperwork to assist them and those that work with them. One valuable item is the loudspeaker plot.

Just as you create a plot for your sound and music content, it is necessary to create a plot for your sound delivery system. As you begin to auralize the elements of your design (auralizing is imagining the sound in the theatrical space, as it takes place over time), you will begin to understand where you need to locate loudspeakers in order to create the aural illusions or effects that support the production.

When you listen to music or sound from your home stereo or headphones, you'll probably notice that some of the sounds appear to spread out in front of you. In some situations you might perceive sound from behind, above you, or even in your head. If this level of illusion is possible with two loudspeakers, consider the complex imagery that might be possible with multiple loudspeakers. In an extreme example, Jonathan Deans designed a sound delivery system for Cirque du Soleil's Las Vegas production of *LOVE* using 6039 custom loudspeakers. Can you imagine the illusory possibilities of that system? You, however, might consider a simpler arrangement of loudspeakers around the perimeter of your theatre. With a sixteen-channel delivery system, it will be possible to create a number of workable aural illusions. Of course, the more loudspeakers you add, the more control you will need. The bottom line is that it will be necessary for you to learn how to arrange and control multiple loudspeakers in order to create the desired effect. Drawing these loudspeakers positions in section and plan view will constitute a loudspeaker plot. This is an essential part of any professional sound design.

Another possibility when designing an arrangement of loudspeakers is to group a number of units doing the same job into a distribution area. Having a number of loudspeakers working together can

77

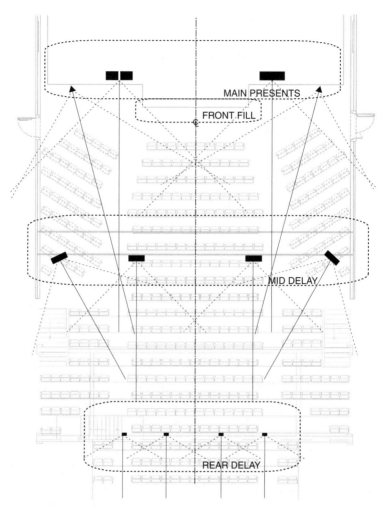

FIGURE 5.7 A loudspeaker distribution area drawing.

be a very effective way of creating either a directed or diffuse aural image, depending upon how the loudspeakers are arrayed or placed.

Figure 5.7 is a plan view drawing identifying distribution zones. This drawing shows four zones: main presents, front fill, mid delay, and rear delay. The solid line from each speaker is the on-axis point, which shows how to aim the loudspeaker on the horizontal plane. You'll need a section view drawing to present the focus of the loud-speakers on the vertical plane. The dotted lines are the 6 dB down points—where the volume of the loudspeaker becomes 6 dB lower than the volume at the loudspeaker.

The needs of the production and the preferences of the designer will determine the format of the sound plot. Because different designers want different information to be readily available, the composition of a sound plot will be an individual choice. Regardless of which setup you choose, in the end, a sound plot is an invaluable means of organizing your work.

79

6

Working with the Theatre Company

In the mid-seventies I was hired as the resident sound designer, music director, composer, and sometimes-performer at a struggling theatre. I performed all of these functions simultaneously. I was not alone in this multi-faceted atmosphere—the stage manager, whom I thought must have been a wizard, also served as the lighting designer, technical director, master electrician, master carpenter, and occasionally the wardrobe mistress and janitor. He was fond of telling all staff, when asked for any assistance or out-of-the-ordinary request, that it was simply not possible—and then he would do it. —DK

Theatre is a collaborative art. No one works in a vacuum. Ideally, everyone depends on each other to give his individual artistic input and to interact in a supportive manner. For example, loudspeakers can't be built into set pieces without the guidance and support of both the set designer and technical director. A director might ask for a special effect that would cause you to exceed your budget, but only the production manager, producer, or business manager has the power to adjust your budget. In the same way that you expect your needs to be given full consideration, so must you be mindful of the artistic and financial needs of the production. Let your needs be known early in the process, especially in theatres that have not worked with a sound designer before.

Your needs will probably be related to budget and rehearsal matters, and can include such items as:

- Paying for studio time
- Hiring musicians

- Buying recordings and blank media
- Renting special equipment or instruments
- Hiring a sound operator
- Securing a workspace
- Renting and reserving music rehearsal space
- Scheduling time in the theatre for dry tech rehearsals
- Supplying a dedicated communication channel and appropriate headset/handset
- Allotting quiet time for initial soundchecks (including sound system focus and balance sessions) in the theatre prior to first tech
- Providing additional quiet time for setting rough cue levels and musician mix balances
- Duplicating performance conditions during level setting (any fans or air conditioners that are on during the performance should be on at the time of level setting)
- Guaranteeing absolute quiet during tech, as required for cue adjustments
- Running difficult sequences outside of tech with your sound operator
- Ensuring that your sound operator has time for a soundcheck before every performance

---

I was invited to be a guest artist at a large university that assured me that they had an adequate sound system. A conscientious technical director had made sure that the theatre had decent equipment—but that had been fifteen years earlier. Since then, it had not been updated, maintained, or even used much, so the booth and the equipment were disheveled and disorganized. The first thing that caught my eye upon entering this booth was a dusty sign made to look like a sampler hanging over the mixing console. It voiced an attitude that seems to prevail at many theatres: "Everyone in the theatre knows two things. Their job—and sound." The same could be said for music.   —DK

CONTRACTS

Your design and/or composition fee and contract should be on par with those of the other designers. As a professional, don't be short shrifted because the powers-that-be don't understand the time and energy required for your work. Also, make sure that your program credit and bio are treated in the same manner as the other designers.

Don't be surprised to find a lack of awareness at any level of theatre, because knowledge about sound design, although improving, can be limited. Affirmatively, in 2008, the American Theatre Wing (Tony Awards) instituted two sound design awards, one for Best Sound Design of a Play and another for Best Sound Design of a Musical.

In 2002, United Scenic Artists Local USA 829 began to accept sound designers under the collective bargaining agreement with the League of Regional Theatres (LORT). The 2005–2009 LORT agreement and examples of an artist's coversheet are available on the USA website. Even if you are not a union member, these documents can still serve as guidelines for salary and benefit expectations.

The producer typically attaches a rider to the coversheet of your contract that defines your work schedule, production sound budget, travel expense, hotel, designer expense lines, bio, billing, per diem, and other contractual obligations. For more information about United Scenic Artists Local 829, go to http://www.usa829.org/.

Artist's contracts and riders are continually renegotiated, but they usually include much of the information listed below.

- *Production schedule:* The production schedule not only lists the dates of your commitment to the production, but also includes important dates like design meetings and technical rehearsals that you are expected to attend.
- *Fee schedule:* This schedule details when you'll get paid. Often, you will receive a percentage of your fee at a specific milestone in the production. Payments could be made at contract signing, acceptance of initial sound plot, final preview, opening or closing night, or some date agreed on during the run of the show.
- *Additional fees:* You may be compensated or reimbursed for your assistant's fee, additional weekly compensation, out-of-pocket expenses, and transportation. You should receive additional weekly compensation (AWC) in the event the production of the play extends beyond its scheduled run. AWC provides the designer an additional fee per week (prorated for partial weeks) for each week of the extension period. Reimbursements are often subject to approval by the production manager/ director of production. The producer should agree to pay (or provide) your round-trip transportation and possible additional transportation costs incurred by you and accommodations convenient to the theatre or working place during any residence period. This may not be the case in certain metropolitan areas, as a designer is expected to be "local." The policy for

reimbursement for other personal expenses incurred that are directly related to the production (such as telephone, fax, postage, and shipping) should also be detailed.

- *Responsibilities:* Some producers specifically delineate what your duties are, such as producing the design or composition, showing up for meetings, or completing your work within the authorized budget. They may also ask you to provide detailed cue sheets, hook-ups, and a sound plot. The contract may state that errors or mechanical problems, including but not limited to board operator mistakes or power failures, shall not constitute a breach of your agreement.

  There might be a clause that states that if the designer cannot perform because of fire, strikes, riot, act of God, war, the public enemy, or any other cause of the same general class that could not be reasonably anticipated or prevented, then neither the theatre nor the designer shall be entitled to any contractual compensation for the time during which said services were not able to be rendered.

- *Rights and intellectual property:* Be sure to include a clause stating that the producer agrees not to make any of your sound design available to any third party without your written consent. The producer should also agree to make all best efforts to return your original materials at the end of the production. The producer should agree not to make any changes in your design without prior permission. You may agree to be available for consultation with respect to any requested changes.

  The theatre must agree that all rights in and to the design conceived by you in the course of your services to the theatre shall be your exclusive property, and that you hold the copyright for the design of the production. The production materials are your property. Some theatres may include a clause stating that the design remains the property of both you *and* the theatre. Do not accept this clause. You are the owner of your design. You are the owner of your intellectual property, excluding previously published materials. If the producer requests a copy of your design for their archives, you should produce it and include that cost in your production expenses.

  The theatre must agree not to alter nor permit anyone else to alter or make substitutions for any portion of the sound design without your prior consent and approval. However, the theatre may claim to have a perpetual and irrevocable license to use such designs in any production of the play from which

83

the designer receives a royalty. All such changes would become your property.

The theatre may agree that in the event the play is subsequently produced, alone or in association with others, it will offer you the same job.

- *Billing and marketing:* You should have the right to approve your biography, as it will appear in the program. Your contract should state that you will receive billing in the program on the title page or cast page, on a line alone, or on a line with set, costume, and lighting designers. Your billing should be of the same size, type, and prominence of the other designers' billing.

  The producer may state that she will not film, televise, or otherwise transmit complete or partial performances of the play, or authorize or permit others to do so, without first negotiating and executing a written agreement with you, providing for mutually agreeable compensation. This might not apply to commercials or publicity related to items of fifteen minutes or less, provided the producer shall receive no payment except for actual out-of-pocket expenses.

- *Insurance:* You may be asked to agree that the theatre is not responsible for the security of your personal property or effects unless such property is deposited with the theatre for safekeeping. However, if you are providing equipment to the production, you may request that they insure your equipment in the form of a rider to their policy. The producer may agree that you shall be specifically named as an additional insured under the theatre's general comprehensive liability insurance policy. You may be asked to agree to look only to the insurance company in respect of all claims.

The reality of the situation is that you might not be offered a contract or given the opportunity to negotiate *any* of your demands. Then you must ask yourself if you want to work with this producer, and whether doing so is worth the uncertainty of trusting a handshake. Some theatres operate very casually, and nothing is ever signed by anyone. You might stress to the theatre that the contract is to protect both you and the theatre, but if their operations are along the lines of "My father has a barn, . . . let's put on a show!" then you need to determine whether the project is of enough interest to you. Very early on in your career, there may not be enough of a fee for you to even quibble. However, certain points for your protection can be presented to the theatre and you might want to give them something in writing even if a contract is not forthcoming. (Please refer to the Sound Designers' and Composers' Forum at the end of the book, where our distinguished colleagues discuss their views on contract negotiations.)

PRINCIPAL POSITIONS IN THE THEATRE COMPANY

Theatres vary in their organizational structures, but there is a basic setup that many theatres follow. Understanding your relationship to each person in the "chain of command" can save you unnecessary confusion when you're trying to sort through the bureaucracy and determine who does what. You should know how many people are affected by decisions you make, and who will be affronted if you don't clarify your actions to them.

As a general rule, the larger the theatre, the more likely it is that they know how to accommodate a sound designer. For smaller theatres, you may be among the first sound designers they have ever hired. Before having a sound designer, sound effects may have simply been burned to a compact disc as a last-minute consideration by an intern, stage manager, or the director himself. Now, even though they have hired you, they may not have considered all of your requirements. If you know your needs and who is likely to fulfill them, you can help the theatre accommodate your design responsibilities.

85

THE ARTISTIC DIRECTOR

Every theatre, no matter how small, is headed by an artistic director who decides which productions will be included in the season, selects and approves the artistic and design staff to be hired, and reserves the final say-so on all artistic decisions. The artistic director may or may not direct shows within the season. She may function more as an administrator, fitting the right staff to her chosen projects. She answers to the board of directors of the theatre and confers with the managing director on money matters. She may hire you and be your contact for working on another production at the theatre. The artistic director may come to rehearsals at any point during the production process and ask for changes, either directly through you or through the director. Do not, however, ever feel compelled to make her suggested changes without the director's knowledge. She may mediate artistic differences between you and the director or other designers, although rarely should you ever need to take your problems as high as the artistic director. Your interaction with the artistic director may be so limited that you could go through an entire production without ever meeting her.

THE MANAGING DIRECTOR

The managing director is responsible for the seasonal budget and operating costs of running the theatre. He also works directly with the theatre's board of directors and is usually the chief financial officer of the organization. Your contract was probably approved (though not offered specifically) by the managing director, so he must clear any addenda or alterations to it.

THE PRODUCER

Most theatres in the commercial arena have a producer who is responsible for the overall execution of the production. The producer has many of the responsibilities of the artistic director and managing director. Producers put together the entire production, which includes financing, securing the space, and hiring the director, actors, and design staff as well as the other members of the management team. In the world of not-for-profit theatre, it's not uncommon for the artistic director or the managing director to serve as executive producer.

THE DIRECTOR

The director oversees a particular production, but her aesthetic decisions may be subject to influence by the artistic director. Generally, she casts the show herself (or with a casting director), but is sometimes presented with a complete cast and crew. She may be given free reign over her design staff, or may be presented with the theatre's resident staff. She may not even be previously connected to the theatre. If she is a resident director, she may be able to assist you in persuading a budget-conscious managing director to accommodate your needs for sound design. If you're an unknown entity to the director, you may not have an easy rapport with her, and you may have to struggle with any preconceived ideas she has of what sound design can do. The more a director knows and appreciates what creative sound—and particularly your design talents—can do for her production, the more work that will generate for you.

THE PRODUCTION MANAGER

The production manager (sometimes called the director of production) serves as the liaison between the technical and creative staff and the management of the theatre. It is his responsibility to make

86

sure that the designs for the production are executed on time, within budget, and as the designer intended. All technical department heads report to the production manager. Not every question you have will be addressed by him, but he is the one person on staff who has a full overview of how the theatre runs and how to best coordinate your design. Although the managing director approved your contract, the production manager was probably the person who offered it to you. You'll see him to request increases in budget, changes in scheduling, or revised deadlines.

THE COMPANY MANAGER

The company manager should see to most of your creature comforts. If you've been jobbed in for a production, she might handle your travel accommodations, living situation, special considerations, and ground transportation. See her for information about banking privileges, grocery shopping, daycare for a child, and needs of a visiting spouse (or even a pet).

THE PRODUCTION STAGE MANAGER

The production stage manager's responsibilities depend on the size of the theatre. At regional theatres, he is in charge of arranging rehearsal times, fittings, recording sessions involving actors, and similar activities when there are numerous productions in rehearsal and performance. The larger the theatre, the less responsibility he has to a specific production. Although qualified as a stage manager, he may not ever run a show. Sometimes he's the head of the stage management department.

On Broadway and off-Broadway, the production stage manager's production book is the one used to call the show. He was the original stage manager as the show developed, although his book may be passed along to subsequent stage managers. He coordinates production meetings and the activities of the designers. The production stage manager may assign the maintenance of the blocking, tracking props, and other technical elements to stage managers, production assistants, or interns. He also supervises understudy rehearsals.

If the show is a long-running one, the production stage manager's most important duty is making sure that the production doesn't deviate from the director's intentions. He'll periodically sit in the audience to take notes, maintain the technical aspects, and check the blocking. He deals directly with the music director regarding changes he observes in tempo and any problems with live music; he also listens for speaker quality and sound levels. In this capacity, the production stage manager can correct any deviations from your original design.

THE STAGE MANAGER

The stage manager schedules rehearsals, records blocking, and runs tech rehearsals. She is, in sum, your link to a smooth production. Besides calling the cues, once the show has opened, the stage manager also preserves the actors' performance level and maintains the integrity of the designs. She takes over where the director has left off and holds the show together with her constant ministrations.

If the stage manager understands your job and needs in tech rehearsals, she can field interference with the director and the actors to ensure that tech time is not wasted. This is especially helpful when working with directors or actors unaccustomed to working with a sound designer. A stage manager who is savvy about sound affects your experience completely and wonderfully. There are dream stage managers, who anticipate the calls as if they have an innate feel for your design. There are stage managers who have a sophisticated musical sense—after hearing the music once or twice, they can recognize where cues are meant to happen and adjust their calls appropriately. Because of their respect and appreciation for your work, they understand your needs during tech rehearsal and allow for both the quiet and the time you require. This type of stage manager recognizes the importance of your work in rehearsal and makes every effort to assist you. She can identify deviations in your sound design during performances—even over a monitor loudspeaker—and can correct a problem with a cue even as it plays. When you are a distance designer (a New York designer working on the West Coast, for example), the stage manager can be a vital link to the rehearsal process and the day-to-day changes that might affect your design. Having a strong rapport with a good, musically adept stage manager will greatly improve your work experience and, hence, the production.

Other stage managers, while aware of sound design, nonetheless lack the skill or musicality to correctly call your sound cues. There are very few options by which to remedy this situation. You may be tempted to ask your sound operator to compensate for late or missed cues. This is less than ideal and may not be completely ethical (by all rights, the sound operator should not run a cue until it is called). You may ignore the imperfect calling, grin and bear it, and pray that you'll never have to work with this stage manager again. You could also try to tell her exactly what was wrong about the late or missed cue, and suggest another place for her to call it. In some situations you could ask her to use a stopwatch to time an event if she cannot feel the music of a moment. In any case, you may never hear the show exactly the way you intended it to be.

If the cues are missed frequently, consider cutting them altogether, since a poorly executed cue is worse than no cue at all. Some sound designers choose not to have stage managers call sound cues. Arguments have even been made by some distrustful sound designers that it is better not to use a stage manager to call the cue, because it's one too many links in the chain of events, and because her reaction time causes the cue to be executed inaccurately. On the other hand, to require a sound operator to keep track of where he is in the script—and at the same time run all the cues in the show—is an unnecessary burden. A competent stage manager should be able to judge the reaction time of the sound operator. On extremely tight cueing, the sound operator may be advised to initiate a cue himself after being properly warned and readied by the stage manager.

Be sure to let the stage manager know from the start what your rehearsal needs will be. Inquire about production meetings so that there is no doubt in anyone's mind about your interest and your need to be there.

To help the stage manager incorporate your work into the production, take the following steps. Before first tech, talk through the cues with her as she marks her production script or prompt book. Try to make rehearsal recordings easy to use; when changes are needed, supply revisions as soon as possible. Let the stage manager know when you'll be attending rehearsal to obtain timings. If she knows that you need to get an accurate sense of the flow of a sequence, she can keep the actors or director from interrupting the scene until you complete your timings.

THE TECHNICAL DIRECTOR

The technical director's job is to assist all members of the production team in carrying through their designs. At smaller theatres, he may be the person who supervises the set construction, hangs the lights and loudspeakers, and wires the sound equipment. In other situations, he may be responsible only to the set designer.

The technical director can inform you of any aspects of the set or lights that affect your loudspeaker placement. He'll be familiar with the layout of the theatre and may know any peculiarities of the sound system. Should you not have an assistant, the technical director may assist you or have someone on his staff help you set up your equipment. Usually, the technical director is well versed in sound equipment, but if he is not, someone on his team probably is.

THE SOUND SUPERVISOR

The sound supervisor is the head of the sound department. While this is typical of larger theatres, the term has begun to infiltrate all levels of the industry. She is sometimes part of the design staff, but in general, she serves in a purely technical capacity. All sound department personnel report to the sound supervisor. One of her most important responsibilities is to act as a liaison with guest designers. She is responsible for maintaining the equipment and will help in familiarizing incoming sound designers with the acoustics of the theatre, the equipment, and the sound operator. You should provide her with all your production paperwork, including schematic block diagrams, plan and section drawings, shop orders, a hook-up, patch schedule, as well as microphone and RF schedules. She will coordinate the load-in of your design, so be specific about the placement and particulars of the equipment. For example, when specifying that loudspeakers be placed upstage, your production paperwork should indicate the position, pan, and tilt (focus) of each loudspeaker.

THE SOUND ENGINEER

Smaller theatres may not define a position called sound supervisor and instead will define their primary audio position as sound engineer. This person will most likely be part of your labor pool when loading in or configuring your sound system. He will help build cables, set up your system patch, configure your console, build practicals, or anything necessary to execute the load-in. If the producer has more than one venue, he might assign a sound engineer to each performance space. In theatres with more staff members in the sound department, the sound engineer will work under the sound supervisor and is sometimes referred to as the A1.

ASSISTANT SOUND ENGINEER

In larger theatres, it is common to have an assistant sound engineer, or A2. This is usually a seasonal position or possibly an internship position. The responsibilities of the assistant sound engineer will vary depending on the size of the venue. She will generally assist with every aspect of the load-in, strike, run-of-show tasks, and general maintenance. In smaller venues she might be the sound operator or sound mixer on a production.

THE SOUND OPERATOR

The sound operator runs the cues and mixes live sound during tech and performances. He is responsible for the daily soundcheck (loudspeakers, microphones, playback, and special effects), maintaining communications systems, and faithfully executing your design throughout the run of the production. Being a good sound operator requires a certain finesse and is similar to playing a musical instrument, so give careful thought to the expertise of your sound operator when designing a show. Timing and style are talents that may not come naturally to the sound operator. The best thing you can do is to instill in the operator a feeling of confidence and appreciation for his efforts. When possible, include him in as much of your preparation for the show as possible. If the operator expresses interest, see if he can be hired to assist you when producing the cues. This will bring him into the creative process earlier, offering him a greater understanding of how the cues fit into the entire production. Such involvement may pay off in a greater sensitivity to your work and better operating skills. At times, you might be stuck with a totally inept sound operator, one who cannot lend any consistency at all to the design that you have set. This may be due to inexperience or to a bad attitude. Either ask that he be replaced or try to work with him and the stage manager until he develops a feel for the equipment and running the cues. With the advent and increasing adoption of computer-controlled playback systems, sound operators have become more like light ops. They often just press "GO" buttons except when there are live mix elements and, of course, in musicals, where they are not called sound operators, but production sound mixers.

91

PRODUCTION SOUND MIXER

The production sound mixer is a specialized sound operator who must be quite musical and is able to take direction from the sound (reinforcement) designer in conjunction with the musical director in a music theatre production. Her role is essential in making a musical sound good. She artfully blends the orchestral accompaniment and the singers through a sound reinforcement system that is intended to faithfully amplify the live performance. Some sound designers might work with their operator to create a very subtle reinforcement that is extremely effective, but barely noticeable. Other designers will want to create a visceral experience, where the audience is immersed in the performance. Therein lies the art of the mix. In smaller venues, the production sound mixer may be the sound engineer. On Broadway and on tours, these mixers are specialized individuals and the key person the designer relies on to represent his work throughout the run of the production.

PRODUCTION MEETINGS

Production meetings are useful for addressing immediate and eventual design issues with all department heads and designers present. Questions and needs that arise during rehearsal can be addressed, and matters like having to place a speaker in a prop—as well as other crossover considerations—should be discussed at these meetings. Avoid lengthy discussions that involve only one other department in a production meeting. There's no need to take up the time of other departments. But feel free to introduce these issues in a production meeting, since many problems can be solved efficiently when all decision-making entities are present.

At some theatres, the stage manager writes up rehearsal notes after each rehearsal day. These notes are divided up by department and consist of information and questions for which the director and stage manager will need answers. If these questions aren't addressed by the following production meeting, they are brought up again for immediate attention.

Not all theatres have regular production meetings. Some are sufficiently small-scale that the logistics of communication and decision making are simple and direct.

In situations where you are designing remotely, see if the theatre can provide a teleconference phone device or even a webcam so you can participate in the meetings in real time, even over great distances.

BUDGETARY LIMITATIONS

One of your considerations when working with a theatre is its financial health. The fiscal stability of the theatre will be reflected in your budget, the type and range of equipment you have to work with, and what shape that equipment is in. You'll have to produce your design within the time and budget parameters of the theatre.

It's crucial that you estimate what your budget requirements are prior to first meetings. This may seem like fortune-telling, but with experience, you can learn to judiciously determine how much certain services cost and how far your budget will stretch.

You may find that the quality of the sound equipment at the theatre is deficient. In that case, either make do with what is there or, if necessary, start accumulating your own equipment to rent to the theatre. If you know that the theatre is safe and that your equipment will not be mishandled, the latter choice may turn out to be a fine investment, since your equipment could eventually pay for itself from rental fees.

TOURING CONSIDERATIONS

When you are contracted as a sound designer for a tour, be aware of the differences in the organizational structure of the production. In this situation, the company manager may be concerned primarily with the cast, and you may simply be supplied with a per diem allotment. In that case, you might have to find your own housing. Instead of a production manager, there may be a production supervisor responsible for scheduling and for the overall flow of the tour. The budget has already been set and, short of disaster, it won't be increased, so all of your design considerations must be agreed on before you begin to work with a tour.

When a show that has been playing in a theatre is then adapted for touring, a different staff may be required. It's common for well-funded tours to be fully equipped and staffed specifically for the tour. But it's also common to expect that in order to tour successfully, the sound design must be tailored to limitations of equipment, staff, and the unknown properties of the varied spaces in which the show will play. Keeping your touring design as simple as possible could be advantageous. Unless you or a trusted operator is to travel with the production, and unless there's a large budget to provide for the upkeep of primary and auxiliary equipment, you have no way of ensuring that once it is on the road, your sound design will be maintained as you originally intended. A smaller touring production sound design may have to be run through different loudspeakers, played on different equipment, and executed by a different operator at each location. Ideally, you would be involved with the setup in each new space, but if this is not possible, have someone in the company help with the soundcheck and keep an eye on and an ear open to the integrity of your design.

If you move from a nonunion theatre to a union house, you'll have to conform to specific rules regarding hours that can be spent working each day and what nonunion persons are allowed to do. In most union houses, for example, the sound designer is not permitted to touch the equipment, plug in a cord, or pick up a wrench—although you are encouraged to make coffee and donut runs.

Whether the theatre company is knowledgeable about your design area or not, remember that your purpose is to enhance the quality of the entire production—ultimately, your goal is to help the production company present the finest theatrical work possible.

94

7

Preparing to Build the Cues

A brilliant sound design or composition is only a collection of ideas and concepts—until it is produced and performed. The art of sound design involves the selection or creation of the proper sounds for a theatrical moment. The science of designing sound for theatre consists of gathering sounds and reproducing them faithfully within the style of the production. It is also essential that the aural elements be played back musically and consistently, while allowing for the subtle shifts within individual performances.

In the not-so-distant past, providing sound for a play used to mean copying sounds from an effects record to tape and editing them. Now that the digital age has arrived, bringing with it expansive aural experiences, audiences expect sound and music for the theatre to be more sophisticated—and at least as high-quality as what they hear at home. More theatres are hiring sound designers and investing in better sound equipment. As a result, technical standards—and audience expectations—for the sound and music in a show keep rising. From the earliest conceptualization through the editing process to the final technical rehearsal, the sound designer must know how to produce what the production needs. A sound designer has to be aesthetically adept and organized, while also possessing the resources that enable him to achieve the design technically. No matter how good your equipment, it will not yield an effective sound design without an aesthetic sensibility behind it.

As the editorial process begins, your design starts coming alive. You hear its voice emerge. The creative process does not stop here. Much experimentation and discovery lie ahead if you have the resources, time, and talent to transform your raw tracks into sonic wonders. If the equipment you're using is more a mystery than a tool, it will interfere with your experimenting and creating. The exciting part of designing sound is when a sound in your mind's ear becomes a reality because you know how to produce it.

The current generation of sound designers seem to be remarkably comfortable with sophisticated audio production tools that provide an extraordinary vehicle for creating music and soundscores. Many of these scores are being reproduced through equally sophisticated theatrical sound delivery systems. Once out of reach to most, now computers, digital audio workstations, and software like Digidesign's ProTools, Apple's Logic, or Mark of the Unicorn's Performer are used by almost every designer or composer to produce their work. Playback systems such as Meyer Sound Laboratories' Matrix3 offer unlimited possibilities for presenting the work of designers and composers.

You don't have to use ultra-fancy digital equipment and super-expensive microphones to produce crisp, clean sound—what you do need is an understanding of what the equipment you have will do for you. Most designers produce their music and effects on equipment that they own. The tools of a sound designer can consist of a laptop, an audio hard drive, a modest pair of loudspeakers, a simple mixer, a good microphone, and one of the wonderful pieces of creative software that have been written for recording and manipulating audio. The alternatives to using your own tools include using equipment owned by the theatre and renting time at a commercial recording studio. Most theatres cannot afford to build, support, and maintain an independent recording/production facility. Renting studio time can be costly.

The ideal situation is for you to produce your own cues. As you record, mix, and edit each sound, you have complete control over the design every step of the way. This allows you the freedom to experiment as you work, without having to articulate new ideas to another person.

This doesn't mean that all talented sound designers are engineering geniuses. It isn't necessary to know all the ins and outs of audio equipment (no pun intended) to become a successful sound designer or composer for the stage. Many designers and composers collaborate with engineers and technicians who can lend their unique creative strengths to the designing process.

ORGANIZING YOUR WORK

Knowing that a cue is required is not the same as knowing what constitutes that cue. After conceptualizing the sound design, you start collecting the sounds that will become cues. Yet before you can even gather your effects, you must determine the specifics of each cue.

What does each cue require? Is it made up of a single sound, a layer, or a number of sounds and layers mixed together? For instance, if your show needs a night ambiance, what does it sound like? You could find a selection in a commercial sound effects library that is called "night ambiance," but it might not be the proper atmosphere for your production. A night ambiance cue could be a single cricket, a field of crickets, or a blend of crickets, cicadas, and owls, with an occasional lonely dog barking in the distance.

Once you've determined the specifics of the cue, then you can plan how to create it. Do you gather it yourself with a portable field recorder? Do you set up a session and use the theatre's equipment to record your source material? Do you transfer the sounds from existing commercial recordings? As you look at your sound plot, you may want to make a separate list of where you'll be getting each sound. If you keep a list of effects and their sources, then you can plan your approach methodically. Treat the whole endeavor like a shopping trip. If you develop your design using a cue database, one of your fields could be "source," detailing where you will get that sound.

Remember that the sound plot is a list of all the aural ideas you are considering for use in the show, in the order of their occurrence. It's supposed to offer an easy reference to the flow of the show, but it's not organized to help you plan the collection of your effects. A separate collection list (see Figure 7.1) is better for that purpose. The collection list presents an overview of how many sound elements— not cues—you are looking for. A show with fifty cues may need only thirty different sounds because there will be many identical cues (doorbells, for example). The collection list will indicate this, and help you gather the sounds more efficiently. You could even cluster together effects that have a similar source on the collection list, especially if you're designing sound for a huge show.

Creating any cues needed in rehearsal is a good place to begin, particularly if a cue's timing depends on the performer's actions (when, for instance, actors are working with underscoring or sound effects to which they react). It's easier for the director to work with the cue while rehearsals are going on, since once technical rehearsals begin, there won't be as much time for either of you to make adjustments.

GATHERING THE SOUND SOURCES

You will have to either pull the sounds that make up your design from available effects libraries or record them live. The longer you work as a sound designer, the more sounds you'll amass in your

EFFECT	SOURCE
Clock ticking	My library of effects disks for my digital sampler
Clock chimes	Field recording of Uncle Bob's grandfather clock
Planter crash	Field recording
Night ambiance	Field recording
Dog for first night ambiance	Sound effects CD
Door chimes	Field-record each chime used on the set and then play the doorbell on the digital sampler
Bottle break	Transfer from my sound-effects library
Beethoven	Transfer from CD
Scratchy record surface	Make recording and loop
Jazzy slow pop tune	Transfer from 1960s jazz recording or compose it
Martha's laughter	Recording session with the actress
Dish crash	Field-record in my kitchen
Bird for dawn ambience	Transfer from sound library

FIGURE 7.1 Collection list.

own collection. As you get to know others in the business, access to their personal sound libraries is often available on a reciprocal basis. Other sources of prerecorded effects and music are museums and universities with collections of natural sounds, the Internet, train buffs who collect recordings, and collectors and stores specializing in unusual, old, or rare recordings.

Finding an effect is only half the work—being satisfied with it is another story. For example, you might need an elephant trumpeting, but try as you might, you can't find any recordings that you like.

Your choices are to either record a real elephant or try to re-create the sound. The first option is not as impossible as you'd think—with one or two phone calls to a local zoo you might be able to arrange a recording session with an elephant and its trainer in exchange for program credit and some free tickets. There might also be someone with the show who can imitate the elephant, but you'll never know until you ask.

I designed a production of *Love's Labour's Lost* a few years ago. The composer I was working with asked me to provide the sound of doves cooing to accompany some short music cues. A few days after I got the request, I was complaining to my friend, the production manager, that I had looked everywhere for a good dove recording and didn't know where I was going to get that sound. He replied, "I do great doves," and proceeded to do an extraordinary imitation of the most contented doves I had ever heard. Surreptitiously, I recorded his imitation, knowing that if the composer or director knew the source of the cooing, they would hate the cue no matter how authentic it sounded. I was worried that they would feel it was an obvious fabrication. When I played my final, edited dove coos, I let the tape speak for itself. The composer loved the cooing, and the director thought the music cues were fabulous.   —JL

RECORDING YOUR OWN EFFECTS

When you can't get the right sound from a library, another option is to record it yourself in a studio or make a field recording. One advantage to a studio is that you can record the effect in a quiet room; another is that the recording gear and microphones available in the studio may be better than the field equipment you have at your disposal. Frankly, though, contemporary field recorders have improved remarkably and have become so affordable that they have become a staple of many designers' gathering process.

Even if the sound you are looking for is available, there is always a chance that you could make a more suitable recording yourself. City ambiance from a sound library may be adequate, but if you live in New York City and have access to good field recording equipment, you can do much better on your own. Choosing where to record will be based on practicalities. You can't get a fighter jet into a studio and it doesn't make much sense to record refrigerator doors opening and closing when that sound could be achieved more quickly and cheaply with a portable deck. Recording your own effects often gives you a wealth of material from which to choose, and sometimes you'll pick up sounds that you had not even considered using.

I was recording a late-night urban ambiance for a production of Philip Gotanda's *Fish Head Soup*. This ambiance was for some scenes that take place in the courtyard of a Buddhist temple. As I was recording the background, a firehouse a half-mile away responded to a call. The sirens echoed off the buildings in an eerie fashion. As I listened, I realized that this section of ambiance would be perfect for the scene where one of the characters has a disturbing Vietnam War flashback. I doubt that it would have dawned on me to use distant sirens in that scene if the possibility hadn't approached me first.   —JL

Recording your own effects is useful for producing variations of the same sound. If a show you are designing calls for ten cues of a subway train entering and then leaving a station, you may locate one recording of the perfect train. But if you repeat it ten times in the show, it will become both boring and obvious to the audience that it was the same recording. Yet if you used two or three different recordings, all from different sources, they wouldn't sound like they were from the same subway station. By recording your own train sounds at one location, you'll have a number of versions to choose from, each with its subtle differences and character, but all from the same station.

If you find yourself doing a lot of field recording, invest in some decent equipment. A basic field recording setup includes a portable recorder, microphones, windscreens, headphones, microphone cables, and one or two microphone stands. There are also many all-in-one field recording systems with good-quality microphones built right into the "head" of the recorder. If you're on a very tight budget, a portable MP3 recorder is an affordable way to start recording in the field. But don't expect a cheap MP3 recorder to match the recording quality of a more expensive recorder. For not much more money, you can obtain a much better unit that has superior microphones, preamps, and the ability to record WAV files at high sampling and bit rates. Regardless of which format you choose, be sure that your portable deck has lighted VU meters and indicator lights that make it easy to use in the dark, as well as a record volume limiter. A limiter gives you added protection against distortion when recording in unpredictable situations.

What type of microphone to use for field work depends on what you'll be recording. An omnidirectional microphone works well for recording ambiance when you want to pick up everything around you, but a directional microphone (cardioid or hypercardioid) is better if you want to be selective about what sounds you're picking up. Because it is sometimes difficult to know ahead of time what microphone to use, you might want to carry a number of different microphones or use a microphone system with interchangeable elements. In about the same space it takes to carry one microphone, you can carry a base unit and three microphone capsules, each with a different pickup pattern. If you are recording ambiance, you might choose to use a stereo microphone because a stereo recording might sound more realistic than a mono recording. Stereo microphones can be used to record spot effects, although most spot effects are played back in mono. Recordings made with a good single point stereo microphone system can be mixed down to mono without experiencing comb filtering. Another choice you'll need to make is whether to use a dynamic or a condenser microphone. Dynamic microphones are very rugged. They can tolerate the abuse of live performance, loud volumes, as well as inclement weather. Condenser microphones tend to be brighter and can make more detailed recordings. They have a louder output, which means that you don't have to boost the microphone preamp level as much as with a dynamic. That's important if you're using a moderately priced recorder that might not have the quietest microphone preamp.

101

Specialized windscreens are necessary for most outdoor recording situations because wind blowing across the microphone produces noise. Most microphone manufacturers make foam rubber windscreens for their particular equipment, although windscreens made by manufacturers that specialize in only that product usually provide superior results—they provide noise-free operation at higher wind velocities.

When buying a set of headphones for the field, consider those that are designed to isolate the ear from outside sounds. When you record, trust your ears to determine whether you are getting the sounds you want. It's hard to know what your microphones are picking up if sound is leaking in around the headphones' ear pads.

Microphone cables are a necessity, unless your microphone comes with its own permanently attached cable or the microphones are built into the recorder. A 25-foot microphone cable is long enough for most situations, and four 25-foot cables in your stock of equipment will assure you that you have longer cable lengths if you need them. Note that extending the length of the cable attached to a cheap dynamic microphone will probably open you up to interference. Typically, these microphones use unbalanced cables, which use two conductors. Balanced microphone cables use three conductors, which by their design cancel out interference trying to get into the cable.

One or two lightweight microphone stands are important to have since, generally speaking, microphones should not be held while recording. Imagine trying to record five minutes of ambiance without shifting the microphone in your hand. Handling can easily be picked up on many microphones. If you don't want to bring a full-sized stand with you, there are short, folding microphone stands, small enough to fit in a pocket. If you're recording in stereo with two microphones, you can buy an adapter that screws onto the top of the stand, allowing you to attach two microphone clips to it.

In addition to your field recording gear, bring a flashlight, a pencil, and a notebook or tracksheet to write down any details that will make your work easier once you return to the production studio. You can even log field session information right into a database on your laptop.

ASSESSING CUE PARAMETERS

Before your raw sounds can be made into finished cues, you have to plan how to manufacture and reproduce them. You already have a good idea about what each cue is and where it happens in the action of the play—now you have to determine method of playback, how to mix the cue elements (layers), and the aural imaging in the performance venue. (See Chapter 5 for a discussion of figuring out how to organize the playback of a cue). Refer to your sound plot with specifics about how you intend to build each cue. You should now have decided:

- How long the cue will be (duration)
- On what source channel(s) you'll assign the cue
- On what kind of playback device the cue will be played
- What loudspeaker or group of loudspeakers you plan to use
- If the cue will be executed live or as a practical effect
- If the cue requires significant processing, such as radical equalization, heavy reverberation, or other digital signal processing
- If the cue is an operator-triggered MIDI event, sequence, processor, or special effect
- If the cue is literally triggered by an actors action

Most importantly, make sure that you know under what conditions your design will be performed before you build your cues. Don't design a thunderstorm soundscape that calls for fifteen cues played from ten sources if those playback devices aren't available. Even if the playback devices are available, you need to know whether the sound operator is competent enough to operate such a complex show manually, and whether the theatre's mixer can accommodate all of those playback decks. As you plan how many and which playback devices to use and other details, keep in mind the amount and condition of the equipment you're working with, the budget, and the expertise of the running crew. For smooth operation of complex sound designs, it is advantageous to use a computer-based playback system. The manufacturers of these systems have built in a range of sophisticated control features. You can play back many sounds simultaneously from a single, relatively compact computer system. Usually, the more you can spend on the system, the more sounds you can play at one time. A basic system should be able to play eight sounds at a time, whereas more expensive systems have practically no limit on how many sounds they can play concurrently. The basic versions of these systems allow the designer to control the number of sources, level, position, and movement (panning) with ease. You can initiate a complex series of cues with a single click of a button. In the more advanced (and yes, expensive) systems, you can add equalization, delay, digital signal processing, and other parameters of a sound in real time, giving you an extraordinary tool set to shape your designs.

103

THE EQUIPMENT

Find out what equipment the theatre is providing for the production. Many companies keep an equipment list that they give to designers, but be aware of the possible inaccuracy of that list. Sometimes the production office sends it out without the sound department having updated it. You don't want to set up your show only to find out that some essential item broke last year and was retired—and you hadn't known because the equipment list wasn't kept current.

PLAYBACK

Ask the theatre specific questions about its equipment. You should know how many simultaneous playback tracks are available. If the theatre uses a computer-based playback system, find out how much sound file storage space is available.

AMPLIFICATION

You should know the brand and model of house amplifiers, how many total channels of amplification are available, and how those amplifier outputs are distributed around the theatre. Some theatres are hard wired and some use portable cabling for all their hookups. If it's a small theatre with limited resources, find out whether the amplifiers are professional power amps or home stereo amps.

LOUDSPEAKERS

Familiarize yourself with the theatre's loudspeakers. Are any of the loudspeakers self-powered? Again, knowing the manufacturer and model number will allow you to easily research individual specifications and determine how you might be able to best use the unit. If you've never heard of the brand and model number of the loudspeaker, look it up. The Internet is full of specifications on current and what have come to be called legacy (older, no longer manufactured) products. If that fails, ask about the number of drivers and size of the woofer. Knowing the size of the loudspeakers won't tell you if they sound good, but a general rule of thumb is that larger speakers with big (fifteen-inch and up) woofers are better for reproducing the deep, low frequencies and volume needed for cues like thunder and explosions. When checking out these systems, bring some prerecorded program material and listen to the individual units. Make some notes about their performance and, if necessary, use that information to ask the production manager whether renting better or more appropriate loudspeakers is possible. It's also important to know which loudspeakers are permanently mounted and which ones can be moved. You'll also want to know how many specialty loudspeakers are in stock for practicals, under-balcony fill, front fill, and other unique applications.

ACOUSTICS

If you are designing sound for a theatre you're not familiar with, try to spend some time listening to the room before you start to build your cues. Sitting in the house and hearing music or effects over the theatre's loudspeaker system will help you evaluate the overall quality of the system and give you a sense of how your cues or microphones will sound in that particular space. Knowing the sound of the space can be an important part of your design. Long reverberation times can cause problems with the intelligibility of the actors' speech. If you sense a problem related to excess reverberation, try to reduce the problem. Experiment a little by hanging a thick velour curtain in a strategic location to absorb some of the sound that is bouncing around. Don't deaden the room too much, though, because actors rely on a certain amount of "lift" from the acoustics of the room to carry their voices into the deep recesses of the house.

AURAL IDENTIFIERS

Let's say you're doing a scene that takes place at a beach. Your inclination might be to provide soft ocean waves throughout the scene to support the location. But if the performance space is highly reverberant, the actors' words will never have time to die out between lines so that the sound of the waves can be heard. If you know that a soft ambiance won't be heard in that space before you enter technical rehearsals, don't waste your energy building something that won't work. Instead, try improving the acoustics of the performing space or saying "beach" with a few well-placed seagulls. These *leading* sounds added to a characteristic foundation layer are called *identifiers*. There are many circumstances where identifiers are extremely valuable.

MIXING SYSTEMS (CONSOLES, DESKS, AND CONTROL SURFACES)

If the theatre has a manually operated mixing console or mixing desk, check into how many inputs and outputs it has, and how the mixer routes the input signal to the outputs. Some manufacturers' mixers allow you to have access to the outputs in any combination, while others will let you work with only two at a time. Most semi-professional and professional mixing desks provide a high degree of flexibility as well as many input and output points. For analogue and digital mixers, inquire about the number of effects sends and returns. These pathways are used for sending a signal to a reverb unit (or other processing equipment) and directing that processed signal back into the mixer. Effects sends and returns can also be used as auxiliary outputs and inputs. Many smaller digital consoles have a modest amount of built-in effects, such as reverberation, equalization, and delay. You should still understand the effects send and receive structure on this type of mixer in case you'd like to add another piece of outboard gear. If the theatre has a computer-controlled mixing system, find out its full capabilities. Can it trigger playback devices or does it just mix tracks? Is it capable of show control that would allow it to trigger lighting effects or other stage machinery? Don't assume anything. If the mixing system has lots of bells and whistles, make sure that you or the sound operator knows how to utilize those features. You might be the most ambitious sound designer to work in that space in a long time and the operator may not have had to learn all the functions of the mixing console.

OUTBOARD GEAR

Does the theatre have any specialized signal-processing gear, such as reverberation systems compressors, equalizers, or delays? If so, you can embellish the cue later if you were too conservative in the studio. If not, you'll have to pay close attention to your recording approach and to the amount of processing given to the cue when mixing.

MICROPHONES

The number and types of microphones available is extremely important if your show calls for sound reinforcement or a need for a specialized microphone. When considering the house microphones, look at pickup patterns, sensitivity, and sound quality. What might not be included on an equipment list are the microphones that many theatres have pointed at the stage for use with the backstage monitor system. If the playback system can access those microphones, they could be used to add reverb or other effects to the actors' voices.

INTERCONNECTIVITY

Ask how much cable the theatre has. If you're doing something out of the ordinary, like using a number of live microphones or putting loudspeakers in unusual locations, you might have to rent or purchase loudspeaker or microphone cable out of your show budget. Contemporary sound delivery systems have a lot more than microphone and loudspeaker cable. Loudspeaker cables alone have a number of variants in capacity, length, and connector type. Connectivity is not just about connecting loudspeakers and microphones. The control side (or the "front end") of many systems will make use of Ethernet, video, coax, display and keyboard extenders, optical fiber, and even proprietary cable systems. Cable runs and their associated connectors can be very expensive. Staff sound engineers must consider building their house inventory to cover an increasing number of sound situations.

ADDITIONAL GEAR

Equipment that the theatre doesn't have may be rented or borrowed. Some theatres have wonderful relationships with vendors who want to support the arts by lending or renting at a reduced rate to a not-for-profit organization. Ask the production manager whether any such relationships exist.

If the theatre has gear that you are unfamiliar with, such as a digital sampler, a multitrack playback device, or a multi-effect digital sound processor, ask the sound engineer or sound technician about it. Most likely, she'll not only teach you how to use it, but will also show you how to get the most out of its capabilities.

THE BUDGET

In venues that have a good house sound delivery system, the bulk of your design budget will go to the cost of producing the sound cues. These expenses could include your studio time, research materials (music CDs, sheet music, stock sound effects), and blank media like CD-Rs and DVD-Rs. Other costs you may incur include equipment rental, batteries, supplies for creating live effects, fees for musicians and engineers, commercial studio time, and purchases of equipment specific to your production. When working on the production of a musical, you'll find the majority of your budget will be directed toward system rental: loudspeakers, radio microphones, and associated microphone costs including batteries, microphone elements, and materials to mount microphones on actors. A supply of batteries is essential if you're using wireless microphones. Even if a theatre owns wireless units, it doesn't mean that you can afford to use them. Over the course of an eight-performance-per-week, six-week run, one wireless microphone could consume 48–96 batteries.

In some venues, you may find that the only way to execute your cues is with extra equipment. Some theatres don't own much house equipment, preferring to augment their system by renting extra equipment for the season. The problem is that most productions don't have budgets big enough to afford renting the equipment you might need.

For live effects, expect to pay for items such as pots and pans for a live crash effect, or for the wood to construct an offstage door slam unit. Miscellaneous items like a small loudspeaker, a boom box, or a doorbell may be needed for your show. Depending on the scale of the company, the theatre's annual budget may provide for some equipment purchases, but don't expect the money for your item to come from that budget just because a particular item you need can be used in future productions. If you can justify it, the production manager may allow that to happen, but don't count on it.

107

Additionally, if you spend money out of your design budget on recordings, you will have to negotiate as to whether you will keep them or return them to the producer.

THE RUNNING CREW

A well-established and well-paying theatre usually offers a competent staff. Theatres generally go out of their way to hire an experienced stage manager because so much of each production is his responsibility. You'll find that the better theatres see the wisdom of hiring experienced running crew, too. But this is not always the case.

Find out how long the operator has been running sound, in general and at that theatre, specifically. Designing the show with the operator in mind lets you decide the best way for the cues to be executed. With a computer-assisted playback system, the operator's resume isn't as critical as it is for a manually operated system. As a rule of thumb, the more experience the operator has, the more flexible you can make your design. Unlike an operator who gets flustered when there is more than one device playing at a time, a talented sound operator can run a large number of separate cues in a sequence. If you're working with a less experienced operator, you may have to make a sequence of cues into one cue. The difficulty with this approach is that the actors will have to time themselves to the recording, and consequently will have less flexibility with their performances.

Early in my career designing sound, I created extremely ambitious sound cue sequences that had to be operated manually. Frank, the best sound operator I had ever worked with, seemed to take each new design as a competitive challenge. One cue sequence required controlling an eight-track tape deck, five auto-cueing DAT players, and two CD players while mixing all twenty-two channels of audio manually on an analogue mixer. With me at the tech table and Frank in the booth, we worked intensely until he memorized the FIFTY+ moves within the sequence. It was not possible to read this cue sequence off cuesheets while executing it. Everyone was so impressed with his masterful execution that the entire crew and cast erupted into applause at the completion of the sequence. I was surprised and delighted. At the run-through later that evening, I peered through the doorway of the booth to observe the running of this cue in real time from his perspective. I was astonished to see a gymnastic ballet, with Frank using nearly every part of his body to make the effect work in concert with the stage manager. I was impressed!   —DB

While the story above harkens back to a time when there was a significant art to being a manual sound operator, today, significantly more complex sequences can be triggered by computer-based playback systems that provide incredible precision and repeatability.

No matter what the sophistication of the technology at hand, the art of our discipline remains in how the designer builds and arranges the cue elements, in the stage manager's musicality in calling the cues, and in the precise way the operator responds to those calls. The current tools of our trade simply allow us to make incredibly complex and well-developed cues seem effortless.

109

Recording, Editing, and Refining Cues

All of the sound and music cues need to be prepared for performance conditions. Once you've collected the sounds for your design, they can then be put in their final form. Prerecorded cues need to be gathered, mixed, and edited. Original music or soundscore elements need to be recorded, mixed, and prepared for the production. Live effects and practicals must be set up, listened to, and refined.

PRERECORDED CUES

Under most circumstances, theatre sound calls for using the same recording and editing techniques that are employed in other genres, such as film or music recording. As in these other fields, it's important to make your cues as clean as possible. Recordings with imperfections or noticeable digital artifacts are a big problem in theatre because a noticeable edit or hiss clearly identifies recordings to the audience as being artificial. Consider that the only other sounds the audience hears (along with its own coughing and candy unwrapping) are the performers' voices, which are obviously not accompanied by sonic hiccups or background noise. Because the actors' voices are what your score or effects accompany, your recordings must be as pristine as possible.

If you mix your playback devices live on an analogue mixer, there are some things you should consider. By using a *lower* recording volume on your mixed cue, you can make it easier for an operator to fade in a cue to a very soft level. It's often difficult to gracefully execute a manual fade of an effect or music to a very low sound level if it means that the operator is moving the volume fader only a small distance. The usual way of avoiding this is changing the mixer's output volume or reducing some other volume control in the sound system. If that solution is not possible, you can give your operator a little more "fade distance" by recording the effect at a lower volume than normal. Computer-based playback systems nearly eliminate this problem by allowing the user to program a fade up or down, at almost any rate (measured in fractions of seconds) and you can even program a compound fade. For example, if you're fading in a sound from infinity (off) to -20 dB in a twelve count, you could program the first part of the fade-in to be a four count to -30 dB. Then you'd program an additional fade-in, eight count to -20 dB. In some systems you can create customized fade contours for any cue. This provides a wonderful amount of control for the shaping of your aural ideas.

Mixing sound and music for the stage is similar to mixing for records in that you strive for the best balance of sounds and processing (equalization, reverb, delay, and so on). There are, however, some major differences to bear in mind. Always listen to your cues in the studio at the same volume that the audience will hear them in the theatre. Put your mix together at a normal listening volume, but check your final mix at a volume that resembles what you think you will be hearing in the house. What at first may sound like enough reverberation at a moderate listening level may disappear when played back at a soft level. Just as some people use the loudness control on their home stereos to boost bass and treble frequencies at low volumes, you might want to adjust the equalization. On the other hand, the louder a recording is played, the more the imperfections can be heard. A slight thump in an edit may be imperceptible at soft listening levels, but could become apparent at a louder volume. Listen for imperfections in a recording (like noise or the fadeout at the end of a cue) at a slightly louder volume than you expect to hear it in the theatre—that way, you'll know that it will sound unblemished at most volumes. If you're unsure of how to mix a cue, give yourself some leeway by making one or two alternative mixes to try in technical rehearsals. As you become familiar with a particular theatre, experience will tell you how your cues will sound in that house.

When executing final mixes, I put a small pair of loudspeakers in an adjacent room to audition sounds "at a distance." This creates a listening environment that more closely resembles a "theatrical distance." This technique has saved a lot of remix time.   —DB

SPLITTING TRACKS/ALTERNATE MIXES/ PROCESSING

You may be undecided about which elements are needed in a cue or whether the director will like your choices. For example, suppose you've created a night ambiance consisting of a field of crickets, an owl, and a dog barking in the distance. If you built it as a single cue (with all elements on one track) and the director doesn't like any of the elements, you'll have to go back into the studio and rebuild the cue from scratch. If the tracks and channels are available, lay down each effect on its own track, a technique called layering—that way, any one element can be mixed lower, higher, or eliminated completely. If you don't have the tracks available, make alternate cues that are variations of the first. Record a few takes without the dog or the owl and have them at rehearsal. Make sure your choices are readily accessible. When you play the cue in the first technical rehearsal, tell the director that you have alternatives for him to hear. Unless things are very hectic (or the director is a dodo), he'll appreciate alternatives. A computer-based playback system allows you to layer as many cue elements as you require. You can even treat the layers as if they were tracks on a multitrack music recording. This type of system allows for the greatest flexibility and subtlety. Track counts (the number of available playback tracks) can be limited by the speed of your hard drive, computer processor, or the software you are using.

For two track playback systems, splitting the tracks or creating alternate cues are also good ideas if you're unsure about the amount of processing you want to add to a cue. Record your cue without reverb on one channel, while laying down a reverberant track on another channel. (This method comes in handy when the theatre doesn't have a reverb unit.) The cue can always be made more reverberant by adding more of the reverb track in the mix, but it can't be made less reverberant. Consequently, if you've gone too far with processing, it may be impossible to compensate for it later without rebuilding the cue.

In the best of situations, using an artificial reverberation processor in real time allows a designer the ability to sculpt the reverberation to the theatrical need as well as change reverberation characteristics over the duration of the cue.

BUILDING THE SHOW

Some designers like to gather and prepare all of their cues before they load them into the playback devices. They believe that this is a more efficient way to work and it helps them focus on the operation of the cues. This consideration can lead to a show that is easier to operate.

Not too long ago, a sound designer had few choices as to how to play back his design in the theatre. Reel-to-reel, cassette decks, and cart machines were the norm, and digital technology was just starting to appear in the form of samplers. Digital audio can provide clean, hiss-free sound as long as the signal path is free of noise and distortion. The days of splicing cues together into a show reel have faded away, replaced by terabytes of hard disk space and computer-based playback systems. The nightmare of a broken splice mangling your show reel has been replaced by the equally invigorating nightmare of having a hard drive crash during performance. Fortunately, data backup systems with instant recovery have significantly minimized that problem. Today, designers have many options when it comes to playback equipment, including digital samplers, MiniDiscs, compact discs, DAT players, digital cart machines, hard disk playback, digital audio workstations (DAWs), and dedicated computer-based systems. However, the basic concepts behind how you prepare your show for operation haven't changed significantly—only the equipment has.

What *every* cue has in common is that they must all be defined or encapsulated so that only the cue called for plays; they must be easily identified; and there must be a backup copy of the cue in case of disaster. These cue attributes are best achieved by the use of a sound designer cue database (your software for creating a sound plot) and computer-based playback system. The database is also essential when using manual playback, especially when constructing operator cue sheets.

PLAYBACK SYSTEMS

MINIDISCS AND COMPACT DISCS

MiniDisc and compact disc playback devices are still popular in theatrical playback because they provide inexpensive digital sound. Many players start immediately when you hit the play button. Professional models of both units will allow you to play only one track with its own cue, and then will cue up to the next track without playing it. Some consumer models have a single playback mode that will play only one track at a time, avoiding the chance of accidentally rolling into the next cue. Barring these features, you can leave a few minutes of silence at the end of every cue, which will give your operator enough time to cue up the unit. If you look at the playback specifications of a MiniDisc player, you can see that the format is a bit of a compromise in audio quality. Using a MiniDisc player would be acceptable under circumstances where there isn't a need for impeccable playback, such as a soft ambiance. But music or loud sound effects can reveal the shortcomings of this format.

MiniDisc players do allow you to change the running order of the cues by reordering the discs' table of contents, and because MiniDiscs and CDs are so easy to use, they are often used to play rehearsal cues. A MiniDisc player allows you to give a name to each track, which will show up on the machine's display. Many designers will name a track by its cue number and will include a brief description. Although CDs don't allow you to name a cue, by putting only one cue on a track you can locate a cue by its track number. For CD playback, include track sheets with each disc.

DIGITAL AUDIO WORKSTATIONS AND HARD DISK PLAYBACK

Although it's common to edit, process, and mix your cues utilizing a DAW with software such as Logic, Digital Performer, Nuendo, Sonar, and ProTools, DAWs generally do not make great playback systems. In the past, these units were used for multiple track playback and they were reasonably effective, if a bit clunky, in theatrical operation. If you choose to use one for playback, you'll want to have a specific file (often referred to as a session) dedicated to playing cues. If your session has multiple cues in it, utilize the memory location feature of the software to allow you quick access to each cue.

Cues played on a hard disk playback deck need to be referenced to "locate" points. Hard disk decks work similarly to multitrack tape decks except for the fact that they are random access devices, which allows you to go from one cue to another very quickly. Tape-based systems must fast forward or rewind through the tape to get to different cues. Both DAWs and hard disk systems have the advantage of allowing you to play multiple tracks at the same time. DAWs allow you to do anything from automating fades to redesigning the cue.

DIGITAL SAMPLERS AND CART MACHINES

Digital samplers and digital cart machines take sounds and play them back at the touch of a button. In the case of a sampler, that button is usually a key on a MIDI keyboard, whereas a cart machine has assignable buttons to play specific sounds. Digital cart machines are modeled after the tape cartridges that were used for years by radio stations to play commercials. They look similar to an eight-track cartridge from the 1970s. Both of these units were often used to play short sounds. Although they can play longer sounds, they are limited by the amount of memory they have.

When you play a sound out of a sampler, assign one key on the keyboard to play that sound. The envelope can be adjusted so that the operator can hit the key and the sound will run for the full length of the sample. If the sound plays for six or seven seconds, adjust the envelope of the sound so that the operator does not need to keep the key held down for the duration of the cue. The envelope of a sound represents how fast the sound fades up to volume, how long it stays at volume, and how long it takes to fade out.

Samplers have many other features that make them good tools for both design work and performance. You can play more than one sound at a time, letting sounds overlap. If you have a series of thunder cues assigned to different keys on a sampler, you can begin the next cue before the first one has finished playing. Samplers are ideal for cues that are repeated often. Once loaded into the sampler, the sound can be triggered as many times as you want. For example, if there are fifteen identical doorbell cues in a show, it would be simpler to have those cues played by a sampler than to edit them into fifteen separate cues.

COMPUTER-BASED PLAYBACK SYSTEMS

MiniDiscs, compact discs, DATs, hard disk players, and DAWs each have their value depending on the scale of your production. But it should be noted that these devices have generally fallen out of favor for playback use. They have been replaced by computer-based playback and mixing systems such as QLab, SFX, Meyer Sound's LCS Matrix3, AudioBox, and Cricket. The URLs for these companies can be found at our webpage at www.elsevierdirect.com/companions/ 9780240810119. Most of these systems are capable of playing back more than a dozen stereo tracks of audio simultaneously, and on some systems, track counts are limited only by your budget. Some systems allow you to mix live microphones and process effects, while others only play back multiple sound files.

Portable DAWs have become the creative tool of choice for every professional sound designer. These tools provide flexibility and power when creating or recording music, soundscores, soundscapes, and sound effects. They can easily "talk" to any of the computer-based theatre systems listed above and allow for the seamless transfer of sound and control files in either direction, facilitating backup.

BACKING UP YOUR WORK

The importance of having a backup copy of your work cannot be stressed enough. A substantial amount of work could be lost if a hard drive crashes or a CD or DVD is irreparably damaged. Making backups (or clones) of your CD or MiniDisc is simple. Most good MiniDisc players have digital inputs and outputs for copying. You can go back to the source files on your hard drive to burn another CD once the show is locked. Backing up a DAW can be as simple as copying the performance hard drive to another drive or using backup software. There are several automatic systems that back up in the "background" and others that can be scheduled to back up overnight. The bottom line is to make sure you do regular backups and make sure they are dated or marked in a way so that you know what they are.

LIVE AND PRACTICAL EFFECTS

Live and practical effects need the same preparation for performance as do prerecorded effects. Live effects, such as gunshots and offstage crashes, should be heard in the theatre before technical rehearsals so that there will be time for refinements. Directors especially like to hear gunshots before tech because it often takes time to locate and determine the right combination of firearm and blank charge size. Even if the set isn't complete, a listening session in the house lets you ascertain the quality of an effect.

Crash box effects usually require a lot of experimentation before finding the right sound. If the crash sounds too small, more items should be added. Another solution might be to make the crash box bigger or construct it out of a different material. Refine your materials, then work on the "crashing" technique. Timing and intensity are vital. Believe it or not, there are many ways to drop a crash box, and the attitude of the dropper is as important as the technique of an instrumentalist.

Try to experiment with the person who will be performing the effect. Allowing time to do so outside of technical rehearsals gives you and the operator a chance to work on his technique and finesse without being rushed. Explain the action that the effect is supposed to imitate, and describe the artistic intent of the crash. For example, tell the operator that he is producing the sound of a trunk full of family heirlooms falling down a flight of stairs, picking up momentum along the way. This will conjure up a visual image in his mind and, hence, a sound image. Show the operator how you would work the effect and have him try it a few times until you get the sound you want.

Phone rings, doorbells, and other practical effects also need listening time. A realistic effect, such as an actual phone ring, will often sound small in a large theatre, in which case you may have to augment the effect. If you can, prepare the practical effect before tech by wiring it up to its power supply and activation switch; make sure to use enough cable to reach the power outlet, the operator's position, and the location of the effect.

Regardless of how a cue is executed, you should play, experiment, and try things. Bang on a dumpster in search of the right "bang" effect. See whether cascading pots and pans sound funnier than tumbling pie tins and ironing boards.

Manufacturing effects is a major part of your craft, but it is not the last step. Until you enter the technical rehearsals, your beautiful music and glorious sounds are only discs and drives sitting on a shelf. When you add your cues to the production, your design becomes whole, as does the production. This final phase in the development of your design or composition is just as important as all of the hours spent researching, recording, and editing.

Rehearsals

Rehearsals are the preparation process that leads to public performance. The sound designer/composer needs this time to polish her craft in the same way that the actor needs rehearsal time to develop his character. If the actors rehearse with all of the design elements in mind, those elements seem integral to the production, rather than embellishments tacked on as afterthoughts. When the actors and director have an opportunity to interact with the sound designer's work, the door to improvements and enhancements is opened.

Sound can help breathe life into rehearsals. As the actors work with the score or effects, they can respond to sound as if it were another character onstage and draw motivation from it. Very often, the only way for you and the director to tell if a piece of underscoring or ambiance works for a scene is to hear it in the context of the actors' performance.

There is no set rule about when to add sound to rehearsal—each production has its own needs, and directors have their individual preferences. Most directors want to wait until the show has been "blocked"—that is, until the actors have worked through the play and the director has made preliminary decisions about stage business and where and when the actors move. Some directors will wait until the actors are familiar enough with their lines that they no longer carry scripts. When a production has many props and costumes and little sound, the director may not want to give the sound much rehearsal time. If the director is using sound as an intricate element of the production, then she may ask to have it as soon as possible.

Sound should be part of rehearsals no later than the week before tech (the days before opening when all remaining design elements are added to the show). Tech week is not the time to decide whether a cue is working; rather, it is the time to make the final cues sound exactly as you wish them to sound. The importance of incorporating sound into the rehearsals in advance of tech week cannot be stressed enough. Feedback obtained before tech week allows you to develop and refine your sound design without the time pressure of doing so during technical rehearsals. Attending different stages of rehearsal is the best way to understand the production and its development. You should make every effort to be at the first read-through and first run-through to help develop your decisions about the sound design. In some situations, when the sound is considered a character in the production, you may be required to be at all rehearsals. If you're unfamiliar with the atmosphere of the play— the traits of the actors, the overall spirit of the production—attending more rehearsals will be advantageous. It is also helpful to have a strong line of communication with the stage manager. He can provide a lot of important details that will help your process. This is especially important when you are a guest artist, designing at a distance.

Optimally, you'll be able to attend numerous rehearsals that include pertinent details about your design, and observe the actors and director developing their work. You can gain new information at each rehearsal by better understanding how the design works within the context of the scenes. Use these opportunities to make important choices about the timing of cues, their placement in the action, and the location onstage from which the effects will originate. You can decide whether a cue is necessary at a specific moment or, if sound seems to be missing, you can choose a particular point where a cue might be added.

Whenever possible, provide the stage manager with rehearsal recordings of music, effects, ambiance, or voiceover announcements. Supply simple phone ringers or doorbells—any cues that can be used in rehearsal. Don't put off giving the stage manager something because the timing or the quality of the material is not up to performance standards. Even a rough cut of a cue can be helpful—whatever can save the stage manager from saying "ring," "honk," or "oink" will certainly be appreciated.

In some situations, you might encounter resistance from the stage management staff about running rehearsal recordings. Since they're busy moving props, giving lines, and watching the flow of the props and actors, they could find it difficult to do more than they are already doing, and they might consider running rehearsal cues an imposition. With their workload in mind, consider limiting the number of cues to be run. You may need to choose which cues have priority. Nonetheless, you should avoid running the sound in rehearsal yourself. If you're focusing on that task, you won't be able to pay attention to how the cues are working.

There are two things you can do to encourage a stage manager to run rehearsal cues. First, explain to her that rehearsal cues are just as useful as rehearsal props or costumes. They can help the actors

119

prepare for their roles and enable technical rehearsals to go more smoothly. Second, make the recordings as user-friendly as possible—if all the stage manager has to do is set a level and press play, it won't require much of her attention. An ideal rehearsal system would include a simple computerized playback system with a simple mixer and self-powered loudspeakers capable of reproducing sound with good fidelity. Some rehearsal spaces have remarkably high-quality systems. On the other hand, a boom box is adequate for many rehearsal sound systems because it is compact and portable. Many portable systems include a cassette and/or CD player. Remember, these are usually not performance quality.

Rehearsal cues are best played back on a CD player, MiniDisc player, or computer-assisted playback system. The latter will require you to program it, but all the levels and fades are programmed in, making it the easiest for the stage manager to operate. Additionally, the programming you do in rehearsal might become the foundation for the cue sequence you build during tech. This can be a big time saver.

Figure 9.1 shows a configuration of three windows of the SFX computer-assisted playback system. Note the big "GO!" button in

FIGURE 9.1 A screenshot of Stage Research, Inc.'s SFX application.

the lower left-hand corner. At the top is the transport window. This is especially handy in rehearsal, as its controls allow you to start and stop or find a specific point in an audio file. Below that is the cue list window, which shows the cues and highlights the next cue to be played. Note that cues aren't necessarily just the initiation of a sound file. They can be volume adjustments or any combination of actions. Below the cue window is the active matrix window, where the volume levels of the cues are set.

MiniDiscs are also great to use in rehearsals because they are simple to cue up, they have a display that can show the name of the cue, and they can be easily modified to incorporate changes. CDs are also simple to cue up, but the stage manager will have to reference the track numbers on the CD to a cue list to know what track to play. Additionally, if you want to make changes to a rehearsal CD, you will have to burn a new one. As a rule, always rehearse with copies of the CDs or MiniDiscs containing your show cues. You can never be absolutely certain that the equipment won't fail or the operator won't damage your media.

Because many CDs or MiniDiscs cue up to the next track, it is preferable to prepare each occurrence of the same cue rather than continuously recueing the same track. If the sound operator will be fading in a cue in performance, record that fade into your rehearsal cue. That way, the stage manager will not have to worry about adjusting volumes.

If a cue is meant to crossfade to another sound onstage, you will need to consider having more than one CD or MiniDisc.

You may find that you have a manually operated sequence of cues that is impossible to run in rehearsal as designed. In this case, have the stage manager play as much of the cue as he can and call out the missing portions, or rehearse the sequence in parts small enough to operate. Don't expect to work short sections of the play to accommodate sound at every rehearsal. After all, one of the primary purposes of rehearsal is to run sections of the play without interruption so that the actors get a sense of the show's pacing. Again, using a computer-based playback system will solve this problem elegantly.

PREPARING FOR TECHNICAL REHEARSALS

Virtually all performance spaces have a designated control area. Many have appropriately designed control booths or rooms that accommodate the people and technology necessary for the execution of a theatrical production. In some situations, you have to set up

121

your own control area or sound booth. Setting up the sound booth usually precedes setting up the in-house equipment, since much of the onstage installation cannot begin until the set is completely built. It may be no more than a card table placed behind the back row of seats, but it's usually an enclosed room with windows overlooking the stage. Some theatres with limited space have the sound operated from a separate room; the sound operator's only contact with the stage and stage manager is via a production monitor loudspeaker and a communication headset. Other theatres have sound control areas that are open and located in the audience, allowing the sound operator to appropriately mix live microphones as well as run prerecorded cues. Keep the following items in mind whether you're creating a space in which the sound will be run or simply preparing the existing booth for tech week.

EQUIPMENT LAYOUT

Equipment should be placed so that the sound operator can run the sound without having to dash all over the booth or control area. Be sure you confer with her on the equipment layout in the booth if she is not involved in the actual setup. She could foresee problems that may not occur to you. You might consider building shelves or a special table to hold playback decks, the mixing console, radio microphone racks, signal processing, or other equipment.

Place whatever equipment you use the most in the center of your setup. Locate the gear in a manner that will allow the operator to see the stage, then position the other equipment in close proximity to the mixer, with the playback devices or their remote controls closest to it. Once you've determined the layout of the equipment, start patching it together.

Equipment that doesn't need to be adjusted throughout the running of the show does not have to be centrally located. If you need a bulky digital sampler for playing just a few cues, hook it up to a small keyboard with a MIDI cable, allowing the operator to play the keyboard instead of the sampler itself. Route cables neatly and label them all. This will help you to track down and replace a faulty cable if the need arises.

THE BOOTH WINDOW

When working in an enclosed control booth, position the equipment so that the operator has a view of the stage through a booth window. Most cues are called by the stage manager, but occasionally the sound operator will have to initiate the cue himself from an onstage action. Also, many sound cues are coordinated with lighting cues, so unless you are using a system that communicates with the lighting board via MIDI (allowing either operator to trigger effects simultaneously), the operator will have to see such cues executed. If there is difficulty synchronizing a sound fade with a light cue, have the sound operator watch the light fade and try to coordinate the sound with the lights. This is a more efficient solution than running the cue until you find the right count or instructions to the sound operator about how to make it happen correctly. Ideally, you should be able to open the booth window, allowing the operator to listen to the sound coming from the house, if necessary.

SOUND ISOLATION

The audience should not be able to hear the mechanical noise (such as button clicks or fans) of the playback hardware or the conversations of those running the show. If the controls on your equipment are particularly noisy (something that might happen with a cassette deck), there are several complex solutions, including placing the deck inside a soundproof box with a Plexiglas cover and operating it with remote controls. A simpler way to minimize the noise is to make sure the equipment is not on a resonant surface that mechanically transduces the sound. A two-inch-thick piece of foam or a swatch of carpeting between the deck and table will help to dampen the sound. When operating in an open control area in the house, you'll have to make sure all your equipment is silent by design.

123

PRODUCTION MONITOR LOUDSPEAKER

When working inside a booth, make sure there is a production monitor loudspeaker near the sound operator. The only way the operator can hear the stage when the windows are shut is over the production monitor system. Although this doesn't provide a perfect reproduction of what the audience hears, it does give the operator some information about his cues. The monitor loudspeaker lets the operator know if the sound is getting to the stage. If the monitor is always set at the same volume, the operator will know if a cue is playing too loudly or too softly.

MONITORING FROM THE MIXER

Place the monitor loudspeakers in the booth so that the operator can hear the sound coming directly out of the mixer. This way, the operator can listen to the output of playback devices and processing gear without that sound playing in the theatre. Listening to the mixer output is important if the sound operator needs to troubleshoot problems with the equipment during the show. It is also useful if the operator has to listen carefully to the sound going out to the house to execute the cues. For instance, if he has to fade in another deck after the sixth measure of a piece of music, it will be easier to hear the music if he listens to it directly out of the mixer, as opposed to turning up the volume on the production monitor and hearing the cue along with the actors' voices. If the operator is in an open control area, he will need a set of isolating headphones to audition or *solo* microphones or playback devices.

LIGHTING DIMMERS

Place the sound booth's equipment as far away from lighting dimmers as possible. Dimmers radiate an electromagnetic field that the sound equipment can pick up if everything in the sound system is not properly shielded and grounded. When you're dealing with sound setups using ten to fifteen devices with hundreds of interconnections, it's likely that one of those components will let some interference into the system. The further the equipment is placed from the dimmers, the less effect dimmer-generated interference will have on your equipment. Fortunately, most modern theatres have the dimmers set up away from the booth where the lighting board and soundboard are located. The light board communicates with the dimmers over a thin control cable that can be several hundred feet long.

Be sure that the lighting dimmers are not introducing a hum into the system by having the master electrician bring up the lighting instruments to a level of about thirty percent. At this intensity, the dimmers are emitting their strongest electromagnetic interference. Listen to the loudspeakers to hear whether the dimmers are introducing noise into your system. Fortunately, manufacturers of modern lighting dimmers have added substantial filtering to their systems that reduces the transmissions that adversely affect sound systems.

ADEQUATE ELECTRICAL POWER

Insufficient power can cause failure of the equipment, blow a fuse, or trip a circuit breaker. The sound equipment should be drawing its power from a circuit separate from any other devices. In most professional venues, it is now common for the house infrastructure to

124

include isolated sound power that is demarcated by orange-colored AC receptacles in appropriate locations. It is common for sound power to be run to all the necessary points in the theatre, including the mix position, the tech position, the communications rack, the amplifiers, onstage in various areas to accommodate live musicians who might be using electronics, and other places best suited to the production style of the venue. The house electrician should know whether the venue has proper ground isolated audio power. Lighting dimmers, refrigerators, or electric motors on the same circuit can introduce noise or voltage fluctuations that may cause problems with the sound equipment. If you're experiencing problems with insufficient or noisy power, try to tap electricity from another outlet by running extension cords to your equipment. If you do this, however, make sure that you use extension cords rated for drawing the amounts of power that you're using. Be aware that local fire regulations may prohibit running extension cords for this purpose. Route and secure cable carefully to avoid tripping hazards. Use white gaff tape or glow tape to identify potential hazards.

PROPER LIGHTING

The lighting in the sound booth should be bright enough for the operator to see the equipment she manipulates during performance. Supporting sound equipment that is not usually adjusted during the performance, such as power amps and the patch bay, need not be illuminated. If something unusual happens (such as a cue failing to play) and the unlit equipment needs to be checked, the operator can use a flashlight or an appropriate dimmable/switched lighting instrument such as a Littlelite.

Make sure that the booth's lights aren't so bright that they disturb the audience. There is nothing more distracting than sitting in the house when the lights fade to black and having your eyes drawn up to the control booth, which is shining like the beacon of a lighthouse. Instead of trying to cover a large area with a few lights, illuminate the sound equipment with several low-wattage fixtures, each focused on a specific area. You may use a blue-tinted light bulb or cover the light fixture with blue gel to make the illumination subtler. The master electrician will often have scraps of used gel saved just for this purpose. Beware of putting your lights on a dimmer. Although this seems like a great idea for controlling the intensity of light, some dimmers can produce an electronic interference that some sound systems intercept, producing noise. However, there are small lighting fixtures with dimmers specifically designed for use near sound mixers and other audio equipment.

PAPERWORK

Make sure there is a clear space in the booth for cue sheets, a script, or a prompt book (see Chapter 10). The cue sheets should be kept in an area that is well lit and close to the control equipment. Ideally, you should have enough room to let the operator lay out a few sheets in case there's a tight sequence that doesn't allow him time to flip pages. There is often an area on the mixer big enough for this purpose. Some operators use a music stand, which has the advantage of adjustable angles and height. Even shows that utilize computer-based playback systems are likely to have some operational paperwork that needs to be referred to during the performance, even though they would not be using traditional cue sheets. During load-in, you will also have other organizational paperwork in the booth, such as a schematic block diagram and a system hook-up, that you'll want to have ready access to.

WRITING SUPPLIES

The sound operator should have a mechanical pencil and a straight edge with her in the booth. If your show is manually operated, you'll also want to have some colored pencils for color coding and highlighters or markers for underlining. Self-adhesive colored marker labels also work quite well and are easy to move around your cue sheets and script. If you are not using computer-generated cue sheets, the sound operator will need either blank cue sheets or a legal pad on which to handwrite her cues. She should have a dependable eraser handy before she starts tech so that she can erase items completely and leave no confusion as to what note was last written. In addition, a folder, notebook, or manila envelope will help to keep all paperwork together.

STORAGE SPACE

There should be a designated storage place in the booth for show media and backups, as well as emergency supplies. A kit for emergencies should include a flashlight, light bulbs for running lights, gaffer's and electrician's tape, a screwdriver, fuses for every piece of equipment in the sound system (labeled accordingly), extra cables, and phone numbers of whom to contact in case of emergency. Include your contact information and that of the audio engineer.

SAFETY PRECAUTIONS

Make sure that the sound setup in the booth doesn't create any fire or tripping hazards. The equipment should not impede access to fire exits out of the booth. Outlets should not be so crammed full of plugs and power taps that they look like a bad example from a fire safety film. Cables should be secured so that it is impossible to trip over them. Provide a place for the operator to put drinks where they pose no threat if knocked over, or prohibit food and beverages in the booth altogether.

SETTING UP IN THE HOUSE

The sound system needs to be installed in the theatre prior to the start of technical rehearsals. You can assume there will be some equipment already installed, unless you're bringing a production into a roadhouse—a theatre into which touring shows customarily bring their own equipment—or designing at a theatre with meager facilities. Most small theatres have some kind of house system, usually consisting of various loudspeakers, a mixer, several amplifiers, cabling, and some playback devices. Under most circumstances, you'll be supplementing and repatching this sound system to meet your special needs. Larger venues can have substantial inventories as well as production budget lines to rent gear that they don't have.

127

The degree to which a designer must actually set up her own system depends on the availability and expertise of the theatre's staff. Your experiences may range from having to set up everything yourself to handing a diagram of the system you want to a sound technician and coming in later to double-check his work, focus loudspeakers, and start setting levels. If the theatre employs a union crew, however, you may not even be allowed to plug in a single cord.

The first step in system setup is choosing loudspeaker locations, which you should do several weeks before bringing in the equipment. In fact, you should have a clear idea of loudspeaker placement as you build your cues. Get a copy of the ground plan of the set. It will be useful for determining exact loudspeaker location. Make sure that the stage manager, director, lighting designer, and technical director know your intentions well ahead of load-in. The stage manager and director can anticipate any backstage traffic problems posed by loudspeakers placed on the floor, and can either work with your placement or alert you to any problems so that you can pick alternate positions. Should you need to hang loudspeakers, tell the lighting designer so that you can negotiate for the positions you need to serve the production. If the master electrician is more accessible than the lighting designer, tell her about the loudspeaker placements that work for you. She usually keeps the lighting designer apprised of any changes. It's also a good idea to confer with the technical director before making final decisions on loudspeaker locations, to avoid misinterpreting the ground plan or model. It would be advantageous for you to share your loudspeaker plot with the lighting designer as soon as it is developed and approved by the technical director. Letting the technical director know of your plans allows him to keep your needs in mind should there be changes in the set.

Determine how the sound system will be patched together long before technical rehearsals begin. Regardless of whether you're putting it together yourself or with the aid of a crew, by planning well ahead of time, you can make sure you have all of the equipment, cable, power cords, batteries, and other items required by the design.

One common way to depict an equipment setup and present it to others is a block diagram (or a line drawing), which is a visual representation of how the system components will be interconnected (see Figure 9.2). The drawing doesn't detail items like extension cords or

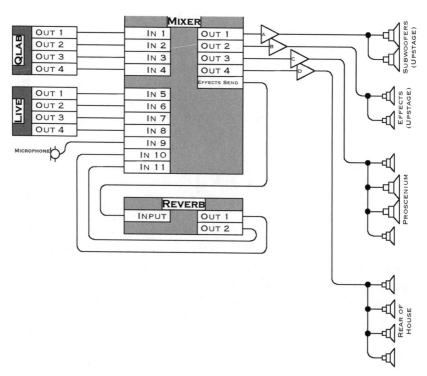

FIGURE 9.2 Diagram of a simple sound system setup.

where the equipment will be located in the booth, but it does provide all of the information needed when considering those details.

A block diagram tells whoever will patch the equipment together exactly how the designer wants it done. It contains such information as which mixer output feeds which set of loudspeakers, and what is patched into each mixer input. The block diagram should specify the brand and model of the gear. However, it does not indicate the precise placement of the equipment. These details are usually worked out beforehand by the designer, the producer/theatre, and the sound equipment rental company (if one was involved before the diagram was drawn). If a rental company is used, they will expect to see a detailed equipment list that defines every single piece of equipment, cable, connector, and adapter, as well as expendables—absolutely everything that will be needed. You could also draw a key to identify each piece of equipment on the block diagram, but with relatively small systems such as those shown in Figures 9.2 and 9.3, it wouldn't be necessary to go into such detail. Additionally, with larger systems you may need to provide a text document, called a hookup. This document lists all the parts of the system in great detail, including all input devices, cables, and connectors including cable length, the mixer, outboard processing, loudspeaker management systems, output paths, digital signal processors, amplifiers, loudspeakers, powered loudspeakers, and practicals. With either a block diagram or an equipment list, you or the sound technician can check the theatre's

129

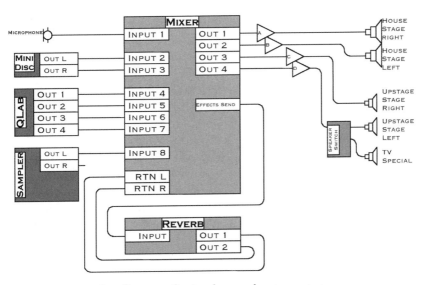

FIGURE 9.3 Another diagram of a simple sound system setup.

inventory and verify first that the equipment actually exists, and second that there is adequate cable, adapters, running lights, tables, intercom, and power outlets to accommodate your needs. Don't forget a high-speed Internet connection, preferably wireless.

It's important to coordinate the installation of the sound equipment in the house and onstage with the other departments setting up their respective portions of the production. You lose valuable time waiting to share a ladder or tools. You don't want to work when the lighting crew is focusing lights, plunging the theatre into darkness.

Pay close attention to safety and concealment when installing the loudspeakers, microphones, and offstage effects. Make certain that the loudspeakers and cable do not present a safety hazard to the actors, audience, running crew, or technicians; securely tape down cables in heavy-traffic areas. You might also consider safety cable troughs that protect your cable runs, minimize the trip hazard, and allow equipment to be rolled over the cable without causing damage. If you have loudspeakers within sight of the audience, be sure the cables are as inconspicuous and neat as possible. Check the sightlines of the audience to make sure that loudspeakers and effects meant to be unseen by the audience are indeed so. If you're next to a loudspeaker and can see a seat, you can be sure the audience will be able to see the loudspeaker.

Hanging loudspeakers is one of the most difficult and potentially dangerous jobs of an installation. If you're not experienced with rigging techniques, get assistance from those who are—don't injure yourself or the crew by trying to mount a heavy, bulky loudspeaker many feet above the floor. People with rigging experience will know how to secure the loudspeaker so that it won't come loose from its position. An experienced rigger will also know how to hang the loudspeaker with the exact focus you desire. Always use safety cables to secure any hanging unit as an extra precaution. If a loudspeaker needs to be positioned and plugged in during the course of the show (possibly during a scene change), make sure that the connector is reliable and easy to use. Look for connectors that lock together, like the Neutrik NL series of connectors.

A number of manufacturers make self-powered loudspeakers that have an amplifier built into the enclosure. You will not have to run speaker cable from the amplifier, but you will need to run a line-level signal and AC power to the back of the powered loudspeaker.

Keep in mind that using an XLR connector for anything other than patching microphones or line-level devices can be dangerous for your equipment. Ideally, the plug used for patching in a loudspeaker will be distinctive and not easily mistaken for anything else. Current practice now is to use Neutrik NL series loudspeaker connectors also called

130

Speakon connectors. These connectors come in a number of versions for single or multiple loudspeaker circuits. XLR remains the standard for most single circuit line and microphone level connections. When it comes to multicable, there are quite a number of workable variations, from multiple runs of copper to digital fiber-optic cables. The scale of the production will help to determine the appropriate choice.

When all the equipment has been positioned and patched together, you can perform a comprehensive soundcheck. For larger scale installations this process is called "focus and system balance," and it makes use of *quiet time*—a time when nothing else is going on in the theatre, a time when you use the valuable commodity silence. During this process, you'll make sure that every playback device, mixer component, cable and connection, signal processor, amplifier, microphone, and live effect is functioning properly. (Refer to Chapter 10 for more information on the soundcheck.) When you schedule your load-in, leave sufficient quiet time for a soundcheck, since troubleshooting can sometimes take hours. Don't forget that you'll want to schedule some quiet time for setting cue levels. The larger the show, the longer the time you'll need. If you are planning to use a computer-based playback system that is programming intensive, make sure you schedule the good part of a day to rough-in the cues so that during tech you can move a bit more quickly.

131

YOUR TECH POSITION

Once the booth is set up and the soundcheck is completed, the equipment is ready for technical rehearsals—now prepare yourself and the operator for tech. Choose a suitable spot in the theatre for setting up your tech position. You need to be centrally located, yet free to move around easily when necessary.

Set up your tech position so that the director is close at hand, but bear in mind that the director is usually dashing from one location to another during tech and rarely sits still. Don't set up at the tech table, where the lighting designer and stage manager are, because their conversation can be distracting when you're trying to hear the sound. If possible, try to find a central location where you can play the part of an average audience member.

At your position, the following items will be helpful:

- Writing and erasing implements; mechanical pencils
- Cue sheets and other corresponding system paperwork, including magic sheet, schematic block diagram, hookup, loudspeaker management system, programming schedules

- Table work lights
- A stopwatch
- Your communications headset (or handset)
- Notepads
- A large, flat surface on which to write and put your script
- Your personal digital audio workstation (DAW) including digitized sound/music libraries
- Power strips

If you are working with a computer-based playback system, you'll want to have your own display to see the programming, and if house/union conditions allow, a keyboard to let you write, play, and modify cues. Most union houses don't allow you to touch the equipment, but many will, once you build appropriate mutual respect and trust.

All of that paperwork listed above will really come in handy, especially for focus and system balance days. That's when you'll make most of your paperwork as you reference all your connection points and log specifics about the processing, delay, levels, EQ, compression, and so on.

At first, you'll be on the headset a great deal, giving cueing notes, EQ adjustments, and volume changes. It won't be easy to leave your position unless you have a good assistant. When setting cues, pick one basic spot from which you set all initial levels. Check other locations to see how the sound plays in other parts of the theatre.

Because the headset amplifies every sound you make, always shut off the microphone control button when you put the headset on or take it off. The stage manager usually has the volume turned up on her headset, so gum chewing, eating, laughing loudly, or coughing into the headset can be irritating. Technical rehearsals are stressful enough, so every bit of consideration and courtesy helps—the words "please" and "thank you" cannot be overused.

In most situations, you'll find a multichannel communications system that will allow the stage management, electrics, and sound and deck crew to have their own independent channels. In a less-than-perfect situation, you may have to share a headset channel with the backstage crew. Try to work out a mutually agreeable system by which you can communicate with your sound operator and the stage manager can speak to his crew. Some designers own walkie-talkies to use in cases like this or when they need to communicate with someone who can't be on a headset (like a backstage wireless microphone coordinator). Most headset systems have a call button. When pressed, it illuminates a light on the base station or belt pack. During

132

a run-through or performance, it's best to flash the light first and let the stage manager acknowledge with either a "go ahead" or "wait" before talking on the headset. You may not know when the stage manager is in the middle of a cue sequence, and you don't want to inadvertently disrupt a cue call.

PAPER TECH

At *paper tech*, the stage manager, director, lighting designer, and sound designer talk through the show before going into technical rehearsals. Paper tech does not necessarily happen at every theatre, but when it does, cues are placed in the stage manager's book and assigned letters or numbers. If you won't be doing a paper tech, confer with the stage manager about assigning cue numbers or letters. This has to be done before tech so that you have the appropriate letters or numbers for the cues and cue sheets. Otherwise, the stage manager will have to abide by your cueing information.

Most of the called cues in a show are light and sound cues, some of which are called together, especially at the beginnings and ends of acts. Try to get a sense of how the lighting designer and director want the cues to work. By learning as much as you can about the length and intent of scene transitions, you can avoid having to start from scratch as you rough-in counts the first time light and sound cues are played in tandem.

133

LEVEL SET

When using a computer-based playback system, you need to do an appropriate amount of preprogramming before your level set session. If you are operating manually, prepare plenty of blank cue sheets and start writing in some preliminary information about the cues. By this point, you should know each cue's number or letter, the device on which it is played, what input on the mixer it's assigned to, whether it starts at a set volume or fades in, and what loudspeakers or areas it will be assigned to. Have the operator enter this information onto his cue sheets or into the computer before the level set session (or if you don't get one, before tech). Then instead of him having to write out all of the specifics of the cue, he'll just need to write new information, such as volume or equalization. You can also use an assistant to write or type this information into cue sheets prior to tech. Never waste the cast and crew's time waiting for your operator to fill in information that could have been noted prior to tech. This doesn't mean that the operator can't take time to write new information during tech carefully and completely. That's also part of his job. (See Chapter 10 for more on training the operator.)

Roughing-in the sound levels should happen at least twenty-four hours before first tech, with the director present to hear the cues in the space. If the director is not available, you should still rough-in your levels. If you are planning to use a computer-based playback system that is programming intensive, do not forget to schedule enough time to make this go smoothly.

If the set has moving pieces, the location of the pieces in relation to the loudspeakers may affect the sound. Make sure someone is available to move the scenery or to show you how and where to move it.

You'll need absolute quiet at your level set. You may allow the painters to quietly continue their work, but you should not be expected to fight against the sound of hammering, drilling, or banging. This is one instance when sound must take priority over the other design elements.

FIRST TECH

The first time the actors are onstage may be considered a "spacing rehearsal" and not a tech. During this rehearsal, the director and actors will be exploring the staging and there might be a lot of conversation about making adjustments in the blocking. This is probably not the best time to be playing cues. You might sneak some in, but observing these blocking adjustments may give you information about adapting your cues to better fit the situation. Sometimes the first tech "crawl-through" will be merely an opportunity for the design teams to go from cue to cue with the actors present. At first tech, your goals should be getting the sound operator familiar with the material, equipment, and your manner of writing cues and hearing how the cues fit with the production at this rather shaky phase of rehearsal. On computer-based systems, you might be double-checking your basic programming and loudspeaker assignments.

Until this point, you've heard your cues set at preliminary levels in an empty theatre or studio. This is the first opportunity for you to gauge the volume of the cues in relation to the actors' voices. Be advised that you still will not hear the design as a whole. There's a great deal of "hurry up and wait" going on from all the design elements. You certainly will not be able to get accurate timings at this rehearsal. Concentrate instead on fine-tuning the execution and placement of the cues and the volumes and equalizations.

As a designer and not a technician, you should be presented with problems to solve, not given orders by a director who believes he knows the proper solutions to problems. For example, the director might say, "Take the volume down on this cue," because she thinks that the cue is too intrusive. However, the problem may not be with the volume, but with the calling of the cue, its placement in the aural landscape, or, in the worst case, its content. One solution might be to start the cue in a less obvious moment in the action. This isn't to say that the director can't recommend that a volume be raised or lowered—you may hear her complain, "I can't hear the cue. Where is it? It was there a moment ago." Try to relay to your director that there are more options in dealing with the cue than "louder," "softer," "there," or "not there."

The director will ask for changes in the volume, timing, and placement of cues, but it's not always necessary to make the changes and rerun the cues right then and there. Don't waste valuable rehearsal time listening to minor adjustments. Take a note and give the changes to the operator later. However, it is a good idea to give the stage manager changes immediately so that any confusion can be discussed while the details are fresh. If you're working on a sequence that does need to be run again (for lights or actors), and one cue in the sequence needs an adjustment, take the time to have the operator write down the adjustment so that he can run it correctly in the next pass.

It's important to confirm that the timings of spot cues and ambiance (including any extra ambiance intended as a "safety buffer") that you made in rehearsals are long enough. Cue-to-cue rehearsals often have many interruptions, and it may be impossible to get an accurate timing of scenes to know if the ambiance is long enough. Timings can be achieved at the first tech run, which is usually the dress tech. Cue to cue is the proper place to confirm that the lengths of spot cues (a train's passing, a dog's barking, a thunderclap) are correct.

When hearing a cue, possibly for the first time in context during tech rehearsal, you may find fault with how it sounds. First determine that the sequence or cue was heard as written, because the problem may not lie with the design, but with the execution. Check the cue's EQs and volume, and make sure that the stage manager is calling the cue at the correct point in the script. Also confirm that what you originally indicated for the cue's call is indeed where it should occur. This is the time to make adjustments and fine-tune. You may reach a point where it's better to leave the cue and come back to it later with fresh ears. Make a note to yourself to pay careful attention to this section at the next run-through.

MAKING CHANGES

What do you do if the director wants to cut your favorite cue—the one that took you forty-seven actors, three days, and two cases of beer to build? Find out what the director didn't like about it or what, specifically, wasn't working. If there's something about the cue that can be adjusted immediately, try that before starting from scratch. If the director has simply changed his mind about including *any* sound at a particular moment, don't throw the cue away when you remove it from the current cue list—he may change his mind yet again. He may eventually want the same cue back where it was or inserted somewhere else, either as is or in modified form. Keep every cue and variation of that cue at hand through the tech and preview process.

136

I was hired to design the sound for a production of a new play centering on a goat from Virginia that decides to become an actor, stands on his hind legs, and moves to New York to star in *The King and I.* The sound, as well as all other aspects of the production, was decidedly odd. Out of the original fifty-nine cues requested by the director, only twenty-three remained by first tech. Eleven of the cues cut were flushing toilets, meant to be heard from an offstage bathroom. The director's decision to cut the flushes was based on the obvious distraction of having to hold the action onstage while the plumbing said its "lines." After the rationalization that the bathroom was far enough away from the onstage room that the audience wouldn't need to hear what transpired there, another dozen cues involving running water and doors and windows being opened and closed were cut. None of this became definite until I was asked to splice all the flushes and some of the faucets back in and cut them out several times. Because the company became so fond of and familiar with these sounds, I gave out the lengths of tape with the flushes as opening night gifts.   —DK

Be prepared to accept the fact that some cues may never be part of your production at all. This idea can be hard to swallow when you're particularly proud of the work you've done in building the cue. But keep in mind that your design is tailored to the production, and that the director reserves the right to change his mind. The director will gain a new perspective on his work as rehearsals progress, and as a result, there will be changes, cuts, and additions. Use the same artistic attitude and openness that you had when developing the project. Don't feel that you can't discuss the merits of certain changes, but keep in mind that the director has a lot going on, especially at tech time. Try to accommodate the director whenever possible. Sometimes a director will have to hear a cue in context before he can tell if it will work.

Once in tech, don't be surprised if you want to make a change and the director tells you not to. He may not want to try something different if he feels the cue works, or he may have enough problems to worry about without fixing something that isn't broken. In addition, some directors hesitate to put something new into a show too close to opening night for fear that the actors' performances will be adversely affected.

Typically, a designer's commitment to a production doesn't end until the show opens, and until that time, you must stay open to changes. Only when you get into the theatre will you be able to consider your work as a whole. At this point, you'll hear the show run on the proper equipment and not just on the rehearsal system. Occasionally, what seems like a good idea in the rehearsal hall is not as effective when heard in the theatre. Perhaps some cues will seem completely wrong and you'll need to fix or cut them—or you may realize how to make a merely mediocre cue into a perfect one.

137

DRY TECH

When running sequences of cues that are difficult to execute, try the cue a few times and then move on to other cues in the show. Once you have a sense of the pacing of that sequence, arrange time with the operator for a *dry tech*—a separate rehearsal outside of tech rehearsal in which you both go over these problem cues and figure out a smooth way to run or reprogram them. Repeat particular sequences until the operator is comfortable with executing them. Some stage managers are more than willing to find time to call sequences in a dry tech. It both gives them the opportunity to become more familiar with calling the cues and allows them to be part of the troubleshooting. These stage managers have a special place in heaven.

If certain cue sequences depend on timings of the actors, first dry tech with the operator, and then ask the director if the cue may be worked at a later rehearsal with the actors available. If the equipment is new to the operator or if she is inexperienced, anticipate that she may be a little nervous when there are tight or tricky sequences to run. Be patient and assure her that there will be a chance to work on these problems without the pressure of tech rehearsal.

DRESS TECH

Dress tech is the first real run-through of the show without constant stopping. You want to be able to hear the show without a headset on, but don't remove it until you feel confident with the way the show is being called. You must also be sure that the operator doesn't need your help to get through a run.

Dress tech is a good time for you to move around the theatre and hear the sound from different locations as you further refine it. Start paying close attention to EQ, smoothness of fades, coordination with lights, volume, integration with action—in essence, the way the design works as a whole. If you've questioned anything about a particular cue, now is the time to determine if you should make changes.

After dress rehearsals and previews, you'll have gathered notes relating to the operation of the show. Find a time for you and the operator to discuss these notes, which will include level changes, count changes, and cuts/additions of cues. The sound operator should have been taking notes about any problems encountered during the performance. This meeting is a good opportunity for you to discuss her notes as well. Throughout this note-reviewing process, make sure that the cues were properly executed before you adjust them to compensate for what you heard. The operator may have been distracted by a problem in the booth that prevented her from executing the cues as intended.

PREVIEWS

Many elements of a show are altered when there is a first audience. The acoustics in the space change, and the actors' reaction times are different. During previews, the show starts to solidify. You'll never truly know how your design works until it plays before an audience. Because an audience changes the acoustical properties of the house, you'll probably think that a number of cues are too soft, so make notes on cues that should come up in volume. They may sound too hot in the next day's rehearsal, but hear them again with an audience to see if your adjustments work. Although many of your volumes depend on being balanced with the actors' voices, the actors often don't speak at performance level until there's an audience present.

You may have found a certain place to listen to the show during rehearsals. At the first preview, listen to the show from this same point to see how the presence of an audience affects the volume level. During the course of previews, check out how the show sounds from different locations.

FINAL REHEARSALS

Unless your design or the entire show is still in a state of flux, the final few rehearsals before opening will be spent refining subtle aspects of the cues. These rehearsals generally take place during the days that previews are scheduled. As the actors get used to having an audience, they'll develop rhythms around which you can adjust the cues' timings. Remember, though, that there is a cut-off point when you must stop fixing. The director should stop giving notes at opening, when the show is said to be "frozen." So should you. Have your operator redo and clean up his cue sheets or playback cue list when there are no more cuts or additions.

139

When opening night arrives, make sure you have backed up the show materials. After all, if something happens to your playback media or device, it's easier and quicker to use a copy of the original cue than to remanufacture it. If you are using a computer-based playback system, you can easily back up the entire production every day—and you should.

Save any outtakes that might be valuable in the future. Unless your contract specifies that the theatre owns the sound design, you should get your materials back when the show closes so that your effects or the whole design cannot be used without your permission. Your design now becomes the latest addition to your sound and music library.

If you live in the same area where your show is having a long run and have the opportunity to see it, you'll find it interesting to hear how it sounds after several weeks or months. With an attentive stage manager and conscientious sound operator, the cues will have solidified and gotten tighter and cleaner. The reverse may happen, of course, and a few precise notes about execution and intention from you to the sound operator or stage manager might help matters. But don't overdo the notes—the show is no longer in your hands. It is under the capable (you hope) guidance of the stage manager. It's splendid to attend a show on which you worked, and to be able to sit and enjoy it without being constantly aware of your cues. Look forward to it!

140

10

Running the Show

The sound designer and operator work together as a team, so they must have a relationship that involves good communication, patience, and trust. As they work together, a common language will develop that will enable them to understand each other more quickly and clearly. A good designer helps the operator learn about the sound system and the intention of the cues. The operator, for his part, should know that things will be changing right up to opening, and that it is the designer's desire and responsibility to exercise different options before settling on a way to perform or run a cue. Performance is the key word here, whether the show is operated manually or via a computer-based playback system. When working with a computer system, a great programmer understands the subtleties and idiosyncrasies of the software and can translate your cue instructions into appropriate coding that will allow you to realize almost anything you hear in your mind's ear. Like the actors, the operator must take his task to heart with each show.

I had to design some sounds that would accompany the movements of an actor's body. When he arched his back, we had to hear his joints creaking. When he bent over, we heard the sound of his blood flowing through his veins. I didn't feel that the actor was going to be consistent with those movements every night, so I couldn't make those cues a specific length, and I didn't want him to be constrained to a length I would dictate. I decided those cues were best executed by the operator playing random, short sounds, laid out within an octave of keys on a digital sampler. The operator would simply tinkle the keys as long as the performer moved. After an hour of rehearsal with just me, the director, the actor, and the operator, we concluded that the cues weren't synchronizing well. The sounds would play too long or they would start late. Then the operator asked me if he could "play the faders" instead. He wanted to raise and lower a volume fader instead of trying to play the keys. I questioned in my mind whether he would be able to do that any better than he was doing with the keyboard, or whether the fades would sound too obvious. But the way it was going, we needed to try something different anyway. I made a sequence of random notes for each sound, assigning the joints to one output of the sampler and the blood to another. When that section of the show started, the operator started the sequencer with the faders out. Sure enough, all of the cues started right on time and played perfectly. While the operator didn't feel comfortable playing a keyboard, he could play the mixer like a Stradivarius. The operator and I worked as a team and I learned to trust and respect his judgment.   —JL

Until opening night, the operator should take changes only from the person with whom he teched the show (the sound designer, the associate sound designer, or composer, for example). After the first preview, a director may feel that all the sound is too quiet, and mention to the operator that it should come up a point. But the operator should never accept that kind of recommendation without checking with the designer, who has the best ability to translate the director's requests into specific instructions. After opening, the stage manager may consult with the designer and make changes according to her judgment on how the cues are working within the show.

The sound operator's primary responsibility is to execute the sound design. This involves preparing for each performance (the soundcheck), running the show, and shutting down all the equipment at the end of the performance (if appropriate). His job also includes preserving the artistic intent of the sound design throughout the run of the show. To do this, the operator must run the sound precisely and maintain the sound system. He should have an adequate grasp of the technical aspects of sound so that he can identify and correct problems quickly and competently.

Early in my career, I was running the sound for a production of *My Heart's in the Highlands*. During one performance, I suspected that one of the input channels on the mixer had gone bad because one of the dog bark cues didn't play. I checked the board to make sure that it wasn't just an operator error on my part. Just as I got the "ready" from the stage manager for the next dog cue, I bypassed the bad input by patching into an open channel on the mixer. "Ready," I responded, proud that I had figured out how to get around the malfunction. When the stage manager said, "GO," I played the cue. It sounded like there was a nineteen-foot miniature poodle backstage. That was bad. I was certain that the stage manager, known for running an extremely tight and well-executed show, was going to leap over his console yelling, "What's that? FIX IT!!!" Well, the audience completely lost it when the actor onstage delivered his next line. Peering out the front door, he said, "It's not a very big dog, Johnny." Horrified, I looked over to the stage manager, who was laughing so hard he had tears rolling down his face. Somehow, that made me realize that even though I had made a mistake, people would understand that I was only human. After the show, I figured out that when I bypassed the bad input, I had plugged into an input that was calibrated hotter than the bad channel. A level of three on the new channel equaled ten on the faulty channel. After that production, I trimmed all of the inputs on the board to the same value.   —JL

THE SOUNDCHECK

Before each performance, every piece of sound equipment used in the production must be checked thoroughly to be certain that the sound equipment is set up and functioning properly. If a sampler hasn't been loaded, it won't matter if the volume has been set correctly—the cue won't play. If an amplifier hasn't been turned on, the loudspeakers patched into it will never make a sound. If the equipment isn't preset properly for the top of the show, the cues will not play properly. The first three steps of the soundcheck are

- Setting up/turning on the equipment
- Checking the equipment for hardware and software integrity
- Presetting the equipment to run the show

The soundcheck should start well ahead of the house opening so that if there is a problem, there will be enough time to fix it. A basic rule of thumb is to allow an extra half-hour. If the soundcheck takes thirty minutes to perform, then it should start an hour before the house opens. Plan on allowing more time as a cushion on musicals or shows with lots of equipment or an inexperienced sound operator. Large- and even medium-scale musicals can easily add an hour or more to the soundcheck.

The most thorough way to do a soundcheck is to have a written list of the duties that need to be performed. A soundcheck list helps to delineate which equipment has to be checked and what the procedure is for checking that equipment. However, there's no such thing as a generic soundcheck list—every sound system is different, and the setup of each sound system changes from show to show. How detailed the information is should be determined by the situation. If your operator is experienced, then listing what needs to happen in order might be sufficient. If, on the other hand, the sound operator or the backup operator is inexperienced, then it would be a good idea to have a thorough step-by-step list of duties.

FIRING UP THE SYSTEM

Start the soundcheck by properly placing and plugging in any equipment that isn't kept in its performance position between shows. Equipment such as loudspeakers or microphones on stands may have been moved to accommodate the resetting of scenery or to prevent theft. If you need to plug in a loudspeaker, do so before turning on the amplifiers. This minimizes the chances of shorting out the amplifier in the process.

There's a definite logic to the order in which you turn on all the equipment. Some components may emit an electronic "pop" when turned on or off. This pop, or transient sound, is actually a loud, very brief signal produced by the equipment because the electronics are not at normal operating values at the instant of turning on and shutting down. The amplifiers—which are near the end of the signal path—should be turned on last, so that if there is a pop, it isn't amplified through the loudspeakers. The pop is dangerous to loudspeakers because the transient signal can be much stronger than the typical signal the amplifier was designed to receive. When the amplifier tries to reproduce this signal, it sends the loudspeaker a distorted, extremely strong (loud) signal that the loudspeaker tries to reproduce. In trying to reproduce that signal, the loudspeaker may be damaged.

As you turn on your equipment, check any controls that are normally left in one position throughout the show to make sure they are set properly. On amplifiers, check output volumes. Indicate the proper position of a knob or a switch by marking the equipment with a small piece of board tape (white paper tape) marked with an arrow pointing to the correct position. These visual guides are called "spike marks," a term that more commonly refers to positioning furniture on a set. It might be helpful, for an inexperienced operator, to list all the switches and knobs that are to be checked on each device or draw a diagram.

If there are controls that will not move throughout the run of the show, tape them down to their correct position. Consider whether

144

any equipment in the setup will be used at times other than performances. In some theatres, the equipment used to run sound during a show is also used to produce recordings for the next production. All controls that do get changed throughout the show must have their settings checked when you set up for the top of the show. These controls could include (but are not limited to) EQ, output assignment, effects processors, and loudspeaker controls.

CHECKING THE EQUIPMENT

There is no standard order in which to check the equipment, but as you become more familiar with your sound system, the most efficient procedure for checking will become clear:

- CDs, MiniDiscs, samplers, computer-assisted playback systems, and other sources
- Microphones, wired and wireless
- MIDI gear, triggers, synthesizers, and samplers
- Mixing boards
- Auxiliary equipment (reverb units, equalizers, digital delays)
- Loudspeakers
- Practical sound effects (phone ringers, door bells, and buzzers)
- Equipment that may be the responsibility of the sound operator (headsets, production monitor system, the stage manager's paging system)

The most precise way to check the loudspeakers is to move around the house and listen to each one. Music is useful for checking loudspeakers because it usually has a wide range of frequencies. You should also use the show recordings for this test. If there is no music in the show, choose a piece of music with which you are familiar. Listen to make sure that the loudspeaker is reproducing the music clearly. If the loudspeaker sounds like it's working properly, then you also know that the amplifier powering that unit is functioning properly. A muffled, tinny, or distorted sound might indicate that a component in the loudspeaker has failed, that something is wrong with the amplifier, or that there is a bad connection somewhere.

If you are using a computer-assisted playback system, you can build a loudspeaker and effects check. This is similar to the technique that a lot of master electricians use to perform a dimmer check. This check can be built for a one- or two-person operation, but it's common for the sound operator to do it by herself. The following is a guide to how the sequence might be created.

145

First, select a broad-band, fairly compressed music selection without a lot of variation. This will make it easy to consistently hear content from each of the loudspeakers units or distribution areas.

Second, identify how many units need to be checked and note their location.

Third, build a sequence that crossfades between each of the loudspeakers or distribution areas. Set an appropriate wait time between each loudspeaker cue to allow the operator to walk around the house and check each unit, even if there are multiple units in an area. If you use real-time effects processing, you can create cues within the sequence that check microphones and effects levels. You should also test complex sequences using the sound cues built for the production.

The next phase of the soundcheck is to make sure that sounds coming from the playback devices, microphones, effects units, or any other equipment are being routed to the proper amplifier at a consistent volume. Volume controls need to be checked to make sure that each control fades up as smoothly as it did in the previous performance. While music is playing through the input, move the fader up and down, listening for a sudden jump or drop in volume. Also listen for static, which would indicate a dirty fader. Test each input channel used in the show by playing something out of each piece of equipment and moving the individual faders up and down. By checking each fader used in the show, you'll also be checking all of the sound-producing devices (decks, samplers, microphones). If you are working with a digital mixer, you'll want to check all of your saved scenes.

If you're using a digital sampler, load the show sound bank. Setting up a test bank that has data routed to each output separately is another good way to check the integrity of each output. If you are using more than one disk or bank in the show, make sure they all load. It is rare for a hard drive not to load, so if a drive reads properly when checked, then it will most likely read during the show. Of course, all drives and disks should be backed up in case of an emergency. When playing a digital sampler with a keyboard, make sure the keys work, and if you're using a sequencer in conjunction with a sampler or other MIDI equipment, make sure that the sequencer is working properly. Set up one or two specific cues with which the sequencer is used, and run the sequence to ensure that all the equipment and sounds are triggered properly.

Do the microphone check after the loudspeaker check—that way, if there are problems with the sound quality, you'll know that the loudspeakers are not the problem. Whenever possible, have someone onstage talk into a microphone while the sound operator listens in the house.

Many times when I've asked someone to talk into a microphone, they reply, "What should I say?" My stock answer is, "Tell me what you had for lunch yesterday." If they skipped lunch yesterday, then I ask why. Between the two questions, I can usually get someone to start yammering enough to check the equipment.   —JL

If equipment such as a reverb or compressor is used with the microphone, make sure it is patched in and tested. When wireless microphones are used, check the batteries, antenna, reception, integrity of the microphone cable, as well as the sound quality of the microphone element. Walk the microphone around the playing area while testing it through the loudspeakers. Even the best wireless microphones are susceptible to interference from outside radio transmissions or blockage because of metal objects. For example, a metal ladder placed backstage in a different spot than that used on previous nights could change the characteristics of the reception onstage. It's not a bad idea to turn all the wireless transmitters on during the RF (radio frequency) system test. This will help you to see if there is any interference due to transmission frequencies being too close together. Go to www.elsevierdirect.com/companions/9780240810119 for links to more detailed information available on the web about using wireless microphones.

All practical sound effects should be tested to see if they are hooked up and whether the switches operating them are functional.

Communication headsets, along with their belt packs and cables, probably receive more abuse (from dropping and yanking) than any other type of equipment in the theatre. Put on the headset and listen to yourself to make sure that the microphone works. Press the page button to make sure that it is functioning, and wiggle cables at the connectors to check for shorts in the wires. Once you've checked the headset, make sure the microphone switch is off. When you put the headset back in its resting place, see if the headset cable needs to be coiled. A long cable lying haphazardly on the backstage floor is a tripping hazard.

In most houses, the production monitor—the system that allows the stage to be heard backstage—and the stage manager's paging setup are parts of the same system. Common to these systems are loudspeakers in various positions (combined with a volume control), a microphone over the stage, and a microphone enabling the stage manager to page various locations throughout the theatre. Some systems also allow the stage manager's microphone to address the house. This comes in handy during technical rehearsals and emergencies. As with the other equipment, all of the components of the production monitor system need to be checked, which means that loudspeakers, amplifiers, and microphones need to be tested and preset to their performance values. In the same way that actors should check their props before the show, the backstage crew should test every piece of equipment that will be used during the performance. Normally, the stage manager will confirm that her own system is functioning and ready for performance, but the sound operator must incorporate the production monitor system into the flow of his setup. The sound operator should determine that everything is working properly before the stage manager checks her own equipment.

Once all of the equipment has been set up and checked, the operator should preset the controls and equipment that he'll be using and changing throughout the show.

148

TOP-OF-SHOW PRESET

The top-of-show preset refers to setting the controls on the sound system for the beginning of the show. How this is done depends on the configuration of the system. For example, it's always necessary to have the decks routed so that their sound comes out of the proper speaker. If you're using a home stereo amp for the center of the system, the tape monitor or input selector must be set in the proper position. If you're using a mixing board, each input must be assigned to the proper output, and that output fader has to be put at its performance setting. Even digital mixing systems require a detailed top-of-show preset check. You should check your opening "snapshot" or "scene" against a printout or list of exact numerical values as opposed to the specific position of a fader or switch. Don't forget that it's good practice to back up your settings regularly. All could be lost in a catastrophic hardware failure.

In manually operated systems, a concise and efficient way to preset the equipment is to develop a top-of-show preset sheet containing all settings. Sound systems vary as much as the composition of the top-of-show preset sheet, and there are many ways to display the same information. Whatever the format, though, the preset sheet should provide the sound operator with clear and complete information on how to set the equipment. For a very basic sound system, the preset sheet can be as simple as a list of a few settings, but a more complicated setup requires a layout that clearly charts the information.

Figure 10.1 is a preset sheet developed for presetting a 16 × 8 mixing board. Here, the numbers 1 through 16 denote the input channels. ER1 and ER2 stand for the echo (or effects) returns available on this particular mixing console. The EQ column tells whether the equalization section of the input is engaged. On some mixing consoles, there is a switch that allows you to bypass this section, so that the setting on an equalization knob has no effect on the signal passing through that input (it's like having the high, mid, and low controls set at flat). For each channel, the EQ column is marked "in" or "out." Suppose there is no equalization needed on an input channel at the top of the show, but the channel has equalization later. With the EQ section bypassed ("out"), you can set the equalization knobs to the proper settings for later use, then engage the EQ section

CHANNEL	ASSIGN	EQ	HIGH	MID	LOW	NOTES
1	2	OUT				
2	2	OUT				
3	1	IN	——	+ 3	– 6	
4	3	OUT				
5	7	OUT	+ 3	——	–6	
6	8	OUT	+ 3	——	–6	
7	3+4	OUT				AREA MIC
8	6	IN	——	——	– 3	
9						
10						
11						
12						
13						
14						
15						
16						
ER1						
ER2						

FIGURE 10.1 A top-of-show preset sheet.

later. Channels 5 and 6 show how this would look on the top-of-show preset sheet. Some other operators might want a column for each input channel's volume setting. The operator who developed this particular sheet wanted to set the volumes by looking at his cue sheets. He thought that having to look over the first sequence of cues would help him get ready for the show.

Other information that could be indicated on a preset sheet includes the following:

- Output to loudspeaker assignments
- First cue number for each playback device
- Pan pot positions
- Auxiliary equipment settings
- Output fader levels

It's simple to enter such information on the top-of-show preset sheet.

With a blank sheet in front of you, go through the cue sheets for the show (see p. 151) and find the first instance for each input channel on the chart. If the first cue that uses input 5 has no EQ, mark the EQ column for input 5 "out." Continue through the cues until you find the first instance of input 5 using equalization, and then mark those settings under the high/mid/low column.

With all of the equipment set up and ready to go, the sound operator needs to check the cue sheets to make sure that they are all there and in order. As a final precaution, some operators like to play the first cue that appears on each deck or the computer so that they know the show will start off flawlessly.

Finally, the sound operator needs to turn on all of the running/work lights and tell the stage manager that he is ready for the house to open. The sound is now ready to be run for the performance.

POSTSHOW

For the post-show shutdown, the equipment should be turned off in reverse order from which it was turned on, which means shutting off the amplifiers first. All production playback media should be stored in a safe place. Although keeping them in their players won't hurt them, securing them away prevents them from being mislaid if someone uses the equipment outside of performance. And if the equipment is stolen, your cues won't disappear as well. For computer-assisted playback systems, it is not necessary to pack up and remove the hard drives when you power down. It is very important to keep

Mixer Input to Output Patch Schedule
Sound Design: Production

| Mixing Console Preset Schedule | | | | | Production: Spiderman the Musical | | Date: 8/16/07 |
| Mixing Desk: Yamaha 01V | | | | | Portland High School | | |
Item	Input Label	Sound Source	Input Trim	Inpu tCH	Output Assign	Signal Processing	Note
1	CD1 Left	Denon DN600F	-10	1	1-8 ST	none	
2	CD1 Right	Denon DN600F	-10	2	1-8 ST	none	
3	CD2 Left	Denon DN600F	-10	3	1-8 ST	none	
4	CD2 Right	Denon DN600F	-10	4	1-8 ST	none	
5	MD1 Left	Tascam MD-350	-10	5	1-8 ST	none	
6	MD1 Right	Tascam MD-350	-10	6	1-8 ST	none	
7	MD2 Left	Tascam MD-350	-10	7	1-8 ST	none	
8	MD2 Right	Tascam MD-350	-10	8	1-8 ST	none	
9	Mic 1	Shure Beta 58	-35	9	1-2 M	EQ: -10dB Shelf @ 120Hz	Offstage Vocal
10	Mic 2	Shure Beta 58	-35	10	1-2 M	EQ: -10dB Shelf @ 120Hz	Offstage Vocal
11	Mic 3	Crown PCC160	-45	11	1-2 M	EQ: -12dB Shelf @ 90Hz; -3d3 @ 10KHz	SR Floor Mic
12	Mic 4	Crown PCC160	-45	12	1-2 M	EQ: -12dB Shelf @ 90Hz; -3dB @ 10KHz	SL Floor Mic
13	Reverberation L	TC 3000	-10	13	1-2 ST	none	Vocal
14	Reverberation R	TC 3000	-10	14	1-2 ST	none	Vocal
15				15			
16				24			

FIGURE 10.2 Another top-of-show preset sheet.

151

one backup of the show in a location that is not the control booth. Keeping a complete copy with your digital audio workstation is the norm. Making DVD archives will preserve the show for the rest of your life (or so we're told).

OPERATING THE SOUND

As a designer, you want the operator to have the best chance of running the show properly. You've built the show so that the sound is as easy as possible to operate. Still, when you are working with a manually run show, the operator must have both concise instructions on what she is to do and a feel for the technique of running the show. While cue sheets provide the instructions, becoming comfortable with the equipment, developing a feel for fades, and understanding the artistic intent of the cues can only come with experience. Of course, with computer-based playback systems, this is less of an issue. But there is still an art in the musicality of pressing the "go" button, especially when the operator is taking the cue on an actor's action and not a stage manager's call.

Nothing about running the show should be left to memory. This is not to say that there won't be a sequence of cues that requires the sound operator to memorize certain moves—but all of those moves should be in front of the operator to review before they are called. Having every move down on paper will also help the operator jump accurately from one part of the show to another during technical rehearsals.

CUE SHEETS

Cue sheets now must be looked at from two different production paradigms: the computer-based playback system and the manually operated setup. Since a computer-based playback system remembers all of the details of each cue in its memory, the paperwork involved with running a show can be rather simple. However, the sound operator of a manually executed show has to have clear instructions to follow.

CUE SHEETS FOR MANUALLY OPERATED PLAYBACK

The format of cue sheets commonly used to operate the show varies greatly. Since cue sheets are tailored to a particular sound system, it's difficult to present a universal cue sheet. What is common to all cue sheets, however, is that they are clear and comprehensive. An operator's instructions must be organized so that the cue can be located quickly, with the moves she must execute for each individual cue laid out in sequence.

Ideally, the cue sheets should be so understandable that someone with a working knowledge of sound and that particular sound system could step in for the operator in case of an emergency. Sound operators do not get understudies, but some theatres make sure that someone else on the staff has an overview of the operation for each production's sound.

Figure 10.3 is an example of a cue sheet devised for use with a sound system that included an analogue console and different playback devices (which were referred to as "decks"). This cue sheet was developed from a collaboration between the sound operator and the designer. Other operators devised completely different cue sheets for the same sound system. Always provide space on a cue sheet for the cue number, the cue sheet page number, the name of the production,

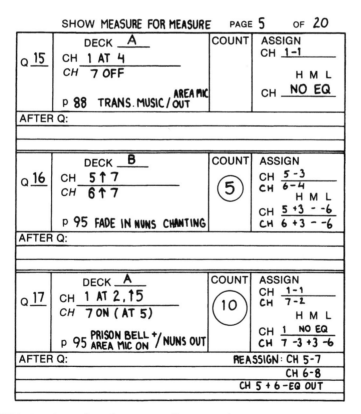

FIGURE 10.3 A cue sheet for a manually operated system.

and the action of the cue—including the volume at which a fader is set or moving, the count on which an action is executed, and which deck to use. The cue number should be the most prominent information on the cue sheet, so put it in an uncluttered area. Because the eye is used to reading from left to right in Western culture, most designers and operators put the cue number on the left-hand side of their sheet. Numbering all of the individual cue sheets assures that they are kept in order. It is good practice to write the name of the show on each sheet. This is useful when the theatre is doing more than one show at a time, the show goes on tour, or the show is to be archived.

Other information that might be shown on a cue sheet (depending on the needs of the production or the desires of the operator and designer) include the following:

- Description or name of the cue
- The script page on which the cue appears
- The act and scene of the cue
- How to operate a practical effect
- Input and output assignments
- Equalization settings
- Changes that must be performed while the cue is running or after the cue is completed

It's always preferable for the operator to be aware of how the cues being executed relate to the production, so write in what the cue entails on the cue sheet. Figure 10.3 shows that Q15 is the cue for the transition music and includes taking out the area microphone. This helps the operator associate the execution of a cue with an event in the play, not just with a group of numbers and instructions. That connection will help him recall the cue and how it has been performed in the past.

In most cases, including the script page number on which the effect or music appears will help the operator gauge the pace of the cueing until he gets to know the show and feels comfortable with it. Most operators approach a show as a series of clusters of cues. An operator might look at running a ninety-cue show, for example, as a few ten-cue sequences plus a number of three or four-cue sequences. As the operator gets close to a sequence, he will review only that group of cues. By using the script page numbers to show him where the "non-cue areas" are, the operator can easily anticipate an upcoming group of cues.

154

The most common adjustment involved in manually running a show is moving a volume fader. The operator needs to know which fader is involved, to what level the fader should be set, and at what rate (count) this happens. In Figure 10.3, Q16 has Channels 5 and 6 fading up to a level of 7 on a 5 count (CH___ is the area on this cue sheet for writing levels of input channels). Note that the cue sheet does not say where Channels 5 and 6 started. In this case, the operator set up a convention whereby the volume fader starts at 0 (complete attenuation) unless a specific volume is indicated.

Q17 has the volume for Channel 1 set at 2. When the "go" is given for Q17, the operator starts the deck and immediately fades Channel 1 up to a level of 5 on a 10 count. At the same time (or right after starting the deck), Channel 7, which was preset at 5, is turned on (in this setup, Channel 7 is the input channel for the area microphone). Q15 is a spot effect. Its volume is preset before the go is given to start the deck.

The term "count" may seem subjective. Ideally, one count equals one second, but that will never be the case unless your cues are being executed by a computer. In the real world, a count is a unit of time that the operator uses consistently to determine the rate of speed at which an action is performed. As you, the designer, work with an operator, you develop a feel for whether he counts slowly or quickly.

In Figure 10.3, the sound designer and operator determined that if a deck/device is started at the top of a cue, an indication of which device will be used is entered next to DECK. When a cue does not include starting a device, that space is left blank. Instead of writing "deck B—go" as an instruction within the cue, the operator knows that, if a tape deck is listed in that location on the cue sheet, then he should start that deck on the "go." If the cue called for the operator to start a fade of an input and then start a deck three counts later, then the "go" for the deck might be written as an instruction below the input channel information (CH___).

Remember that there are many different devices that store or emit sounds. An operator needs instructions on how to operate devices as diverse as a practical phone ringer and a digital sampling keyboard. Explanations on the cue sheet for how to manipulate these devices

155

should be concise. For example, a cue may be stated simply "Press red button marked phone bell – 2 counts." The operator needs to know what to move in what direction and for how long.

The assignment (ASSIGN) section of the cue sheet contains information pertaining to how the sound is being routed to the loudspeakers. Depending on the sophistication of the sound system, this information might list an output number (or letter) assignment, or simply a loudspeaker that has been switched on. It is good practice to write in the assignment for each input used within that cue and not just when it changes. This allows a quick double-check before the cue is performed, and it is helpful when jumping around the show during tech week.

When equalizing a cue, make sure that it is clear to what channel the settings relate. In Figure 10.3, there is a space in the ASSIGN box for high, mid-range, and low settings. If you were using a home stereo amplifier in place of a mixer, you might prefer to refer to treble, bass, and possibly mid-range settings.

Space should be left on the cue sheet for writing notes. Operational notes, pertaining to the execution of the cue, should be kept visually within the main body of the form, but actions that happen after the cue is complete, or once it has been executed and is running, can be placed in an adjacent space. In Figure 10.3, the AFTER Q section is for that purpose.

Figures 10.4 and 10.5 are other examples of cue sheet layouts. Note that the cue sheet in Figure 10.4 applies to one particular act and scene, and dedicates a block of space for the decks' volume and EQ settings as well as speaker assignments for that particular sheet. An advantage to this cue sheet is the adjustable amount of space used to write a specific cue, depending on the length of data. The cue takes as much room on the page as is needed to write the instructions, whereas the cue sheet in Figure 10.3 limits the cue to a specific block of space on the sheet.

Many designers and operators make up a blank cue sheet and duplicate it, using it as a standard form for most shows. This doesn't mean that you can't write out all of your cue sheets by hand on a legal pad, although it is helpful to be consistent in the layout of the information. Other designers use a database for logging all cue information and then print out a report that contains individual sheets or a full set of cue sheets needed in a production. This also helps keep the process a bit smoother when having to insert a cue into a page that is already full. Once she is familiar with the layout of a cue sheet, the operator will know what part of the sheet to immediately go to in search of specific information.

PRODUCTION ROMEO AND JULIET Page 6 of 15

Act 2 Scene 3 Date 12/4

PRESET: Deck A Cue # 19 Deck 13 Cue # 20 Speakers ALL TO HOUSE

NOTES:

CUE #	PRESET VOLUME	VOLUME ADJUSTMENT	COUNT	DECK	DESCRIPTION	EQ	NOTES
19	2	↑6	4	A	TRANSITION MUSIC ACT 2, SC. 3 TO 4	BASS +3	
20	0	↑5	4	B	TRANSITION MUSIC ACT 2, SC. 4 TO 5	BASS +3	
21	3			A	CHURCH BELL TOLLS 9:00	TREBLE +6 BASS -3	

FIGURE 10.4 Another cue sheet example.

Revels '98 Sound Cue List Pg. 6

	Cue Description	Chan.	Level	Pan	Bus Assign	Aux 1	Descrip
7	**#32 Eclipse**	**1**	**-7db**	**L**	**1-2**	**OUT**	PT 1
		2	**-7db**	**R**	**1-2**	**OUT**	PT 2
	PT: #32 Eclipse	**3**	**-7db**	**L**	**3-4**	**OUT**	PT 3
		4	**-7db**	**R**	**3-4**	**OUT**	PT 4
		5	**-7db**	**C**	**None**	**U (post fader)**	PT 5
		6	OUT	C	5-6	OUT	PT 6
		7	OUT	C	1-2;3-4	2	E3 Main L
		8	OUT	C	1-2;3-4	OUT	E3 Main R
		9	OUT	C	1-2;3-4	OUT	E3 Sub 1 L
		10	OUT	C	1-2;3-4	OUT	E3 Sub 1 R
		11	U	L	1-2	OUT	Panner Rtn 1
		12	U	R	1-2	OUT	Panner Rtn 2
		13	U	L	3-4	OUT	Panner Rtn 3
		14	U	R	3-4	OUT	Panner Rtn 4

FIGURE 10.5 A different cue sheet.

Figure 10.5 is a cue sheet that was produced using a spreadsheet program on a computer. "U," which is found under the Level and Aux 1 headings, stands for unity (a level that neither boosts or lessens the signal's volume). "PT" refers to ProTools, the digital audio workstation that was used as a playback device in performance. The designer that developed this cue sheet used the convention that anything that changed in a cue would be shown in boldface.

When I began designing theatrical sound professionally in 1980, I realized that there wasn't an established language for sound designers to use. Lighting designers had some standards, but sound designers had a wide variance in the language and terms they used. When writing cues manually, it became extremely important to have the designer, assistant or associate, and operator speaking the same language. So by 1983, when I started teaching at Yale, I developed a list of terms (shown in Figure 10.6) in an attempt to standardize sound design cueing communication. As with all languages, this is a living document that changes and adapts with different creative teams and production styles. —DB

There are many ways to abbreviate the information contained in a cue sheet. Figure 10.6 is a chart that proposes a common language for the abbreviations that are used for cue sheets.

The list of terms in Figure 10.6 can express both simple and complex command statements. The terms can be adapted for use in contemporary computer-assisted playback systems as well as in manual playback systems. Not listed here are many new terms that manufacturers of cue control software have developed that reflect their own control architecture.

CUE SHEETS FOR COMPUTER-BASED PLAYBACK AND MIXING SYSTEMS

In 1985, Richmond Sound Design introduced the Command Cue, a computer-assisted playback system developed for the theatre. Early systems, such as the Command Cue, were limited to basic features, including starting a playback deck or sending a MIDI note message to a sampler. The technical advances in computers, audio, and show control since the mid-1980s have allowed a number of new systems to come to market that have revolutionized and advanced the art and craft of sound design. These new systems eliminate the need for individual stereo playback devices or deck-based playback by providing multiple channels of playback and mixing. They provide automated mixing, panning, and imaging of sound sources as well as automated control of microphones and effects. These systems

158

Language for Cueing
Also for use in the Sound Designer Organizational Database

This cue language is made up of standardized symbols that can be arranged to describe any cue operation. The Designer, Assistant/Associate Designer and Operator must be familiar with these symbols and understand how to use them during technical rehearsals and "run of show".

Symbol	Label	Description	Example
B	Bump	An immediate start up or stop of a cue or event	CD1: B@L25; CD1: B out
@	at	Used to connect symbols in a "sentence"	CD4: B@L10
C	Count	The "C" is used, preceded by a number representing 1 second in time	SFX 1/2: B@L20, 3C to L40
L	Level	The "L" is followed by a number that represents a position on a linear fader	10C to L40
AF	AutoFollow	The expression "AF" indicates that the next action will immediately follow the current action	CD1: 3C out AF CD2: B@L30
CD, MD, SFX, LCS	Source Playback Device	The source playback device identifies any playback device that is NOT referenced in the initiating cue event. The device label is followed by a colon	MD2: 10C to L20, MD1: B@L10
M or RF	Microphone	Indicates a wired or radio microphone followed by a number designation	RF14: B@L25
Samp #	Sampler	Labels any type of Sampler followed by a number designation	Samp 1 or Samp 2
W	Wait	This is a pause. The "W" is followed by a number that represents seconds	B@L20, W3C, 5C to L 30
A	Area	This may be used when an "AREA's" level changes within a cue	A 5/6: 3C to L30
Grp	Group	Like Area, the GROUP is identified when a level changes within a cue	Grp 3/4: 5C to default
CH	Channel	Used to identify a specific input channel within a cue sequence	CH2: 3C out
MSTR	Master	Used to identify a MASTER fade within a cue sequence	MSTR: BO
SM	SubMaster	Used to identify a SUB-MASTER fade within a cue sequence	SM5/6: 3C to +5
/	Slash	A slash separates pairs of numbers	Grp 9/10: 3C out
Aux.	Auxiliary Send	Combined with a number, used to identify an Auxiliary Level (or change)	Aux.1 @ Unity
Rcv	Effects Receive	Combined with a number, used to identify an Effects Receive Level	Rcv2: B@L20
LINK	Link	Used to start multiple events using a single cue number	Q101,203,103 Linked as Q101
OUT	Out	Represents turning off an audio path	CH2: 5C out
To	To	Used to connect count and level designations	CH5/6: 3C to L30
BO	Bump Out	Used to indicate an immediate STOP of an event	CD1, CD2: BO
PO	Play Out	Used to indicate a cue that once started, plays out completely	CD2: B@L20 PO
12:00	Of the Clock	Used to indicate the position of a rotary control (volume, pan, etc.)	Aux.6 @ L1:00
Default	Default	Used to indicate the default level as listed in the default settings chart	Grp 9/10: 3C to default
▲ ▼ ▼	Level Change	Arrows are used to indicate a fade up/down in level as well as OUT	MD3: 3C ▼ L30
,	Comma	Used to separate instructions in a command sequence	B@L50, 3C to L20
:	Colon	Used to separate a device from an instruction	MD1: 3C to L35

FIGURE 10.6 Language for cueing chart.

159

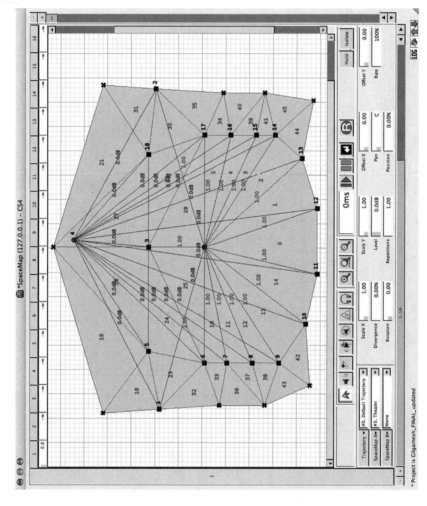

FIGURE 10.7 SpaceMap window from the Matrix3 audio show control system.

can automatically back up your work, preserving your design in the event of a catastrophic equipment failure. Probably the most important reason to use this technology is that it can provide consistent playback of very complex sequences.

Meyer Sound Laboratories' LCS Series Matrix3 audio control system is one of the most advanced products for theatrical playback. This integrated software and hardware package allows you practically unlimited control over volume, panning, EQ, and multiple audio file playback, just to mention a few features.

The SpaceMap window is where the sound operator can define speaker locations within the theatre and then draw a path showing where she would like the sound to travel.

The capabilities of the most sophisticated systems are limited only by your budget. Of course, the larger systems can be very powerful and allow you to more closely realize what's in your mind's ear when conceiving a sound design. Technologically, they can perform just about any task that the designer asks. They can also be quite expensive, but are well worth the money. However, don't overlook the less expensive or free programs that are available.

QLab is a versatile, affordable computer-assisted cueing system that is in use at many theatres. It's easy to learn and use, plus it's very reliable. Because it's not dependent on external audio hardware, you can build an extremely portable and useful playback system with just the software and a laptop computer.

There are many other products you may want to become familiar with. These include Stage Research, Inc.'s SFX and ShowBuilder programs and Richmond Sound Design's SoundMan software and AudioBox hardware.

{You can find additional information about computer-assisted playback systems on our webpage at the Focal Press website – www. elsevierdirect.com/companions/9780240810119.}

Computer-assisted playback systems don't require a physical operator cue sheet. The cues are displayed in a list that is part of the operational software. The detailed cue information that would be on a cue sheet (if the show was run manually) is all stored as a part of the cue.

Although you won't need to make operator cue sheets for running the show, you should provide the operator with a cue summary as you would for the stage manager. The cue summary is a useful reference for your operator and comes in handy when you're building cues with him. That said, you should still track your cue running information by either making a printout of the computer data or manually tracking it in a database or spreadsheet application.

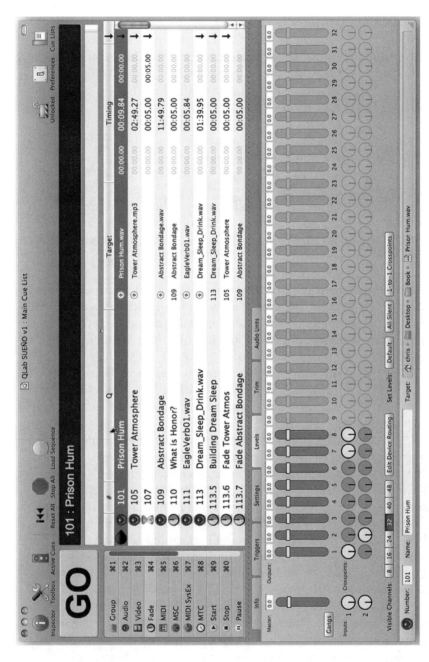

FIGURE 10.8 A screenshot of a cue list from Figure 53's QLab application.

You want to have a backup of the cue instructions in case the worst should happen, your primary and backup computer systems fail.

TRAINING THE NOVICE OPERATOR

The first step in training the novice operator is to make her familiar with the equipment. Identify each piece of equipment and describe, in terms as simple as possible, how the various pieces of equipment are hooked together to form the complete sound system. Show her in detail the complete setup and preset of the system—where the power switches are, how to load the CD and MiniDisc players, how to set up for computer playback—even how to recover from a crashed computer. Explain the actual mechanics of running the show, stressing to her that operating sound is different than running another aspect of the show (use the lights as an example). Once a fade into a lighting cue is complete, the lighting operator can relax while in that cue. When running the sound, some devices will continue to play unless stopped by the operator.

Chances are that training the novice operator will happen during tech week. If you can do it earlier, you should. Impress upon the new operator how crucial the soundcheck is. Let her know that if she is running behind, the soundcheck still must happen and that you'll help her through it. Remember, a technical rehearsal without a proper soundcheck could be fraught with problems and could waste more time than it takes to do the soundcheck correctly in the first place.

Go over all the paperwork with the operator, especially the cue sheets. Make sure that you give her guidance on how to fill in her cue sheets. Explain to her how counts are used in running the show; have her count out loud and adjust her tempo, if necessary. Impress upon her the importance of double-checking the equipment against her cue sheets.

Go to the booth and have the operator run a few cues in your presence. Watch the way she runs those cues, and give pointers where necessary. If there is time, try running the hardest sequence in the show—working those cues by her side, where you can see what she is doing, is better than trying to figure out her problems from the other end of the headset cable. Explain to the operator who the stage manager is, how the cues will be called, and the proper response to the calls.

One word of wisdom to pass on to the new operator is to not become complacent. Even experienced operators tend to become relaxed as they get more confident with the show. Between the terror of running the first shows and the feeling of confidence after running a number of flawless performances lies a transitional phase in which many operators make careless mistakes.

TRAINING A REPLACEMENT OPERATOR

If the current sound operator or mixer has to be replaced, there are some measures to take that will help the transition to her replacement. Assuming that you have advance notice of the operator's departure, you have the opportunity to train a backup operator. If a backup operator is familiar with the show, then any instance of an operator leaving a show should not become a disaster. In many ways, training a replacement operator is similar to rehearsing an understudy.

Have the replacement operator watch the current sound operator run the show—not just the actual operation of the cues, but also the soundcheck and strike. The replacement operator should have his own copy of the cue sheets (if used) so that he can follow along without looking over the shoulder of the current operator to see her sheets. If he needs to make notes for himself, he can do so on his own copies. If the show isn't too demanding, the current operator can give a running commentary on what to watch out for.

With this training, the replacement operator should then be given a chance to run the cues outside of performance (dry tech). With the current operator watching, the cues should be called with the same rough timing in which they are called during performance. With difficult sequences, the calls may need to be slowed down to allow a replacement operator time to get the moves down pat. An excellent technique to help the new operator learn the pacing of the show is to record the stage manager calling the show and use that tape during this dry tech.

Once the replacement operator has mastered this phase, it's time to work him into the show. His first performance behind the controls should include the previous operator standing by to catch any problems and give reminders. Only the judgment of the original sound operator and the stage manager can determine when the replacement is ready to go solo.

TOURING

There are additional tasks that the sound operator may have if he is taking a show on tour. He'll probably be responsible for setting up the equipment from scratch, or incorporating the equipment into existing equipment at the performance space. He'll have to devise a procedure for setting up and striking the equipment at each theatre, and he'll need to prepare packing lists. Plan on allotting a sufficient amount of time for an extensive soundcheck. If you're using equipment belonging to the performance space, make sure that it is working properly. Often, there is a contact person at the theatre who can clue you in about the idiosyncrasies of the space and equipment.

Microphone and playback levels will change from theatre to theatre. The designer will not always be present on these tours to set new levels, in which case the operator sets levels in the tech session before performances. It's difficult for the operator to do this if he is isolated in a booth, far away from the stage—and as we've seen, to properly set sound levels, he has to be familiar with the volume of the sound in relation to the actors' voices. Using a house position would be preferable, whenever possible.

Sometimes there will be no designated sound operator, and members of the touring company will be responsible for the equipment and running the sound. Because the assigned person lacks the background of a sound operator or technician, a thorough system for performing the soundcheck and setting levels will need to be developed. Even if a number of people are involved with the setup and operation, one person should be designated to maintain the equipment and the consistency of the execution. This person should be given a complete overview on how the cues work within the production.

It's imperative to have backups for everything when on tour, because there is usually no way to remake cues while on the road. Carry copies of all playback media. Make sure that there are copies back at home base. This way, if your cues, backups, or the equipment holding the cues is stolen, a new set of cues can be sent.

IN CASE OF EMERGENCY

Problems and emergencies always come up—fuses will blow, a deck will freeze up, a cue will be patched wrong. Steady nerves and preparation will keep these situations from becoming any worse than they already are. "Grace under fire" isn't something that can be taught in a book. Experience is the best teacher. The longer an operator has worked, the more comfortable he will be with the equipment. It is this understanding of how everything works together that allows an operator to troubleshoot a problem quickly and identify the solution.

When a cue doesn't play when called, the stage manager will be aware of it as soon as the operator is. The stage manager will probably jump into the situation and decide whether to pass over the cue or to play it. If the problem is an incorrect volume, it's best to try to get it

165

to the proper volume, and not just to an arbitrary value. The point is to try to cover mistakes as smoothly as possible. It would be impossible to detail all of the technical difficulties that might occur. Some items that it would be wise to keep on hand in case of an emergency are fuses, screwdrivers (all types and sizes), backups, cables, and a flashlight.

AFTER THE SHOW CLOSES

Once the curtain comes down on the final performance of a show, all technical departments strike their equipment, removing their elements from the theatre. There are some extra duties that the sound operator should perform during her portion of the strike. The production playback media and cue sheets must be returned to the designer or composer. If agreed upon in advance, a copy can become part of the theatre's archives. Ideally, a full copy of all production paperwork was completed after opening, as part of the production archives.

All equipment should be removed from the stage to allow a clean area for the load-in of the next show's set and lights. Striking the equipment keeps it from being damaged by the next show's load-in. The sound operator should make sure that all borrowed or rented equipment is returned or given to the person on the theatre's staff responsible for it. Leave the theatre's booth and equipment in as good or better condition than you found it.

There's much more to running sound for a show than just pressing the go button. The designer must supply the operator with a show that is possible to run, and with complete instructions on how to do so. For his part, a sound operator should have a sense of his artistic contribution to the show and be technically adept and level-headed. When all of these elements come together, the sound design or composition can be presented at its best, working as a vital part of the production's success.

11

Approaches and Techniques

There's no textbook way to prepare a design or composition for a production. It's not as easy as saying, "Take a storm, add some underscoring and scene change music, and you'll have a wonderful sound design for *The Tempest.*" Every production of a play is different, and each production presents a different set of possibilities for the composer and/or designer. At one end of the spectrum, there are straightforward productions containing a handful of realistic effects taken directly from sound libraries. At the other end, there are productions that call for numerous unrealistic effects, each one needing to be created from scratch. This range of needs and diverse approaches is not limited to sound effects. Compositions can call for something as uncomplicated as a solo piano or as involved as an ensemble of experimental instruments. A sound reinforcement job could be as simple as providing one microphone for a mime to covering the needs of a Broadway musical.

Because of the varying nature of the designs you may be asked to create, you have to learn many different techniques in order to manufacture the cues. Such techniques include:

- how to record and edit sound and music into a cue
- how to make field recordings
- how to manufacture effects from prerecorded or gathered sounds
- how to create a sense of distance in your effects
- how to prepare live sounds
- how to use live microphones

Deciding on your design approach is as important as perfecting your techniques. For example, if you were designing *The Night of the Iguana*, one of the sounds you'd need to create would be the iguana trying to free itself from its confinement under the veranda. Assuming that you wanted to record something that sounds like the clawing and scratching of an iguana, you would use a portable recorder to gather those sounds, then edit them into a specific idea and have them play through a loudspeaker concealed on the set under the veranda. There are, however, other approaches. One option would be to get an iguana, put it in a box with some leaves, and record it trying to get free. Or you could decide what the iguana would be clawing through, collect those items, and record someone moving and scratching through them, her hand imitating the sporadic movements of an iguana. Or you could not record at all, but do the effect live, with someone under the stage making those sounds. Any of these choices can work well if the designer knows how to execute it.

Let's say you want to record someone's hand imitating the sound of the rustling iguana. There are still many choices to make. What would the reptile move through, and why? What will the human hand move through, and how? The script indicates that the iguana is tied up below the veranda near the "cactus clumps." Cactus doesn't make much noise when moved—and the iguana isn't likely to rub against it—but there's certainly other vegetation around, since the play takes place in a Mexican rain forest. The set design may also offer clues about the terrain on which the iguana moves. You've decided, then, that the iguana is moving through dry, dead leaves, old beer cans or bottles (depending on whether cans or bottles are being used in the production), and wooden crates—items that could conceivably be found under the veranda. The iguana would be trying to claw its way free from its constraints.

With this knowledge, you can collect the items you need to create the "iguana hand." Gather some dry leaves and a plastic shopping bag, both of which sound like dry vegetation when moved. A few empty soup cans should simulate period beer cans, which were constructed of heavier metal than those in current use. Some bottles and a small wooden box should fulfill your needs. Place these items in a mini-landscape simulating the layout underneath the veranda. Once the recording equipment is set up, you're ready to make the iguana sounds. Imagine that your hand is the iguana—move around, struggling to get yourself free. A flick of a finger might bang two cans together while you run your hand through the dead leaves onto a plastic bag. This should provide an interesting variety of sounds. Don't forget to experiment with different microphone placements. You might not get exactly the right sound you want if your setup has been miked too closely or too distantly.

The following discussion of design techniques can help you create cues, and offers various approaches to your work as a sound designer.

CREATING STYLIZED EFFECTS

What is the sound of death? You can't pull that cue off of a sound effects CD. This sound can only come from your imagination. Many stylized effects can be found and produced by manipulating already existing sounds. Radically changing the speed and/or pitch at which a sound is heard, for example, can give it a completely different character.

I was designing effects for a collection of monologues, the topics ranging from everyday events to nightmares. One was a canoe ride down a river after a nuclear holocaust. I had to invent a menacing presence to add to the scene that would embody the destruction of the land and convey an omnipresent threat in the air. I thought about what aspects of a canoe trip might be annoying or threatening, and I came up with insects. Then I decided that there should be a slow, bass sound to represent the water and the "remnants" of the explosions. I started playing with some of the sounds I was already using for the show, trying them at four and eight times their normal speed and slowing them down to 1/4 to 1/16 speed. When I tried this with a city traffic recording, I felt I'd come up with the perfect effect. The sound of the cars passing at eight times normal speed sounded like evil insects, while the very slow traffic sounded like deep turbulence. —JL

169

Effects made up of very low frequencies are felt more than they are heard. A chilling presence can be added to a scene by using rumbles with frequencies from 80 Hz and below. Adding a low-frequency boom into an explosion completes the effect. Imagine the impact on an audience of children if the footsteps of the giant from *Jack and the Beanstalk* actually caused the room to vibrate. (They would wet their pants!) Placing loudspeakers on the floor and/or against walls can accentuate lower frequencies, but to reproduce frequencies such as these, you usually have to use a substantial, high-power subwoofer.

You can lower the pitch of a sound by using a sampler, pitch shifter, or software. If you assign a sample throughout the entire keyboard, you can "audition" the sound at different pitches very easily. You can also play more than one key at a time and hear how combinations of pitches mixed together will sound. Blending sounds together on a sampler can be an effective design tool (pun intended). Note that pitching a sound up on a sampler will make it play back faster than the original, and pitching it down will make it play slower. If that presents a timing problem, you might consider using a pitch shifter, which changes the pitch of a sound but not its speed. Pitch shifting, a feature found on some digital effects units, can yield great results—some units can move a sound's pitch as much as two octaves, which should be enough to transform any sound. Pitch-shifting software allows you to raise or lower the pitch of a sound over a wide range. You are given the option of preserving the length of the sound. Trying to maintain the length of a sound that is being radically pitched may create what is referred to as *artifacts*. Artifacts, or glitches, are generated when the pitch shifter or pitch-shifting software is asked to work outside the limits of its musical range. Pitching a sound down may cause an effect called *aliasing*. Aliasing sounds like a high-frequency sizzle has been added to the sound. It can be attenuated from the sound by filtering out the high frequencies of the sound. Just as a weed can be defined as any plant (even a rose) growing where it is not desired, these artifacts and imperfections may show up unexpectedly and can transform a sound in a way that you can use to your advantage. A good designer stays receptive to new sounds, even if they weren't what he was looking for.

Often, when I'm trying to make new sounds, I'll play all sorts of things through various software processors (known as plug-ins) on my digital audio workstation. I'll tweak all the parameters, trying to alter the sound. One day, I was playing the sound of slowed-down breathing through a pitch-shifting plug-in. I had every slider adjusted radically so that the breathing sounded like it was being processed by a Cuisinart. The phone rang and I stopped the workstation. About ten seconds later, bizarre blasts of sound started coming out of my speakers. At first, I didn't know what was causing this. Then I discovered that the sound was coming out of the workstation. Evidently, I had set the parameters in such a way that even after stopping the workstation from playing, the sound was recycling inside the plug-in, feeding back on itself, until it exploded in glorious distorted noise. It wasn't something that you'd want playing at your wedding reception, but the sound was full of power, emotion, and excitement. It was just what I needed for the paranormal scenes I was designing. "How appropriate," I thought, "the 'ghost in the machine' is coming through." I would use these sounds for the appearance of a character that was supposed to be dead. I wound up sampling forty-five minutes of these new sounds, changing the settings on the plug-in to vary the results—playing the workstation like some kind of beast/instrument. When I named this sound file, I called it "Frankenstein." —JL

You should also explore other techniques to create new sounds. Try mixing unrelated sounds together, playing sounds or music backward, using subliminal sounds, or processing sounds with radical amounts of equalization, reverberation, delay, or other effects.

AVOIDING UNIDENTIFIABLE EFFECTS

There will be times when you'll listen to an effect from a sound library and find it hard to recognize what you're hearing. Prime examples of this are noise-based sounds such as rain and fire. Recordings of fire often sound like radio static or white noise, while prerecorded rain can sometimes sound like bacon frying. Listen to every cue with fresh ears. When playing back the sounds you've created, ask yourself if you'd be able to recognize them if they were heard completely out of context. Certainly a dog bark or a police siren would be easy to identify, but how do you approach less distinctive sounds like fire and rain?

In Chapter 2, we discussed finding the essence of a design. In order to avoid unidentifiable effects, you have to determine the essence of the sound you are creating. You need to comprehend what qualities or characteristics would most clearly identify that sound. The essence of a car crash might be the sounds of squealing tires, metal hitting metal, and breaking glass. You would combine those sounds to create a car crash effect. If you can break down a certain sound into its primary elements, then you can find a sound similar to one of those elements. For example, part of the sound of fire is its crackle. Years ago, soundmen working in radio discovered that if you crinkled cellophane in front of a microphone, it sounded like fire. The faster the cellophane was crinkled, the bigger the fire sounded.

171

The essence of rain is the individual drops of water hitting a surface. The usual rainstorm recording, however, doesn't sound real, because the rain is hitting only one type of surface, so all of the drops sound alike. A richly textured rain cue might be built from a combination of a downpour on cement; slow, large drops hitting an upside-down bucket; and other drops hitting various surfaces like aluminum cans, a plastic tarp, and a car. If the drops hit enough distinctive surfaces, the audience will perceive that recording as rain. When you know the essence of the sound you are trying to produce, you don't always have to use the real sound.

When I entered technical rehearsals for *Our Country's Good*, I had two options ready for the sound that would accompany the flogging at the top of the show. (Using a real whip was never an option, since it was impossible to achieve a consistent sound with it.) The first option was some carefully prepared digitally recorded samples of a whip swooshing through the air and snapping sharply as it hit a hard surface. Played loudly in the booth, it sounded very realistic. The staging of this production was "organic"—the audience saw actors change from one character into another as they made visible costume changes. I decided to prepare an acoustic effect, something we could see being executed, as opposed to this sound coming from loudspeakers. I chose a long garden stake (a metal rod sheathed in green plastic). I experimented with slapping the stake on different surfaces of the set. As it turned out, the best place to slap the stake was behind the set where the audience couldn't see it. The garden stake produced a sharp, painful slapping sound, evoking an uneasy reaction from everyone in the theatre. A preview audience member was overheard saying, "How can he stand that?" Even though it couldn't be seen, the effect was perfect. The beautifully crafted, digitally sampled whipping cues—produced with equipment costing thousands of dollars—were upstaged by an 87¢ garden stake. —JL

BUILDING/EXECUTING COMPLEX SEQUENCES

As with any single cue, when creating a complex sequence of cues like a storm, you need to find the sounds that comprise the essence of the phenomenon. What is it that gives the storm its characteristics? Imagine that you have to build an ominous storm. How do you construct it so that it can adapt to the actors' performances?

The constant elements of the storm can be rain, wind, and distant rumbles of thunder. Specific events that could be cued individually are loud thunderclaps, toppling trees, and gusts of howling wind. The constant effects are the foundation of the storm. This bed track can be played on a stereo or multitrack playback device. With the latter, you have more control over the balance of the different sounds.

Cues that have to happen at specific moments in the action need to be cued individually, instead of being mixed into the ambiance. This allows the actors to perform at their own speed without having to pace themselves to the recording. A digital sampler or a computer-assisted playback system can be useful in a situation like this. Producing the sound bed track may call for building and mixing long segments of sound that can be continuously repeated or looped.

A good loop is seamless; it's impossible to tell where the splice is and there are no overt "landmarks" that stick out every time the loop repeats. The term *loop* comes from when reel-to-reel tape decks were used to produce sustained sounds or music. The beginning of a section of tape would be spliced onto its tail, making a continuous loop. Today, loops are made using either a digital audio workstation (DAW) or a sampler. There is no ideal length for a loop. As a rule, the longer the loop, the less obvious it is that the sound is repeating. One way to keep loops from sounding monotonous is to mix two together. For example, if you mix a seven-second loop and a six-and-a-half-second loop of rain at the same time, chances are the two loops would never repeat exactly. In some cases, this technique can mask an imperfect edit. If the sound at the edit isn't seamless, mixing in another loop of the same sound can smooth out the rough edges by burying the imperfection in the mix with the other loop.

It's simple enough to build a storm with a bed track and the big thunderclaps individually cued, but there may be times when you'll want to take one effect and split it into two cues to accommodate variations in the actors' timing. Suppose you have the sound of a car starting up and pulling away. You cannot build this as one cue because after the car is started, the two characters in the car talk for about forty-five seconds. A solution would be to split this effect into two cues, one with the car starting and idling and the other with the car leaving. The operator can "dump" the sound of the first cue under the second, once it starts. This will work especially well if the cue of the car leaving starts with a big sound, like the rev of the engine. It will overpower the idle and mask the fade.

When producing a complex cue that might require you to commit to a mix of several elements, see if you can keep those elements separated as individual layers. With computer-assisted playback devices, you can mix these layers in the theatre, eliminating the need to go back to your studio after rehearsal and remix a cue. You can even add optional layers, and if they don't work, you can delete them or turn them off. While this won't work for all types of cue situations, mixing layers in tech can provide you with more subtlety and precision in the final "mixed" cue as well as keeping you from having to work all night revising your cues.

ADJUSTING THE LENGTH OF CUES

How long to make a cue is always a concern. If it's too short, it may not have enough impact; too long, and it can get in the way. Over

173

the course of rehearsals, you've probably come up with a good guess at the timing for each cue. As you hunt around for the right sound, keep its length in mind, but remember that with a little editing or mixing, most cues can be tailored to the proper length.

A script may indicate a series of applause cues. You may have made a number of different recordings that you like, but some are too short and some are too long. Applause usually has at least one section in it that sustains at a constant level. If the cue is too long, cut out some of this constant applause; if the cue is too short, try recording the cue twice. Cut near the end of the sustained portion on the first take and near the beginning of the sustained portion on the second, edit the two together, and you should have a seamless length of applause. If your recordings were made all at the same time with identical recording volumes and microphone placement, it will be easy to find good sections of applause to splice together from different takes to obtain the right length. The only thing you have to match up at the splice is the intensity of the audience. But be careful, because even if the VU meters are showing the same volume for each take, if the audiences' "performances" differ in their emotional content, the edit may not work.

If splicing doesn't work, you might be able to crossfade from one recording to another to get the right length. This technique works well with nonsegmentable music, and different sections of music that can't be edited together can sometimes be mixed to crossfade gracefully.

THE DOPPLER EFFECT AND PANNING

When a fire truck with its wailing siren passes by, it sounds as if the pitch of the siren drops. This is the Doppler effect, named after physicist Christian Johann Doppler, who published a paper describing this phenomenon in 1842. When you create sounds that move within the theatre, the pan (movement from one speaker to another) must happen at the same time and speed as the shift in pitch—otherwise, the effect sounds unrealistic.

The easiest way to ensure that the pan from one speaker to another will happen at the correct time is to build the movement into the cue. Let's say you have a wonderful mono recording of a cropduster passing closely overhead, and you want that sound to travel from behind the audience to the stage. One way to accomplish this is to "stereo-ize" the recording. Using a DAW or other playback device, transfer the recording into the playback device so that the approach of the plane plays on only the first track of the device. At the point in the recording where it sounds like the plane is passing by, pan the plane to the second track. Assign the first track of the playback device to the rear house speakers and the second track to the stage speakers. Note that using a stereo recording as is may not be discrete enough to make the pan convincing. Unless the movement of the plane from one channel to another is very obvious, the effect won't be believable. The more of the same sound on each channel, the less the sound appears to move.

One alternative to producing a two-channel pan is to use a mono recording in performance and have the sound operator move the pan pot from left to right at the correct time in the cue. This won't be as foolproof as building the pan into the cue. Another drawback to this scheme is that you may have to adjust the input volume of the cue as you pan to compensate for differences in volume between the two sets of loudspeakers. To work around this problem, you could adjust the levels of the outputs before the cue begins. If that isn't possible, record the mono effect on two channels at the same time. Assign one channel of the playback device that plays the effect to the "incoming" speaker and the other channel to the "outgoing" speaker. When the effect starts, the level of the incoming channel can be preset. As the plane passes, the sound operator fades in the outgoing channel to the proper level and then fades out the first channel. Keep in mind that there is a point in the pass when both channels are up. These techniques work not only for planes, but also for sirens, cars, and other sounds that you want to move. The faster the pass, the faster you have to move the pan pot or faders.

Using two mono channels to operate a pan is also a great way to crossfade music from the house into a practical unit onstage. Suppose you wanted to start a play with a recording of Elvis Presley singing *Blue Suede Shoes* playing over the house loudspeakers. As the scene lights come up, you want the music to travel to a jukebox on the set. Record Elvis in mono to two channels. Assign one channel to the house loudspeakers and the other to the jukebox. In many instances, you can have both sets of speakers playing because the volume of the house speakers will probably be loud enough to mask the sound of the jukebox playing at its volume. To make the sound travel to the jukebox, fade out the channel feeding the house speakers, and the music coming from the jukebox will be "revealed." The rate of this fade must be exact or it won't create the illusion of movement. Too fast a fade would sound like a loudspeaker was turned off, while too slow a fade would make the pan imperceptible. Of course, if you are using a computer-assisted playback system to control the volumes, pans, and assigns, then you can program pans just the way you would with a mono recording.

You can also add the Doppler effect to recordings of stationary objects. Say you are building ambiance for a scene that takes place on a fast-moving train. In addition to the rhythmic sound of the wheels, you want to provide the occasional sound of a railroad-crossing bell. Unfortunately, you only have a recording of the bell from a fixed location. All you need to do is find a way to change the pitch of the recording and record that. Digital samplers have a pitch-bend control that allows you to change the pitch of a sound as needed. Just about every DAW today will allow you to do the same thing. To achieve the sound of passing a crossing bell, fade up the sound of the stationary bell. As you get to the loudest volume you want, quickly lower the pitch of the bell and immediately start fading out the sound. Coordinating the peak of the fade-up with the drop in pitch is what makes the effect convincing.

Another situation might call for the sound of a distant old mail plane passing overhead. If you can't find a recording that sounds like a vintage plane, you can loop a lawnmower engine and slow it down, and it might sound like an old, large motor—which would work well for the airplane. You could then complete the illusion by building the pan on tape with a Doppler effect.

BLENDING PITCHES AND CHANGING MUSIC

If you have a basic background in music or are working with a composer or music director who can assist you in determining the key of the music you are using, there are ways to blend the respective pitches of recorded and live music. For example, if you have prerecorded music for either a preshow or an entr'acte leading into live singing (either *a cappella* or accompanied), you can adjust the key of the entire composition by adjusting the pitch of the recording so that the last note will be the same pitch used as a cue for the singers onstage. This technique gives a feeling of continuity to what happens *before* the action onstage, and works especially well when the prerecorded music is instrumental. Most audio software programs have pitch shift or time-shifting capabilities. These programs let you adjust either pitch or length without necessarily changing the other. Regardless of how good the software, too much alteration tends to make voices sound unrealistic.

To alter the length of a piece of music so that it better fits a situation, you may sometimes have to tack on different endings or beginnings from other sources. There are production techniques that allow you to take chords or notes directly from the piece itself and lengthen them—isolating the note or chord, looping this small segment, and adding it on to the existing recording. Suppose you have found the perfect piece for a theme, and all that's missing is a fanfare to introduce it. If the only suitable fanfare you can find is not in the same or a complementary key, you can adjust its pitch to fit the original.

FIELD RECORDING

The techniques employed in recording effects and music in the studio are the same as recording in the field, with one exception. In the studio, extraneous noises are controlled, but in the real world, sounds that you don't want to record often surround the effect you're trying to capture. Unwanted bird chirping can make it difficult to record the sound of a car leaving. In most places in the United States, it's hard to record outdoors without picking up the sound of aircraft. And don't be surprised if while you're recording urban sounds, people say "Hi" or ask, "When is this going to be on the news?"

One way to reduce extraneous noise is to use the proper microphone. Omnidirectional microphones are good for recording ambiance because they pick up sounds all around them without focusing in on any specific location. A cardioid microphone is more selective in its pickup pattern, but is useful for most recording situations. For recordings where you need the most isolation from extraneous sounds or when you can't get close to the source of the sound, use a hypercardioid microphone, a shotgun microphone, or even a parabolic dish/shotgun microphone combination. Selective microphones such as these can be used to record specific birds, for instance.

Wildlife, like birds and crickets, tends to produce sharp, shrill sounds that may not seem very loud if you look at the VU meters on the recorder. But those sounds contain very high frequencies that can easily overload a system and cause distortion. Regardless of whether you are making analogue or digital recordings, always check your recordings while you're in the field. You want to make sure that your recording levels are correct and that your recorder is working properly. If possible, purchase high-quality headphones to use when field recording. The better the headphones, the easier it will be for you to tell how your recordings will sound in the studio or theatre.

COMPRESSING UNDERSCORING

It's often a good idea to compress the volume of underscoring. The concept behind underscoring is to play music under a scene to support the moment theatrically. Music obtains much of its emotional variation through changes in tempo and volume. Obviously, an orchestra playing *presto* at its full volume will carry a different emotional value than a serenely plucked solo harp. When you underscore with music that has a wide dynamic range, it's difficult to set a constant volume to the cue that won't play too loudly at times and/ or inaudibly at others.

Compressing the music as it's transferred to the deck automatically reduces the dynamic range of the recording so that the loud sections aren't as loud and, in comparison, soft passages aren't as soft. This is much easier than having the operator listen to the music and control the gain manually. Beware of using too much compression. If you squash the dynamic range radically, the music may sound artificial.

BUILDING A FADE INTO THE CUE

When a cue must fade in or out, have the sound operator (or the computer-assisted playback system) do the fade instead of building the fade directly into the cue. The reason for doing this is that it's hard to compensate for the speed of a built-in fade if you need to change it. There are several exceptions to this rule. If building in the fade makes a difficult sequence of cues easier to operate, then by all means help the operator. Perhaps the operator needs to cue up and reset faders for an upcoming series of cues at the same time he is supposed to be fading in another cue. If the fade is built into the cue, the operator is then free to set up the next sequence once the deck has been started.

TIMING CUES

When building ambiance or any other long cue that doesn't end naturally, remember that it's important to build the cue longer than the timings you get from rehearsals. You don't want to run out of the cue if the performance is paced slowly, or if something unusual happens that makes the scene longer. Anything can happen, from an actor forgetting lines to a stage door sticking, delaying an entrance. There is no perfect formula for how much "fudge factor" to build into your timings. When the timing for a cue is thirty seconds, doubling the length of material should be a sufficient safety measure. A cue timed at four minutes probably needs only an additional forty-five seconds.

Figure 11.1 was developed with the reasoning that the minimum amount of extra material that provides a degree of safety is thirty seconds. But if a cue was timed to run twenty minutes long, then thirty seconds, percentage-wise, isn't much of a pad. If you added twenty percent to most long timings, you'd have plenty of sound. As the length of the timing increases, the multiplier decreases from two down to 1.2, at which point the graph becomes a straight line, not a curve.

If you're creating the ambiance for a scene involving an actor who usually hams it up over the course of the run, you may want to build more time into the cue. Slowly fade out the ambiance before you stop your transfer of the final cue. That way, if something really unexpected happens and the ambiance does run out, at least it'll fade out and not just end abruptly.

Unexpected delays can happen even before the play begins. If your show has a fifteen-minute preshow that leads into the top of the act, build it so that if problems come up before curtain, you won't run out of music. A good way to approach a preshow—whether it is music, montage, or spoken words—is to divide the cue into two parts. Part one contains the material you want the audience to hear until curtain, built long enough so that you won't run out of material if the show starts late. The second part, cued up on a second deck, is what you want the audience to hear last, possibly leading into the action. Crossfade to this cue when you're ready to go into the top-of-show sequence. You might want to start it a minute before the houselights dim so that the audience is less aware of the change, or you might want it to start big and herald in the beginning of the play. Regardless of your strategy, splitting the cue into two parts lets the preshow be flexible enough to compensate

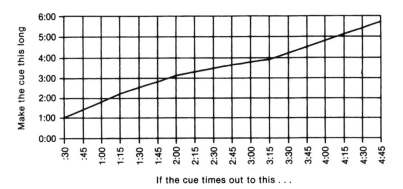

FIGURE 11.1 Cue length guide/chart.

for house or backstage problems, while still letting you have control over what is heard at the top of the show. The stage manager will appreciate having the option to hold the curtain without running out of preshow. The entr'acte should employ the same safety methods.

PROCESSING THE PERFORMER'S VOICE

Voiceovers are usually either narration or a character's thoughts represented by a disembodied voice dripping with reverb. This is one example of how a performer's speech may be processed for a production. When you produce a voiceover, make sure it's obvious that you are heightening a theatrical moment. Although this convention is commonplace in film, it may not be immediately apparent in a stage production that a voiceover is playing.

Adding processing to an *onstage* performer's voice can be useful when you want a character to become different from others on the stage. Imagine you have a stylized scene, where an adult actor has to sound like a child. You could try using a body mike on the actor and processing his voice so that it is four semitones higher in pitch. It might be an interesting (or very peculiar) concept with which to experiment.

Microphones don't have to be used just for reinforcing the actor's voice. A microphone hidden on the performer or on the set allows you to change his voice quality or even the sound of the whole stage.

180

One scene in *The Normal Heart* takes place in a dusty meeting room in the basement of a New York City municipal building. One of the characters describes the room as a tomb. When I designed the sound for a West Coast production, I wanted that scene to have a certain cold, hard edge to it, as if the walls of the basement were as unfriendly as the city's response to the early stages of the AIDS epidemic. To do this, I had a microphone above the stage pick up the actors' voices and feed that signal to a digital delay. I processed that sound with a small amount of echo and delay and played it softly through a set of speakers placed above the back row of seats. The slight reverberation gave a chilly ambiance to the scene. The effect acted subtly as a kind of set dressing that went beyond the fringes of the stage.   —JL

PLAYING SOUND CUES WITH A MIDI TRIGGER

In comedy, as the saying goes, "timing is everything"—and the same applies to executing sound cues. A mistimed sound cue can destroy the theatrical illusion faster than a sandbag dropping onto center stage during Cyrano's death scene. Virtually any sound cue can be called by a competent stage manager, but there are those moments when a stage manager can't anticipate the call of a cue with enough lead time for the operator to react and play the sound. In this situation, the stage manager might allow the operator to initiate the cue herself. There are those rare instances, though, when an operator cannot anticipate her cue, and her reaction time will not be fast enough to start a deck or press the key on a sampler.

In a production of *Who's Afraid of Virginia Woolf,* the audio master suggested I use a MIDI trigger with a digital sampler to execute a cue that would have been difficult for the sound operator to run flawlessly at every performance. A MIDI trigger is an electronic device that is mainly used with drums. A microphone plugged into the trigger's input picks up surrounding sounds. When the intensity of the input signal passes a selectable threshold, the unit generates a MIDI message, signaling "play a particular note" and then "stop playing." Any MIDI-capable device can then be told to play a note by this unit.

At the end of the first act, the script indicates that George breaks a bottle over the bar. One way to protect the actors and the audience from flying glass is to use a stage bottle for this effect. Made from a fragile plastic, stage bottles disintegrate when struck and leave a harmless residue of dust and very small pieces. Unfortunately, when broken, they also sound harmless.

Reproducing the sound of glass breaking and shards hitting the floor wasn't hard—a small speaker near the place of impact and the right sound were all that were needed for the stage effect to sound realistic. What was difficult was timing the playing of the effect with the action on stage. A good sound operator using a digital sampler to play the effect might execute the cue at the right time seventy percent of the time. This intricately timed cue played too soon or too late would seem odd or comical. Neither would have been the effect the playwright intended.

Fortunately, the director had blocked the moment upstage, near a staircase, to hide the fact that the bottle pulverized and didn't break into pieces. Near the location where the stage bottle was to be smashed, the audio master concealed a small microphone. I assigned the sound of breaking glass to a note on the digital sampler that the trigger would tell the sampler to play. When the bottle hit the banister, it triggered the sampler to immediately play the sound of breaking glass. The prop department's coating the top third of the bottle with flex glue so that only the bottom two-thirds disintegrated when the bottle hit the banister further heightened the realism. What remained in George's hand was a jagged remnant. The use of the MIDI trigger gave us the exact timing of the effect for every performance.   —JL

RELATIVE DISTANCE

One consideration when manufacturing an effect is the relative distance of audience to the effect. How far from the stage should the sound appear to be? For example, is a gunshot supposed to be heard coming from outside a window, or is it coming from a gun a quarter of a mile away? Making an effect sound realistic is rarely as simple as turning down the volume for distant sounds and cranking it up for close ones. Although volume is one of the qualities to keep in mind when trying to create a sense of distance, another characteristic is reverberation. When climbing up a long stairwell, you've probably noticed that if you're right next to someone talking softly, his voice doesn't bounce off the walls very much. But if someone two floors down is calling up to you, her voice will reverberate throughout the stairwell. The farther from the source of sound, the more reverberation and echo accompany it. Sounds heard from a distance also lose some of their lower frequencies. An explosion right outside will be very sharp and loud, causing glass to break and the floor to shake. That same explosion from a half-mile away will be quieter, with a tinny boom that might have a bit of echo. Creating this realistic sense of distance in the theatre can be accomplished through loudspeaker placement, reverb/equalization, and distant miking.

- *Loudspeaker placement:* Place the loudspeaker playing the distant effect far away from the stage. You can further distance the sound by pointing the loudspeakers away from the house. Prerecorded voices yelling and other loud sounds played at a normal volume from a loudspeaker removed from the immediate playing area work better than playing them softly. Some of the natural reverberation of the space in which the loudspeaker is playing may help to create a realistic sound.
- *Reverb/equalization:* Record the sound up close, or use close recordings, then thin out the sound with an equalizer. Add a touch of reverb to heighten the realism.
- *Distant miking:* Record from a distance. It's hard to do this without picking up extraneous sounds, but if you need the sound of a distant beach, recording from a distance will give you a sense of an expanse because no one sound will take prominence.

BLENDING LIVE AND PRERECORDED SOUND

When assembling sound effects and music for a show, most designers and composers consider whether a cue will be live or prerecorded as an either/or proposition. But there are many opportunities when prerecorded and live sounds can complement each other and produce a sound superior to either alone.

Imagine having to produce the sound of a tornado picking up a house and dropping it back down to the ground. All of the complex sounds—the wind, the house ripping loose from its foundation and hitting the ground again—can be prerecorded. You can augment the recording, though, with live breaking glass and crashing pots, pans, and other metal objects. The sharpness and clarity of live effects can give the completed cue an added realism that may be difficult to achieve if the entire effect is prerecorded. (Mixing live voices into a crowd recording is another example.) You can also add prerecorded material to a live performance, filling out the sound of a small ensemble or supplementing an onstage chorus.

TIPS FOR PRODUCING LIVE EFFECTS

There are times when it will be preferable to use a live effect instead of a prerecorded one. Live effects can sound better than prerecorded ones, and are usually inexpensive to produce.

PHONE BELLS AND BUZZERS

One way to make live phone rings or doorbell ringers louder is to augment the practical effect with another bell. Another way to adjust the volume of a practical bell or buzzer is to change the location or the way the unit is attached to the set. Obviously, the farther away from the audience the effect is played, the softer it will sound. But it will also sound distant and removed, which isn't the same thing as just being softer. If you attach the bell or buzzer to a flat, which is part of the set, the flat will act as a sounding board for it. Damping or isolating the doorbell or buzzer from the flat by placing some foam between it and the flat will lower its volume.

CRASHES

Thrift stores are wonderful places to collect crash sounds. Because of their many moving parts, old metal ironing boards make a fabulous clatter when dropped, and they can be purchased for just a few dollars. Old pots and pans, metal serving trays, metal ice cube trays, and very breakable china are cheap and abundant at thrift stores.

I was shopping for crash sounds at a thrift store in San Diego one summer. My assistant and I roamed the aisles, looking for items that would produce a raucous cacophony. My assistant told me when he'd found some promising noisemakers on the next aisle, and together we went over and dropped them one by one to see how they sounded. We must have seemed like very clumsy shoppers. After gathering a metal ironing board, some old dishes, and a few pie tins, I felt that my sound palette was complete. We got some strange looks at the checkout line and they were well deserved, but the crashes worked perfectly for the show.   —JL

DOOR SLAMS

The best way to make the convincing sound of a door slamming or shutting is to use an offstage door unit. Practical door units can be as simple as a half-height door complete with doorknob and latch built into a frame; more elaborate door units are full height, with the frame anchored securely to the stage floor. Attaching the unit to the floor gives the door slam a solid sound. Sometimes, in cases where backstage space is limited, alternative solutions can be found or created.

The Porter scene from *Macbeth* calls for someone knocking on a very heavy castle door. I designed the show at a theatre with virtually no wing space. In order to get a suitably heavy door knock to fit the castle, a hollow, shallow wooden box was constructed and turned upside down on a wooden floor. Several strips of steel were mounted to the top of the box, which was then placed in a stairwell directly offstage. A stagehand standing on the box and striking down on the steel strips with a flat-ended metal pole simulated the rapping on that huge door.   —DK

PRACTICAL LOUDSPEAKERS

If you're creating the effect of a radio or television playing on the set, it's best to use the unit's original speaker to help the effect sound realistic. Many old TV speakers had a thin, tinny sound. Although you could equalize the signal sent to the speaker to imitate the original sound, the speaker itself can often provide the proper EQ. It's usually as simple as disconnecting the leads that link the electronics inside the unit to its speaker and running your own speaker line to the built-in speaker. Make sure that the rewired speaker works properly, and that it will play as loudly and clearly as you need. Even if the speaker sounds fine at a normal listening level, it may need to play quite loudly to be heard adequately in a large theatre. Also, bear in mind that an effect may have to be of unrealistically high fidelity if the audience needs to understand what's heard over that speaker.

AND FINALLY...

With a talented ear and an artistic sense, the sound designer and composer develop ways of shaping the emotional core of an audience. As you build upon your experience, you'll learn innovative techniques and explore alternative approaches, always keeping your work fresh and exciting. Your design experiences will present opportunities—often from necessity—to create new tools for artful and practical expression. Keep experimenting, taking risks, and moving the knowledge and creativity of your field forward. Use the concepts and suggestions in these chapters as your tools. As you work, you'll continue to refine our ideas for yourself and improve upon our discoveries and techniques. Unseen technologies and your own unique innovations will ferry you beyond these pages—and give you a refreshing voice in redefining the sound of the theatre.

185

Feedback: A Directors' and Playwrights' Forum

Certain sounds may be dictated in a production as early as the playwright's first draft of a script. As he develops his concept, a director may hear sounds he feels are necessary to the production. Both playwright and director hear the call of sound, and respond by incorporating it into their work in the many ways their craft and unique personalities allow. Theirs will be primary voices in your sound design, so consider their perceptions well.

The following section involves directors and playwrights focusing on sound—its conception and design, and its impact on their work in today's theatre. Their views were gathered in either personal or phone interviews or in written responses to specific sets of questions designed to reveal their philosophies on the use of sound. The authors extended the privilege of choosing which questions to consider to the individual respondent.

Since the first edition of this book was published in 1992, in the interest of updating the forum, we have added some new contributors and retired some as well. The very talented Gerald Gutierrez passed away in 2003 and we have kept his responses here intact. They are timeless, and we remember him and his important, creative voice as a director.

THE DIRECTORS

Joe Brancato is the Founder and Artistic Director of the Penguin Repertory Company, a professional theatre that has been dedicated to developing new works for over 30 years. The *New York Times* has called him "one of America's most insightful directors." Productions in NYC include *Tryst* (Outer Critic's Nominee, Best Play); *Cobb* (Drama Desk winner), produced by Kevin Spacey at the Lucille Lortel Theatre and coproduced by Mr. Spacey and Garry Marshall in Los Angeles; *Door To Door*; *Escape from Happiness* (starring Marsha Mason); *One Shot One Kill*; *The Big Swing* (starring Madeline Kahn, Sarah Jessica Parker, Matthew Broderick, Marisa Tomei); and *Dr. Valentine's Waltz* (starring John Turturro, Laura Linney, Gina Gershon, Jane Alexander) at *Naked Angels*. Regional credits include Seattle Rep, Williamstown Theatre Festival, Houston's Alley Theatre,

Hartford Stage Company, Westport Playhouse, Capital Rep, Boston's New Rep, Hartford Theatreworks, and Florida Stage.

Roger T. Danforth has extensive credits as a director, producer, administrator, and educator. He has been the artistic director of the Drama League Directors Project since 1996. Prior to this he spent seven years at Cleveland Play House as resident director and associate producer, and as the acting artistic director of the 1994–95 season.

Best known as a playwright, **Athol Fugard** is also a director and actor. He has been seen onstage in South Africa, London, and on Broadway, off-Broadway, and in regional theatres in this country. His plays are regularly produced and have won many awards, and some have been filmed. Fugard made his directorial debut in 1992 with the film version of *The Road to Mecca*. In 2006, the film *Tsotsi*, based on his novel of that name, won an Oscar for Best Foreign Language Film. Other well-known plays of his include *The Blood Knot, Boesman and Lena and Master Harold…and the Boys, A Lesson From Aloes*, and *My Children! My Africa!*

A Juilliard graduate, **Gerald Gutierrez** was an Associate Director of the Lincoln Center Theatre. He directed plays by David Mamet, Peter Parnell, Ted Tally, and Wendy Wasserstein in New York. He twice won Broadway's Tony Award as Best Director (Play), in 1995 for a revival of *The Heiress* and again in 1996, for a revival of Edward Albee's *A Delicate Balance*. He was also nominated in the same category in 1994 for a revival of Robert E. Sherwood's *Abe Lincoln in Illinois*.

Des McAnuff is Artistic Director of the Stratford Shakespeare Festival in Stratford, Canada, and Director Emeritus of La Jolla Playhouse, where he was Artistic Director from 1983 to 1994 and 2001 to 2007. His production of *Jersey Boys* received four Tony awards, including Best Production in 2006, and he has received Tony Awards for his direction of *The Who's TOMMY* and *Big River*.

Artistic Director Emeritus of the Old Globe Theatre, **Jack O'Brien** has staged productions on Broadway, in the West End, and regionally. O'Brien directed the London production of *Hairspray*, which won the 2008 Olivier Award for Best Musical after being nominated for an unprecedented eleven awards, including Best Director. He was the recipient of the 2007 Tony Award for Best Direction of a Play for his work on Tom Stoppard's trilogy *The Coast of Utopia*. In addition to garnering consecutive Tony Awards for his direction of the acclaimed Broadway productions of *Henry IV* (2004) and *Hairspray* (2003), O'Brien received the 2002 "Mr. Abbott" Award from the

Stage Directors and Choreographers Foundation, one of the country's most prestigious directorial honors. He also received the 2001 Drama Desk Award and a Tony Award nomination for his direction of Tom Stoppard's *The Invention of Love*. Notably, he was also nominated for the Tony for *Dirty Rotten Scoundrels* and *The Full Monty*. O'Brien was inducted into the Theatre Hall of Fame in 2008.

Tazewell Thompson is a theatre and opera director, as well as a playwright and an actor. His play *Constant Star* has had more than a dozen productions in regional theatres throughout the United States. He has been commissioned to write plays for Lincoln Center Theatre, Arena Stage, South Coast Rep, and Peoples Light & Theatre Company.

Jerry Zaks has directed more than thirty productions in New York, on Broadway, including Chazz Palminteri's *A Bronx Tale*, *The Caine Mutiny Court Marshal*, *Little Shop of Horrors*, *The Man Who Came to Dinner*, *The Front Page*, *Laughter on the 23rd Floor*, *Assassins* (Drama Desk nomination), *Sister Mary Ignatius...*, and *Beyond Therapy*, and received Tony Awards for *Guys and Dolls*, *Six Degrees of Separation*, *Lend Me a Tenor*, *House of Blue Leaves*, and *La Cage aux Folles*. He was nominated for the Tony for *A Funny Thing...Forum*, *Smokey Joe's Café*, and *Anything Goes*. He received the Obie for *The Foreigner* and *The Marriage of Bette and Boo*. In London, he directed *The Philadelphia Story* at the Old Vic, starring Kevin Spacey. Mr. Zaks served as resident director at Lincoln Center Theatre from 1986 to 1990 and is a founding member of the Ensemble Studio Theatre. He was the recipient of the SSDC's George Abbott Award for Lifetime Achievement in the Theatre in 1994.

THE PLAYWRIGHTS

Michael John Graces is the Artistic Director of Cornerstone Theatre Company in Los Angeles. He has directed and written plays in New York and regionally. Michael is the recipient of the Princess Grace Statue Award and the Alan Schneider Director Award and is proud to be a resident playwright at New Dramatists.

Amlin Gray's plays, eight published in acting editions by Dramatists Play Service, include the Obie-winning *How I Got That Story*. He has translated and adapted plays from German, Spanish, and Ancient Greek, and has worked extensively as dramaturge, both staff and freelance.

Philip Kan Gotanda has been a major influence in the broadening of our definition of theatre in America. Through his plays and advocacy, he has been instrumental in bringing stories of Asians in the

United States to mainstream American theatre as well as Europe and Asia. Over the last three decades he has created one of the largest Asian American-themed bodies of work. He is also a respected independent filmmaker.

Wendy Kesselman's plays include the Broadway production of *The Diary of Anne Frank, My Sister in This House, The Foggy Foggy Dew, The Notebook, I Love You, I Love You Not, The Juniper Tree, A Tragic Household Tale, Becca, Maggie Magalita, Merry-Go-Round, The Executioner's Daughter*, and a musical adaptation of *A Tale of Two Cities* and *The Black Monk, A Chamber Musical.*

In addition to his plays, *Missing Persons, Reckless*, and *Three Postcards*, **Craig Lucas** worked with his longtime collaborator, director Norman René, on three films: *Blue Window, Prelude to a Kiss*, and *Longtime Companion.*

Eric Overmyer has been affiliated with Playwrights Horizons and Baltimore's Center Stage, and has also written for network television. His best-known play is *On the Verge, or, The Geography of Yearning.* Other plays include *Dark Rapture, Native Speech, The Heliotrope Bouquet by Scott Joplin & Louis Chauvin, In Perpetuity Throughout the Universe*, and *In a Pig's Valise.*

DIRECTORS' QUESTIONS

What do you perceive as the most important function of sound as a design element of theatre art?

DES M: Sound has to be considered equally with the other design disciplines, and I think we're finally reaching a point where that's beginning to be the case. The theatre was just as slow to recognize lighting's vital role. For a long time, lighting designers were thought of more as technicians and not as real designers. They weren't considered of the same importance as scenic and costume designers. The key idea to recognize here is that sound and controlled sound plays a large role in our cultural vocabulary. It is a critical aspect of live performance. I don't think sound should just play a role where it is aiding in the creation of verisimilitude, like car doors slamming. It's important that sound design works creatively and abstractly in the theatre whenever it's appropriate. I believe sound should accompany the human voice. I don't think we should be shy about sound as underscoring, because all of the audio elements are truly wondrous and should routinely be considered part of our palette.

When lighting instruments were first invented, I'm sure people were horrified at the notion of using electric light because it was so unnatural. I'm sure this was also true when they dragged candles onto the stage, when theatre moved indoors and stages were lit with candlelight. Actors were outraged—they insisted that theatre was meant to be played under the open sky. Basically, the theatre is a reactionary art form, and there's always going to be great resistance to technology. Also, in this age, actors spend so much time in the mechanically reproduced mediums where they are dealing with technology all the time—technology that's out of their control—that there's a substantial amount of resistance to making use of technology in the theatre because of the times we're living in. This is understandable. But I think it's important to press on and do it, nonetheless.

TAZEWELL T: In the ninth grade, I was extraordinarily lucky to have a truly inspirational teacher: Daisy Aldan. A published poet and editor, she would bring great writers to read to our class: Allen Ginsberg, Anais Nin, Norman Mailer, John Ashberry, Kenneth Koch, Storm DeHirsch, etc. I was struck by how each individual writer chose specific words not only for their meaning but for the aural impact they had. Each had a distinct vocal style and dimension that they employed to great and sometimes exaggerated effect to communicate with and engage their audience. From these experiences, I discovered the often symbiotic relationship of the printed word and the human voice/sound giving life to the word. As a child, Ms. Aldan was a cast member of the radio program *Let's Pretend*, a series of weekly radio plays. She invited this program's sound effects person to recreate for the class the live sound effects that were used over the years for the radio show. He also gave us a seminar on how far back sound effects were used for story telling. For example, sounds created by slapping the human body with one's hands; different formations of the mouth to create varied effects; the rattling of bones; twirling sticks in the air to mimic wind sounds; etc. For the months that followed his visit we were assigned the challenge to write a short play that boldly emphasized the use of sound. No recordings were allowed. This is the earliest and favorite memory I have of the function of sound in the theatre. Of course, I went on to become the "sound man" for the school productions. Remember the days of cutting reel-to-reel tape with a razor blade and slicing it on a small contraption?

For me, sound is equal partner with set, costume, and lighting design. It serves multiple purposes in advancing the narrative of the play: setting the atmosphere, place and emotional tone of the work.

ROGER D: The more I direct, the more I'm convinced that sound is one of the most crucial elements of a production. It is absolutely essential in helping me set the right mood, intention, ambiance, and emotional values in a scene. Sound is often the first design element to bring us into the events onstage, it sustains the event during blackouts and scene shifts, and it's often used to bring the conclusion to its full ripeness. As an audience member, though, I often feel the sound is setting a mood or tone not shown by the rest of the work on stage.

ATHOL F: Sound should function in much the same way as the other design elements—supportive of the final statement of the play. My concept of theatre is to subordinate everything to the play—to serve the play, to convey its message, its story.

JOE B: Film is art. TV is furniture. Theatre is life. We live in a soundscape—let theatre reflect that life.

JACK O: Sound is playing a more important function all the time. First of all, our ears are more sophisticated. People constantly walk around with little earphones and little speakers in their ears, in cars, on the golf course, at the gym, at the supermarket. If the individual theatre is well equipped, then you can do lots of interesting things. But like any other element, sound should never become self-conscious and done for its own sake.

JERRY Z: To enhance the production with sound that is music, effects to make the storytelling as successful as possible. Amplification of the human voice, used discreetly and effectively so all the audience can hear are the actors and so they feel that their voices are coming from their bodies, not the speakers.

When you begin a new production, how are the ideas for sound and music usually generated? Do you look to your sound designer or composer to offer suggestions for concept? Do you usually have preconceived ideas?

TAZEWELL T: Both. From the moment I read a play I develop a feeling, an instinct, from what I feel the playwright is telling me. Some playwrights have very specific instructions for what is required to tell their story. Even still, within these parameters, I allow my imagination and impulses to guide me, at times even sweep me away.

I make detailed notes in the margins or on a separate pad. I am currently preparing my work for a production of *Sweet Bird of Youth* that begins rehearsal nine months hence. On the first page of dialogue, as a character is opening the window shutters in a hotel suite, Williams writes, "we hear the cry of birds." Then the bellboy, responding to the question "I didn't know it was Sunday," says "It is Easter Sunday morning. The bells are from the Catholic church and the singing is from the Protestant church." So here sound brings us to a specific time, place, and atmosphere. While I am excavating the script my sound designer and composer (usually Fabian Obispo, with whom I have collaborated on countless productions) is already responding with a list of his own ideas and thoughts about the play. We then continue to have open-ended discussions about how to proceed with the creative execution of the project.

JOE B: If the script has indicated playwright preferences, that is my first source to just "get on the same page" with the playwright's intentions—if there is no indication of sound, the ride is far more joyous from the outset and the collaborative meetings with the sound designer will take us to places that neither the sound designer nor I could anticipate.

ROGER D: I usually have a "sense" of how a production should look and feel. When I'm not sure, I'm still pretty positive about what I don't want. I always rely on all my designers to help me find and/or hone a vision for a play. Even the ones for which I have very strong images or sound ideas. In fact, I've never done a play without finding and using many ideas I'd never thought of until a designer suggested them to me. That's their job and that's why I want to work with good designers—to help us all realize the writer's words and images to the fullest extent possible.

JACK O: First of all, if it's classical, I look immediately in the script for what is indicated in terms of sound effects. Or in a modern script, what the script itself says or what is asked for. And I may or may not decide that I want to have music. Actually, it is rare for me not to have music in a classical play—transitions are so much easier when cushioned by imaginative sound. As a relationship evolves with a sound designer I trust more and more for him to come up with things on his or her own. In the case where lots of sound has to be pulled, I don't usually even screen the ideas. I just sort of plug them in, and if I have an adverse reaction to them, then we discuss it. But I assume that my sound designer, like my costume designer and my set designer, is bringing a point of view with individual ideas and feelings to the sessions, so I need to hear from that. I may ask for a specific idea based on a concept I have myself, but I'm also very often receptive to the ideas of the designer I'm working with.

ATHOL F: In *Master Harold… and the Boys* there are very specific stage directions about a jukebox, which plays a very specific piece of music at the end of the play. But then also, over and above that, is this idea that sound can be a major dramatic device in terms of underscoring or highlighting the action of the play. The sound designer is usually the best person to lead me to see those possibilities. The designer comes along and says to me, "Well, you know there is this moment, there's that moment, and then there is also this moment, and would you like me to try and show you what I think can be done with those moments?" Starting with that sort of a dialogue developing, we end up with a sound design for the play.

DES M: If I really know somebody well, I might first want to get his intuitive or creative responses to the piece. And I might want this uncluttered by any ideas from me. But I think that most of the time, the sound and music concepts come out of a series of discussions with the designer and composer.

193

What I generally like to do is talk about the reasons that I am doing the play and the qualities that are important to me about the play, and perhaps the ideas that pertain to a particular situation or event in our lives and times—something to do with our own world. That's vitally important to me. And I like to start talking about the content and the themes of the play and how they apply. Hopefully, thoughts then develop—thoughts about sounds.

I like the sound designer and composer in the room working with the actors. Sometimes a concept evolves over the first several weeks of the rehearsal process. Frankly, I prefer to work as we go, even if we already have a battle plan. After we work through the play, we can go back and sketch out a more formal plan and talk through it.

GERALD G: Sound has always been a very big element of my pre-production planning. I can't recall a production I've done that didn't use some sound design elements. The sound designers I work with, I work with a lot. When one of them reads the script, he knows the way I work and the kind of things I look for and want. By the time we come to our first face-to-face meeting, he has a whole list of things that either corroborate what I've thought of ahead of time or are things that I may never have thought of before.

JERRY Z: In early meetings with designers, compare script notes. I have preconceived ideas but I'd be stupid not to listen to their suggestions. The number of times my ideas have been improved upon by sound designers is far too numerous to list!

When did you start thinking of sound as a design concept? How did you happen to begin working with a sound designer?

JOE B: My experience of entertainment frankly was as a child watching films, never entering a professional theatre until I was 12, so of course everything had a score to it in my mind's eye.

GERALD G: A lot of what I think about the theatre is a direct result of how I was trained for it. And also the fact that I grew up in New York. As a high school student, I would cut classes just to go to matinees. It was in the era of the APA-Phoenix, and I remember thinking that when I grew up, I wanted to be a member of this company. Ellis Rabb always used a lot of music in his plays and he underscored his work, and so my point of view about the use of underscoring came out of the fact that I was a teenager sitting in these theatres, being swept away by the emotional possibilities of sound.

DES M: I started with musicals. So my first work was starting back when I was a youngster with *Hair*. Then I wrote a musical when I was in my late teens, which was a very precocious thing to do. I think that is when I first learned about sound reinforcement and what music and underscoring could do under scenes.

I can remember when I was about nineteen or twenty watching a sound designer named Bill Fontana work in Toronto—a brilliant guy, a composer as well as a sound designer. And it was impossible to cue him, because all his work was improvisational, although you'd never know it in performance. It always felt like the sound was cued, because Bill's cues were going off somewhere in his head. No stage manager was calling them—no stage manager would dare. But Bill did remarkable things with sound. Once he taped the live actors' voices on several machines and then funneled them all into a loop on one machine so that at a certain point late in the performance of this particularly terrifying play called *The End*, these voices would suddenly build slowly and eerily and finally sound like a strange human siren going off. It was completely unnerving—you'd want to run screaming from the theatre. He would do staggering things with cymbals, bells, bottles, chimes, gongs—you name it—as well as with tape. I think he was a definite inspiration for me to use sound in the theatre I've done.

From the time I was first writing and directing, I think there's always been somebody responsible for sound and often for music, too. I can't think of any production I've ever done that didn't involve sound on some level.

TAZEWELL T: From my earliest childhood memories, I have always been super sensitive to sound to the point where now, in my adulthood, I live with a strange and sometimes debilitating dichotomy: the slightest sound will wake me from a deep sleep and yet, I cannot fall asleep in a quiet environment. I must have the sound of voices from a radio or recording in my room. So it just seems a natural progression that sound and music design would always play a major role throughout my career as a director and writer. I cannot remember a production that I worked on in which sound and music were not integral on some level to the storytelling.

195

ATHOL F: I think my most important sense of sound was when I came to doing a play of mine called *A Place with the Pigs*, which was not all that long ago. It is the story of a man in a pigsty. The play is a mixture of realism and fantasy, and the fantastic elements involved an extraordinary use of the designer David Budries, who is associated with Yale Repertory Theatre. I don't know how to describe the actual technology, but he ended up getting pigs to sing the Russian national anthem and the *Volga Boat Song*—things like that. It was really an extraordinary bit of work. I think that's when I first really appreciated the huge contribution that sound design can make to a production.

ROGER D: I first really took sound design seriously when a designer (Miss Kaye, in fact) designed a show I was directing. She brought me so much wonderful music from the period that it sparked all sorts of ideas in my head about different ways to use it—not just as entry and exit music for scenes, but how to incorporate it into the fabric of the show. That taught me to bring designers into my directing process earlier, so that I could build their ideas and suggestions into the style and tone of the production.

JACK O: I've thought of music a lot, but it was in mid-career at the Globe that I realized music was going to be part of the overall concept of the design. Before, if the sound designer didn't like the levels or wanted to rerecord a cue, I respected it, but didn't know how to take advantage of it. Now I'm eager to. Beginning to work with a sound designer had to do with the fact that I needed music in my productions and the musicians inevitably had somebody that they wanted to help augment their work. First it was a technician, and then suddenly there was the sound operator. After the sound operator was not sufficient, or more sound or sound effects were required, a sound designer evolved.

In what ways do you like to be involved with the developmental aspects of the sound design to be used in your productions?

JACK O: If I know the work of the designer, I don't want to be involved at all. I want the designer to just do it. And then I want to respond to it. If you hear two sound cues that your designer is doing, you can tell whether they're on the right track or not. If they are, you let them go. If they aren't, you have another talk. So I would prefer, in the best of all possible worlds, to hear the sound in technical rehearsal as we set the levels. But quite frankly, that usually isn't the case, and I just need to be checked with as the design takes form.

JERRY Z: When I first began directing in larger spaces. The sound of the actors had to be sweetened in order for the audience to hear and understand what they were saying. I first started working with a sound designer off-Broadway. My interest was more about specific sound effects that the sound designer could come up with to help punctuate or underscore moments in the play. I'd make suggestions to Guy Sherman, my first sound designer, and he'd bring back a tape of possibilities.

TAZEWELL T: When I am working on a play, I listen to music from the period of the play or music that connects me, involves me, inspires me, and takes me deep into the play. Sometimes this music or related music consciously or unconsciously will find its way into the production. Most of the time, I will let the composer know what I have been listening to and this will inspire/influence him in his work. There is constant communication through phone calls, emails as well as in-person meetings. I encourage the sound designer/composer to attend as many rehearsals as possible. Our collaboration is thorough and unending.

JOE B: For the first ten years of my professional career I designed every sound cue that I used on a reel to reel (does anyone remember that?) so my first collaboration with a professional, outside designer was a gift from heaven, in that now I had a partner in creating the soundscape for a project. Now my enthusiasm is piqued awaiting what a good designer brings to the table on their own. So I guess I have grown in my sense of trust over the years.

GERALD G: Because I also trained as a musician, I'm able to communicate with my sound designers in terms of the music. They can understand what I'm looking for musically. I also involve myself in the placement of the sound effect, the level at which it's set, and what speakers it comes from. This is all extremely important to me. It all relates. It's like lighting—all very subtle, but an important element of the production.

DES M: I like to spend lots of time listening. When I worked with the designers on *Macbeth*, Eric Drew Feldman and Stephen LeGrand, we spent a lot of time together at their studio just listening to all of the elements they were working with. In that case, we worked with a number of themes that were suggested by the play itself—doors knocking, birds screeching, the horns and drums of battle. So basically, we created a kind of nightmarish, abstracted universe out of textual suggestions, and we worked with all the wonders you can create with sampled sound.

I had worked previously with Harry Somers, the Canadian composer, on that same play. Harry combined wind and string instruments with natural sounds that he had recorded in a variety of locations, including the Arctic. We used those natural sounds as a foundation for the Canadian production, but then turned them berserk—thereby capturing the rebellion of nature that goes with Macbeth's descent into eternal night.

ROGER D: I like to talk with a designer about the moods and images a play conjures up to me. I also love for them to watch as much of rehearsal as their schedule allows. I hate to have a design meeting or two and never see the person again until tech. That's not a collaboration. That's just treating your designers, and having them treat you, like a gun for hire. I want them to get turned on by my work, have that spark their creative juices, so that they bring me suggestions for music and their own exciting ideas.

ATHOL F: I like to listen to the designer's ideas. I like to define an idea and a concept with a designer. Then I like the designer to go away and to come back to me with one or several examples of that concept, roughly realized. In other words, he should come back, as it were, with sketches, in much the same way that the scene designers or the costume designers do. Then we look at those sketches and start a dialogue based on them, making choices and slowly refining and becoming more specific about the direction we are going in. I find it enormously useful to incorporate rough ideas on tape in the actual rehearsal process. That helps me test the validity of the sound ideas.

JERRY Z: From the beginning—in every possible way. I don't like surprises. I look forward to generating ideas with the designer. I like to create the design prior to going into tech.

198   *What pointers have you found helpful in achieving an effective work-*
       ing relationship with sound designers or composers?

JOE B: To meet and discuss my intentions/goals for the ultimate emotional journey of the play; make that clear to the designer and then allow the designer to feel that any choice can be brought to the table and considered.

TAZEWELL T: There are no set rules. Some designers like to be told exactly what I desire. Others prefer communication in more abstract terms. Still others want to surprise me by bringing ideas to the table before any discussions are had. I think it is important to be open and feel out the personality and the work habits of the designer that you are sometimes given. You are not always allowed to choose. It can be like a blind date. If things work out, you have begun a new relationship. And listen. Listening to each other is critical.

ATHOL F: There are absolutely no rules. These are intensely personal relationships that depend on the personalities of the two people involved. Some designers like to do a lot of talking. Some like to do a lot of listening. Some designers like to do nothing of either and just get on with the job.

JACK O: The way we relate to our husbands, wives, lovers, dogs, family is the way we relate to each other as professionals. I think that mutual respect and mutual consideration are the two most important elements of any healthy collaboration. You have to feel that you are being listened to, you have to feel that you can listen. I have found, over the years, the wisdom of having one set of personal rules for everyone!

GERALD G: It's the same to achieve a good working relationship with any colleague. You have to respect and trust in their talents and abilities to bring you things you never thought of, or to build on your ideas. I think that's the biggest thing—trust and respect for the designer as a contributing artist.

ROGER D: If you don't like an idea, don't just say "No!" Explain why not. Support your positions—not with mindless defenses—but with explanations of how ideas came to you. But be willing and happy to entertain better ideas, from whomever they come. Also, don't abandon your gut feeling for something, even if it's not working out right. Share this feeling. Invite your designer into your innermost thoughts. Their talents can help you make it work if it's a worthy idea. Share and Trust—the key words.

DES M: I think it's important to include a composer and sound designer in every stage of development of a project. You can create a relationship simply by inviting your colleagues to participate in the entire process. The most important way to develop a relationship is to spend lots of time together.

JERRY Z: Listen to what they have to say. Try to be as specific as possible when making suggestions to them. Try to articulate the effect or mood you're looking for.

When using sound in a production, do you rely on it more as a tool to relay information, or as part of the emotional palette to set the mood?

TAZEWELL T: For me, it is ideal when it provides information as well as mood and ambiance. Whatever the play demands. The primary source should be emotional.

JOE B: Emotional palette. I hate off-stage toilet flushes....

JACK O: Both, frankly. In classical plays, sound can swiftly change locations for the scenes being acted, or in highly or complicatedly emotional landscapes, help the actor woo the audience. These are different techniques for different situations.

DES M: I use sound to create an ambiance or a mood more than anything else. It's often not one ambiance for a whole act, but rather something very specific, more moment to moment, shifting and evolving with the action. And there are certain things I don't like to do. I generally don't like to foreshadow with sound. In other words, I wouldn't want the sound to change a beat before an actor did. I prefer the sound to respond to actors, which is why I prefer working with MIDI or multiple tape decks. But I also think there are some wonderful things about samplers and working with live players and keyboards. The technician and the person who is running the show can breathe with the actors much more.

In *A Walk in the Woods*, Michael Roth and Tom Clark miked the actors very subtly and changed the instrumentation from act to act. The second act, for example, used strings, autumn sounds. The first act was flutes and recorders, woodwinds. The third act was completely silent, and we turned the microphones off for that and got a much flatter sound—the kind of sound you get on a cold day. It was a sneaky, subtle little thing. In that case, I would say the ambiance was created partially by the instrumentation in each act, in each scene. We also had a number of layers of sounds. There were particular kinds of bird sounds as ambiance, and then we also had all kinds of specific bird cues which went with cues where we would drop a single leaf. In a sense, we had created this white box and orchestrated nature, spanning four seasons over two hours. Most people never noticed how specifically all of that was controlled. We could subtly play on people's emotions. A leaf dropping at a precise point could heighten and bring meaning to a particular moment. It was an attempt to create a kind of poetry. Sound became a part of that poetry. And sound should be dealt with as that kind of tool or instrument. It's not just something that arbitrarily imitates nature, or that occurs because it's simply mentioned in the text.

ROGER D: Sound provides both mood and information, depending on the need. I will say that I use and like it much more to set an emotional mood, since usually I want plays I direct to work first on the emotions of an audience.

200

GERALD G: Sometimes the sound will tell you place, time, tempera-ture, or time of day. For instance, chickens cluck a different way at the end of the day than at the beginning. Everything clearly comes from the page. Some places in the text demand sound to underscore or heighten a mood. Directors have to know where and how to make that happen.

ATHOL F: Sometimes sound relays information. Sometimes it's just a requirement. Somebody puts a coin in a jukebox and there's got to be a piece of music. There is nothing that you can do about that. But then sometimes a sound design can both create and pass on information about a situation of deep and dangerous social unrest but at the same time work as an emotional underscoring of the moment.

I did a production of *A Lesson from Aloes* in which I used only a lit-tle brushstroke of sound [a radio] at the start of each act. But I could have just as easily not had that. I don't think my production would have been severely diminished. In other words, I directed a play in which I used just the spoken word and silence.

JERRY Z: Both. This is not an either/or question and it's a danger-ously academic distinction. Sound creates mood. Sometimes it relays information. The gun shot that unexpectedly goes off at the end of *A Bronx Tale* startles the audience but it also relays the information that someone's been shot.

Have you miked performers for reasons other than amplification? If so, what effect was desired, and did miking serve the purpose?

JOE B: No. Only to enhance and "sweeten" the voice.

GERALD G: I did a wonderful Trinidadian play called *Meetings* by Mustapha Matura. It is a three-character play that takes place in a kitchen. An upwardly mobile couple hires this peasant girl from the country to cook for them. It was breathtaking and theatrical and ended in a bloodbath. For practical and dramatic reasons, I wanted to show the girl actually cooking. I had her come out between scenes and prepare the food onstage. The smells permeated the theatre and it was very exciting. I wanted to find a way to further heighten all this. There was one dish she prepared where she would have to slice an onion. We developed a way to mike the cutting board with a surface mike. Right before she started to slice the onion, we brought the level up very high. You heard the slice of the serrated knife through the onion, and it was really spectacular. We had to take the level down when she chopped, so that it wouldn't be deafening. But every time she sliced a tomato or potato, we heightened the sound, so that the audience was hearing this sensual, visceral aspect. It was great. Sound can focus and heighten anything you want in the theatre.

TAZEWELL T: For the play *On the Verge,* an extremely literate play where the words played a pivotal role in the storytelling. In fact, words, their usage and invention and how they sounded next to each other, were a key spine of the play, and if lost in performance, would undermine the production of the play. At Arena Stage, where the audience surrounds the actors, and of necessity some scenes were played with the actors' backs to a section of the audience for lengthy periods of time, the use of body mikes to enhance and support the consonants and vowels worked beautifully. I have also used miking to distort voices in productions of *A Christmas Carol, Macbeth, The Tempest, Cymbeline,* and for the voice of God in my own play *Constant Star.*

DES M: I love reinforcing voices when no one in the audience knows we're doing it. The voice can be slightly exaggerated to become larger, deeper, and more resonant—larger than life. And no one really notices that the performer is miked. I did this for a production of *Three Sisters.* We used very subtle miking which gave Olga an otherworldly, slightly unnatural quality in her opening speech. I think this is a wonderful effect, particularly when you use it for just one character. You can sometimes create a little more distance, or cool down the voice just a bit. All of these uses can be very valuable.

ROGER D: I have not personally used mikes in that way, although at the Cleveland Play House I remember we once miked two characters who were ghosts to give them an "other-world" quality. Personally I was not very satisfied with this, though I am not sure if it was because it was not the right thing for the moment, or if it was not executed well.

ATHOL F: At the end of Act I of *My Children! My Africa!,* a microphone was directed at an actor at the climax to a long monologue. The image I wanted to create was a political rally. In the course of the monologue, the atmosphere, the quality of the moment, had changed from something very personal and intimate to something very big, wide, and open. I think the use of a microphone at that critical moment, at that climax, in order to amplify his voice, and the African chant that he came out with, achieved that effect.

JACK O: When the ghost in *Hamlet* spoke, in my second (or was it third?) *Hamlet*, I wanted there to be some odd and intermittent reverberation of sound, yet not picked up by other actors in the scenes. This was very much a surprise. The audience was unable to predict when it was going to happen. Sometimes there was a hollowness in the ghost's speech—a strangeness to the sound, and sometimes not. I thought it was spectacular.

What factors or problems may prevent you from achieving the sound design you want for a production? Conceptual differences? Substandard production of the effects or music? Other difficulties?

JOE B: Budgetary restrictions very often can constrain the effect you want but I have found that even the most basic equipment can be effective with a solid sound design.

203

GERALD G: Inevitably, problems happen when I work with somebody new. There's a point in the preproduction planning where I have to force-feed a concept and then finally say the thing I hate to say, which is, "This is what I want." I hate to do this because it's door-slamming and negative. This problem usually relates to people from whom nothing much is demanded, sound designers who are in-house staff members and who look on my production as one of twelve that they do in a year. Usually, when they're permanently employed by the theatre, they get lazy and really don't give a damn. This happened to me on a production of *Carousel* at the Houston Opera. I wanted to do something that they'd never done before, which is to have sound effects in a musical—wind, the surf on rocks, and seagulls. I felt that these atmospheric things and echo and reverb would help tell the story. Not that the in-house guy fought me on it, but he really didn't do it. The seagulls sounded more like pigeons, and the buoys clanging never really made it, so I started cutting cues, and before I knew it, I had cut all of them.

What I wanted to do was to heighten the storytelling. The problem with doing a musical like *Carousel* is that it comes with so much baggage. We've all seen the terrible movie or bad productions of it. You know Billy's going to die because you've seen it before. But I thought that you could be involved and wrapped up and swept away in the story of this antihero, and that the sound would add to the element of suspense. The designer didn't do it, and it was fine. But I lamented the loss of it.

ROGER D: Usually a lack of imagination on the designer's part. I often have lots of feelings and images that I want a piece of music to fulfill. I hate it when a designer says, "Just tell me what piece you want." If I really am certain, fine. But most of the time, I'm not. I don't have all the answers. That's why I hired a sound designer.

TAZEWELL T: Most sound designers want to know where the speakers are placed in the auditorium of the theatre. They want to know the size and the quality of the speakers. Then they want to know about the experience of the operator and technician. Other than that, perhaps I am unique in this, I have not had problems or difficulties in achieving the desired sound design. The key is having first-rate technical equipment and experienced operators/technicians and, most of all, a highly gifted, imaginative, and industrious designer capable of exploiting them to maximum effect. A designer that enjoys attending rehearsals as well as participating in numerous meetings and discussions so that by technical rehearsals she is fully prepared and on top of her game.

ATHOL F: There's a danger that, because you are using a sound designer, you feel that there has got to be sound or a lot of sound.

DES M: Because I start working with sound in rehearsal, I very rarely find myself terribly dissatisfied with the result. If I don't like a particular sequence or the way something is going, we can always change it. And so the chances are that on some level the sound is my creation, too. I'm responsible for it long before we get into the theatre. I get very few sound surprises in tech week. I have never been in a situation where I would reject an entire score. Ironically, that does sometimes happen with me with light. Because you can't draw light. I have found that it's possible to gel the show the wrong way.

One of the principles I have is that most of the time, the human voice is the solo, the melody. Therefore, sound becomes the bass line, the chords, or even the countermelody. But the melody is the human voice, for the most part.

I have learned that in a musical, you should always mike book scenes with wirelesses, never try to go back to foot mikes, because the book scene will recede psychologically, and dip. And it will anyway, because you're reaching an emotional peak with the music. Underscoring can help tremendously that way if, once a song is finished, you raise the volume of the underscoring, or pick up the tempo, which is basically an elevation. You can actually boost into the book scene psychologically.

Sound is a very powerful element. You have to accept, as a director, that you do manipulate an audience whether you like it or not. Unless you're doing something that is entirely improvisational, whatever planning you do is suggestive, if not manipulative, and I think that once you take responsibility for that, it is very liberating. You can do wonderful things to people psychologically and emotionally through carefully controlling sound.

Where you can get into trouble is when you start pushing actors into places they don't want to go. For example, if you make an early decision that there's an emotional peak three-quarters of the way through a speech and that the sound accompanies that speech in such a way that it forces the speech to peak at that moment, you may never give the actor a chance to change his mind—you may be stuck with that forever. So sometimes it's important to anticipate where things may want to go and leave plenty of room for the actor. In other words, you try to avoid straitjacketing the performers by making dead-end choices. This is why I tend to like cues that are long slow fades. I don't like to do things that will, say, take exactly twelve seconds. I like to allow for timing changes so that a show can breathe.

What scares a lot of people off is that they're afraid they'll get locked into a bunch of cues. I think it's possible to design sound so this doesn't happen, so that you have a lot of flexibility in performance. And in this day and age, there is much more live control than there once was. I'm sure it's going to get better and better.

JACK O: Sound design doesn't work if the speaker placement isn't properly worked into the initial design. Most of my musical collaborators have said to me that I never used to look at where the speakers were going to go in the original design of the set, and I have taken that to heart. In the last several years, I have striven to rectify that omission.

JERRY Z: The only factors are not anticipating what we need. Budget has never been an issue. There has always been enough for necessary sound design.

Please describe a moment from a specific production of yours in which the sound design was most useful or magical.

JOE B: Every tenth production you are lucky enough to find a sound conceit, song, or artist that not only illustrates but enhances your intentions. Such was the case in a recent production of mine, Lyle Kessler's *Orphans*—the use of musical selections by Tom Waits embossed every intention of the director and designers—enhancing every element of the play.

GERALD G: I remember an effect for a play called *Geniuses* by Jonathan Reynolds that took place in the Philippines. There was water onstage and a lot of special effects. A typhoon hits very suddenly, and there's an attempt by helicopters to rescue people out of their hut. We had a series of speakers hanging over the ceiling only for the helicopter effect. The sound traveled from speaker to speaker. You really thought those helicopters were overhead. I loved it so much I used them again at the end of the play for a fadeout. It was a fabulous effect.

206

DES M: One wonderful bit of manipulation was in a production of *Romeo and Juliet*. I believed very much that the tragedy in the play falls on these two families and not on the two characters. When you first read the play you think, "My God, they die!" and then everyone comes on and they talk and they talk and they talk. Friar Lawrence goes through the whole story again. Well, as you study the play more carefully, you realize it is as much about greed and money and hatred as it is about the love between two young people. In my opinion, Friar Lawrence becomes the protagonist, the one who is driving the play, and then the ending starts making more sense as you realize that the tragedy really is falling on the families.

It's amazing that I found, even in rehearsal, that I could watch these two young people die without having as much of an emotional reaction as I would have in the following scene. And I think that's because you're dealing with the horror of their death—there's so many emotions going on at that moment—and you're not really able to register the grief. To let yourself feel freely and completely, you need some distance from the moment. And Shakespeare is such a brilliant dramatist that he would know that, and he would know exactly how to pace himself emotionally through the poetry of that last scene.

Michael Roth's whole score was in a minor key up until that scene. Well after the death of Romeo and Juliet, Capulet and Montague are pledging peace to each other. In our performance this was staged, not exactly cynically, but in a way that, hopefully, made the audience skeptical about whether or not this peace would come. It's kind of absurd because they've both killed off their only living heir. So there's this deeply sad, tremendously ironic scene. Capulet and Montague, even at this moment, can't prevent "money" images from creeping into their speech. And during the last scene, this minor theme that we'd been hearing for two and a half hours suddenly went into a major key. There was an amazing emotional reaction and, literally, you would see the audience pulling out handkerchiefs and weeping inconsolably—even hardened old businessmen. It had a devastating emotional effect. It was a memorable audio moment. I had to smile in the back of the house, watching this happen.

ATHOL F: I would say that moment I've already described of Thami's at the end of Act I in *My Children! My Africa!* The sound really lifted the climax of that act to a level that the actor by himself would have had difficulty achieving.

JACK O: I have to say I think the opening of *Uncle Vanya* was one of the most beautiful things of mine I've ever achieved on a stage. In worklight, an actress walked from the back of the theatre through the set. She pushed a samovar on the stage and as she did, a Chopin mazurka started. Simultaneously, the lights began to change to the most beautiful texture of light and sound on stage possible. That whole opening used to make me just ache with pleasure. For me, the blending together—initiating the theatrical moment, ushering in the play with music that invaded the audience's ear exactly in the same proportion as the light began to change—was enormously pleasurable. On the dramatically opposite end of the spectrum, I would imagine I will never rival the individual or collective openings of the acts of *The Coast of Utopia*—the blending of all possible elements into an unimaginable landscape of water and characters will remain the standard for me for quite some time.

TAZEWELL T: In *Black Star Line* by Charles Smith, a play I directed for the Goodman Theatre, the character of Marcus Garvey was preparing to deliver a very important speech in front of an enormous crowd of his followers. Rather than a sound cue of audience hubbub and chatter, the sound designer, Fabian Obispo, and I decided that while the previous scene was fading away and Marcus Garvey was changing into his tie and tails in front of a three-paneled mirror that rolled on during the scene transition, we would use the sound of a huge orchestra tuning up before the arrival of the conductor. Although it was opposite to what was expected, the sound cue was chilling since Garvey saw himself as a Godlike figure (conductor) leading the masses.

However, the most challenging and ultimately the most rewarding solution of a sound "problem" occurred when I was the stage director for a new Glimmerglass Opera production of Francis Poulenc's masterpiece, *Dialogues of the Carmelites*. The opera is based on a true historical event that takes place during the French Revolution's Reign of Terror: Sixteen Carmelite nuns are sent to their deaths—martyred by guillotine—in the opera's harrowing third act finale. In the concluding, unbearable moments of the opera, the nuns sing a simple, yet ecstatic Salve Regina while, one by one, their voices cease as the "thwack" of the guillotine's blade repeatedly falls, frighteningly off the beat of the music. Every director and sound designer is confronted with the task of finding the sound of the off-stage blade of the guillotine that remains the most important directive-notation in Poulenc's score. Sixteen times! After weeks of experimentation with all kinds of blades, axes, hatchets, various carpenter's tools—including metal mallets smashing cantaloupes and a variety of melons—we discovered the perfect solution: a rather old and rusty metal paper cutter! It was placed in the orchestra pit after the second intermission next to a microphone that was carefully turned off and on in between "thwacks," so as not to pick up and imbalance the sound of the orchestra between "beheadings." The age and rust of the paper cutter blade created a realistic and horrific off-stage character, especially when amplified with a slight reverb. It brought gasps from the audiences. After the final, solo voice was silenced by the guillotine, there was a chilling silence. It was thrilling. This is why we do theatre.

ROGER D: In *The Man Who Came to Dinner*, I wanted a magical way to open the second act, when the huge Christmas tree is revealed for the first time. We had designed a beautiful show curtain, which was a blowup of a large Christmas greeting banner from Mesalia, Ohio, the play's location. I asked my sound designer, Jeff Montgomerie, to look for a terrific version of a great Christmas song from the period. Somewhere he found an absolutely wonderful live Christmas Eve broadcast of a 1930s big band, complete with a fabulous intro from the band to "everyone out there in Radioland," which then swung into "Jingle Bells." Since Sheridan Whiteside, the main character, is a radio personality, it was the perfect piece of music,

208

and so working with the sound and lighting designers together, we built a terrific opening of the act. In several steps, accompanied by the band intro, we gradually lit the room from behind the curtain, which revealed itself to be a scrim. First we had just the tree lights and the star, then the tree area (nestled in the turn of the grand staircase) warmed up to reveal the characters posed decorating the tree in silhouette, and finally light expanded into the entire room. Band intro segued into music—scrim out, characters moved, and dialogue! It was as magical as I had hoped, and got a huge round of applause every night. But as wonderful as this moment was, it all happened because my designer found a very special piece of music that ignited a whole bunch of staging ideas for me.

A totally different issue arose from a production of Lee Blessing's *Two Rooms*, a harrowing play about a man being held by terrorists in Beirut, alone and blindfolded in an empty room. After reading it many, many times, I called my designer and said, "I don't know what to say. Everytime I read this play, I hear No Sound. I've never felt that way about a play before. The main character is totally isolated from everyone and everything, so I keep hearing and feeling No Sound. Yet, if we don't have sound, won't audiences think we just forgot? How do we make No Sound seem like designed sound?" Tony Garfias, my designer, took it as a wonderful challenge, and our work together was very enjoyable. I am still amazed at all the sound ideas and options he brought me, all of which helped to convey No Sound—my favorite being a drip of water, that would fall periodically, splitting the silence of that empty room with a mournful loneliness that was devastating.

209

Do you often have difficulty convincing producers of a need for a sound designer? If so, how have you been able to change their minds and budgets?

JOE B: Never had that experience to date—producers have been supportive in understanding the importance of sound design.

GERALD G: I always try to make the producers see that I've placed the sound on an equal footing with the set, costumes, and lights. And I've had to fight for it. You just try to convince them of the importance of sound, and if you can't convince, then you demand. You have to make them realize how necessary it is.

ROGER D: You just have to be firm and say that any play requires a minimum of four designers—lights, sets, costumes, and sound.

I remember one of my very first professional jobs—I was hired to take over a production of Jules Feiffer's *Little Murders*, which has one of the most complicated sound plots of any show I've ever done. The producer had lost his director about a week before rehearsals were to begin, and knowing that I had directed it previously in college, he called me in a panic and asked me to take it over. When we had our first design discussions, I discovered that not only did he not have a sound designer for the show, he didn't even have a sound system in the theatre! (It was quickly apparent to me that he had committed to this play without reading it.) I told him flat out that this play couldn't be done without a sound designer, and if he couldn't commit to that, then he had to pick another show. The very least the script called for were sirens, street noise, construction sounds, subway noise, and gunfire. He told me, "The other director said he was just gonna hang a microphone out his window." I told him I was not hanging any microphone out my window!

The bottom line was that he did hire a designer and bought a sound system, but it took a threat to quit to get it. I'm certain the producer always felt I had caused him needless expense. Having done that show once, I was unwilling to sacrifice what was minimally required to get it done right. Remember, no one in the audience knows or cares when corners are cut or what compromises are made. If they don't like what they see, it's the director's fault. If you don't demand what you need, you'll pay for it in other ways.

JACK O: I think it depends on the project. If you are doing a musical, producers usually see a need for a sound designer. If you are doing a two-character play that doesn't seem to have any sound effects, yes, it's a problem. I haven't always been able to change their minds. But I always think that as you bring people into the process, instead of pounding your fists and saying "I need this and you've got to get it for me"—if, in fact, you are patient and you show them the necessity and that the necessity is real—people are pretty realistic. They try to accommodate me when they can. When they can't, we compromise.

TAZEWELL T: The pioneers of the American regional theatre movement really did the advance work and paved the way in recognizing the importance of sound designers as a key staff member of their theatres. I am talking about Zelda Fichandler, Jon Jory, Gordon Davidson, William Ball, Tyrone Guthrie, and Joseph Papp. They understood the need for resident sound designers as integral players

210

in the theatre art form. While many theatres today cannot afford to have sound designers in residence, they do appreciate the need for their contribution.

DES M: I have had the experience before where people are surprised that I want a sound designer, particularly if it's a drama and they don't see any sound cues called for in the script. Then I have to explain the way that I like to work. As far as I am concerned, sound is a design element. With *A Walk in the Woods*, I thought of the sound as a major element in terms of bringing the forest to life. Michael Roth was with me for the whole journey. We always thought of the forest as the third character in Lee Blessing's two-character play. Producers are notorious for hiring one operator and expecting him to do both sound and lights. In many productions these days, that's impossible, if you're working with any kind of ambition. Insisting on having a sound designer would be an early battle for me with a producer. It would be on my list of things I needed in order to do the work, and it would come up immediately. I wouldn't already be working on the design and say, "Oh, by the way ...." I think a good producer is going to try to give you whatever you absolutely need. And most producers are much more familiar with sound design now than they were ten years ago.

PLAYWRIGHTS' QUESTIONS

Before a new play of yours is produced or read, do you ever "hear" sound or music as part of your concept?

MICHAEL G: Yes, in fact quite often. There is sometimes a particular piece of music that inspires me during the writing, or is particular to how a play gets structured. This music is sometimes incorporated into the production of the play, but, even if not, it is, I think, useful for director and designer to hear in understanding what I was thinking/feeling/intending during the writing. I rarely see how a piece should be staged or produced while writing; don't think much about set. But I do "hear" the play as I'm writing it, the rhythm and melody of the dialogue. So I am very interested in how sound—and silence— interacts with the music of the spoken word. I also think a lot about non-musical sound as I'm writing, in terms of what the soundscape the play lives in might be, what non-musical sound might be used as punctuation or as bed—the sound of an old air conditioner, or late-night traffic, or a hospital cafeteria at off-hours.

AMLIN G: I often (in my mind's ear) hear the aural element of my plays before getting a visual image. Today we say we go to "see" a play, but we used to say we "heard" it, and we still rehearse a play. I sometimes ascribe the primacy of sound over image in my head to a deficiency in my visual imagination, but the plays I like tend to live very fully in the sound they project. They tend to be terrifically exciting on records, from the works of Shakespeare to *Who's Afraid of Virginia Woolf?* I'm very sorry that radio drama has no audience in this country. It's been a vital developmental venue for the last two generations of English playwrights. The two radio plays that I've written I've found very satisfying to work on. The writer, in (one hopes) close and happy collaboration with the sound designer, has complete control of the imaginary world which the listener receives. That's not true of any other medium.

Hearing is a much more involving sensual process than seeing. Seeing is, relatively speaking, a cool and distant kind of contact with its object. All our metaphors for skepticism are visual: appearances deceive, don't judge a book by its cover. You look askance at something, you don't listen askance.

PHILIP G: I started as a musician before I was a writer and spent about ten years in rock 'n' roll. I played guitar, wrote songs, sang, and performed by myself in clubs. My early works contained a lot of music that I wrote. My first play was a musical and the subsequent one was a play with music.

So as I write a play, I do hear sounds and put them into the script. *Dream of Kitmura* was based on a very vivid dream. The play itself has a dream quality and a mythic quality. I decided that sound was, in a sense, a character of the play, and participated in the play. When I did the play in New York, two Japanese musicians created a very interesting score which they played live that incorporated a classical or traditional Japanese instrumentation.

When the young ingénue is introduced to the male lead, she appeared in a pool of light and slowly, very slowly she folded a paper airplane and then tossed it. The plane itself was carried by a person dressed in black. This kurogo moved the paper airplane very slowly across the stage toward the other actor and while this was happening, there was a rhythmic arpeggio repeating over and over, with Japanese flutes playing over it. All of it had to work together. The movement of the paper airplane was at a very slow speed, and the repetitive music was a little ahead of it in terms of the time signature. The continuously repeating music against that very slow movement created a tension that made that moment compelling. So in this particular play, the sound was really a direct participant in the emotional action onstage.

WENDY K: An anonymous song from the Warsaw ghetto stayed in my mind as I was writing *I Love You, I Love You Not*. I went through many songs of the Holocaust, but that one seemed particularly connected to the two characters in my play.

ERIC O: Sometimes when I'm writing a play, a song will pop into it. That happened in *On the Verge* several times. There were songs that became part of the narrative, that are like artifacts. But I also sometimes hear sounds as underscoring. There is a point in *Native Speech* at the beginning of the scene that I put in the stage directions. I heard a far-off electric guitar in the ether. But I don't do a lot of that. I don't do any kind of stage or design direction; I always leave that to the designer and director. But every once in a while, when I think that something is absolutely essential, I will write it in. Whether the director pays any attention to that stage direction is another question and something I often have no control over.

213

Have you ever drawn upon a specific piece of music as inspiration for a play? Was it incorporated into the script?

MICHAEL G: Yes and yes. I wrote a piece some time ago in which pieces by Jimmy Giuffre, Thomas Tallis, and Thelonious Monk were integral to the scenes, as background and as foreground. The designer was initially very resistant to my ideas, until he and I met; he had brought some samples of what he would like to use instead, and we played all of it, and soon realized that our ideas and inspiration were remarkably similar, and wound up having a great collaboration. He brought a lot to the table which enhanced and deepened my original impulses. He and I wound up collaborating on projects for years. I also sometimes write songs—at least lyrics, with ideas about melody—into scripts. This often influences the approach of the sound designer—who is also sometimes the composer.

CRAIG L: I have frequently started with the idea of a song as either a jumping-off point for the story or as an atmospheric or contextual notion for the world in which the play might take place. Or, in one instance, I have designed a whole piece around a song—*Blue Window*, in which William Bolcom's *The Office Girl's Lament* is part of the script. I knew I was going to name *Prelude to a Kiss* after the Ellington tune before I began writing, and nurtured from an even earlier time a very general notion for the plot and characters. When writing the first draft of *Reckless*, I kept hearing Bing Crosby singing *I'll Be Home for Christmas*, which found its way into Norman Rene's production. Again, it was part of the inchoate germ; how it informed the ultimate product, I couldn't say.

PHILIP G: While writing *Fish Head Soup*, there was one piece of music that I listened to a lot. That was *Like a Rolling Stone* by Bob Dylan. At one point it was in the script, then it was taken out, and then put back in. But that's an example of a piece of music that I heard as a young kid, and it had a great deal of impact on me. For some reason, years and years later, I was listening to it and I wanted to bring it back. As I wrote this particular play, I was listening to it because the play is emotionally based in a period of my life that the song allows me to reenter emotionally. The song allowed me to write the play in a particular kind of mood.

When I used it in the script, it was not so much for the audience as it was for me. I wouldn't have included it, though, if I thought it was only for me, because I do think the song has a peculiar effect on a lot of people. There's a certain cynical sadness to it, a kind of posturing cynicism that captures a quality I like.

WENDY K: For *I Love You, I Love You Not*, I indicated the Bruce Springsteen song *I'm On Fire*, which seemed crucial for Daisy. Gerald Chapman, who directed the reading of it in Boston, commented on what a beautiful stroke it was to choose that particular piece of music. I had never thought of it, but he saw it as symbolizing the ovens at the concentration camps. For a new play, *The Foggy Foggy Dew*, the title itself is crucial in the development of the play.

ERIC O: Other people's research has affected my work. For instance, for *Heliotrope* the musical director did a lot of research finding period music. And he dug up some really wonderful stuff. The play was written. It was really up to him and the director to decide where they wanted music and what exactly they wanted there.

AMLIN G: I've often heard about writers getting plays from a song that may have no apparent connection with the finished work. Maria

Irene Fornes, for example, says that *Fefu and Her Friends* came from a recording of a Cuban woman singing folk laments. She heard the songs in her head as she conceived the play and played it while she wrote. The play is set in America. None of its people are Cuban. But the emotional core of the play is the songs.

Do you often indicate, in terms of stage directions, what music or sound you want to happen within a script? If so, are these incidents usually results of research or your general knowledge? Do you ever consult with sound designers or composers as part of your research?

ERIC O: I'm repeating myself here, but I indicate sound and music very sparingly, and I usually leave that sort of thing to the designer and director. In most of my plays, music is transitional because my plays are verbally dense. It's hard for underscoring to work in them. The underscoring often seems to be competing with the words. The music that has been used successfully tends to be transitional.

I do look to sound designers or composers for research a lot, because I don't do research myself. I'm fairly knowledgeable in a hobbyistic sort of way about certain kinds of folk music, jazz, and American pop music—that sort of thing. I have a big personal collection, and I buy a lot of records. It's all avocational, for my own personal pleasure. I would not know how to go about researching anything. That's what sound designers are for.

215

CRAIG L: I have never done research on music or sound, and I use very few stage directions. In the original script of *Prelude to a Kiss*, I indicated that the song *They Can't Take That Away from Me* would play in the bar before Peter found Rita trapped in the old man's body. It was not my idea to use Van Morrison's *Someone Like You*, a much better choice for the scene.

I consider the use of sound to be the director's province. I have worked with composers at various stages of writing.

WENDY K: I do indications in the script. I've sung a great deal with the guitar and have wonderful source books by Ruth Rubin and Theodore Bikel. A friend gave me *Voices of the Holocaust*, which supplied many ideas for the music of *I Love You, I Love You Not*. I researched a great deal for the French Revolution play I'm working on [*The Executioner's Daughter*]; I listened to many cassettes and was given books of French songs of different periods. There was one song that I fell completely in love with which I'm using in the play.

MICHAEL G: In general, I rarely include stage directions in my scripts. So, other than some musical ideas, or general notes, there is usually not much indication. That said, I recently wrote a play, *Los Illegals*, in which I described in great detail the ongoing, evolving soundscape of the play, which was a big part of my intention for the production (in this case I also described the physical environment). This was as a result of my research, which involved interviewing day laborers at worksites and street corners all over Los Angeles, as well as attending pro- and anti-immigrant rallies. It was crucial from my perspective to creating the right atmosphere for the production that a theatricalized—sometimes altered or exaggerated—version of the particular sounds of these environments. In response to the third part of the question, I have created pieces in collaboration with composers, and sent designers and composers texts for their response in starting to think how they would be articulated in performance, but I've never "consulted" with a designer or composer during the writing process.

216

PHILIP G: Certain sounds that I hear, certain music that I come across, are just in my background as part of my upbringing. And I prefer to draw upon my own general background as a Japanese American.

I don't research music or sounds much for my plays. I do listen to music a lot. In the course of conceptualizing a production, I'll sit down and work with the composer or sound designer or director, and we'll develop an approach.

AMLIN G: I love to talk with music people about the form of plays, my own and other people's (also about the form of musical works). I go along with what Walter Pater (I think it was Walter Pater) wrote, that all the other arts aspire to the condition of music.

Has your research on music or sound ever had a profound effect on any of your plays?

MICHAEL G: Often. As I said before, music has had a huge impact on the writing of many of my plays, and when one particular composer, song or genre/type of music inspires or becomes part of a piece, I often explore other work of the composer or genre, and this in turn influences the course of the writing.

AMLIN G: I've always found it irksome to look at play structure analytically for long at a stretch. I think a good many other people likewise fight shy of extended critical, abstract attention to the form in which they work. But I can spend no end of time in complete fascination thinking about, say, painting, and making half-stabs at applying resultant abstractions to plays. The greatest hit of artistic speculations concerns the Golden Section, used (no doubt not always consciously) in so many visual works. The Section is, of course, the place where you divide a line so that the shorter part is to the longer part as the longer part is to the original, undivided line. A rectangle constructed of the shorter and longer parts is aesthetically pleasing, and has been used as the frame size of paintings by da Vinci, Dalí, and countless others, as well as everywhere within their compositions. But a painting is before its audience all at once. This makes problems for the application of painting principles to theatre, which unfolds over time. All right then, so does music. Composers such as Debussy and Bartok have used the Golden Ratio in their works. Also Chopin, whose etudes and nocturnes are often "cut" at the Golden Section by their point of greatest technical difficulty and highest excitement.

I try and structure my plays in five parts. Worked for the Romans, worked for Shakespeare. The climax, in this synthesis, ideally comes at the end of Part Three. Everything preceding leads up to the climax; everything afterward results from it. Now, this three-fifths point isn't exactly where the Golden Section comes. That would be a little later. But not much.

Lots of musical pieces are structured in five parts. I'm working on a play now with a mind to the proportions of the five sections of Schoenberg's *Transfigured Night*.

The above is all very wiggy and vague. But it's probably best if abstract synthetic thinking stays somewhat on the level of noodling. Get too systematic and you rob concrete imagination of the freedom it needs.

ERIC O: Other people's research has affected my work. For instance, for *Heliotrope*, the musical director did a lot of research finding period music. And he dug up some really wonderful stuff. The play was written. It was really up to him and the director to decide where they wanted music and what exactly they wanted there.

PHILIP G: It's not necessarily that I found it in research but I did rediscover a sound from my childhood that I've ended up using in my plays: Buddhist sutra chanting. I grew up with it, as I attended a

Jodo Shinshu Buddhist Temple as many Japanese Americans have. I find that it's the only sound that allows me to feel something as close to a Japanese American soul that there is. I mean it in a transcendent, vessel type of way. It washes over and through me and lets me fall through a crack back into me and beyond. I'm Japanese American from California and I'm Japanese from Hiroshima in the early 1900s.

WENDY K: Music is always such an integral part of my plays. The folk song sung in *I Love You, I Love You Not* occurs in the first scene and then comes back, in a kind of broken replaying, in the end of the third scene. I don't know if I could say that the song shifted my structure of the play, but it did affect the emphasis.

The French song in *The Executioner's Daughter* has been in and out of drafts and readings, and although other French songs have been eliminated because they didn't seem right, this one seems to stay.

What function do you believe sound design does/could/should play as a design element when developing your scripts?

CRAIG L: I see sound design as an important element of a production, and I will occasionally incorporate a director's contribution into the final published script. But I don't see sound design per se playing any part in the development of my scripts. If a telephone rings, I put that in the original script, but I don't indicate "traffic noises" if a scene is set outside in New York. I find Chekhov's broken guitar string in *The Cherry Orchard* an unhappy shock when I'm watching the play. It sounds like a good idea when you read the play, but I prefer to let the director find his or her own solutions to the sound "design."

ERIC O: I don't think I've ever gone back and incorporated something that the sound designer invented and passed it on to the next production. So really, all the designers start from the basic text every time. I've never worked with a designer from a rough script, although it might be interesting. I should work with a sound designer on a scenario—really develop it together—and see what happens.

AMLIN G: I like everything in a show, as far as possible, to be live. The resulting immediacy seems to me to be of the essence of theatre, and it has increased in importance as film has staked its incontestable claim to the combination of realism and mobility as well as access to an enormous and various audience. What's special about theatre is that it's live, and that its liveness potentially provides the energy to enlist the audience's very active imaginative collaboration on the particular performance they see.

Accordingly, I like live sound. Of course, it's possible to woo the audience to give you license to try for the best of both worlds, live sound and recorded sound. *Kingdom Come* started with a lone violinist coming onstage and playing a cadence of harmonics—damping the string he was playing, so that all that sounded was the sympathetic vibrations of adjacent strings. A very beautiful and unsettling effect. But, as the show went on, taped synthesizer music—string orchestra in timbre—came in strong behind the soloist. We weren't kidding anyone that our violinist was pushing that cinderblock wall of sound at the audience, but they were willing to hear it, as it were, through his visible presence.

PHILIP G: I've always put sound into my scripts; I don't know if that's unusual or not. Sometimes I am specific about what sounds I hear. For example, in *The Wash*, I use two lullabies. They're both traditional, but one is very childlike and the other is a very haunting, somber song. They're used at various points to establish moods of the main character. They then served as a takeoff point to compose music for underscoring other scenes.

WENDY K: I always include music and sound in some form, and I see it as an extremely important part of my work. What happens between scenes is easily as essential as what happens in them. The ringing of a phone, the clanging of a bell, after what line a car horn is heard are all crucial, and the timing of these cues very specific. The sound of a key turning in a lock and the sound of a door fanning in and out are both important in *My Sister in This House*. These sounds sometimes form the segues between scenes. I've always been aware, as I'm writing, when sounds fall—after which sentence, before what scene. Sound must be used carefully, and it is becoming more and more important to me.

MICHAEL G: Often. As I said before, music has had a huge impact on the writing of many of my plays, and when one particular composer, song, or genre/type of music inspires or becomes part of a piece, I often explore other work of the composer or genre, and this in turn influences the course of the writing.

219

Is there a style to your use of sound, or does it change from play to play?

PHILIP G: I've begun to realize that I prefer a very sparse score, not too overproduced, with minimal instrumentation. I use one or two instruments, and I prefer not to use chordal music like piano. I like certain Japanese instruments, like the shakuhachi and the string bass. They are interesting to me because they don't have a precise tone. They can be played in quarter-tones; you can bend the notes. I also like the idea of certain instruments like the shakuhachi, which can duplicate a human wail. It also can reproduce a quality of nature, like the wind. I like that it can bend and doesn't have a heavy tone, unlike the very set piano tonal scale. I also like ambiance and sound effects and percussive instruments.

Even silence is very important. I consider silence to be a type of sound. For example, in *The Wash*, there are certain sequences that could easily be scored, but I've always thought that they work best in total silence. Silence, to a degree, only works if you have some kind of sound before it that sets up the no-sound. Just dialogue can be sound, a type of music, or a lot of dramatic action onstage can create a sense that there is a kind of sound. Then after that, to not have any sound sets up the visual moment. In *The Wash*, the last moment is when the woman comes in, bringing the laundry she has been doing for her husband, even though they are separated. She picks up the dirty clothes and puts them in a brown paper bag and she starts to go toward the door. Then she decides this time that she's not going to take his dirty wash, and leaves it at his home, symbolizing her decision to go on with her life and basically break from this man for good. That moment done completely in silence becomes very compelling. We tried sound then, but pulled it out. It's all done through discovery. Sometimes you make these choices during the course of rehearsal because it just feels right. But for each play, as I work conceptually with the director and the designer, we develop something that I think is consistent.

AMLIN G: My only constant is a strong preference that music and sound be "up front." I always hear that movie music is working when you don't know there is any. I like a live show to put all its cards on the table. An adaptation of *Coriolanus* I prepared and dramaturged for Georgia Shakespeare Festival a few years ago had a great percussion score, by Klimchak, played in full view of the audience. I loved that.

MICHAEL G: It changes from play to play, from production to production, and from collaboration to collaboration. It's part of the fun of it.

Please give us an example of your attending a production of one of your plays and finding that the sound or music offered a fresh interpretation of your work. How about instances when the sound or music was completely off base?

CRAIG L: The whole question of interpretation of a play is the director's prerogative. Whether or not I've approved or disapproved seems to me to be irrelevant. I've always been very happy with Norman Rene's use of sound and music in my plays. I've seen productions, successful or otherwise, that use sounds I didn't like, but I just don't think it's my business.

WENDY K: Some years ago, the Dublin production of *My Sister in This House*, directed by Ben Barnes, used incidental music in an extraordinary way. Some of the pieces I had chosen that I felt were so crucial to the play were probably hard to find. Only one song, a lullaby I wrote, was published with the script. Ben made his own decisions about what music was used and it was quite different from what I had conceived. But he is very musical and has a wonderful ear. It was a beautiful production.

AMLIN G: In my play *How I Got That Story*, I have two actors enact the encounter of a reporter and an event. One plays the Reporter, the other plays the Event: all the people it comprises as well as its sights and its sounds. Since the Event actor was always either onstage in a particular character or offstage madly changing costume, most of the sounds had been prerecorded, though in the first production we made the actor's voice recognizable as much as we could, so as to intensify the sense of a burgeoning presence that finally engulfs the poor Reporter. But I specify in the script that, whenever possible, the Event actor should make the sounds live and in sight of the audience. The best realization of this injunction I know was in a production I did not work on, but saw, in Rochester, New York. The Event was played by Joe Morton. During the scene where the Reporter first goes out into the streets of the (to him) exotic Asian city he's supposed to cover, Joe swung around behind the Reporter in a slow, wide arc making the sounds of tanks, Hondas, chanting bonzes,

221

beggars, arguing soldiers, sirens, etc. The whole city appeared on that bare stage, with all focus bearing down upon the overwhelmed Reporter. All done with live sound.

MICHAEL G: A designer composed a piece, quite different from what I had imagined, for a song (made-up) that a character sang fragments of during a monologue, and then used this music as a basis for transitional music throughout the piece and it worked beautifully, giving a real coherence to the production. It was quite haunting, and very appropriate to the play.

I've had a couple of experiences in which the sound design seemed heavy-handed, either getting in the way of the piece or overemphasizing the themes or mood instead of setting them off or contrasting them usefully.

ERIC O: I don't ever know where the director leaves off and the designers begin. I don't ever really know who to either credit or blame. I have worked with the same director so much, and he controls the design aspect so heavily, that I tend to give all the designers maybe not enough credit. For instance, I thought the sound design for the production of *In Perpetuity Throughout the Universe* was really good.

PHILIP G: I've had instances where it was all off. It usually is that they've used something quite literal in relationship to the activity on the stage. Or, they've used too much or made it too loud. Usually it's someone who really should be driving a truck for a living.

222

More Feedback: A Sound Designers' and Composers' Forum

The responsibility for creating the aural environment for a production falls on the shoulders of the sound designer and composer. Since our reference is to artistic matters, we recognize that everyone has his or her own style, individual creative voice, and techniques. We approached a representative group of sound designers and composers, whose backgrounds range from traditional to academic, and whose work ranges from abstract to highly commercial theatre. Their work represents all aspects of the best their fields have to offer. We sought their views and input on issues that we felt would be compelling to you, our readers. We consciously did not aim questions exclusively for sound designers or composers. The essence and technology of the two disciplines cover so much common ground.

Although we (literally) "wrote the book," we realize that we are not the last word in the processes of sound design and composition. We tapped the expertise of the professionals in this chapter, and in our esteemed colleagues' responses, we were struck by both the similarities and vast differences in style and approach.

THE SOUND DESIGNERS AND COMPOSERS

Todd Barton is the Resident Composer and Music Director for the Oregon Shakespeare Festival. His concert works have been performed by the Kronos Quartet, the Cavani String Quartet, and the Oregon Symphony Orchestra.

David Budries is chair of the Sound Design Program at the Yale School of Drama. He holds the chair of Music Production and Technology at the Hartt School, at the University of Hartford. He has designed sound and composed music for such luminaries as Athol Fugard, Mark Lamos, Irene Lewis, and Richard Hamburger. His work has been heard at Yale Rep, Hartford Stage Company, Center Stage, and La Jolla Playhouse.

Jill BC Du Boff is a New York–based sound designer who works on Broadway, off-Broadway, and regionally. She has also designed for television, film and radio. She has been nominated for two Drama Desk Awards and a Hughes Award and is the recipient of the 2008 Ruth Morley Design Award in recognition of excellence and pioneering in theatre, the first time this award has gone to a sound designer.

Victoria (Toy) DeIorio is the head of the Sound Design Department at the Theatre School of DePaul University. With a BFA in Musical Theatre, and studying classical acting in London at RADA and LAMDA, she transitioned from the performance artistry to the technical. Her compositions and sound design have been heard off-Broadway, regionally, and in the little storefronts of Chicago where she is based.. She has been nominated for five Jeff Awards, winning three; and has received two After Dark Awards.

Michelle DiBucci is an internationally recognized composer working in film, concert performance, and theatre. Film credits include music for Stephen King's *Creepshow* and *Twins* starring Fernanda Montenegro. Concert commissions include the Kronos Quartet and Lincoln Center Institute. She has composed music for over thirty theatrical productions and collaborated on many international projects with director Gerald Thomas, including her opera *Grail*. Ms. DiBucci is on the faculty at Juilliard where she teaches in both the music and drama departments.

Brian Hallas has worked with Ping Chong since 1984 as a sound designer and composer and with Jeannie Hutchins creating music and sound. Other credits include *Golden Child* at the Kennedy Center with Bill T. Jones; Max Roach and Toni Morrison at Lincoln Center; and Fontella Bass on the road. He has produced and performed *Welcome to The New Age of Folk*, a collection of familiar songs in an unfamiliar setting.

Michael K. Hooker is currently a media designer for Walt Disney Imagineering. He created the sound design programs and served as faculty at the California Institute of the Arts in Valencia, California, and the University of Cincinnati College/Conservatory of Music. Michael also serves as a vice commissioner for the USITT Sound Commission.

David Lawson is a sound designer and composer for theatre and dance. His credits include Richard Foreman's *Trilogy*, *The Cherry Orchard* at Juilliard, *The Grapes of Wrath* at Capital Rep, *The Slow Drag* at the American Place Theatre in New York City, as well as productions at La MaMa, BAM's Next Wave, and numerous works with choreographer Carol Blanco and a CD of his music, *The Blanco Dances.*

Phil Lee is a partner in Full House Productions, a production facility specializing in audio for radio, television, film, theatre, and educational and Internet projects. He has designed sound scores for theatre and dance artists including Ping Chong, Eiko and Koma, Marleen Pennison, Meredith Monk, the New York Ice Theatre, and the Talking Band. His work has been heard at the Public Theatre, the Brooklyn Academy of Music, the Vineyard Theatre, La MaMa E.T.C. Dance Theatre Workshop, Town Hall, and ice skating rinks all over America. He is the recipient of a Villager Award for theatrical sound design.

Tom Mardikes has been sound designer for Kansas City Rep since 1982 and has worked on over 150 professional productions including *The Emperor Jones*, *The Deputy*, and *The Tempest*. His work is represented regionally and in national tours. He is the Chair of the Design/Technology faculty for the Department of Theatre at the University of Missouri/Kansas City and is Director of Recording for the Conservatory of Music/Kansas City.

225

Richard Peaslee has composed music for over fifty theatrical and dance productions that include scores for Broadway, New York City Ballet, The Royal National Theatre, The New York Shakespeare Festival and The Royal Shakespeare Company, and Peter Brooke, including *Marat/Sade* and *A Midsummer Night's Dream*. He has also composed the music for the Martha Clarke Music Theatre Groups' productions, including *The Garden of Earthly Delights* for which his score received the Obie in 1984.

Elizabeth Swados has composed film scores and has created over thirty pieces on and off-Broadway, including *Runaways*, *Doonesbury*, *The Haggadah*, *The Trojan Women*, *Jerusalem*, *Alice in Concert*, *Missionaries* at BAM, and *Cymbeline* for The New York Shakespeare Festival. She has received five Tony nominations, Guggenheim and Ford Fellowships, and a grant from The Righteous Persons Foundation to film *The Hating Pot* about racism and anti-Semitism.

Jim van Bergan's New York and world premiere designs include *Robbers*, *Denial*, *All in the Timing*, *Ancient History*, *Bunny Bunny*, and

Nunsense. Other clients include Blue Man Group, The Big Apple Circus, the Metropolitan Opera, New York Philharmonic, and the Martha Graham Dance Company. He mixes the worldwide New Year's Eve Ball Drop broadcast annually from Times Square, *Cats* on Broadway, and received a Drama Desk Award nomination for *Lypsinka! A Day in the Life.*

SOUND DESIGNERS' AND COMPOSERS' QUESTIONS

We asked members of the roundtable for their individual definitions of the role of a sound designer or composer. Their responses to this core question frame a broad spectrum of approaches to the creative process and final product. Their diverse perspectives of the role are evident throughout the entire roundtable discussion.

BRIAN H: As both a sound designer and composer, my role is the same: to create an environment in which the action can exist, and to help establish the emotional atmosphere in which the scene occurs. Sound, more than any other medium, can place you somewhere with the least amount of effort. You hear a sound, and you know immediately where you are. There is no middleman.

MICHAEL H: I try to integrate sound design and composition as one. Composing music is really no different than the process of "composing" a sound cue. In the grand scale, your entire set of cues fulfills the simplest definitions of music—"arranged noises."

RICHARD P: In most of the shows I've worked on, the composer has also been the sound designer because that particular role didn't exist for a long time, and also because producers, even today, don't realize its importance and may not budget for it. As composer, you try to write the music appropriate for the production; as sound designer, you try to maximize its impact on the audience through proper miking and exciting production or reproduction. In the area of FX, I feel the roles overlap. As a composer, I never leave them entirely to the sound designer, although he may initially find the material; the composer often has a better feeling for what's needed, having worked closely with the director.

ELIZABETH S: My role is to serve and interpret text and drama, to highlight subtext, and create sound scenery and light. The challenge is to understand the work of drama and its overtones as thoroughly and originally as possible and translate that understanding into music.

TOM M: Get a bead on where the production is heading. Scenery and costumes have to commit their designs very early in the process. Sound has the advantage of being able to count down to the last minute, and creating something very specific to the production.

DAVID B: As a conceptual sound designer, I am responsible for all aspects of the created aural environment. That's *everything* that makes sound. I treat all sound design and composition as a creative endeavor. The primary difference is source material. I maintain that there is virtually no difference between a carefully constructed door close as a scene turning point and a carefully written and orchestrated musical phrase that serves the same function in the production design. Sound design is a compositional skill. In my opinion, you must give the same care and attention to the creation of music *and* sound props. Some young designers get caught up in the idea of being an "Artist." They look too much to personal motivation and not enough to the shape or content of the entire show. If those folks can lose the idea of being an "Artist" they may find that they can actually create more real art, and in turn be a better partner in the design process.

227

With respect to the physical space, there are practical limitations to what you can achieve with sound and music. Obviously you can't go around redesigning each physical space (although I'd like to at times), but we must work to achieve the dramatic goals of the production as well as possible in a given venue.

Anything that makes sound comes under my scrutiny, from scenic elements and props to music and sound effects. As a result, I will consult with a technical director when necessary to make a moving set piece quieter (of course, only if that is important to the production) and with props people to adapt the perfect prop. I will also work with composers to realize their ideas in three dimensions and with sound effects to create abstract environments or realistic source-specific sounds.

In the composition of incidental music, the goals are still the same. You need to provide an aural character that supports the scene and find creative ways of expressing that idea fluidly within the context of a production. If a singular style emerges for you, it can become a personal trademark and often you are selected for a particular production based on your perceived style within the industry. For others, flexibility, the ability to adapt quickly, and broad knowledge of musical history and styles become valued assets.

PHIL L: My role as a sound designer was to collaborate with the director to help him/her achieve his/her vision. It was to bring my expertise in the field of sound and my appreciation of theatre together to help enhance the production sometimes in ways the director might not have thought about or known was possible.

VICTORIA D: I am both a composer and a sound designer so my roles may overlap in many instances. The overall definition of the sound designer is a person who is in control of everything that makes noise in the production, whether it is practical or recorded. A composer adds to the mood, feeling, and pacing of the piece through music. They add the tension, flow, and motion to what you are watching visually, while working with the sound to inform the audience of where and when the action is taking place.

Describe your process. In developing sound designs or compositions, how do you communicate in first meetings with the director? Have you found a favorite director with whom to work? [Given that everyone starts by reading the script, the answers were quite varied.]

JILL DB: Most of the shows I design sound for are straight plays, so, unless otherwise noted, I will be referring to my experiences designing non-musical productions.

My process in designing sound for a show is twofold. Like most other designers I begin by reading the script and generating ideas. I will then delve more deeply into the script and clarify my ideas, producing what I call a "sound script." This is a list, or grid, really, consisting of my ideas of where every sound effect, transition, under-score, and piece of music will go, what the purpose of that sound is, and any other notes I think the director should consider when thinking about the sound. I usually send this sound script via email so the director can make notes on it and send it back. Based on this exchange I begin designing the cues. I usually start with cues that I think are essential to rehearsal, cues that will need a lot of finess-ing before tech, and cues that the director is not quite convinced of. Often I will put an idea in the sound script that is not obvious from reading the play, and the director may be uncertain that we will need or want a sound in that place. The director will either say, "Alright,

I'll listen to what you have," or "You should see that scene and then decide if you think we will need sound there."

By this point I will have also been in contact with the production manager regarding budget, and what the house and set look like. This shapes the way I think about the sound for the production. If the production doesn't have a lot of money, and we can only afford two speakers and a playback system, I will make sure that we can still have a fully realized design within the budget.

Another hurdle is load-in. If the show only has one day, or sometimes less, with festivals, I will have to prioritize my needs and make sure that the essentials can be loaded in on time. I will also make sure to touch base with the lighting, set, and projection designers, figure out where they will be hanging their instruments, and reserve real estate for my gear. When designing a system, I often take this into consideration, deciding what speakers I will be using based on the amount of space I can get in the grid. This knowledge is also important to take back to meetings with directors. If the production budget doesn't allow for something that both the director and I believe are essential to the show, I will sometimes ask the director to go to bat for me with the producers. This is not a common practice, but sometimes it is necessary, and shouldn't be taken for granted. Conversely, when discussing the design with the director, I will sometimes say, no, we can't afford to have/do that, and come up with a creative alternative that suits the production. These ideas sometimes end up being the best ones.

At the point in the process when the director is in rehearsal and has a better idea of what the show needs, and often times, some new ideas, I try to have a meeting with them. Also, at some point either before or during the first week of rehearsal I will give them a CD to listen to. I then try and push for the director to use the music, underscore, or sound effects in rehearsal. This is key to the design because it gets the actors used to the sound, and the director can hear the sound and give notes before tech, when they are concentrating on all of the elements. I find this makes tech easier and more productive for sound. Some of the best shows that I have worked on were shows where the actors have had sound in rehearsal. This is because the actors learn the timing of the sound, and learn to use it while developing their character and blocking. Hearing the sound and integrating it into rehearsal is invaluable: a director can actually "tech" the sound while working on a scene and give notes about things like tone and length as well as decide if the sound is necessary or if there needs to be more. It helps

229

the director to think about the sound in rehearsal rather than the stressful environment of tech. This can only benefit the design by helping to flesh out the sound and interweave in the play. I am often able to wrangle the stage manager or a PA to run the sound for rehearsal.

I will try to meet with the director one or two more times before we go into tech. Most of the notes during the rehearsal will either be given through email, in a rehearsal report, or over the phone. I will continue to bring in new CDs of sounds for rehearsal, so ideally by the time the show is ready to begin run-throughs in the rehearsal space, they have most of the sound to work with. These run-throughs are often very enlightening for me, and I will continue to shape the design based on what I learn from them.

The next step is generally tech. I try to use the ironically named "quiet time" to suss out the system, refocus speakers, EQ the system, and set levels. I will often invite the director to the second half of quiet time, especially if the show is particularly sound heavy. We will listen through the cues and set general levels and timings. After this final meeting before tech, I will usually come away with pages of notes, but something roughed in for every moment. I can then spend much of tech, while lighting projections or automation is working, to do these notes, and play them for the director. By working this way I am not scrambling to come up with many new things, and I can spend my time fine-tuning the sound. I prefer to work this way because I can spend time focusing on the more difficult moments and, ideally, am less stressed during tech.

VICTORIA D: After reading the script, I begin my research on the time period/genre and place of the play. After I do sufficient research, then I feel I can discuss these ideas with the director. It is always foremost in my mind that it is the director's vision that I am fulfilling. My usual approach is to ask questions, and I try to never leave the meeting without feeling as I though I have some specific direction for me to pursue. Once I hear what the director wants for the feel of the production, I then add in how I feel artistically, and use my research to blend with the information that I received from my conversation with the director.

If I have the luxury, my design process truly begins after I've heard the play read out loud. I like to hear the aural quality of the actors and the speed and flow to really determine how the sound and music will fit in. On a basic level, the sound certainly can help illuminate time and place, but I also see sound as another character in the play. It lifts the play from being written word, said by actors, into the world of theatricality. It helps to guide emotion and suspense in the audience as well as provide something that can provoke a pure and kinesthetic response from the actors. My favorite directors are those who recognize this, and trust my experience and knowledge. These are the people who allow me to truly delve into the process with the experimentation of sound, and in return, I'm able to be a full artistic collaborator who can really influence the overall production.

PHIL L: I almost always began by marking up the script as I read it for possible places where sound would be appropriate. Then in first meetings with the director my first priority was to LISTEN. Upon getting a sense of what it was the director wanted to achieve and making some suggestions if I felt it was warranted at that time, I would revisit the script with the results of those first meetings in mind and begin to formulate an outline of what approach should be taken in the sound design. My favorite directors to work with were those directing their own work, so-called avant-garde author/directors such as Ping Chong and dance-theatre author/choreographers such as Marleen Pennison, Eiko, and Koma.

DAVID L: In reading the play, I'll make note of basic information such as location, time of year, time of day, weather, etc.—whatever indications the playwright has given. For example, *Julius Caesar.* Act 2, Scene 1. Rome. Brutus' orchard. Clock strikes.

Following this initial reading, I'll get together with the director and get their ideas on how they intend to approach the work. Find out what their concept is for the piece. In my first reading of the play I have to be careful not to get too firm an idea of how I think the play should sound. There will be things (hopefully) that I'll respond to on some personal level, that very well may serve as my angle into the work, but ultimately it's my responsibility to interpret and implement the director's vision of the play and to place their needs above my own. Usually, my interpretation of a play and the director's will be pretty much in the same ballpark.

I like seeing the set design as early as possible. It gives me the clearest indication as to the overall style of the production. If it's impressionistic or abstract, I'll start to think of my work along those lines. It is important to me that the sound design fit in with the other design elements of a production.

"Talking about music is like dancing about architecture."—Elvis Costello.

"Language is a virus from outerspace."—William S. Burroughs.

RICHARD P: If you've never worked with the director before, the first meeting is establishing a friendly but professional rapport, general discussion of the work, noting their ideas about it and what they want from you. I don't expect much else at this stage, although sooner or later I want to know how much they trust your judgment vs. how much they may wish to micromanage—also, how they express their approval as well as their tactful or untactful ways of saying they hated something you did.

I guess my two favorite directors and with whom I've had long collaborations are Peter Brook and Martha Clark. First of all, I respect their enormous talent. Also, they know a lot about music and appreciate its importance. Always they listen, they trust, they never dictate, but they edit their own as well as your work fiercely for the good of the whole.

BRIAN H: I grew up in the collaborative world of original theatre, where directors, writers, actors, and designers create new work. A designer's job is to take ideas and transmutate them into realities; to start with a concept and create something tangible. I want to make somebody feel something, but in such a way that they don't realize it's happening, even though it may take a lot of technology for that to occur.

Communicating with directors is an equal challenge. They're often as unaware of the details of your process as is the audience, so it's best to be as concrete as possible with your suggestions, and not to expect them to be able to hear any given cue until you can present it in the flesh.

Since you have to start somewhere, I want to be at readings, writings, and discussions with the director and cast, so I have as complete an idea as the others about where to begin. And then I sit at home, alone with my equipment, where I work up a general set of sketches, music, or effects for the director to listen to, preferably from here to create material with the others.

Developing a soundtrack simultaneously and in the same room while the performers make their discoveries is my favorite approach. Many of the more satisfying elements for my soundtracks have come about at the same moment as a performer made a major find. This happy synchronicity needs be nurtured, which is why it's a very rare luxury, indeed.

If I'm working in a less original style of theatre, where the soundtrack is mostly prerecorded music used in transitions and between the acts, I offer an overabundance of suggestions. There are always a few hard, cinderblock cues to follow you around, so the more you listen to, the better. You're always working to solve problems,

232

fill in blanks, and build bridges to the completion of the work. So I offer up solutions, blank filler, and buttresses.

My favorite director has been my most frequent collaborator, Ping Chong. He wants a soundtrack to be just that—the aural blanket against which the action plays out. He is visual, includes movement and text within his pieces, and expects the soundtrack to be cinematic. We share a similar sensibility in the way music and sound work, and as a result, we're game to try anything.

ELIZABETH S: I read the text and as many books and poets who might be associated with the time and subject of the work. Then I listen to as much music as possible that represents the spirit or time. For instance, for *Cymbeline* I listened to every CD and tape of countertenors in early medieval music as I could find.

Since I'm often the director, it's more what happens when I cast a piece and begin to understand the musical energies and personalities I'm looking for. When I work with Andrei Serban, we discuss the deeper meanings and dramaturgy of the piece and how the music can be an appropriate subtext to his interpretation.

I believe the director should be boss. And if he's good, he knows what he wants. Music should serve his interpretation of the piece and therefore it's no good to try showing off or fighting the emotional tonality. It's because of this belief that I rarely let anyone else direct my musicals and operas—but on the other hand, when I do collaborate, I make a decision to be there for the whole good.

Andrei Serban is the best director I know. He loves music, loves risk, and has an instinctive knowledge of how to use music in original and challenging ways.

MICHELLE D: I read the play several times. The first time I read it I try not to think about anything but the story and characters. The second time through I have a pencil and notebook with me, and I begin to take notes about any thoughts that pop into my head as I'm reading. Sometimes they are musical and sometimes not; however, I have found if it is undecided what "sound world" the play will have, then the answer is often in the play itself. For example, when I was asked to write music for *The Cure at Troy* (a version of Sophocles' *Philoctetes*) by Seamus Heaney, my second time reading through the play I noticed words like cave, volcano, seabirds, lurid, and flame trembles and dialogue such as "Absolute loneliness … The beat of waves and the beat of my raw wound" and " … we're in a maze … shifting sand…. Clear one minute. Next minute, haze." All of these

233

words and thoughts were not only helpful, but were also my source of inspiration for the score.

Meeting a director for the first time with no prior history of introduction or mutual acquaintances can be a bit intimidating. Directors are some of the most well-informed people on the planet. Many I have worked with are both knowledgeable and articulate in history, politics, theology, literature, geography, and *all* of the arts. Some even know more about the specifics of some music than the composer. (Even though you may have had years and years of intensive music training, inevitably it will be a director who will want to speak about a piece you've never heard … like Sibelus' *Second Symphony*!) With this abundance of knowledge comes a very large ego. (Although I am not implying that all directors are egocentric.) But let's face it: directors need to be in charge of performers, designers, and technicians, and the play really is their "baby." Supervising such a birth usually requires a kind of myopic vision where equality in collaboration is put on the side burner and everyone looks to the director to unify the work. Along these lines I should add that when you compose music for the theatre you need to "let go" of your ego and give way to what is best for the production. This means that *no notes can be written in stone.* The director can choose not to use certain cues, or may ask you to revise or rewrite or have the music played so softly it can barely be heard. When the music is prerecorded, he can also chop it up and splice it together in such ridiculous composites that your heart will skip a beat as you hear all the beautiful or sophisticated passages you worked on for weeks get reduced to some collage of sonic babble. If this bothers you, then I advise you not to work in theatre (or film or television or commercials, for that matter). The only mediums that allow the composer to have the final word are the concert world and opera. I have several longstanding relationships with directors who trust my judgment and I can usually persuade them to try and hear it my way, but ultimately their approval is necessary.

DAVID B: The specific situation often tempers how I start and proceed in my process. When working with a new team—director, designers, actors—I spend a lot of time with a script (prior to rehearsal) to develop a familiarity with the piece (play, musical, etc.). I attempt to do this without creating too many "plans," meaning, I try to keep an open mind about the possibilities of the piece. Sometimes this happens before the first meeting with the director, sometimes afterward. In any case, the meeting with the director will

234

hopefully yield some discourse that will inform the potential design road map. After a rough course has been plotted, I go to work developing drafts for the next presentation. These might include musical sketches, found music, soundscapes, or sound props, anything that has essential meaning to the work. This should be done in close connection to the rehearsal process. Some works (plays) require regular attendance at rehearsals. Others require less time. For me, all of them require a tight communication with the production stage manager, who is my touchstone during the rehearsal process. Of course, regular communication with a director is essential, but a good stage manager can provide a lot of "structural" content which is essential for shaping the design to the production. Once the essential vocabulary is developed, then I elaborate and create rough cue ideas that could be used in rehearsal. These are then refined, while I create as many as three or four options for each idea. These options allow you to work quickly in the technical rehearsal process where the cues/music are fitted, exchanged, and edited as necessary to complement or support the desired intention.

This process changes dramatically when working with longtime collaborators. Often, design discussion is minimal and TRUST leads the way. A few essential words are exchanged, some references are made, and the drafting process proceeds. This is a very dangerous and exciting way to design. You still have to do the same legwork, but the result is often something better than you ever imagined. Of course this means that you and your team are very connected to each other's style and manner. It's like working in a very tight family where you know what each member is going to say before it's said. Sometimes, I must admit, you can crash and burn, but it's not usually too far to go to get back on the correct path.

TOM M: In my first meeting with a director, I am usually prepared to go in the direction that they want. My main thing is that I never go into a meeting without ideas. If given the opportunity, I will present them. If not, I just hang onto them for later. Directors, in general, do not have a sound vocabulary. Many have to work with selecting their own music and sounds early in their careers when they don't have the luxury of working with sound designers and composers. So they get used to making choices—kind of becoming sound designers. Not knocking the director, but the choices too often tend to be clichéd. One has to steer them, and this is where it helps to have ideas. I've seen directors get very attached to a piece of music, making it a kind of anthem for a production. It is really just a place to start and begin to grow.

I have several favorite directors. I won't name names, but one director who I work with often (a) has a hearing problem and (b) is the first to admit to know little or nothing about music and sound. I am turned loose. Our initial conversations last a couple of minutes and I go to work. So that is great fun. Another director who I have worked with frequently has it all worked out in their head so my job is to kind of pull it out and realize it. That really is not as much fun. That is more of a technician's job than a designer's job. It is more work. It can be good if there is collaboration.

MICHAEL H: During the first meeting I try and nail topics such as period, style, character development, the director's feelings toward using music (underscore, framing, transitions, etc.), and if he/she would consider using original music. I listen for descriptives (adjectives) that might be part of their process—colors, emotional states, seasons, etc.

I see directors falling into one of two types. The first is an "actor's director." This is someone who seems only to be concerned with the acting, and tech seems to be an added bother. The second (and my favorite) is, of course, the "designer's director." This is someone who clearly wants to inspire and be inspired by his/her design team. The designer's director is a team player and looks at theatre as a collaborative art.

JIM VB: I try to look at the script with a directorial or dramaturgical viewpoint. I note any obvious cues or thoughts about sound that I might have. I'm really trying to get a strong feeling for how I feel about the play, what it is saying, to whom, how the piece speaks, and why. It's kind of the five-Ws approach: who, what, when, where, and why? I read it again with specific ideas and concepts, following them through and taking notes. Then, if I think I have a strong concept idea, I develop it and support it, looking for textual support, outside references, and musical ideas or quotes.

In my first meeting with the director, I try to absorb as much information as I can regarding their feelings and viewpoints about the piece, reaction, and intent on production style and values. Once I have soaked up as much information as I can, I try to share some of my insight and thoughts to find similar grounds or to reshape my thoughts and concepts to follow the director's intent, and provide pointers for advanced or specific research. This meeting is mostly about "bigger picture" ideas and rarely gets specific on single cues, but might if there is a large sound sequence or collage that is integral to the performance or action.

On *An Empty Plate in the Cafe du Grand Boeuf* at the Berkshire Theatre Festival, director John Rando and I spoke at length over the phone about the ideas and concepts in the play and about the production. John told me that he was interested in underscoring several sections of monologues (vague ideas) which we later developed strongly in rehearsal. But in that same meeting, we had a short discussion about sound elements of a bullfight sequence that is integral to the play and needed a few specific ideas to be discussed. We didn't even discuss other elements like miking or walk-in/walk-out music and if they would be desirable. We both wanted time to digest ideas and then meet again—especially after I had done some further research.

I find that some directors want and expect artistic collaboration from the sound designer from day one, whereas others consider us simply overtrained technicians. Regardless, I try to have a discussion on the process, find out how the director likes to work, schedule meetings to discuss research or for listening to sound sketches, or make specific dates to supply rehearsal cues for the director to work with. Once you have a dialogue in place, you understand how that director likes to work and where and when they might be open to listening to ideas. With some directors, you hold their hands while explaining a musical concept. With others, I include vastly different musical concepts with a group of music or sound sketches on rehearsal tapes or CDs, and await reaction. I find that directors will either not know what they want (have not heard/felt it yet) or your ideas are not in sync. Or the director *knows* what they want and can say to any idea: "Yes, no, absolutely not, maybe, or have you tried developing this idea … in this way?" The most important thing is *listening* to the director, since our job is to support their initial concept and ideas. So first you listen, then you advise and make options that will help narrow your options down and strengthen your concept.

I have a couple of favorite directors because they all work in the same collaborative style and we communicate the same way each time. John Rando, Chris Grabowski, Annette Jolles, and Jordan Corngold—all younger directors who know how to use their design teams and like to explore during the rehearsal process.

TODD B: As I go through the script, I observe allusions to music, metaphors, stage directions, etc. I familiarize myself with the possible

237

role music might play in enhancing and illuminating the story. In the case of the Jacobean drama *'Tis Pity She's a Whore*, I catalogued about thirty references to music in the text. All references focused on the concept of music of the spheres, celestial harmony, and the healing and serene powers of music. This was in dramatic contrast to the core of the story which portrayed a degenerate, violent, and decadent society where people's lives meant nothing and a brother actually cuts out his sister's heart! Eventually, most of the music cues were of a very ethereal and pristine character, which when played against the violence and terror on stage actually created more tension and horror than a "deep, dark, terrifying" cue would have.

My first meeting is usually with the director and all of the other designers (sets, costumes, lights, movement and vocal coaches, and dramaturge). It is often a brainstorming session where the director guides the exploration based on his or her sensibilities of the focus of the script. I usually come away from these meetings with a sense of the time, place, and general mood of the piece. I collect this information and allow it to expand and modulate my first impressions from reading the script, all in preparation for composing.

The most important question I always ask directors is, "If music was a character in the play how would you describe it? What is its gender? What clothes would it wear? What is its motivation? Is it onstage all the time, or only in specific scenes?" Such questions allow the director to talk in his or her native vocabulary and it also begins an "inclusive" dialogue with the music and the story.

I also ask directors to give me poetic images for specific scenes. In the case of *'Tis Pity*, the director at one point asked for "horribly beautiful" music. A tricky challenge but one worthy of the subtle and psychological power of music.

The general approach of my favorite directors is to acknowledge music as an active character in the play and to pay attention to the rhythm it brings to a scene. Of course, it is my job to first be responsive to the rhythm of the words and breath of the actors so that the music becomes an integral part of the overall dramatic gesture.

Please describe your style of composition. If you've had to emulate a period or composer, is it a consideration to keep your own style intact?

JILL DB: I didn't come to sound design as a composer, but I have always been a remixer. I quickly learned that although I could make a lot of great music and some pretty interesting transitions using this method, I was limiting myself. I will often compose simple underscoring and transitions. My composing is based on the needs of the play, the energy of a transition, and sometimes, input from other designers. It is not that uncommon for a lighting, set, or automation designer to say to me, I need this transition to be loud to cover scroller noise/loud scene shift/lots of moving scenery. I am generally happy to oblige. I think that learning to compose for the needs of a thirty- to sixty-second transition has benefited me in this way. I do think that being a composer is extremely beneficial, to both the production and the art of theatre.

RICHARD P: What's important is to do a score that is right for the show regardless of what style it may require you to write in. In fact, that may be a blessing, forcing you out of your rut and exposing you to other influences. "Keeping your own style intact" is not only unimportant, since the score will always have your fingerprints on it regardless, but also suggests that you are on an ego trip, not necessarily doing what's best for the production. Since the collective fate of the show is what's probably going to benefit you most, it's wise to keep that in mind rather than making some "personal statement."

ELIZABETH S: I have many styles. I'm a theatrical composer—an actor of sound. My style is to relate passionately to the action and motives of the characters. The only place I am outside of the "play" is when I write Judaica. Then I am composing for my ancestors and their writings. I emulate pure raw chant of every culture where a story is being told or a god is being summoned.

TOM M: I think that an artist develops their "voice" by trying numerous variations of the same thing. A designer studies artists, and takes what is needed for a particular production. Designers are great imitators and synthesizers, and rarely go back to the same well again.

DAVID L: My style of composition is largely environmental. I create the sonic landscape that the action of the play (or the dance) will take place in. My music is low on melody and rhythm and very big on things such as texture, ambiance, and tone color. There's lots of vertical space in the composition. It's a style I began developing in 1986 with The Manhattan Ensemble. We were doing a production of *La Ronde* and the director (Raymond Marciniak) thought it would be interesting to keep me out of the rehearsal process. I was to create a soundscape for the show, based on the few conversations we would have about the play.

Once I began working, I became aware of the fact that I had no idea as to what the rhythm of the play would be, what the actors sounded like reading the text, what the choreography would be like, and a number of other things I would've known (and planned for) had I been present at rehearsals. So I designed a piece that was more about "avoidance" than anything. Music that, I hoped, would not conflict with the other elements of the show. I developed the music around my general observations about set design: the set is always present, it doesn't go anywhere. You notice it and study it, for as long as you like, and then it may be largely ignored as other things (like dialogue) demand more of your attention. But it is still there, resonating in sympathy with the rest of the production. The actors move through it, around it, and stand on it.

In dance I'm given a much broader canvas to work with. There's not as much going on as in theatre. There's nothing really to avoid bumping into. When working with choreographers, I'm able to use more conventional musical structures, which fills up a lot more vertical space and, in turn, requires more of an audience's attention. The music becomes much more foreground.

In 1994, Carol Blanco asked me to write music for a piece she was choreographing called *Edge*. Again I was being asked not to attend rehearsals. (Is there a message here?) Instead I was to base my work on my interpretation of the title. The end result was very beautiful and worked extremely well with the choreography. What was interesting was that there wasn't anything overtly "edgy" about either the music or the choreography.

I've never been asked to try and emulate another composer. That's a musical discipline I simply don't possess the skills for. I've been asked to create any number of locations, such as those of ancient China or Arabia. In these instances, I would more than likely try to avoid making the obvious statement in favor of some evocative suggestion. It's important to leave enough room in a composition for an audience's involvement. Give them just enough information to lead them gently down the garden path, but ultimately, let them discover for themselves what is most meaningful within the terrain.

VICTORIA D: I can't really say that I have a particular stylistic mode of writing music because I really try to create music that lives in the world of each production. I do try to achieve a certain amount of elegance in my compositions, using simplicity and subtlety to get my ideas across. The thing that makes composition for theatre so exciting to me is the chance to write music that spans many different styles and genres. None of my pieces really sound like the others, unless they happen to be set in the same time period and place.

BRIAN H: My "style" is very electronic rock and roll, which, as we know, is quite diverse. However, I must say that one of my biggest surprises occurred last year working with Ubu Rep on a piece with a Jewish theme. I wrote a song which everyone loved and thought was an old Jewish song that I had dug up, and it worked with the show very well.

JIM VB: When I compose for shows, it's because I need something that is not commercially available, and it's often a hybrid of musical/compositive styles, or a soundscape that requires composition to function. So it's much more about function and form for me. I'd rather work with a great composer on an original work than try to be the composer *and* sound designer. That's simply too many hats to wear at once. I feel that composing a show is too much work on its own, and is a whole other job, so I'd rather be the sound designer in a collaborative relationship.

MICHELLE D: I am quite eclectic as a composer; however, I do have a strong aural attraction to bass instruments. Contrabassoons, bass clarinets, baritone saxophones, the lower strings, and the low register of the piano all are beautiful, evocative, and inspiring for me. With regard to composing music with historical references, there are always ways to have fun. For example, if you need to compose music for a Victorian salon, and the music is prerecorded, experiment with vintage microphones or different types of reverbs to add nostalgia to the piece. Or, if the play is set in the Renaissance, keep the harmony and style true to the sixteenth century, but instead of lute and countertenor, make it guitar and kazoo.

MICHAEL H: For me, there are no rules to obey when composing. If a show is locked into a specific period or country I do a lot of listening to existing music trying to absorb it all and "regurgitate" it back into new music. My background in jazz piano makes it easy to imitate and clone styles and orchestrations. I especially love composing for dance. Music and movement are made for one another. I use a stopwatch for scene timings in rehearsal and do a lot of outlining in the script—hopefully, to catch key words and phrases from which to let the music come. I always try and cut the music to fit the action rather than making a director restage to fit the music. My personal style is never a concern—I suppose it is always there.

How and when do you decide on what instrumentation to use?

ELIZABETH S: I select the instrumentation when I figure out what character deserves what instrument. I once scored a movie with Blythe Danner in it and she was, without a doubt, an alto flute. Imogen—in her sweetness and innocence (and pluckiness) was a harp. Shylock is a trombone. My kids are often drums. It goes on and on. Vocal always precedes instrumental whether talking or singing. In film, it's image and expression.

RICHARD P: I decide instrumentation early on since it is integrally bound up with composition. Naturally, it will depend on style and budget.

PHIL L: My instrumentation was always sound effects.

BRIAN H: I determine the instrumentation as I go. The process of writing music is, for me, very subconscious, so I don't usually think of things like instrumentation in an upfront kind of way. I suppose I have my basic palette. Of course, as with the song for the Jewish plays, the instrumentation becomes self-evident. As a self-educated musician, I don't easily accomplish original "period" music, although the older I get and the more I know, the easier it becomes to attempt even this.

MICHAEL H: Sometimes instrument choice is dictated and driven by the script. At other times, I look at orchestrations as being "thick" or "thin"—big emotional moments get big drums, low brass and strings; sad underscores often get solo instruments like guitar or oboe. I love composing with non-Western instruments: *taiko* drums, *mbiras, gamelan, tablas,* and pan flutes. I have often composed with just sounds (not necessarily musical) and blend the line between sound and music. Character themes are fun to work in and out of scores. I often assign a certain instrument for a specific character with their melody intertwined throughout the show.

VICTORIA D: First, I research what the popular music was in the time period specified, and I listen to what instruments were used in those historical pieces. After that, I determine the force of the flow of the production and how I will use instrumental voicings to have the effect that I want on that flow. Finally, I decide on certain characters on stage who might have a particular instrument that either sounds like their voice, or expresses their character. If they have a particular theme that follows them around the play, I then match the perfect instrument to their character and their motives.

TOM M: It is innate. I just know, and have frequently wondered about that decision-making process myself.

TODD B: Often instrumentation is my first consideration. I'm drawn to timbres and textures, so early in the process I spend most of my time finding the "right" musical palette or musical language. The same note or series of notes played on a penny whistle has a completely different impact when played on a prepared piano or an electric bass. The instrumentation is an inseparable element of the music's character.

Please talk about the pros and cons of working with live musicians vs. MIDI instruments.

RICHARD P: Live musicians bring feeling and flexibility to a score— MIDI technology, a whole new array of sounds and manipulation of sound. It's not necessarily an either/or situation, and I'm strongly in favor of the use of both in the same score.

243

VICTORIA D: In music, live musicians are always the preference for me because of their intricate expression that they can bring. There is nothing that compares to the sound of a real human being using their energy and breath to create the sound from their particular instrument that they have worked their entire life to perfect. However, this is not always possible, and there are wonderful computer programs that simulate live musicians very well. In fact, they are getting better all the time.

The ease of MIDI is that it can be changed or manipulated well into the process, unlike a live recording which has to be edited or re-recorded if something needs to change. MIDI is very effective when you can't find musicians that play a particular instrument, or to create an entirely new instrument based on sounds that may not be considered as traditional musical notes.

PHIL L: The only time I was involved in music was when I was working with a composer, recording live musicians for music to be used in addition to the design I was creating. Let me state right here that

I consider composition and sound design to be two very different disciplines and art forms and that I believe one needs the assistance of the other if original music and sound design are going to be incorporated in the play. I've worked in sound most of my life and I know I don't have enough of a musical sensibility or the talent to ever consider myself a composer and I've never worked with a composer or heard the results of sound design done by a composer that made me believe they had any idea what they were doing in terms of sound. I know there are many people on this panel who consider themselves to be both a composer and a sound designer, but I would deign to say that their strengths lie in one area or the other and that if it wasn't for synthesizers and digital recording the sound designers wouldn't be able to compose and the composers wouldn't be able to create sound design. And I hate MIDI!

TOM M: I don't like things that replace real musicians. No theatre affords live musicians for a play (or it is rare), so I at least try to use real musicians when recording the score. I hate scores that use synthesizers imitating real instruments as finished cues for a production.

JIM VB: There are two strict schools, and I've worked with both of them. Both can be extraordinary experiences and both can be failures. My personal preference is to work with live musicians, but that's also because I do a good deal of live recording and broadcast, and there is no substitute for good musicians. Let me reemphasize—GOOD musicians! MIDI can do wonderful things, but let's face it, there are places where you want twenty-five strings and places where you want five keyboardists. I think a good example of the two would be if you look at the score of *Show Boat* and the score of *Sunset Boulevard*— both require large orchestras, but one includes a great deal of multiple synth work, and they have very different sounds. Modern music has a different bent and includes the combination of both pop music's influence on the orchestrations in modern musicals and the technological advances of wireless miking. These have made modern musicals both more compressed and louder by default. On the flip side, they also have made some musicals spectacular—with a greater dynamic range, total intimacy, and raw power when it is needed.

The orchestrations are better if fully controlled by a musician— meaning that whether your orchestra is a forty-plus-piece symphony or a single pianist, you will have better options and opportunities than if using a non-dynamic playback or MIDI orchestration.

MICHELLE D: The pros of live musicians, if they are "live" for the performance, is that they are able to respond to each individual performance as the actors become more comfortable and their performances evolve. The actors may want to take more or less time with certain scenes, potentially disrupting a prerecorded underscore. However, when the musicians are present they are ready to assist the actors rather than limit them to the same performance every night. I find no pros in working with MIDI instruments supposedly simulating a real person, like playing a flute sound on the synthesizer. However, using MIDI instruments for new sounds (new instruments) is always an exciting venture and has opened up so many new color possibilities on the composer's palette.

ELIZABETH S: As I've indicated, my roots are so much in ritual and ceremonial theatre, I believe that instruments talk, comment, and play off of humans. Therefore humans must be playing the instruments. Electronic mediums are only appropriate if the range and world of the drama and its characters warrants ultra-modernization. I did a piece called *Millennium Lounge* about college kids as they face the year 2000. We used MIDI in that because the personal world was being lost to them and replaced by technology. I am a huge fan of Laurie Anderson and by no means judge others who make fabulous use of technology.

245

BRIAN H: MIDI instruments never talk back. Live musicians never get lost without a backup, unless, of course, they drink.

What is key to producing sound designs and compositions that unify as a seamless piece of work?

DAVID B: For me, the key is listening and communication. Once you determine the aural palette of the piece or what the essential elements are, it's not hard to coordinate the music and sound components. If you listen and talk, this process is quite simple and coherent. What sometimes happens is that one partner in the process takes off on his or her own path, ignoring the foundational elements. Other times production partners simply don't understand the general intention. If you talk about the piece in depth with your production partner, it is possible to have regular collaborative successes.

JILL DB: I think that the key to producing sound designs and compositions that unify as a seamless piece of work is different for everyone. A big part of this also depends on who the director is. If the director is open to trying things and excited about the sound for the show, then it is easier to make a seamless piece of work. Sometimes the director is scared of sound, or doesn't know what it can do or how it can be used, and that takes a bit more convincing. I have found that when sound is integrated into rehearsals, it is easier to have a comprehensive design. This is the case because both the actors and the director utilize and integrate the sound ideas when blocking and rehearsing a scene. This makes the overall arc of the deign much more natural and seamless.

PHIL L: I think it's a great mistake and a disservice to the production you are COLLABORATING on to ever think of your design as a seamless piece of work. If it is, why do you need anything else, like a play, to accompany it? It is supposed to complement and enhance an already scripted work (or if not scripted something where another visionary in another area than sound is working with you) and as such should not be seamless or particularly stand on its own.

VICTORIA D: The most valuable lesson I have learned is to maintain the same key signature, or complementary key signatures, throughout a play. Pieces of music can then move around within a production if the flow changes during tech without losing integrity of mood and feeling and thereby literally giving the show a feeling of seamlessness. You can also combine a few pieces together to make a longer piece as well.

I also like to use musical themes in the production. Those themes may be determined by character, mood/emotion, time period, action/pace, or place. You can follow these themes throughout the production, changing with emphasis as the show progresses.

BRIAN H: Unity in design has no magic "key" to its formula. I think you need to be constantly aware of the whole while working on the pieces, although in most shows I've worked on, the whole is yet to be discovered until very late in the game. You just have to be current with the show's progress. On the occasions when I haven't been, it's been very difficult to let go of pieces I loved but that didn't fit.

TOM M: It is important to use musicians and create your own palette. I feel that is the single most important aspect to having a complete design for a production. It has to sound like it belongs together. An interesting production that worked wonderfully was *Les Liaisons Dangereuses.* The director wanted to explore the use of Jean-Philippe

246

Rameau, who wrote in the mid-eighteenth century. We hired a harpsichordist for the recordings. My idea was to have the music progress from being very period and very posh at the beginning, and as the wickedness, shallowness, and deceit of the characters becomes more revealed, the music would deconstruct; still harpsichord, but something unimaginable for the period. I likened this, in my explanation of the idea, to Oscar Wilde's *Picture of Dorian Grey*, which begins very beautifully and the inner ugliness becomes exposed on the painting at the end. So, from CDs we found Rameau selections that worked well for the many different scenes and told the harpsichordist what selections we wanted to use. She had the score for most of Rameau's harpsichord work, and was able to review it before the recording session. The director came to the session and we were able to adjust tempos, timings, beginnings, and endings very specifically. When we completed the Rameau section of recording, the composer then went to work with the harpsichordist recording dissonant chords, noises, and scrapes so that he could build up the deconstruction in ProTools. The final cues worked so that the harpsichord sounded very natural for most of the first act, stereo cues coming from the set, as if there were a harpsichord on stage. The deconstruction begins near the end of Act I and the cues grew progressively from four-track to six-track and eventually eight-track cues. It enveloped the audience and got quite wild. This scene change music worked in conjunction with the attitudes of the actors playing servants, and the mundane activity of moving furniture and chairs developed quite an attitude and commentary.

JIM VB: In reference to the one-woman shows *Keeping the Word* and *The Handshake*, these are prime examples of strong compositions that tie in to the same world as the sound effects, environments, and ambiance. The key is staying in the same milieu, and collaborating on every aspect of the sound with the composer, director, and performer. The audience is always responding to the sound of the music, the soundscape, and the actress—so we must always be on the same page, and have the same intent. Since these works are single, continuous cues, the soundtracks are immense and required huge amounts of work, and a great deal of development, as well as trial and error in the process of creation. But like a great film, these plays then have a life of their own, and develop their own genre. And unlike a normal sound design which would have no life without actors, I feel that these soundscores would be quite interesting to listen to alone. They would make sense by themselves, yet only become extraordinary within the performance, the ultimate collaboration.

MICHAEL H: The key—communication and collaboration.

What is your approach to technical rehearsals? What are your top priorities?

VICTORIA D: My approach to technical rehearsals is to be as prepared as possible. I never want anyone to be waiting on me unless it is completely necessary. It's still fairly new for sound designers to make quick changes to their cues in a technical rehearsal, but I feel it's very important for me to be able to do this. I want to make sure I am well prepared with my cues programmed into the system so that tech will continue to run smoothly. This makes me overprepared at the start.

I believe everyone's priority is teching a show efficiently while respecting everyone's artistic vision. Tech is the point in the rehearsal process where all the creative minds must come together smoothly to achieve the production values of the show. Clear communication and consideration for other designers'/director's ideas is essential to getting through the process efficiently.

I work best when a really focused stage manager runs the tech while keeping an eye on the clock. When there are too many voices trying to run the tech, it can get very confusing and much more difficult to honor the overall artistic vision.

JILL DB: Before tech begins, I will get together with the director, by meeting, over the phone or via email exchange, and make sure that I am totally clear on all of the sound moments. Ideally the director will have heard most of them, and worked with them, or at least approved them by this point. I will also give the stage manager a more comprehensive version of the sound script, which will include the page the sound is on, the word it should get called on, and the purpose of the sound. This ends up being an outline for the SM, and not set in stone. The calling will often change when lights are added, or will be called on an action rather than a line. I will usually go through the cue script with the stage manager before tech.

By the time tech rolls around, I will have also had quiet time, and set starting levels for the sound. I find, however, no matter how prepared I am for tech, the first few cues always take the longest. Learning the language of the show, working with the other designers and putting the show in the space are all elements that can only be done during tech. Once this language is established, tech is a lot of starting and stopping. I use this time to work on notes and setting levels. I try to get as much done before tech so that my *focus* is on refining the sound for the space and creating new cues if necessary.

I will also make sure to stay in constant contact with the lighting designer during tech, either through the SM or directly. I try to make sure that our timings line up and that we are generally on the same page. I have worked on shows where the lights and sound are telling two different stories. By talking to the lighting designer and sometimes even playing them the music or sound, we can make sure we are both working towards the same goal.

The hardest thing about tech is the stopping and starting. When I have a long cue, such as underscoring or background ambiance, it is sometimes difficult to tell if it will work in the show. By stopping and starting, a cue that would normally play for three minutes is played for three hours while the other designers are working on the scene. This can make it hard to gage where certain builds will fall within a scene. Only by running the scene in real time can this timing be figured out, and, generally this doesn't happen during tech. The top priority for tech, I think, is getting through the show and hearing every sound in the space, with the director.

PHIL L: One of the reasons I'm no longer doing sound design is because I hated technical rehearsals. I would be there all day waiting for them to get the lights right while we eventually got to the half-hour or so it took to check our cues. In those circumstances my top priority was to stay awake. In shows with very complex sound designs such as Marleen's or Ping's my top priorities were timing, levels, and usually running back to the studio to make last-minute updates to the cues.

MICHAEL H: I ask for a preliminary cue setting time ("quiet time") with just the sound operator and myself to set preliminary levels, routing, and timing (fades). The house engineer will have had drawings in advance in order to get effect speakers and the mains in place and in rough "focus." This makes the cue-setting process go much faster. The stage manager and sound op will have my cue sheets well in advance of tech.

During tech, my priorities are to nail playback levels with the engineer and cue placement with the stage manager. Second to this, I focus on continuity and blending with the action on stage, scenery transitions, and lighting. I try to sit near the director and involve them in this process to the extent that they feel comfortable. If (after discussion and trial) a director is not comfortable integrating a cue into their action—then I have provided the wrong cue—period.

RICHARD P: What cues come out of which speakers at what level is what techs are about for me. Making sure the sound operator is competent, that he has a clear cue sheet, and that the sound equipment is in good working order is also vital. Other than that, I find having a walkman with some good tapes most useful to kill the many hours while they sort out the problems with lights, set, and actors.

JIM VB: Once a system is installed and tuned, I want to have preliminary time to rough in assigns and levels. I want to get the sounds set so that when we begin tech, I can use the elements of sound as they *should* be used, not to stop, hold, set a level, develop a pan, and change a count while the actors wait. Inevitably you will have to do that, but I want to have the entire show roughed in and have options for every cue so that tech time can become my play time. I'd much rather spend the time listening to a few fade options than trying to set assigns and levels, which are very easy to do in advance. If I have had my pretech quiet time and dry tech time, tech with actors is a lot of fun. My biggest priority in tech is the operation. Have I built the show accurately? Can the stage manager call the sequence right? Can the board operator execute the show easily and consistently? Since the technical process can be a real pain (I always hear it called "Tech Hell," but don't ever want to see the process that way personally) I want the sound team to be together and well prepared, so that when the artistic staff sees that a shift, transition, cue, or even a scene doesn't work, we can address the bigger picture in a collaborative process. To me, that is what the essence of tech should be about.

ELIZABETH S: I like to be completely ready by tech and leave nothing in the music to chance. I'm not one who likes to decide on sound, etc. in the final days of rehearsal.

DAVID B: My approach during the tech process is very organized and full of "options" (some people think *too* full of options). If I can't react quickly to a change in perspective or a new idea on the floor, I don't feel that I am a good design partner. The days are long gone when you can get away with a statement like, "I'll fix it in the studio and you'll be able to hear it tomorrow." You have to act in the moment, or the moment's gone.

In general, when working with conceptual sound design, textural composition, or soundscapes, I work elementally (with individual stereo elements or layers—lots of two-track and four-track layers.

In Hartford I have sometimes used eight-track layers). This gives me the ability to change a mix value without having to constantly run back to the studio and rebuild a cue. This also allows for greater image broadening or spatialization as layers can be assigned to different playback areas within the performance environment, creating depth and distance. By broadening the image and creating depth in the sound design, you can give the audience a very rich experience without having it be too obvious or overstated. You can also make as large a statement as necessary. However, this requires a good operator or an automated system. At this point, I still prefer to use manual operators as opposed to automation; however, I am very encouraged by recent developments in Richmond and LCS system operation.

The listening position for conceptual design is very important. I try to select a location that is somewhat central to the delivery system coverage. The goal is to be in a position that is representative of the general listening area. Moving around throughout the room is also very important. While in communication with my assistant, I will request specific cues be played while I roam the room. This is to confirm the effectiveness of the delivery system design as experienced from several locations.

The reinforcement design listening position is tougher because it is permanent for the run of the production. Ideally, you'd like a representative listening location; however, that is rarely possible due to the practical issues of audience seating. On Broadway, taking up nine seats represents a significant loss of cash over the run of a successful show. In the best of circumstances, audience seats, usually rear-of-house center, provide a reasonable (although not perfect) location. In some productions the sound is considered more important than in others, so it is possible to negotiate for a good position or have an audio perch built that does not take up audience seating. The "perch" approach is quite expensive and only appropriate for shows that expect long runs. Although I have also experimented with remote mixing positions, the majority of production sound mixing personnel do not favor this approach. This is quite understandable. A remote mixing position requires the use of a sophisticated listening system (dummy head or CALREC soundfield) and a monitoring system (like a mini surround monitor) in a remote location. This space is best if it is visually connected, but aurally isolated. These are very tough situations for the mix engineer. It takes a long time to get familiar with that style of mixing and it's hard to get completely comfortable and confident. I know I'd prefer to be in the house.

BRIAN H: In the theatre, sound is the bastard child, very often a second thought. It's consistently the last element to be allotted time in a concentrated period during tech—that sacred "quiet time" (when everyone else is at dinner). Sound often shoulders the blame for rough tech rehearsals. I can't tell you how many times I've had to fight for tech time. It's best to be well prepared for this.

Since tech rehearsals are usually devoted to the lights and there's a lot of time to kill, I try to maintain a sense of purpose and a sense of humor. Basically, I try to get rough levels as early as possible, then worry about fitting in artistically during the run-throughs of different scenes.

TODD B: Cue placement and the level of sound/music is critical—the wrong place and the wrong level and it functions as a completely different piece of music and is completely inappropriate. However, cueing is the most important element. Cueing has to be in sync with the actors' breath. It is the intervals between an actor's breath that ultimately determines the tempo and rhythm of a scene—the music and sound must be responsive to this or you are dead in the water. The people responsible for this finesse night after night (and I'm talking about recorded cues) are the stage manager and the sound operator. They are the "performers" of your music and sound design and should be treated with the same respect and trust as live musicians—it is their responsibility and art to breathe with the actors, to breathe with the story.

Please discuss your aesthetic approach to sound reinforcement. How do you organize your system? Please comment on the amount of reinforcement for musicals.

MICHAEL H: I modify my "aesthetic(s)" for each show, but, in general, I have two:

(1) To make the sound system disappear (both visually and aurally). In this type of show, I want the audience to key into the action on the stage and not focus in on sound coming from speakers. I use very carefully set delays on almost every reinforcement speaker to help with imaging. I want focus to pull toward the stage. I try to keep the mains out of sight lines and often volley for speakers hidden in scenery. For traditional and older musicals (*Oklahoma*, etc.) I go for minimal miking of the orchestra, concentrating mainly on areas and using a more distant (ambient) positioning of microphones. I try to fill in and assist the acoustic sound. For more modern shows

(Sondheim, etc.) I go for a more "studio" sound with each instrument close-miked and careful baffling and deadening of the pit.

However, this transparency only happens to a certain degree. Ultimately, I expect that the audience will accept the reinforcement early on in the musical and hopefully it won't become an issue. Your brain levels out such anomalies and makes them seem normal and acceptable.

(2) Rock and roll! For rock operas (*Tommy, Jesus Christ Superstar,* etc.) I make no attempt to conceal the equipment or the reinforced sound.

My systems come in layers of coverage. I am a great proponent of left-center-right (LCR) systems. If I have an inexperienced mixer, I will keep the voices C and the music in the LR. With an experienced mixer (or automation), I will spread the voices to reduce combing and open up the sound. Sometimes I do a LCR with an A/B center—but I must admit there is some guilt in specifying such a pile of equipment and having more stuff in view than the lighting rig. The next layer is the delay fill system(s) used to provide even coverage (frequency response and sound pressure level [SPL]/volume) to the far reaches and awkward spaces in the theatre. Usually every speaker in the house has a delay in the chain. Many designers don't think about timing as part of their systems—for me, it is just as important as frequency response and SPL. The third layer is the effect playback system. I almost never use the reinforcement system to reproduce sound effects. The fourth layer is the foldback system providing mixes for the conductor, stage manager, and performers (occasionally the hearing assist system, too).

Generally, I shy away from compressors—except on electric bass, close-miked brass, and the occasional uncontrollable singer. Most modern speaker controllers provide adequate protection, so I rarely limit the mains. All of this is, of course, predicated on having a top-notch production mix engineer.

JILL DB: My aesthetic approach to sound design varies based on the space, the show, the budget, and the set. I generally like to have a set of main speakers, an upstage pair, and a pair of subs in my skeletal system. If the show has enough money/space, I will often add an offstage pair, and surrounds. My two favorite playback systems are SFX and QLab. These allow me to do anything, and do it quickly and easily. When I design a show, I will always begin by organizing it in my head for one of these two systems.

253

VICTORIA D: My goal with sound reinforcement is to make it appear as though the sound is coming directly from the voice on stage. I do not believe that, just because there is amplification, it should sound amplified. It should feel enhanced. My aesthetic is clarity. As a designer, it is up to you to make sure the audience hears everything that is happening on stage. For example, take the end of a big chorus number: if there is a quiet scene that directly follows, I keep the level of the mics up louder than I normally would because the audience's ears need to readjust to what they've just heard. Then slowly, during the scene, I bring the levels down to speaking level so that I have somewhere to grow when the next big show-stopping number comes along. I create dynamics by using the physiology of the human ear.

When I organize my system, I think of the most efficient way for the sound engineer to choreograph their hands. Live musicals are fast moving and anything can happen, so I make sure that equipment is placed within reach, and that characters' mics are grouped together on the board in a straightforward and easily accessible way. Each input must have the cleanest signal path in its routing, just in case something has to change quickly during a show.

254

RICHARD P: As far as sound reinforcement goes, the best is when you are totally unaware of it—when instruments and voices sound perfectly natural. This should not rule out adding reverb and EQ, which can help greatly if not overdone. Musicals are tricky because balance between singers and orchestra is no longer in the hands of the orchestrator and can be upset by levels on the board.

BRIAN H: Reinforcement is so often dictated by budget in my world that it has become almost a nonissue. Some of the greatest compliments I've received have been for shows with two speakers, a sixty-watt amp, a 6 × 2 mixer, and cassette decks. It's all relative.

DAVID B: In general, my approach to sound reinforcement is to try to keep it as simple as possible. That doesn't mean that the delivery system isn't sophisticated, but that every attempt is made to preserve spatial information and natural sound quality of the performance unless the objective is otherwise stated. It also means that every attempt is made to minimize excessive equalization by insisting on good loudspeaker positions, carefully aligned delay systems, and careful microphone selection and placement using high-quality radio microphone systems. Whenever possible, I separate the vocal/music reinforcement system from the sound effects system. More often than not, the systems are completely different in focus and flexibility. This separation allows each system to be optimized for their respective tasks. One of the key factors in a successful sound reinforcement design (aside from a well-arrayed and balanced system) is an experienced music mixer.

In general, the Broadway musical production aesthetic seems to be the prevailing trend. That trend is characterized by higher sound pressure levels creating a very visceral experience. For some productions, I wouldn't have it any other way. For others, I'd like to hear more subtlety. This move toward louder productions creates a lot of problems for the intermediate-level producer who wants the Broadway sound, because it is expensive to achieve. Regional theatres are also feeling that pressure as "enhancement money" flows from New York producers to the regional market. Producers are again using regional theatres to test new productions. This trend has made regional theatre audio production grow significantly over the past five years. It has also created the need for more competent and experienced sound personnel.

255

TOM M: I hate miking actors. If it is a must, I try to use PCC-160s as foot microphones and replace what is missing acoustically in the theatre. I never want the microphone levels in a play to sound electronic or reinforced. I believe in separate bussing. I play music through one system, voice reinforcement through another, sound effects from a third. I never cross streams.

I love reading in trade magazines where a sound designer in an interview talks about how they made the show sound like the CD. No show has *ever* sounded like a studio recording.

PHIL L: I've only done one show that required reinforcement and that was a play that had a live jazz band and a singer on stage in front of a stand-up mic. I truly abhor the current dependency on reinforcement and have walked out of many shows because it's done so badly. It's beyond my understanding why stage actors who, just a generation ago, knew how to project their voices without straining no longer seem to have that ability. As for musicals, it's apparent that bands and orchestras no longer have any sense of dynamic range and there are very few musicals where I'm able to hear the lyrics over the music or, indeed, the dialogue because I'm hearing more mic reverberation.

JIM VB: My preferred aesthetic is a subtle, natural reinforcement which is quite uncommon these days. I think traditional musicals sound better when the reinforcement is subtle, the voices are well-trained, and the orchestra is talented and well-conducted. That being said, we know the truth: few people will allow a sound designer to do their job without interference. Instead of realistic productions, we are often told to make the show louder. "Louder is funnier!" I've been told by one writer/producer. Many modern musicals, however, often do not sound better when subtly reinforced, in my opinion. I have found that these scores need a lot of vocal and instrument reinforcement to sound like an intimate recording, not a live acoustic performance. Shows like *Rent, Tommy, Cats, Phantom, Jekyll & Hyde, Scarlet Pimpernel, Footloose, Smokey Joe's Cafe*, and much of Sondheim's work all require a stronger level of reinforcement. I think that shows are becoming more and more like the movies and TV, which is good for audiences and often bad for sound designers. The technical reality of a Broadway show has a lot to do with how it is perceived. Shows that are louder have more sound problems inherently—large numbers of wireless microphones, huge mixes, active monitor mixes, louder monitor mixes, younger (sometimes ill-trained and easily damaged) voices, and composers/musical directors who want a rock-level orchestra!

On the other hand, the louder shows are very exciting, bring younger audiences to the theatre, and sell well commercially. So if we are to evolve with theatre, we had better be capable of what the show requires.

ELIZABETH S: I hate miking except when it is an effect in itself. I believe that the voice particularly is capable of creating magic of its own in open space. I depend on the kindness of sound designers who only amplify the blend that is already there. I despise and abhor the amplification in musicals. I think it's all one overdone, double forté mistake.

How did you develop your skills as a sound designer or composer? Please cite the most important experience of your development or one defining moment.

VICTORIA D: Like most designers of my generation, I am self-taught. I started as a ballet dancer, expressing my body to music and sound, and did that for thirteen years during the early stage in my life. My mother was a classical pianist who would wake us up to Chopin on Sunday mornings. This early formative exposure to music made me very intuitive to musical expression on stage. I earned a BFA in Musical Theatre and then began a career as an actor. I later learned the technical side of the job from being in a band and having to set up and tear down our equipment every night. I took a job as a sound engineer in a high-profile theatre without any prior knowledge of the gear and soon fell in love with the technical process of theatre. I excelled in the job and began my design career not long after. My skills as a composer come originally from writing songs for my band, but they soon grew as I began creating many more styles of music, due to the incredible variety required by specific productions.

The moment that springs to mind was my work on *The Bluest Eye* for Steppenwolf Theatre. That show felt to me like a marriage of design and composition. The compositions were based in Negro spirituals played sparsely with guitar and piano only. They were simple in nature, but were played extremely expressively. We approached the play in seasons, and my compositions were to reflect winter, spring, summer, and fall. What was fun about this was the matching up of what was happening to these characters in the play, and how these seasons felt to them. So when most would think summer would be light and fun, it was actually oppressive and stormy in our show. Because this production had three different runs in three different venues, I was able to tweak the timing and the feel of the music to almost perfection for each venue. In fact, many people didn't even realize that almost the entire show was underscored because the music and sound were so perfectly matched to the production. This experience of marrying design and composition was not only the most rewarding production for me, but also the most informative on how I now approach my work. It's this type of specificity that I strive for in every design, and its grace and subtlety is the crystallization of the elegance that I look for.

JILL DB: I have been very lucky in my career in that I have been able to develop my skills by using them. I began as an engineer and assisted a few amazing designers who taught me many of the skills I needed. For much of my career I have done smaller productions, which allow for more experimentation, more trial and error. These shows generally have smaller budgets, so I am forced to come up with creative ways of making a fully realized design. This has been hugely beneficial in that it has taught me how to think differently and be able to come up with many options, both system-wise and cue-wise. I would also get the chance to work with many different directors and many different types of people, all with vastly different aesthetics. Learning from other designers, directors, and even playwrights is always advantageous.

I think one of the most important experiences in my career was meeting one of my favorite directors, Jeremy Dobrish. He is a director and playwright as well as the artistic director of Adobe Theatre Company. He directed one of the first shows I designed. It was a wacky comedy, and none of the sound was anything close to realistic. Jeremy not only pushed me towards the creation of sound like "if a tiger was a snake—that sound," he would also make me justify my choices. These two lessons have been invaluable throughout my career. To be able to think in an interesting way, not just pull sounds off of a sound effect CD, and to make sure I can justify each choice has made me a better designer.

PHIL L: I developed my skills as a sound designer by becoming a very good sound engineer through a background of radio, music recording, and voice production work and marrying that with a lifelong love of theatre. The defining moment was when someone (and I truly can't remember who it was first) asked me to create sound for their production.

MICHELLE D: As a very young girl, I wanted to be an actress. By high school, I was part of an experimental theatre company in Pittsburgh. Everyone in the company knew I played the piano quite well, since I continually took advantage of playing the Steinway grand in the theatre whenever we had a break. We were working on a production of Buchner's play, *Woyseck*, and I was cast in a very small role as a prostitute and the director, Dennis Aubrey, approached me one day and said there were these "songs" in the play, and since he knew I played the piano, and had such a small role, would I be interested in composing music for the piece? I was shocked by the invitation, yet immediately challenged. "Sure, why not?" I replied, not knowing this was going to be a turning point in my life. A friend at the time told me some composer named Berg (pronouncing it like "burg" as in *Pittsburgh*) had written an opera based on this play and I should "check it out." I went to the music library and asked the librarian, "May I please have a recording of *Woyseck* by Burg?" He tilted his head a bit, and in a most affected manner replied, "You must mean *Wozzeck* by Berg!" "Sure," I meekly answered. I sat at one of those listening stations, took out the first LP of several, put on my headphones and gently put the needle on the record. It never crossed my mind it would be in a foreign language. As soon as the piece began I heard the Captain sing "Langsam, Wozzeck. Langsam." But, because I was so familiar with the play, I understood everything being sung, and not just that. The music. *The music!* It was like no music I had ever heard before. It was incredible. It was perfect. And it was at that moment I knew I had to become a composer! I left the library with an orchestration book, and proceeded to not only write music for *Woyseck*, but also the whole score for orchestra, which my high school orchestra played and recorded for our performances. My entire life had been changed!

ELIZABETH S: I traveled many places studying ethnic music. I acquainted myself with many cultures. Then I began making troupes of kids and other "outsiders" (new Americans, mideasterners, etc.) and myself to learn the music of the raw human intention. In my thirties, I taught myself notation and Western orchestration. I also kept abreast of the rock and roll and jazz scenes. I think a defining moment for me was when I heard a Muezzin sing the call to prayer from a tiny minaret in a small village in Algeria.

259

TOM M: Before I ever worked on a play, I was a good recording engineer and music producer. My goal was to produce albums and I have, to date, produced a lot of CDs and radio shows. My undergraduate degree, however, was in English and dramatic literature. I specifically loved Shakespeare. I never thought at the time that I wanted to work in the theatre, but be more of a Shakespeare scholar. In 1982, Missouri Rep was going to do a production of *Macbeth* and I spent a year trying to get on that show. At the last minute, they agreed, but I had to accept a two-show contract and do another play first. I was green for the theatre but was great with production and sound. The first show was a horrible experience, and if it had not been a two-show deal, I would have never worked on another play again. *Macbeth*, however, was a fantastic experience. Music. Sound. Shakespeare. It all happened for me and I still love it.

RICHARD P: I developed as a composer through formal training and composing as a "sound designer," often by default, because the sound operator was often an inexperienced ASM or an incompetent union hack. In some cases as a composer, I found myself designing the sound system.

TODD B: In my early years at the Oregon Shakespeare Festival in the 1970s, there wasn't a budget for composers. Yet directors needed music, so I would use music that they wanted from LPs. I would then compose additional incidental music in that style. I've always loved getting into other composer's minds and seeing what made them tick. Composing in many different styles honed my analysis and compositional skills. In fact, when I wasn't working I would get up each day and write a short piece in a specific style with a specific mood, like a serene piece in the style of Ravel or a chase sequence in the style of Steve Reich. It was great practice!

MICHAEL H: I came from the recording studio. Those skills (other than playback systems) are a big part of me. One of the best recording skills is the ability of a great recording engineer to work with people at a human level, making them feel at ease, and inspiring confidence. Nobody likes working with egos and we all know there is no shortage of overbearing personalities in theatre. The second thing from the studio is the ability to listen. Critical listening is a skill that best comes from the studio. Critical listening is at the heart of my teaching. You have to be able to discern and comprehend what you are hearing, both technically and at a musical level. I hate "meter-readers"! Pegging the meters isn't a bad thing as long as the result still sounds good and no equipment is being damaged.

DAVID L: I began my theatrical training as an actor. In school, when I wasn't performing in a production, I was usually working on the sound for it. This is the late 70s we're talking about. It wasn't called sound design just yet, at least not in Columbus, Ohio.

After moving to New York in the early 80s, I spent a year or two pursuing work as an actor. I noted that technicians on a production were getting paid, while the actors seldom were. This is off-off-Broadway and showcase theatre I'm referring to. Well, the prospect of earning some kind of income outweighed my need to be seen on stage, so I decided to stop acting and make sound design my specialty.

Sound design became a convenient way for me to combine several of my interests: love of the theatre, fascination with recording equipment, and electronic music. I'd just gotten my first couple of synthesizers in 1983, and I began incorporating them into my designs. At first I used them for special effects—explosions, wind, space ships taking off—pretty conventional stuff. As I started to get involved with more experimental forms of theatre, my work with the synthesizer became more tonal.

In 1985, thanks to an introduction by Deena Kaye, I began working with The Manhattan Ensemble and their director Raymond Marciniak, the person I credit as having the largest influence on my work. For the next four years, I worked with Raymond and the Ensemble on a variety of performances. The greatest thing about working with Raymond was the freedom he gave me. Mistakes were honorable.

BRIAN H: The show where it all came together for me was Ping Chong's *Elephant Memories*, in 1991. It was the show where I felt my apprenticeship was complete. It was wall-to-wall sound and included songs from The Residents and James Brown, with my own complementary music, presented (hopefully) in a seamless form. I used tape, a sampler, keyboards, CDs, and even did live voiceovers. It was great fun and I realized that I knew what I was doing, which was quite satisfying.

DAVID B: My background was primarily as a musician, starting piano at the age of eleven. I played by "ear" as much as possible and really pissed off my piano instructor, but my ear was what I was most comfortable with. In fact, it opened a new world for me. Then theatre nabbed me in junior high and senior high school, with a passion that was unparalleled at that time. I wasn't only doing sound, I was doing everything I could. Concurrently, I played in several rock bands, which I also loved, but theatre really hit me hard. At the time, I knew there were no "real" opportunities in theatre, so I went on to explore my other interests which were biology, electronics, and photography, leaving dreams of theatre behind. As a teacher in two universities, I really shouldn't say this, but undergraduate school really bored me. So I took the cue and fell into an opportunity to build and design a new sound reinforcement company called Mantra Sound. OK, it was my hippie days. In any case, my partner Steve Washburn (an electrical engineer) and I built a funky and *very* nice sounding reinforcement system which we geared toward acoustic musicians. That meant quality (HiFi) first, volume second. So for many years I honed my ears mixing a couple of one-night stands and mini-tours for acoustic acts like Oregon; Gary Burton; Keith Jarrett; Peter, Paul and Mary; David Bromberg; the Hartford, Springfield, and New Haven Symphony Orchestras; and many other bands too numerous to mention. I was doing too much of what we *all* seemed to be doing in the 70s, so I decided to quit the reinforcement business and "settle down."

261

In 1980, I got a call from the Hartford Stage Company and I remember thinking, "Wow! A call from a real theatre!" They asked me to help with the reinforcement for a new musical titled *Is There Life After High School?* In brief, I solved their problems effectively, had a great time, and felt good about the work. I finally had gotten my opportunity to work (even if briefly) in a professional regional theatre.

Then another call came. Mark Lamos asked me to provide sound for another piece at Hartford Stage. This time it was a straight play called *The Portage to San Cristobal of A.H.* So I said, "What kind of help do you need?" He told me that of the twenty-two scenes in the play, twenty of them were set by sound. Did he say, *set by sound?* I remarked to myself that I had never done anything quite like that before, but that it would be a great challenge. So off I went to explore scene sound and incidental music for the production. Well, a challenge it was! I was thoroughly exhausted by the time we finally finished the project, but at the same time, I realized that I had never felt better. After the show on opening night, Mark came to me, hugged me, and thanked me for the contribution to the production. I was exhilarated. He said, "You know, Budries, you're a sound designer." I had never heard the two words put together before. "A sound designer," I repeated to myself.

So from these fragmented beginnings came a nineteen-year exploration that now, in many ways, defines who I am. I have not looked back and I continue to explore the possibilities of designed sound. I'm always learning.

How did you start as a sound designer or composer? Do you have some advice for breaking into the business?

MICHELLE D: When you are getting started, say yes to everything! There is no project too small, and any experience will be of value. Money should not concern you in the beginning. Get a job doing something else, anything else, so you can start building your resumé and creating a demo tape for future propositions. I wrote music for nine plays before I ever made a cent. Trust me, the transition into earning better and better fees will happen. Also, see all of the work of people you most admire. Be assertive and try to meet these people. I first saw a production by Gerald Thomas in 1987 at La Mama in New York and I was awestruck by his work. The music for this play was composed by Phillip Glass, and I learned from reading the program notes that Gerald and Phillip were regular collaborators.

Unintimidated, I wrote Gerald a letter introducing myself as a great admirer of his work, adding quite wryly, "If Phillip Glass is not available for your next project, then please call me!" Well … he did! It took six years, but in 1993, we had our first collaboration and have worked on four additional projects since then.

VICTORIA D: I started sound designing because I had friends who asked me if I could compose music for a play. I thought that it would be fun to marry my theatrical background to what I loved the most: music. From that point on, I've never stopped working, but the point of my life where I truly accepted this as a career was when I assisted a sound designer in a regional theatre. I finally understood what my goals should be. He had so much passion for the art of his work, the organization of his life needed to accomplish that work, and the ability to gracefully express himself collaboratively, that I felt as though I finally understood what it meant to be a sound designer and to have a career doing what I loved. So my best piece of advice is to find the busiest sound designer and ask if you can work as their assistant. That's the best way to see if that's how you want your path to go.

263

PHIL L: As I stated in the previous question, I evolved into it. My advice for breaking into the business is run the other way as fast as you can. As audio equipment gets cheaper and easier to use, sound design will go the way of music engineering. Music studios have been closing in droves the last ten years because musicians can do it all in their basements. In theatre, more and more, directors will feel they can successfully create the sound they want themselves if they're working on a small scale and have a clear vision of their piece. Since that's where designers cut their teeth in theatre it will be more difficult to get the experience needed to advance and the "art form" of sound design, at least, will evolve into nothing more than reinforcement and playing with synthesizers. The reinforcement is much more an artisan's work done by skilled technicians and leave the synthesizers to the composers.

JILL DB: I broke into the business in a very roundabout way. I was studying dramaturgy in college when I went to visit a friend of mine who was stage-managing an off-Broadway play. She went to call fifteen minutes and told me to talk to the sound designer who was standing in the lobby with us. He asked me a few questions and told me that the best way to break into theatre is to do everything you can and meet as many people as possible. This designer, Jim Van Bergen, hired me to assist him on a play during my winter break. I got along well with the theatre company that was producing the show, and they hired me over the summer to do box office and house managing. Over the next year I left school and did everything in theatre from wardrobe to assistant directing. I realized that I like sound the best and got a gig running shows around town. I met David Van Tieghem, who used me as his board op on a few shows. At this point, I was board op-ing at night, and a casting director during the day. I was looking to do sound full-time and asked David if he needed an assistant. He said he wasn't sure if he had enough work to warrant an assistant and I told him that he did need an assistant because I wanted to quit my job and work for him. He hired me for thirty hours to clean his studio; however, the show we were working on propelled him to the forefront of design and he ended up needing me more than he thought he would. I would assist David, who is now my mentor, and run shows to make money. Eventually I got a national tour, quit my board op gig, and went out on the road. I was able to save enough to live for eight months after I got off the tour, so I decided to try designing full-time, and if I didn't make it, I wouldn't starve or get evicted. Being able to devote myself to design and getting my name out there was essential to my career. I would still assist David and take sub gigs around town for extra income, but my focus was on my own designs. I was able to climb the ladder from "a friend's show" to Broadway.

The most important thing I have learned so far is persistence and staying power. If a young designer can figure out a way to stick it out through the lean times, eventually the show will come along that will showcase their skills and set them on the right path. Also, be pleasant. People like to work with other people who are nice and have a good attitude as well as a few options for each sound cue.

MICHAEL H: I was sound designing in high school before I ever knew there was such a title. I was the young geek who always set up sound systems, recorded crickets and thunderstorms, and played in the pit orchestras. Back then, it never occurred to me that it could become a legitimate profession. In college, I was primarily in the music school and spent half of my time in their recording studios but was hired to tour with a university musical theatre review. Four years later I was still with that group and also ended up designing for mainstage musicals and dinner theatre, too. The drama department was always hiring me to fix and rewire the sound systems in their theatres, cut sound effects, and run shows. It was the design faculty that explained to me what a sound designer was, and I've been hooked ever since! I was an avid jazz pianist in high school and always dabbled in composition. I nailed my accompaniment skills playing in pits and did a lot of composing for theatre in undergraduate school. I have always found directors to be eagerly open to having original music. The MIDI revolution happened during my college years and made the possibility of original scores much more accessible and practical. This all came together when I was asked to put the musical *Working* on tape for a mainstage show as music director, performer, and sound designer. I have created ten canned scores since then.

As for breaking into the business, I say that you should always let your passion and art come first and the paycheck will eventually follow. I have learned the hard way never to burn bridges. If you get stuck in a no-win design situation you should always see it through and then never work there again. Having a mentor and returning the favor by being a mentor to someone else really makes the world go round. I have been exceptionally fortunate to have had wonderful mentors— all of whom are still good friends to this day. Their guidance and advice have had profound influence on what I have accomplished in my career so far.

When my students graduate, the last thing I tell them is that they haven't really "made it" until they hire me for a gig!

BRIAN H: I started on the road to sound designer as a volunteer for Ping Chong in 1963. I owned a car and offered to go anywhere to fetch anything. That was more valuable at the time than any real skill I may have possessed. It then turned out that the guy who ran sound couldn't do it for the next show, *A Race*, so I was asked to. On opening night I was given an envelope with a check for $125.00, making me an instant professional.

As a result of that gig, Phil Lee, the sound designer, showed up, liked what I was doing, and offered me a job. I was asked to do the sound for Ping's next show, which was my first. I've been working with sound ever since.

TOM M: I began as a designer working with a crew. I have *never* operated a show, which is unusual. For my students, I see the hardest thing for them is to make the transition from operator/engineer to designer. People need to work hard, think hard, and be positive. Unfortunately, a lot of people only deliver two of the above three.

JIM VB: I began as a musician and actor, and was asked to compose for a show. Along the way, the cursory door buzzer, phone ring, birds, and crickets got added. I found that I really enjoyed doing sound, and that in contrast to what the professors at my undergraduate school had taught, in my opinion, sound design was a very real and satisfying design element which is integral to the theatrical experience.

As for breaking in, I think any student should get a college degree, then apprentice or intern with a designer they would like to emulate and learn as much as they can in a six- to twelve-month period— then try to branch out. It is not an easy life, but it has certain rewards. I also find that being a sound engineer helps tremendously in a designer's awareness and performance, so that is something to do early on.

RICHARD P: Very little advice—"just do it"—it's the experience, not the money, that counts.

ELIZABETH S: I began writing music in college for theatrical productions. I had bands of my own. I stayed loyal to relationships and took risks teaming up with arrangers. I don't encourage students to break in to the business. I tell them there's only time to make what possesses you and what you *must* hear, and work with people who inspire you. Make lifelong artistic friendships and don't be ashamed of a day job.

What was your favorite or most satisfying design or composition? Please tell us a favorite "war story."

JILL DB: It is hard to think of my favorite design, but all of the shows in my top five are shows where the director was really excited about using sound, and integrated it into rehearsal early. They were the most difficult and time consuming, but the most rewarding as well.

I have many war stories, but I think this is one of the only ones I can tell without getting in hot water with someone I may work with again. I was designing a show out of town as part of a festival. It was a show about high school students, and it took place in many locales. The director and I chose lots of current music, which the characters would have listened to, and he choreographed elaborated scene shifts to go along with the music, so the audience would have something interesting to watch while things like desks were being struck and benches brought on. We had our invited dress, and although the playwright had been in most of the rehearsals, she came away from the dress in hysterics. She was appalled that there was so much music in the show, and thought it detracted from her script. The director lost the battle and we had to get rid of a lot of the transition music. This was sad, but the kicker was that the scene shifts still needed to happen, so instead of compromising, the director and playwright were at such odds with each other, the shifts ended up happening in a clunky silence.

PHIL L: Again, my favorite designs were for work I did with Ping Chong and Marleen Pennison. Probably my favorite of Ping's was for a piece called *Nuit Blanche* where there was a sound environment throughout the whole piece that was imperative to the creation of the mood. I enjoyed all of the half-dozen or so designs I worked on for Marleen but the one I remember most clearly was a seven-minute car race I created to which Marleen and one of her dancers performed. Marleen had already created the dance using beats and told me at what points in time certain events had to happen to match the dance. I was able to incorporate various sounds such as the revving of engines, the start of the race, various crashes, and tire squeals to match the timings. It was very exciting mixing that piece, and when I saw it performed I had the same feeling I had with many of Marleen's and Ping's works, that I was an integral part of it and was actually performing along with them.

DAVID L: One of my most satisfying designs was a production of Samuel Beckett's and Jasper John's *Foirades/Fizzles* performed at La MaMa E.T.C. In this production we incorporated body mikes for the three actors, recorded voiceovers, musical composition, and sound design. The body mikes were used not for the purposes of enhancing vocal but to create an invisible wall—a barrier between the performer and audience. The production was highly stylized and presentational. We didn't want the audience "falling in love" with our performers or feeling that they could personally relate to any of the characters. The body mikes kept everyone at arm's length.

One benefit to miking the actors was that once amplified, we could treat the voices in interesting ways. We could place each voice in its own sonic environment. We could place one voice in a deep reverb, add echo to another, and experiment with equalization. The transition from live voices to the recorded voices became seamless. Having everything at line level allowed us to create a really beautiful and rich sonic environment.

My war story: I was working out of town at a regional theatre (somewhat respected, but which shall remain nameless). We had rehearsed the play in New York the previous month and I had been hired to compose music for the production. The play was really dreadful. Lots of long meandering monologues, ridiculously stupid dialogues, etc. My job was to supply a diversion to the text, to give the audience something else to listen to while trying to create a supportive environment for the fiercely talented actors trapped in this nightmare of a production. All my work had been written and approved before we left New York. At the final tech/dress rehearsal, the night before opening, the author shows up. He hadn't been part of the rehearsal process at all. Next morning, I walk into the theatre, eight hours before opening, and I'm informed that all my work, over an hour's worth of music, was being cut from the show. The author hated my work. Couldn't stand the electronics. The only sound cue heard in a three-hour production was one doorbell. I still received my full fee and the play's review accidentally got printed in the local paper's obituary column.

VICTORIA D: In a war story, it's all about the battles. What battles are you choosing to ensure that your artistic vision is accomplished? I only like to choose one or two battles per production in order to never appear demanding and not collaborative. One of my favorite war stories is one that resulted in one of the most satisfying moments in my design career. I was designing *Fiddler on the Roof*, and fighting many battles, trying to impart my aesthetic of enhancement instead of amplification for the production. Luckily, I had a director who was willing to allow me to create the vision I wanted. The conductor and I had a discussion of putting a microphone on the actual fiddler in the show, which I needed to do to make the fiddler pop out over a thirty-two piece orchestra, while he was at the furthest upstage position and also twenty feet up in the air. The conductor was resistant to this idea because he wanted the integrity of the instrument to remain intact. I assured him that this was my goal as well, and eventually just yelled "at least let me try it so you can hear." Thank God I got it right the first time we tried it, and I won the battle. But the biggest moment I did without fighting at all. At this point in the process, I had fought enough and decided to take matters into my own hands without telling anyone. (I don't necessarily agree to this way of working; however, sometimes you have to do what you have to do.) We got to the point in the show where it was time for the Shabbat dinner. We had already determined, after a long discussion with the conductor, that this was one of those places where the orchestra was to be at their quietest. The cast began to sing their prayer, and I took out every single microphone that was on, both for the cast and musicians. The result was the most beautiful moment I remember hearing on stage. A mass of singers heard, as their natural voices would carry in the space, made the moment incredibly reverent and, without the use of any amplification at all, it sounded like perfection.

BRIAN H: I don't have a single favorite experience, although I've enjoyed some shows more than others because the discoveries were more interesting. For example, in two shows with Jeannie Hutchins, we collaborated on songs. She wrote lyrics both to music I had previously written and for music I had yet to write. It was a real thrill to see these things take shape.

Sound design became more fun as I learned how to be more economical. Creating a soundtrack that someone else had to run, eliminating *my* shorthand of methodology, was one of the biggest lessons I learned. It represented a "giving up" of my work to that of the whole that I hadn't yet experienced.

269

RICHARD P: I don't know that they were my favorite or most satisfying, but certainly the two biggest shows soundwise were *Indians* and *Frankenstein*, both on Broadway. A brilliant young FX guy, Bran Ferren, designed the largest (till then) sound system ever on Broadway for *Frankenstein*—sixty-four speakers including subwoofers (earthquake speakers) with three sound men running eight decks for music and FX. For the other show, *Indians*, I experimented with "surround sound," traveling music and FX around the theatre from speaker to speaker. One obviously benighted member of the audience, not in tune with the wave of the future (at least as I saw it), walked over to the speaker nearest him and pulled the wires off. Another incident: the climax of the production was Buffalo Bill's Wild West Show, the action of which was all carefully choreographed to lots of rousing music and crowd noise on tape. With the full cast of thirty about to come on stage, the tape broke! "The rest is silence," as Hamlet once said—although the actors did their best singing and yelling *a capella*.

ELIZABETH S: I have no favorites. I live very much in the present and fall in love with each piece as I work on it. I remember when Serban and I were doing *Good Woman of Szechuan* at La Mama. He decided two weeks into rehearsal that he wanted everything *sung*. So I sat on the third floor of La Mama writing different songs to teach to the actors *as* I wrote them. Then they'd dash downstairs and Andrei would stage the stuff. It was a mad creative assembly line.

JIM VB: Two one-woman shows I have designed, called *Keeping the Word* and *The Handshake*, feature continuous two-track sound designs that are seamless and I'm quite proud of them. The soundtracks include all music, effects, background environments, and scoring for the shows. The entire show travels quite lightly, with few costume pieces and a tiny unit set and a compact MiniDisc player. The performer can fly from locale to locale and perform just about anywhere with a minimum of setup time. The plays are wonderful, meaningful pieces. The huge amount of work that they require in preparation and production is very evident upon close inspection, yet serves the show subtly and smoothly. These are among the projects of which I am most proud, as single, sixty-five-minute cues!

MICHAEL H: I did a production in a thirty-three-seat venue for a theatre company which specializes in avant-garde and new works. The production was *The Shrew*—Charles Marowitz's adaptation of Shakespeare's *Taming of the Shrew*. The production values were set around the design team's interpretation of the Theatre of Cruelty genre, which gave us the ability to break our expectations and social mores surrounding the theatre "experience." My design was, at times, literally painful! I gave the director a cassette with one hundred different sounds ranging from grating industrial to ocean sounds. She picked about thirty of them that she felt had relevance to the production. I composed the show's music and sound score using only these sounds. The net result was a show so powerful and a design so collaborative and integrated that my design was mentioned (positively!) in four reviews.

My war stories all revolve around other production areas that make NOISE! Moving lights, color scrollers, lighting ballasts, rolling scenery, air casters, etc. etc. etc. These are all battles that I usually lose.

MICHELLE D: One of my favorite experiences in the theatre was composing music for *The Oresteia Trilogy* by Aeschylus, directed by Jorge Guerra, Dean of Drama at New World School for the Arts. I was able to hire a children's choir, which was prerecorded along with a battery of synthesizers, as well as six live musicians for the show. For several of the shows I acted as a seventh musician, adding

270

percussion and woodwind elements. For most performances, only one of the three plays was done, but on Sundays the entire trilogy was performed. This made for about six hours of theatre and music. Concentrating for that long and being so intensely involved was certainly a peak experience for me.

This production also brought about an interesting war story. The musicians were onstage and very much a part of the set and action for the entire piece. However, six hours of theatre and music cannot be memorized by the instrumentalist. Therefore, music stands with ample lighting were imperative. The lighting designer kept complaining that the stand lights were getting in the way of his design and especially prohibiting fades to black when the music had to keep playing. We experimented a bit with different gels on the stand lights, but whatever he liked had my musicians complaining that they couldn't see their music and were getting headaches from squinting and straining their eyes for so many hours. We had reached an impasse. The director stepped in and, eventually, with some reblocking and incredible patience from my band, we arrived at a solution we thought everyone could live with. On opening night, the lights go down and the music is supposed to start, but the musicians realize the lighting designer has, without our knowledge, changed the gel on the stand lights to a much darker shade. None of the musicians can see their music! In the panic of the moment they tear the gels off their stand lights, hence making the musician area very well lit, to say the least. This of course impeded all lighting design, and there was nothing to be done until intermission. The gels we had agreed on were substituted, and the second play proceeded as planned. It seemed as if backstage was where the real Greek melodramas were happening.

TODD B: My most recent favorite is the score for the Oregon Shakespeare Festival's production of *Measure for Measure*, which was edited down to seven actors, each playing multiple roles. The production was done in our smallest theatre with a seating capacity of about 140. What was so satisfying was that I was present at almost all of the rehearsals from the first reading on. This allowed me to sit next to the director and have a continual dialogue about the character of music. Each day after the rehearsal I would create cues based on that day's work and also create cues in anticipation of the next day's rehearsals. Every day actors became used to cues, and I would have a chance to try new or modified versions just like the actors would be trying new readings and blocking of their text.

In this particular case, I was creating both music and sound design. The sound effects were derived from "musical sounds" and the musical palette was abstract enough to embrace both music and effects. I chose to work with a modified tone row for the melodic and harmonic content. The textures, or orchestrations, were developed from prepared piano, extended soprano vocals, and waterphones. I collaborated with a soprano who was able to see some rehearsals, then would come into the studio and improvise vocal effects and musical phrases, record musical themes I had composed, and overdub herself to create dense and sensual vocal textures.

My war story: Even though *Measure for Measure* was the most satisfying, complex, and rich project of this season, it was not free from major bumps and challenges. Between first and second dress rehearsals, the director and choreographer decided to cut the opening dance cue by two-thirds! This is a cue that they had been working with for four weeks and musically the cue introduced the character of music and sound. Usually I have no qualms about altering a cue, but this one had been used for so long and all of the other cues in the play referred to it and resonated with it. The original structure was ABAB. The new structure that worked for the choreographer (at least in the number of beats) was BAB and he also wanted some new hits. But if I just used the BAB structure with some new hits, then its musical structure would have no meaning or impact. So ... to make a long story short—in one eight-hour session I rewrote the opening cue and recorded new vocals. It should be mentioned that instrumentally, this cue was the most complex of the lot and used sixteen tracks of musical material, which to rerecord took hours and hours!

At second dress rehearsal we played the cue and it worked perfectly. Though recreating this cue was one of those "all-night pressure cooker" situations and a difficult change to make, ultimately the new, shorter cue allowed us to get to the initial dialogue sooner, which is always my first impulse—start telling the story as soon as possible.

DAVID B: *A Place with the Pigs* (1983) was the first show I designed for Athol Fugard and it was an intense combination of wonderful and scary. It was essentially about what fear can cause you to do. Athol subtitled this piece "a personal parable." It is a rather dark but very interesting piece. In this play, aside from creating general realistic pig atmospheres, I created three pig nightmares to represent the passage of forty years, ten years at a clip. My original goal was to make the pigs laugh demonically at the main character, Pavel, as he slept. This was in reaction to the fact that Pavel treated the pigs very poorly. It was an attempt to have the pigs get back at Pavel for his abuse by giving him bad pig dreams or nightmares. It turned out that I couldn't make the pigs laugh. The sources I had gathered over six hours of "living with pigs" couldn't be manipulated well enough to make believable laughter. But I could make them "talk" and "sing." So I selected 110 pieces of pig vocabulary (from my remote sessions) and turned them into three silly and somewhat grotesque nightmares titled *Volga Boat Pigs, The Piglet Dementia Waltz,* and *Military Pigs.* The result was successful. After that show opened, I got many letters from pig fans and farmers around the country who saw the humor in the grotesque little transitions and requested copies of the nightmares.

Peer Gynt was a tremendous challenge in both scale and content. This Hartford Stage production, directed by Mark Lamos, was six hours in length and was meant to be seen in two parts. It was one of the most exhausting and rewarding experiences I have had in the theatre. One of my favorite sections of the play was the aural realization of "The BOYG," a representation of Peer's inner self. In this scene, Peer comes face to face with his inner self in a rich and scary multilayered experience. Peer was played by Richard Thomas. He and I worked in the studio for many hours recording sources, primarily produced by Richard making sounds with his mouth. I took these elements and others to make eight stereo layers of FX that represented the BOYG. They were played back in eight stereo pairs of loudspeakers, all focused from different locations within the house. It created an exciting ride for the actor and audience. An intense, visceral, and moving experience.

273

How and with whom do you negotiate your contract? What items do you insist on including? Do you maintain the rights to your work?

PHIL L: I never negotiated a contract. I was very happy if the producers had something they could give me at the end of the process.

MICHELLE D: I always negotiate my contract with the producer. NEVER discuss it with the director! Directors will promise you things most producers would have a heart attack over hearing. Always make sure you've spoken to the producer before you start composing and always make sure you have a signed contract before any of your music is used. I have recently started insisting on both a creative fee and a production fee as separate issues to be discussed and negotiated. All too often the producer will say, "I have $5,000 for music." Well, that's great, but is that for me, for my musicians, or for all my other additional costs? Producers don't say to set designers, "I have X amount of money." The set designer is given a fee, and the construction of the set involves another fee. It's about time composers are dealt with in the same way. Insist on separate discussions regarding these two issues or you'll end up using live musicians rather than prerecorded sound, only to make zero money yourself.

I have always kept the rights to all of my music for the theatre. The fees for theatre music are not substantial enough to warrant giving one single note away.

RICHARD P: Generally, you negotiate contracts with producers or general managers. I always try to retain copyright to the score, get copies of all the tapes (if they retain the masters), make sure my billing and any assistants' billing is correct, and work out a deal on free seats to performances. Any show may have an unforeseen future, so either have a clause in there about renegotiations for any other use of the score, or get a good lawyer to go over the whole contract—probably the best idea and worth the 10%. Money-wise, go for a fee plus royalty arrangement.

JILL DB: I use an agent, Seth Glewen at Gersh, to negotiate my contract. There is so much in the contract that I wouldn't even think of fighting for, or have time to fight for. He does a great job, and is also very supportive of my career. He will tell me when he thinks I'm overextending myself, or if there is a director I should work with, and he comes to see my shows and gives me his honest opinion.

BRIAN H: I negotiate my own contracts, which are usually quite simple, and I insist upon getting paid. I also maintain the rights to all of my work by the mere fact that possession is nine-tenths of copyright. At the end of the run, I take all of the tapes, including rehearsal tapes, and head home.

VICTORIA D: I do my own negotiations and contracting. The budgeting of sound is varied and usually does not take into account how expensive it truly is to do this line of work. I feel as though I can try to insist on certain things, but it's not always possible and you walk a fine line with being too insistent and getting what is respectfully due to you. I would hope to have a budget that matches the needs of the production. If there is travel and housing involved, the goal is to have that reimbursed. If there are musicians and studio time, it would be nice if there is money that is completely separate from my fee. There is a teaching process for theatres, so that they understand the supplying of compositions to a production is separate from the design of the show, but this is still very blurry in some theatres. I do retain all rights to my work, and if it is to be used in subsequent productions, there is always reimbursement for its usage.

TOM M: I generally work out contracts with the general manager of the theatre and base them on the USA designer model.

I always maintain my rights. They are not for sale. Unless the theatre has you on as a full-time employee, with health insurance and a pension plan, and they have you sign a document stating that you are doing a work-for-hire as a designer, they do not own it. My contracts usually give them a deal for the design on a remount (lots of *Christmas Carols* show up here) but they have no rights to the design and cannot sell it to another producer. With music, we arrange it so that the composer owns the composition copyright and the sound designer owns the sound recording copyright.

275

MICHAEL H: For me, contractual negotiations have always been with either the producer/executive director or the production manager. I insist on the following:

- The producer will obtain all song clearances
- I get quiet time to set cues before tech starts
- I get equivalent playbill and poster billing with the other designers
- The producer does not own any rights to my material
- A fair design fee—and hopefully studio time reimbursement, too
- 50/50 payment (half on signing of the contract, half on opening)
- Supplies budget

JIM VB: The rights are absolutely imperative in most cases, but the ones where they are *not* include former design elements (i.e., previous designer has cues still in show) and reinforcement designs that have little original sound cues (in my case, the Big Apple Circus is a good example of one of the few clients who "buy and own" my designs outright). Regarding negotiations, I have a lawyer who will negotiate any contract I want, according to my terms, but does not require me to use him for every job. I can forego his expenses, especially on small, favored-nation contracts. Some of the items I insist on in my contract are billing, hold-harmless clauses (equipment), ownership rights, right of first refusal, and royalties for extensions in noncommercial shows.

ELIZABETH S: The contracts for most of my shows at the Public Theatre were signed months after opening. I really need to get paid, so I'm precise about when *that* happens. Other than that, the idea is not to be bought out brain and soul.

When teaching sound design or composition, what do you cover in your curriculum? What exercises or practical experience do you give your students?

MICHELLE D: I tell my students that the first question a composer needs to answer is, "What is the *purpose* of the music for every cue I am composing?" And then, "Is it to foreshadow? Is it to set the period? Is it to invoke memory? Is it to help define or develop a character? Is it to help make the audience laugh? Cry? Is it to cover up that noisy scene change?"

Not only are these questions crucial for a better understanding of the play and what kind of music should accompany each scene or scene change, but also, once you have a clear idea of the function of the music, then you can begin to tackle the next problem—"How do I incorporate all these disparate cues into a score with shape and meaning beyond some isolated music cues?" Ah ha! Now it gets challenging. On a practical note, it is very important for the theatre composer to be well-versed in many musical styles, periods, and genres. Say a play is set in the 1930s. That really gives the composer nothing. Where is it set? In New York, Iowa, Mississippi, Germany, Russia, China, Brazil? Can you imagine how different all these scores would be? Also, are the characters rich or poor? City or country folk? Sane or insane? Every little detail is crucial for determining the appropriate sound world for the play.

VICTORIA D: There are two sides to teaching sound design, the artistic and the technical. You cannot afford to have one without the other. I have exercises that I use to teach the artistic manipulation of an audience. These include terms like natural/abstract, themes, repetition, build and decline, punctuation, time of day, and tension.

The exercises soon show that all of these terms can exist in every cue. The only way to learn them is to do them out of context and then in context. After those ideas are explored, there is then the learning of speeding up or slowing down the flow of a show, the convention of design, how to remind your audience of a moment that happened before, and the overall cohesiveness of the design.

Tuning the ear to hear the sounds that occur in everyday life is essential. Not only do you need that knowledge for realistic settings, you also need to know how to abstract those sounds in an unnatural piece.

The technical learning process encompasses how to work with computer programs to edit and sequence sound files, the set up of your system, creating a speaker plot, choosing the special effects tools you will be using, how you will reinforce specific moments in the play, and, of course, mastering the actual tech process. Plus, one must learn how you discuss your art with others involved in the rehearsal process with you, as well as how you represent yourself in the theatrical community, either to acquire more work or maintain relationships with your peers.

MICHAEL H: I split courses into technology, design, and business. Sound technology must be taught hands-on—you learn by doing. I run classes in digital audio systems and critical listening as part of the technology sequence. In sound design classes, I run exercises in synesthetics (relating sound and color), a story-without-words, radio dramas (with all practical effects), and complete "dry" sound designs. I place much more emphasis on in-class critique and the students' ability to explain their concept rather than on the actual material itself. I stress that designers never speak in sound lingo to the director. I openly discuss design fees, contracts, union issues, how to operate a business, and setting up proper tax structure to survive as an independent designer. I highly favor seminar classes as opposed to traditional lecture classes.

ELIZABETH S: I always have my students write and perform original compositions—whether they want to be composers or not. I encourage them to set poetry and unexpected prose to music. I dare them to do their own staging and choreography, their own arrangements. I want music to be a literary and whole-body experience. I also work a great deal on vocal sounds with my students so their imaginations go past the habitual ideas of recorded media-influenced sound.

TOM M: Since I teach in the same art complex where I design for Missouri Rep, students can study my designs (past and present) and then work in the same production studios and performance space. Our MFA program is based on modeling the experience of teaching hospitals.

JIM VB: My class includes system design, conceptual design, basic studio techniques, and "modern scenarios and sound politics" as major elements. We do not deal with composition at all, and I find that students need to understand how a system works before they know how to edit complex multitrack cues. Students must be able to pass written examinations as well as practical (completing a system flow drawing, and determining the pattern of a microphone, for instance), and projects which include detailed script analysis, full design and cue paperwork, and sound cue selection.

PHIL L: I don't teach sound design and don't believe it can be taught. I don't feel you can teach talent. You either have a feel for it and want to do it or you don't.

278

BRIAN H: I concentrate primarily on getting people to be aware of the way sound alters one's perception of the action. I'll have students read a scene with a variety of backgrounds to show how each affects the action.

I feel the experimental nature of sound, even just to discover various tempi and moods, is often left undone in rehearsal, yet it can really make or break a scene. I find it important that designers, directors, and performers all have the need, but perhaps not the knowledge, to do this kind of investigating, and I should leave them with the knowledge.

DAVID B: I assume that this question relates to conceptual sound design and composition, rather than reinforcement design.

Because there is so much material to cover in a three-year graduate program (including practical design opportunities), the selection of appropriate student candidates is extremely important. Students who possess a balance of compositional skills, basic physical sciences, music/sound technology, and an understanding of theatre are difficult to find. Of course, these are all areas we expand on over the course of the program; however, we can't start from scratch with every student. There simply isn't enough time. There has to be an assumption that some relevant experience has been attained prior to entering the program.

Students are expected to have a musical sensibility. From that base, we teach the students how to use their aural imagination to develop ideas in response to a particular text. This can be a lengthy and difficult process. Engaging one's aural imagination is often complicated by a young student's tendency to think about their ideas (or conceive their designs) backwards, starting with a sound delivery system. This process may seem practical, but it often limits the possibilities before you get started. The design of a physical delivery system should be in response to the artistic goals of the production. It is important to encourage or engage the creative process without physical limits. Once an appropriate set of creative responses has been articulated, the goal becomes "realization" or the creation of rough drafts for presentation to the director. In this part of the process, we now attempt to define how a sound might be presented to the audience in a three-dimensional theatre space. We ask questions such as: Is the sound "source specific" (identifiable to a single location only, e.g., a phone ring)? Is the sound representing an external influence? Is the sound representing an internal conflict? Is the sound a transition? Is the sound a framing cue? Is the sound an underscore? Does the sound define a physical space or time? Does the sound describe an imaginary space and time? Answering these questions helps to define an aural palette for the production as well as a manner of distributing that sound to an audience in an appropriate manner. The production budget and other practical considerations can now influence the design. At this point, you may have to get *very* creative in order to execute your ideas faithfully. It should be understood that the development of these ideas isn't done in a vacuum. Regular collaboration with the design team and director is essential for success.

I attempt to explore students' aural imagination through exercises which are designed to make the students "think" in sound and music. Students are given a word or simple phrase, such as "New York" or "hot," which they must respond to with music or sound (text to aural conversion). In the introductory classes, these responses may be composed or found. In the advanced classes they must all be composed. We also view "art objects" (visual to aural) and explore similar responses from each student. In another exercise, I play a musical example and ask the students to draw something that they "see" in the music (aural to visual). I will also play a variety of music excerpts and discuss potential meanings implicit in the sound or music. Text excerpts for many plays are also explored and roughly designed. In the later classes, more advanced creative tasks are assigned and production problems are posed and solved.

Advanced problems are solved, including a sound cue listing, hook-up, ground plan, and section with delivery system components articulated.

You must give the students practical opportunities to design or compose music for productions. This is the most important vehicle in the learning process. Students are assigned three full production designs during each of their three years in the Yale School of Drama program. Additionally, students may elect to design other smaller productions for director workshops or the Yale Cabaret. This represents as many as six designs a year (while in school). These productions offer necessary opportunities for exploration and development of personal skills. Verbal skills must also be developed in order to ensure regular and appropriate communication between design team members and directors. Additionally, the professional alliances you make at this time can become the foundation for development of a successful career in the theatre world.

Of course once you develop your ideas for a production, you must find practical ways to realize them (in a production studio or with live musicians) and ways of presenting those ideas to the audience (through the sound delivery system). I feel it is most effective to learn how to use these production tools through a combination of introductory lectures and practical assignments. Play excerpts are used to create a context for the practicals. Using these exercises, we provide learning experiences in: on location source gathering; stereo and multitrack music recording; SFX recording; microphone technology and techniques, including RF systems; loudspeaker technology and techniques, including focused arrays and distributed systems; amplifier technology and techniques; mixing desk operations, including routing, EQ, matrices, balancing, automation, inserting devices, mixing in layers; playback devices, including CD, MiniDisc, samplers, DAWs; signal processing devices, including outboard EQs, compressor/limiters, delay-based effects processors, artificial reverberation, MIDI, and more.

I encourage students to take elective music classes in composition, history, or performance (as appropriate to the individual). Electronics and acoustical architecture are also important classes providing necessary background information for practical work in the theatre. These electives provide exposure and balance to the program.

And I wish this had been available when I was going to school.

JILL DB: I have taught master classes and been a guest lecturer. Many of my classes have been for stage management students, and some have been for general theatre classes, which include actors and design students. In the stage management classes I will often go over what is expected of a stage manager to benefit sound designers. I will explain the importance of the rehearsal reports, how they are our lifeline to the daily ins and outs of the production, script changes, new cues, the general vibe of the show. I will also walk them through an SFX or QLab program, so they know how the designer is working, and how to think when calling cues. With this knowledge, they will know what they can ask for: cues built together, timings for fades, and anything else that will make calling the show easier and smoother. I will also share pet peeves of mine and many of my colleagues, and what we look for in a good stage manager.

What do you perceive as the most significant changes in theatre sound technology in the past ten years? Has the advent of digital sound changed the way you work? What's been overrated? Are there advantages to how things "used to be"?

DAVID B: Fortunately, we have seen many significant technological advances that have provided enormous benefits to the execution of professional sound designs. They include highly accurate loudspeakers with a variety of dispersion patterns, powerful amplifiers, better wireless microphone technology, sophisticated mixing systems, automation, smart analysis tools, etc. If I *had* to narrow down to the most significant technological advances for my style of design, it would be the digital audio workstation (audio computers, in general) tied for first place with digital sampling. These devices have provided me with the most important set of creative tools to realize what is in my mind's ear. The intention of my work hasn't changed significantly; however, the ease of creation, development, control, documentation, and archiving is truly incredible. I can't imagine how I worked prior to the development of these tools. Actually I *can* imagine and I'm very glad to be the beneficiary of these advances. With these devices, I have finally been able to adapt immediately to developments in a production, almost in real time. That means I can be a better collaborator and constructively influence the course of a production. As a creative person, this is very important to me. The future holds even more promise as control automation gets even faster and operators become accustomed to that style of working.

RICHARD P: I think the advent of samplers, computers, DAT, and MiniDiscs has helped a lot technically. Nevertheless, the bottom line is the musical raw materials we work with, and no amount of state-of-the-art sound equipment can write a good score.

MICHAEL H: At first, I would say the most significant change is automation, but automation has been out there (i.e., Richmond) for years now. I think two areas of growth have affected me most. First is a significant increase in speaker technology—speakers have tighter coverage, higher efficiency, smaller size, and greater accuracy than just ten years ago. Second is the digital revolution.

There is a new generation of sound designers out there who really have no grasp of the art they are creating. To them, sound design is about the toys. I am just as comfortable working in a ninety-nine-seat equity waiver house with two cassettes or a LORT-B house with everything. For dramas, it really is the thought behind and the content of the show tapes that count. I can honestly say that I really miss reel-to-reels and the ritualistic nature of editing, cleaning, and aligning the deck!

BRIAN H: The changes of the past decade have enabled audio playback to be achieved as easily as the lighting. I think the one technological advancement for playback in theatre that affects me the most is the MiniDisc player. Cheap, accessible, with great sound (and no telltale *kerchunk* to give away the cues).

VICTORIA D: The most significant change is the ease in which one can manipulate sound during the technical process. The ability to be as fast, if not faster than the rest of the design team has fundamentally changed how I work and how I approach design technically. Before, if I had a storm cue that was being played back on reel to reel, the changing of where a crack of thunder happens in the storm would be a long and involved process that I would not be able to produce in context until the following day. I would be up all night hoping to get it right for the next day. Now I keep my effect cues separate in my computer programming of a show, and, as a result the changing of a placement of a thunderclap is quick and easy. It makes it possible for my design to remain fluid and change in real time with the production, instead of holding things back, and to specifically punctuate the action on stage with my sound.

What sometimes seems overrated to me is the dependence on a huge amount of microphones and outboard gear to create a sound that could be captured much more simply and effectively. Sometimes, there is beauty and simplicity in just having one microphone in a room to record a band live the way they would sound to one set of ears. This is a technique that I still incorporate into my recording and it's a series of questions that I always consider when creating sound systems. Do I really need all this gear? Is there an easier, more elegant way? It's always worth asking.

PHIL L: The most significant changes are amplification, most specifically overamplification, and it's terrible. Since I'm still working in the field of sound, I can say that digital recording has changed the way I work phenomenally. It makes the work much easier than it was with analog and the possibilities much greater. It takes much less skill and is much less satisfying. As an engineer, although I would never go back to analog, I miss the tactile experience of handling audio tape, the satisfaction derived out of making a perfect edit using a razor blade and the thrill of doing punch-ins knowing that if your finger hit the record button a moment too early what was recorded previously was erased and the only fix was to re-record. As a studio owner, I love the fact that where it used to take me six months to train a new editor, today everyone who comes to me is computer-savvy and able to use Pro-Tools to a certain extent. It takes, at most, four weeks to get an editor up to speed.

TOM M: For sure, the most significant change is the digital audio workstation. CDs and MiniDiscs are nice, too. I got started in the age of the tape recorder, using many decks, and working in multitrack. Digital audio workstations are so much faster and allow much more creativity. When I did *Three Tall Women*, it was only improvised piano for the scene changes. I recorded piano straight to fifteen IPS analog tape, backed up on DAT, and used the master analog recording as the show tape. Sounded nice, but I don't think it sounded better than if I had put it into ProTools and played back from MiniDisc. I used analog just for the fun of it, keeping things exciting!

MICHELLE D: While sampling and music synthesis have opened up whole new frontiers for composers, there is definitely less *human* contact involved in the making of music. Composers have always needed isolation when writing music, but now, since they are also playing all the parts, the idea of coming together with others to make music has taken a back seat. Budget considerations haven't helped this either.

JILL DB: The most significant changes over the last ten years have been in playback systems and laptops. When I began my career, reel-to-reel was very rare but still in use, although most theatres were using cassettes, CDs, and MiniDiscs. This made for very long days in tech. I would sit in tech all day, with all of the options I could bring, and try them out in tech. If a cue needed to be longer, or something entirely different, I would take a note and work on it at home on my desktop after tech. Needless to say, I didn't get much sleep during those days. Once laptops became the norm, I was able to take care of many notes during tech, but I still relied on an operator who (hopefully) had some skill. Depending on the person, the fade times would always be different, and I was limited to four or five MiniDisc players. This would force me to come up with some creative editing for more difficult shows. When SFX and, later, QLab came on the scene, many theatres were dubious, but once the system was in place, it became possible to do anything. Sound could fly around the room, as much sound as I wanted could come from as many sources as I wanted, and a lot of editing could be done with the click of a button. It made the possibilities endless, and I was able to bring in any sound I thought I might need and load it up on the computer and edit it on the spot. Needless to say I got more sleep. Digital technology has given sound design the ability to be more creative and limitless.

I don't think that there is much reminisces for the way things used to be as far as playback is concerned. I do find the need to reinforce actors in smaller and smaller spaces disconcerting. I think that actors have become more accustomed to film acting and can sometimes forget that projecting ten rows to the back of the house is not that big of a challenge.

JIM VB: The digital audio workstation has made *major* changes in the way we create sound effects, and has made a huge impact. Digital has trickled down to make things much more affordable for mass markets, but the big shows have gotten extremely complex and are unbelievably expensive. Yet, a producer does not want to spend the same money for a sound designer's fees and the weekly rental that is spent for scenery, costumes, or lighting.

Something I find quite overrated is the importance we place on technology as a society. I can make a system of cheap gear run with old analog tape cues sound just as good as the latest gear with all-digital signal path. Tools should be unimportant. Technology should be of less concern than it is. Choosing to do theatre sound means you have a method, a reason, and a desire to do something different. The tools are simply that—tools. The tools matter so little. It's what we do with them and how we look at doing things that will make an impact. The theatre embraces noble ideas, and I feel we need to teach that to our students.

DAVID L: There was a time in New York during the early 90s when it seemed every theatre's reel-to-reels weren't working properly or were outright broken and all anyone had for playback equipment was cassette decks. Not my favorite period to look back on.

I'm very happy that the MiniDisc player came along to fill the role of reliable playback medium. I can do about 90% of my editing in the theatre with those decks. They're fast, dependable, inexpensive, and they honestly sound superb. As a rule, I absolutely detest the idea of audio data compression, but I have to admit that for theatre work, the advantages of the medium far outweigh any philosophical objections I may have regarding how audio gets recorded.

I cut my teeth on reel-to-reel and I'm very proud of my tape editing abilities. At heart, I'm an analog kind of guy. The advent of digital audio has certainly made many things much easier. Nondestructive editing is really quite wonderful. But I do strongly caution against the idea that digital is necessarily better. Analog tape is a mature medium. The decks work great (if serviced regularly) and walking into anyone's studio ten years ago, you could pretty much find your way around. Mixing consoles were of a uniform, conceptual design as were the tape decks. Today, all digital audio software does fundamentally the same thing, but the user interfaces are less than intuitive. The problem with digital audio is that it's no longer in its infancy stage. It's more of a precocious teenager who demands to be given much more responsibility than it's capable of reliably handling. The computer is a very hostile environment for audio. Things get lost, moved, or corrupted. There are few things in my professional life more annoying than my computer asking me "Where is audio file 23?" *I don't know. You had it last, wha'djya do with it?* And just as you've figured out version 6 of your software, here comes version 6.2 that promises to fix the bugs in the previous version while it inadvertently creates new ones. Document as much as possible and make two backups of absolutely everything, is my advice.

We're making our machines go faster and faster and creating software that taxes more of a CPU than the IRS would dream possible. Life's not easy on technology's bleeding edge. But my biggest complaint by far is not having a reliable long-term storage medium. I recently pulled some ten-year-old quarter-inch masters off the shelf to have a listen. The tapes sounded absolutely wonderful. In perfect condition. I have DAT tapes less than three years old that sound

285

horrible. There are drop-outs, tracking problems. They're unplayable. Fortunately, the cost of burning a CD-R is now a feasible and affordable mastering alternative. That is until we standardize higher sampling frequencies of 96 kHz at 24 bits and I have to remaster all my old 44.1 kHz 16-bit recordings for the sake of potentially better sounding fade-outs.

Would I go back to the old way of recording? What?! And miss out on all this fun?

What one piece of equipment do you depend on the most?

MICHAEL H: I hate to say it, but it is the computer. My cue sheets, source material, mixes, effects, research, and drafting all involve a computer now. The computer is now the mixing console, effects processor, multitrack, and CD-R burner.

MICHELLE D: I depend mostly on my computer and sequencer. However, I usually begin my compositional process at a desk, work my way to the piano, and then end up at the computer.

TOM M: Today, it is the ProTools (digital audio workstation). That is what I work with for building cues. I am very flexible about what I have to work with in the theatre for playback. I think that high-end, expensive playback equipment tends to be overrated.

VICTORIA D: My MacBook Pro connected to the Internet, and my external hard drives, which are loaded with sound effects and samples.

PHIL L: ProTools and a computer.

BRIAN H: Besides the MiniDisc player, the sampler and digital workstation have made things like looping a designer's dream rather than a nightmare.

DAVID L: My ears. Other than that, not much. When I'm hired for a job, one of the first things I ask for is an inventory list of the theatre's sound equipment. If all a theatre owns is a cassette deck, an amp, and a speaker or two, then that's what I'll design for. Obviously, if tightly timed events are required (such as gun shots), or things have to happen with any real precision, then there's going to be a problem. If the needs of the production can't be realized with the equipment available, then it's my job to make recommendations as to what needs to be rented, borrowed, repaired, or whatever. Then there are those times when I think, "Wouldn't it be great if we could do this or that? If only we had a ..." and I'll look at what I've been given for a budget, talk about it with the director, and see what can be done about it.

Besides considerations about the equipment, probably the most valuable thing I could ask for would be a competent and enthusiastic sound operator. They're the ones who will be living with the production on a nightly basis after the show has opened. It's important that they feel the show is their own and that they're given some sort of a personal stake in the production.

TODD B: My imagination. In terms of electronic hardware, the most flexible and useful piece of gear I have is my hard disk recorder/editor. It has allowed me to artfully redesign cues in minutes while keeping the integrity of the music and sculpting it to fit the rhythm of the scene.

JIM VB: That gray matter between my ears. Nothing is as valuable as knowing how to handle a situation or people. Second to that, I like a sense of humor. Third, a sense of perspective. Gearwise, the technical thing I really depend on the most is a set of reference sounds (not music, though I use that, as well), but tones of gain, frequency, and phasing information. Because when setting up a system, the gain structure has to be perfect, or it's not worth doing. And once I have a flawless system with an ideal gain structure, my job gets a *lot* easier.

JILL DB: I depend on my laptop, and by extension of this, my editing software and hard drives. I think that it might be a tie between that and a digital playback system.

RICHARD P: The pencil.

ELIZABETH S: The human spirit.

No More Feedback: A Sound Reinforcement Forum

The art and craft of designing sound for theatre and entertainment has many faces. For those of us that focus our art on creating pre-recorded sound and music, sound reinforcement designers are like a second cousin. We know them a little and they are related to us, but we really don't know what they do or how they do it. To truly explain their world, we would need to write another book. However, an excellent starting point to understanding this discipline can be found by reading the answers to the following questions poised to some of the leading designers in this field.

In this forum, we focus on the kind of work that is typically associated with musicals, spectacle, and other large-scale entertainment venues. This work combines elements of conceptual sound design and sound reinforcement engineering. These productions generally work with larger budgets and require a significant amount of labor. As you'll read, along with this expansion of responsibilities comes a greater need for a good sense of production politics. The professionals that we polled have an enormous range of practical experience. Or, we could say, a "dynamic" range of experience.

THE SOUND REINFORCEMENT DESIGNERS

Tom Clark has been a theatrical sound designer for 26 years. He is the founder of Acme Sound Partners, nominated in 2008 for the first-ever Tony Award for excellence in Sound Design of a Musical (*In the Heights*), winner of the 2003 Drama Desk Award for Outstanding Sound Design (*La Bohéme*), and the 2001 Entertainment Design Magazine EDDY Award for excellence in theatrical sound design. Acme's designs include the Broadway and National Touring productions of 2008 Tony Award-winning Best Musical *In the Heights, Legally Blonde, A Chorus Line, The Drowsy Chaperone, Dirty Rotten Scoundrels,* 2005 Tony Award-winning Best Musical *Monty Python's Spamalot,* 2004 Tony Award-winning Best Musical *Avenue Q,* and *The Full Monty,* among others. Acme has designed all of the New York Shakespeare Festival's productions at the Delacorte Theatre in Central Park since 2001. Mr. Clark taught sound system engineering and theatrical sound design at the Yale School of Drama and served as resident sound designer for Yale Repertory Theatre from 1987 to 1989.

Originally from England, **Jonathan Deans** has focused his work on the live entertainment side of sound. In London, he worked at Pye and Morgan recording studios in London and the Royal Opera House in Covent Garden. Later, in the West End as mixing engineer and then as sound designer, his sound design work included *Mutiny, Time, Blood Brothers, Kiss Me Kate, Jean Seberg*, and *On Your Toes*. After moving to America, he started work on different forms of live entertainment that needed to have a more soundscaped and dynamic approach. This led to sixteen years of work with Cirque du Soleil on productions such as *LOVE, KA*, and *Zumanity*. His productions for Broadway have included *Young Frankenstein, Lestat, Seussical*, and *Fosse*. Jonathan continues to teach sound design at UCLA.

290

Peter Hylenski's Broadway credits include *Shrek, Cry Baby, The Times They Are A-Changin', The Wedding Singer, Sweet Charity, Martin Short: Fame Becomes Me, Little Women, Brooklyn*, and *Laughing Room Only*. Other credits include *Le Reve* at Wynn Las Vegas, *Ragtime* (London's West End, Olivier Award nomination for Best Sound Design), *Walking with Dinosaurs, Mame* (Kennedy Center), *Opening Doors* (Carnegie Hall), *Applause* (Encores!), *Princesses* (Goodspeed), *Annie, Children's Letters to God, Go, Diego, Go!, Dora the Explorer, Ovations!*, and the *Spoleto Festival* (1999–2002).

Tony Meola's many Broadway credits include *The Ritz, Laugh Whore, Wicked, Man of La Mancha, Sweet Smell of Success, Copenhagen, Kiss Me, Kate, Footloose, The Lion King* (Drama Desk Award), *The Sound of Music, Steel Pier, A Funny Thing Happened on the Way to the Forum, The King and I, Moon Over Buffalo, Smokey Joe's Café, Guys and Dolls, Five Guys Named Moe, She Loves Me, The Red Shoes*, and *Anything Goes*.

Otts Munderloh has worked with Michael Bennett, Bob Fosse, Mike Nichols, Gower Champion, and Jerome Robbins. His many Broadway shows include *Harold and Maude, The Glass Menagerie, Big River, Dreamgirls, Hurlyburly, The Real Thing, Sophisticated Ladies, Whoopi Goldberg, Ain't Misbehavin', A Day in Hollywood — A Night in the Ukraine, Barnum, The 1940's Radio Hour*, the revival of *Sweet*

Charity, The Search for Signs of Intelligent Life in the Universe. The Front Page, Cabaret (1986 Joel Grey revival), *Macbeth* with Christopher Plummer and Glenda Jackson, Jerome Robbins' *Broadway, Tru, Grand Hotel, The Secret Garden, Crazy for You, Jelly's Last Jam, Ain't Broadway Grand,* and *Passion.* Other projects include Edwin Drood at the New York Shakespeare Festival's Delacorte Theatre, Brooklyn Academy productions of *The Gershwin Celebration, Nixon in China,* and *The Gospel at Colonus.*

Brian Ronan has designed the Broadway productions of *Curtains; Spring Awakening; Grey Gardens; The Pajama Game; All Shook Up; Twelve Angry Men; "Master Harold"...and the Boys; The Look of Love; The Boys From Syracuse; Fortune's Fool; The Tale of the Allergist's Wife; The Rainmaker; You're a Good Man, Charlie Brown; Little Me; Cabaret; Triumph of Love; 1776;* and *State Fair.* Regionally Brian has designed *A Christmas Carol* (McCarter Theatre); *Wild Party, Time and Again,* and *newyorkers* (Manhattan Theatre Club); *Into the Woods* (Ordway, St. Paul, MN); *Bleacher Bums* (Royal George Theatre of Chicago, IL); and *A Little Princess* (Theatre Works of Palo Alto, CA). Off-Broadway designs include *10 Million Miles* and *Bug,* for which he won an Obie and the Lucille Lortel awards.

291

SOUND REINFORCEMENT DESIGNERS' QUESTIONS

What do you consider to be the primary function or goal of your sound designs? (This seems like a "duh" question, but we are curious to know if there are any subtle or significant philosophical differences between designers.)

BRIAN R: To allow the writers, composers, players, and actors to sound their best in a way that compliments the style of the specific show I've been hired for.

JONATHAN D: It has to interest me. I need to be a part of the creative team or at least feel I am.

TOM C: With respect to musical theatre sound reinforcement, I am part of the team to make sure that words and music are heard with equal quality and loudness by all members of the audience.

TONY M: To assist in telling the story.

OTTS M: Non-offensive amplification.

PETER H: My designs strive for two goals: the first is adding depth and realism to a scene. Much like a lighting designer might emulate key light sources to add realism, sound designers can also add touches such as sound effects and reverb to further convey to the audience a realistic aural setting. The second goal of my designs is to appropriately extend the energy of the performance to the listener through reinforcement. By "appropriately" I mean fitting to the musical genre. I wouldn't approach a design for an orchestral piece the same as a rock musical. The foundation for each of these goals is storytelling through the use of sound.

Are there different design styles or approaches when creating a sound reinforcement design?

TONY M: Yes, of course. Elton John's music requires a different approach than, say, Richard Rodgers. Electronic instruments became part of the music in the 60s. I remember my father saying on opening night of *Les Mis*, "I liked it except for the rock and roll music". Rock influences were so common by then that it never occurred to me that *Les Mis* is a rock musical, but it really is.

TOM C: Some projects want to seem as unamplified as possible, others require significant overt amplification. Most often the musical style sets the tone. If the size, shape, or acoustic personality of the auditorium is the only reason amplification is required, subtlety is the order of the day. Modern works sometime defy mainstream stylistic categorization, in which case the creative team has to determine the level and obviousness of the amplification. Technological choices follow stylistic choices.

BRIAN R: Every time I approach a musical, I try and wipe the slate clean and respond to the script, the size of the theatre we're playing, the budget, and the style of show we're doing. I try to determine what role the sound will play in the performance. This translates into what speakers to use, what mixing board to order, how many mics, etc. The approach to a play is similar. It's just that musicals require much more pre-planning and generally much more work.

PETER H: Absolutely, I uniquely tailor my systems to the material it is purposed for. The amount and type of loudspeakers for a pop type show can vary greatly from a show requiring only subtle reinforcement. Which microphones I use in the pit and the technique for placing them on each instrument is guided by the style of the show.

JONATHAN D: Yes, although they may use the same basic equipment, the intention and application can be quite different.

In the past, some directors or producers have felt that sound reinforcement design is all craft or technical and isn't an artistic endeavor. What do you feel is your balance between the "art" and "craft" of design?

TOM C: We are called on to make an endless series of choices, both predictive and reactive, as we hack our way toward opening night, solving literally thousands of problems along the way. I think most of the art comes from making the process unobtrusive and carefree for the production. We are sometimes applications inventors—A-B Systems, mics mounted on actor's heads, dynamic insert or system delay to enhance localization, etc., and we are sometimes able to provide an audio system solution for a story-telling challenge such as a subtle reverberation effect that accompanies a purple light that connotes an otherworldly character. Most of all, though, we are collaborators, appending our expertise to the shared artistic vision of the creative team to make the final product better than it would have been without us.

293

BRIAN R: I lean more to the craft camp myself. There are indeed choices made while mounting a production that are purely artistic— they respond to inexplicable emotional needs. A perfectly placed sound cue or a harmony so well balanced it gives you shivers is as artistic to me as a well-designed hat. However, I think the utility of a working sound design satisfies the strictly commercial needs of a production more so than the other design disciplines. I think the road to becoming a sound designer creates a culture of craft more than art. Very few lighting designers, for instance, have spent a great deal of their professional lives acting as electricians. Set designers aren't required to know the craft involved with moving their lovely scenery around. Most sound designers, on the other hand, have been professional board ops for some time in their career. Me, I can supply your soundscape but, if need be, I can solder your headset so that it works again. I believe the term "blue collar artist" applies perfectly to sound designers.

TONY M: I don't know these directors and producers that you refer to. I think it is difficult for a scenic designer to design without having first a knowledge and ability to paint a picture. It's the same with sound.

PETER H: Sound in general, whether recorded or live, has often straddled this fine line. There are theories and formulas and laws of physics that we follow, but our end product must still relate to the heart of that particular show. In a way, we can equate ourselves to a record producer. We are facilitating the technical requirements of the production, while infusing our own artistic taste along the way.

JONATHAN D: I feel that you should run away from these directors and producers. This is an archaic point of view, which belongs to the archaic producers, general managers, and directors. So thinking that you are going to be able to work with them is misguided.

294

Is there a particular part of the design process that is more difficult than another? Please consider any of the following: system design, the politics, working within a budget, RF congestion in urban environments, the communication system, sound effects production, and other issues.

PETER H: I think the most challenging part of designing is departmental integration. As a sound designer, there is still a bit of voodoo surrounding our jobs. Explaining why you need a speaker in a specific place, or why you need "that many" can become frustrating. So much of our work is not tangible which makes it difficult for others to grasp basic concepts like speaker coverage angles. Luckily, as our department evolves we are able to educate those we work with, so with a bit of patience these growing pains should work themselves out.

TOM C: The biggest challenge differs from show to show, sometimes between different productions of the *same* show. Everything has to be right in the end, and the more quietly you get it all that way, the more popular you will be.

OTTS M: These days, the politics.

BRIAN R: The hard part for me is dealing with the many layers of ego and politics that come with the pressure of mounting a production. This pressure can come from various directions. I think that every production has a soul of its own and a distinct personality. One show may have frustrating budgetary constraints, one may have a very insecure director, one may have a diva bass player who calls in the union rep because the percussionist he sits in front of is too loud or a star who feels their performance is being compromised. These are the intangible, unsolvable issues that require bedside manner and support that are often difficult to summon amidst the stress of creating a show.

There is no technical facet of a sound design that I find more difficult than another.

JONATHAN D: The design process does not involve budgets, RF, comms and these common or utility services. These items are things that we just have to deal with in the same manner that a choreographer has to have a bottle of water, jock strap, and band-aids for their feet. If you are thinking of budgets or utility equipment during the sound design, you will probably miss your design opportunities. The most difficult part for me is the conceptual design as it is at this point you commit to the intention and use of your equipment for the entire production. Perhaps a bit like a painter who has to decide on the size of the canvas and what type of paint to use.

295

TONY M: Politics. It's the thing that I dislike more and more as I get older.

Are there any "golden rules" to follow when designing sound reinforcement?

TONY M: First, try to make the sound come from the performer. Second, the more you put between the actor and the audience, the more you take away from the live experience.

JONATHAN D: Experience, so you can go with your first impression or hunch.

PETER H: It may sound clichéd, but use your ears! Remember that we are aural storytellers—if a particular method isn't quite giving you the moment or the excitement you heard in your head, don't be afraid to experiment and try something different.

BRIAN R: A wise man once told me that to be considered a good sound man, make sure the paging system works and the intercom is clear and buzz-free. The rest is subjective. I'd also add that in terms of what the audience needs to hear at a musical—that no one ever stormed up to the box office and demanded their money back because they couldn't hear the oboe. By this I mean there are many important elements to the sound of a show that require emphasis, but if the words are lost to the audience, all the storytelling falls apart.

TOM C: Don't work against the goals of the production. Highly visible microphones between the eyes of actors wearing period costumes being a classic example of what *not* to do.

Do you have regular contact with the director or producer? If so, what are their chief objectives or concerns?

TOM C: This varies with each production. We are there to serve—sometimes that means regular conferences with the director, sometimes it just means a greeting at the beginning of the day and a good night at the end.

TONY M: Yes. Usually that what is being done onstage and in the pit is what is being seen and heard clearly in the audience.

OTTS M: Absolutely, producers, budget, audience complaints, directors—countless concerns.

JONATHAN D: Yes, I have contact with directors. Their main concern is that you bathe and look like someone they can be seen with.

BRIAN R: I'm the worst schmoozer in the business. I hang in the back and quietly get my work done. I wait till the director's not busy and ask my questions or impart a concern. My contact with the director is based solely on how much she or he needs to be kept inside my decision-making process. This is different for every director. I just make sure they know I'm available to them.

Producers I avoid at all costs. I don't recommend this as a career tool. Instead I'd suggest you learn to play golf, go sailing, or whatever it takes to get producers to know you. You'll probably get more work than me. I don't mean to be glib in my answer, it's just that I'm not confident in my ability to "sell" my work. That being said, I'm often forced to deal with the producer due to proximity. The sound board is usually located in the back of the house and on successful shows there is no place for the producer to sit, so we often inherit them.

PETER H: We certainly have contact with both the director and producer. I find that the director is developing the show on a daily basis, refining the storytelling, so as a designer you are collaborating with them regularly on each small detail of the production. If I had to generalize, I'd say that the producers are interested in more of the big picture. Most producers will talk to you about the overall sound of the show, its final volume level or maybe ask you to help out a particular character. I say "most" because there are exceptions who might put input into every detail of what you do!

How much variance is there in how a director might approach a production?

OTTS M: More than there are productions of the same show.

JONATHAN D: Massive, from zero input to where you want to shoot them because they do not leave you alone. Either type of director does not mean that they do not care or understand sound design.

PETER H: Just as each director has a unique way of speaking with the cast and conveying his/her desires to them, the same holds true for sound design. There are some who understand the mechanics of what we do, and can express in clear terms what he/she is looking for in a particular moment of the show. Some will simply list what sound effects they want where, while others will get more involved and may actually have mix suggestions.

TONY M: A great amount. I hate when they use the word, "cinematic." It ain't the movies.

BRIAN R: Huge variance. In terms of sound, particularly musicals, different directors have their areas of focus. Some are very concerned and therefore vocal about instrumentation. Postshow note sessions will consist of very specific direction in what instruments need to be heard and when. Others leave all that to the sound and music department to fight about and trust they'll get what they want in the end.

Some directors lean on the actor hard to deliver all nuances of a performance, some rely on their technical staff to fill in. In my case, a weaker singer may become my problem to fix.

Probably the largest difference between directors' approaches to sound in a production is their tolerance for imperfection. I think sound is the element that takes the longest to gel. No matter how much money we spend on gear, it still comes down to clean operation. The sound mixer bears that burden more than anybody on the technical staff. Directors have very different limits of patience for the inevitable "growing pains" of a sound design.

I've had the great fortune to work not only with some great directors but to work repeatedly with them. Like all relationships, trust is an earned process. My third experience with a director can be much different from my first. Hopefully the trust is earned. With all they need to deal with, a director basically wants to know that their best interests are being looked after and their vision is being supported. The specifics of good sound can be hard for some to articulate and that results in varying forms of communication.

TOM C: With respect to sound, it is somewhat unusual to find that a director has a particular point of view other than wanting to hear the words clearly and have the music sound right for its style. There is more variety in the director's interest in the nature of sound effects than of amplification. Except of course for the dead person reverb thing.

Does the director ever make a request that goes against your better judgment? Can you provide an example and the resolution?

PETER H: Sure, I think this happens in all departments. Sometimes, however, it turns out that the director's request wasn't so farfetched after all and your "better judgment" maybe was a bit extreme. I usually approach these situations in one of two ways. First, if it isn't going to hurt anyone to try it, then I'll give it a go. Often the only way to prove your point is by demonstration. Secondly, I may ask what the director is trying to achieve in that moment. Understanding why the request was made might better equip you to suggest alternatives that might fit both the director's and your vision. These requests might not be limited to just the director, but often extend to the producer as well. In my experience, one of the most discussed topics is the overall level of the show. Many times the director, producer, or choreographer, even, has a differing opinion on how loud things should be. What do you do when you'd like it natural, and they'd like it loud? That's still a battle many of us fight... and often lose.

BRIAN R: I'm often asked to make things louder than I think they should be. Usually during the last performances before the critics come. Everyone is nervous at that time and louder and brighter are easy things for the senses to detect. In press reviews, musical sound designers will sometimes be critiqued for overamplifying. I'm willing to bet that most often that excess volume is driven by an anxious producer or director. I've also been asked to supply sound cues that I don't think serve the storytelling (one involved bodily functions). Ultimately, I serve the director. I may suggest my opinion but I'm there to support their vision.

TOM C: The most common conflict comes with respect to how loud a show is. Most often the director wants it louder than I do. Sometimes the problem is clarity or punch or tone rather than volume, and the goal becomes getting the sound *right* without allowing it to get too loud. There is a real lack of common vocabulary here, and often not a great deal of patience with the details of something as amorphous as sound waves. If you have the director's trust, you will have the time to fix the problem without simply "making it louder." If you don't have the director's trust, you are in trouble. The worst situation to be in is to discover that multiple members of the creative team (particularly, producer, choreographer, composer, lyricist, orchestrator, music director) have conflicting views of how the sound should be delivered. A strong director who trusts you is your best defense here. Otherwise, you are f**ked, unless of course you get it right the first time.

JONATHAN D: Yes, quite often, but we need to abide to the one vision approach which the director must have. Usually it is about overall level, especially when an audience first comes into the theatre and the director is suddenly standing at the back of the theatre and their visual perspective is quite different even though the sound is similar to their rehearsal seats. One might discuss this but really there is no resolution, as one needs to be directed.

OTTS M: Yes, in modern times much more so than in the early days.

TONY M: On *The Red Shoes*, Stanley Donen asked me to make one number MUCH louder than it ever should have been. I didn't refuse, but I told him that I wasn't comfortable with my name remaining on the show if it remained like that. Everyone eventually calmed down (including me) and it got back to listenable levels.

Regarding the challenge of localizing to an actor in a large-scale venue, do you see directors adapting their blocking or staging to help focus attention on the person singing or do they leave the localization problems to you?

TONY M: That's a really good question. It depends on the director. Some get it and some don't.

BRIAN R: That is so venue specific. I don't go crazy about localization and I haven't encountered many directors who do. I like the sound to appear to come from the actors on stage, but I don't pan the sound around to follow the actor. I believe that benefits only about 10% of the audience. Frankly, I think the lighting designer bears the brunt of localization.

In a large, commercial venue I also think the necessity of 3,000 or so people to hear all the words supersedes a slight in localization.

PETER H: It seems inherent in modern musical staging that there is some semblance of focus on the necessary performer. Blocking helps, but on a very crowded stage it can still be difficult to pick out the two principals who are singing. Often lighting plays a key role in this through the use of frontlights or specials. Unlike film, where the director points out exactly what you are looking at in each moment, theatre still allows your eyes to wander. It's a group effort to guide the audience throughout the evening.

JONATHAN D: No and never. It will be up to us to supply tracking systems.

TOM C: The smart ones do it with movement or lighting, often commenting wryly that "with microphones we can't tell where you (the speaking actor) are unless you raise your hand." The problem of focus in large halls has to be addressed in many ways in addition to sound.

OTTS M: No, the very fact that sound can do part of this work allows directors to be oblivious.

300

Do you have any techniques or specific technology that help with this issue?

JONATHAN D: I am working with tracking systems. This is still in its infancy.

OTTS M: No, I'm too old.

BRIAN R: I employ a very basic method of using a phase popper and an onstage speaker to simulate the actor's voice. I time the various speakers to that source pop. I do most of the tune up of the initial session throughout the preview process.

TONY M: The best one is to get the actor to project. Good speaker placement helps enormously.

PETER H: There are a few systems on the market that address localization. Many of the theories behind these units relate to basic delay/attenuation ratios. With any sort of localization, it's important to always think about how these moves affect the entire audience. Be sure you aren't creating fantastic imaging for 50% of the seats, while destroying intelligibility for the other 50%. There are also a few basic techniques that work quite well. It's pretty astounding what simple linear delay (upstage/downstage) will do when used with a well-tuned system.

How "hands-on" do you get with your actors/singers/talent?

BRIAN R: Funny you should ask. Not five minutes ago I was in a dressing room of one actor discussing the onstage sound, I had to hit up two other dressing rooms to play with mic placement, and the hairstyles of another two actors. This is pretty typical backstage behavior. I find most technical sound issues are best handled in the dressing room, face to face. The cast and musicians need to know you're on their side.

JONATHAN D: As much as possible.

PETER H: It's important that your cast members feel comfortable when they're onstage. I'm not shy about jumping onstage during rehearsals to hear what the cast is listening to. Getting to know them,

301

asking if the foldback is sounding good to them, or maybe just fine-tuning their mic position can help a performer feel more confident in their performance.

TOM C: I try to make sure that they know I am there to help them sound great. Some require care and feeding, but most are quite self-sufficient and are content with a hello, and goodnight. From time to time, there are issues with mic placement or foldback.

TONY M: In production, I usually speak to the actors throughout rehearsals. I spend a lot of time onstage so that I can hear what they're hearing.

OTTS M: The better the show, the more hands-on I find myself allowed to be.

Are there any challenges to training actors in the proper use of RF mics and placement of bodypacks?

TONY M: Rarely. Everybody usually wants to sound good.

OTTS M: Willingness of performers to adapt.

BRIAN R: I try to instill a feeling of transparency when I encounter an actor who hasn't worn a mic (a rare thing these days). I don't want them to alter their performance at all. The basics apply: don't get hairspray in your mic, don't get water on your mic, and don't drop the transmitter in the toilet. These are universal truths.

Basically I want them to put their mic on, get it in the place we've agreed to and then forget they have it on and just go do their performance.

PETER H: There are numbers of challenges. The main thing an actor needs to understand is that the microphone is their lifeline to the audience. They should treat it accordingly. Once an actor is aware of microphone positional sensitivity and how it helps or hinders their sound, they will pay more attention to it. One common misconception, however, is the confusion between a microphone and a microscope. Performers can sometimes fall into bad habits thinking the mic will do all the work for them. If there isn't enough level coming from the stage acoustically, our job transitions from reinforcement to straight amplification, often not the goal of a theatrical experience.

TOM C: The biggest issues are getting them to allow us to hide the microphones—the younger ones tend to think it should be just above the bridge of the nose, and are quite surprised when we back them up into the hairline. It takes a bit of work to convince them of the importance of a center position. Hair loss concerns sometimes become an issue with respect to mic cable mounting on the head— we have a bit of a fight to get away from ear rigs, which don't sound as good and are more visible.

JONATHAN D: No, RF mics on actors should be as low key to the actor as possible.

Do actors have any problem regarding the use of head-worn boom mics as opposed to lavs in forehead, ear, chest, or other mounting positions?

JONATHAN D: This is a design approach and decision between the director and sound designer. It is not an actor's choice.

BRIAN R: The opinion of actors about their mics has softened over the years. In my first years as a mixer (mid-80s) you still had old school actors who felt insulted by the mic. On the chest was intrusion enough, but in their hair? The newer breed of actors, though no less talented, have grown up with mics and are pretty open to whatever creative decision has been reached.

303

PETER H: In my experience, the use of boom mics is usually a decision based on the musical concept of a show; and it certainly is a bold visual statement. An actor may have issues with such a device if it isn't fitting with the style of the piece. It creates a disconnection between their character and the audience by having this appendage on their face. There are some shows where it is completely accepted; I don't think I can picture the cast of *Rent* without the signature boom mics.

TOM C: Mostly not, assuming they make sense for the show. They are easier to put on and take off.

What attributes do you look for in your front of house mixing personnel?

TOM C: Everything! They must have tremendous focus to mix cleanly, good taste to mix artfully, good technical chops to keep the system running, and great people skills to cope with stars, ensemble members, directors, producers, stagehands, music directors, musicians, and wardrobe and hair folk. It may be the hardest job in the business to do really well.

OTTS M: Ability to learn, logic, good sense of volume.

BRIAN R: Mettle. Positive attitude. Talent. Fast fingers. Their main task is to make my job easier. That may sound obvious, but I don't think any technical job is harder than a musical engineer's. Not only does that person have to possess technical know-how, but they must also balance the demands of composers, conductors, guitar players, producers, actors, and, eventually, me. This balancing of demands must occur during long production hours and in the face of often immense pressure to perform flawlessly. It takes a special talent to do all this and then sit in post-show note sessions and have your day's work criticized. I'm proud of this often underappreciated group of stagehands.

TONY M: Kindness. Knowledge of the theatre. Ability to get along with others. Smarts.

JONATHAN D: Never to say "NO!." And of course can mix the s**t out of the show for every performance.

PETER H: A great set of ears connected to some fast fingers! Well, that and a bunch more. I look for great social skills; someone who will be able to speak with the cast and musical director in an effort to keep the audio quality at its highest. Engineers I enjoy working with have an innate musical sense and understand how manipulating the faders emotionally impacts the audience.

What do you consider to be the most remarkable or successful design of your career (or, frankly, of anyone's career)?

PETER H: Each show has its own successes, whether it's another designer's or my own. I try to learn a bit from every production, what I think worked or didn't, and file that away in my memory.

JONATHAN D: Currently my show *LOVE* and *The Capeman*, which was a T. Richard Fitzgerald design.

TONY M: I have always loved Otts Munderloh's design for *Dreamgirls* and I've copied it many times.

BRIAN R: Otts Munderloh's *Search for Signs of Intelligent Life* was one of the most impressive uses of sound effects for a show I've seen. I really enjoyed my own job on an off-Broadway show called *Bug*. In that show, the sound acted as another character in the show. It was thrilling to me.

In terms of shows with sound reinforcement, I'd say Tony Meola's work on the revival of *Man of La Mancha* was a perfect fusion of live and amplified sound, Steve Kennedy's work on *Jersey Boys* was some of the best and most creative use of technology to help tell a story and, as for me, I'd say *Spring Awakening* was the right design for that show.

TOM C: *Side Show*.

OTTS M: *A Chorus Line*—the original (Abe Jacob).

Where do you see the future for sound designers?

TOM C: The gear is getting better and better. Our work should, too. With any luck, the addition of the Tony Awards for Sound Design will help to improve pay levels to parity with the scenic, costume, and lighting designers, making the career choice less self-sacrificial.

PETER H: It seems as technology grows, we are more empowered to effect real-time control over the sound of our shows. This, combined with a heightened awareness of audio in everyday life, gives us the opportunity to demonstrate some pretty fantastic sound designs. Each year the digital products sound better and can do more, mics get smaller and easier to hide—I guess our tool box is getting larger. As our art form continues to develop, I think greater acceptance within the theatre community will follow, our final product will become better integrated, and audiences will hopefully appreciate what we add to the storytelling.

OTTS M: Tools for actors without any vocal craft, and the directors who use them.

JONATHAN D: Each year the sound designer and designs become more and more complex and although the general audience has "hearing ADD," they do have high-end equipment in their homes that require something that can exceed their car stereo and 5.1 movie rooms for ticket prices over $100.

TONY M: I think the field will only grow. It should now be taught in high schools since so many use equipment that they have no idea how to use.

BRIAN R: The gear we use will continue to change. The world is going digital with all its lovely benefits and cruel complications. However, the act of amplifying a source of talent, be it an actor, singer, or musician, and delivering that enhanced sound to an audience of paying customers, probably won't change that much.

One issue future sound designers will have to contend with is the shrinking availability of wireless frequencies. Like melting polar ice caps, the abundance of frequencies is being threatened. The growth of digital TV and the desire of mammoth companies like Google, AT&T, and Microsoft to produce products that use commercially available bandwidths is something that could be of real concern. Unlike corporations, we in our democratic theatre world don't speak as one. That will have to change if we're going to continue to provide the freedom that wireless microphones provide to directors, singers, composers, and producers to enhance their performances.

Do you have any other comments you'd like to make or questions we should have asked?

JONATHAN D: Yes, I am very passionate about my work and love my job.

We should all be as lucky as Jonathan Deans. —DK and JL

Glossary

AIFF an abbreviation for audio interchange file format; a sound file format capable of high-quality reproduction.

Aliasing a digital audio artifact typically heard when the frequency (cycles per second) of a reproduced sound is more than half the value of the sampling frequency (samples per second) used to capture that sound.

Ambiance a sound cue that acts as an environmental backdrop to a scene, often a wash of sound without loud or distinguishing elements that would bring undesired attention to the track.

Associate sound designer a member of the sound team who works with the sound designer in a design capacity, making artistic decisions. An associate designer might also be employed when the primary designer is unavailable due to scheduling conflicts.

Attenuate to lower the volume.

Aural identifiers readily identifiable sounds added to difficult to recognize ambiance. A soft, lazy summer wind might sound like white noise, but adding in an aural identifier such as a leaf rustle or a branch creak helps to say "wind" to the audience. These added elements are sometime called "sweeteners."

Auralizing imagining the occurrence of a specific sound spatially and over time.

Autofollow cue a sound cue that a sound operator initiates after another cue, without it being called by the stage manager. Autofollow cues are often used when a sequence of cues happens so quickly that it would be impossible for the stage manager to call them.

Balanced connection an audio connection that is resistant to interference. This type of connection uses a three-conductor cable and connector. XLR or tip/ring/sleeve connectors are examples of balanced connectors.

Bed track a track of music or sound that, when used with a spot effect or specific music cue, allows such cues to emerge naturally from a sound mix. With a soft, early-morning ambiance of birds and distant cows mooing as a bed track, a loud rooster crow would emerge out of the ambiance, rather than seeming to pop out of nowhere.

Bit rate a general term used to express the transmission rate of digital signals. A bit is a binary digit representing two different states, either on or off. The higher the bit rate of a sound file, the better the resolution or clarity of that file.

Board tape white artist's tape used to mark mixing boards.

Comb filtering an undesirable audio effect that happens when a sound from the same source is heard at slightly different times at the same volume. Comb filtering is commonly caused by using multiple microphones to pick up the same source. Combining those signals causes phase cancellation in the waveform of that sound, producing comb filtering.

Computer-assisted playback system   a sound system that uses a computer and software to store, route, and play back audio.

Control surface   a device that connects to a digital audio workstation to provide better control and functionality than simply using a mouse and keyboard. The control surface functions like a mixing console by communicating to the software through touch sensitive faders and rotary encoders that set parameters, write automation, and route tracks.

Count   a unit of time, roughly equivalent to one second, used by sound operators and the designer to express how long a cue should take to be executed.

Crash box   a box designed to hold the items needed to create the sound of an offstage crash.

Crossfade   to overlap the fadeout of one sound with the fade-in of another.

Cue list   a list of the sound cues, in order of occurrence. This either can be found in one of the windows of a computer-assisted playback system or can be produced using the database from which the sound plot is developed .

Deck   any playback device, such as a CD player or sampler. This term originally referred to a tape deck, the only commonly used playback device.

DI   the common abbreviation for a direct input. A DI is often used as an unbalanced input for a musical instrument, like a guitar or synthesizer, into a mixing board. A DI is sometimes routed through a direct box, which has an unbalanced input and a balanced output, the most common input found on professional mixing boards.

Digital audio artifact   an unnatural sound that is a by-product of digital signal processing. Often undesirable, digital artifacts are occasionally so unusual, they become a new and interesting component.

Digital audio workstation   A computer-based sound recording, editing, and mixing system.

Digital delay   an audio device that processes a sound signal to provide special effects such as reverb or vibrato. Originally used primarily to create a delayed audio signal for rear speakers in a reinforcement setup.

Digital sampler   a device that stores sound as digital (computer) information. Incoming sounds are sampled thousands of times a second. The sampler stores the information, and can then play the sounds back at a wide range of pitches or with other modifications.

Doppler effect   the lowering in pitch of an approaching sound as it passes by.

Dry tech   a rehearsal of specific problem sections without actors.

Echo   a distinct repeat or series of repeats of a sound (as opposed to *reverberation*, which is a blend of many sounds).

308

Effects return   the pathway of a sound signal as it returns to the mixer from an effects unit such as a digital delay.

Effects send   the pathway of a sound signal as it moves from the mixer to an effects unit.

Entr'acte   music or sounds played during the intermission of a play.

Equalization (EQ)   boosting or filtering the low, mid, and/or high frequencies of sound in order to make a recording seem more natural, provide clarity, or alter sound so that it seems unusual.

Establish and fade   a technique used with ambiance whereby the track plays for long enough to create a mood or sense of place, then is either faded out gradually or taken out abruptly.

Fill loudspeakers   loudspeakers used to provide coverage to places that the main sound system cannot reach, such as under the balcony or front row.

Focus   the part of the installation procedure when the loudspeakers are pointed (focused) vertically and horizontally (pan and tilt).

Foldback speaker   a loudspeaker typically used in musical performances to play the house mix to the performers. This could also be called a monitor loudspeaker.

Found sounds   naturally occurring sounds that are captured (recorded and/or sampled) and utilized in the creation of sound effects and music. The found sound of a gunshot could be used to replace a snare drum sound in a drum set. The sound of a cork squeaking while being extracted from a bottle of wine could be abstracted into a representation of the chirp or "call" of a bat.

Framing cues   the preshow, entr'acte, and curtain call, which act as the bookends of a production. Framing cues exist outside the actual action of a play; they can comment on what will be or has been seen, but function independently of the actors' presentation of the play. Musically, the preshow is a prelude, the entr'acte a bridge, and the curtain call a coda or finale.

Ground plan   a bird's-eye view blueprint of how the set is to be placed in the theatre that shows where scenery, masking drapes, doorways, windows etc. will be placed onstage.

Haas effect   a psycho-acoustic phenomenon that has to do with the brain's perception of where a sound is coming from, when there is more than one source of that sound. A typical example of this is when a singer is amplified through a sound reinforcement system. Because the ear tends to focus on the sound that it hears first, if the arrival time between the first source (the singer) and the second source (the sound system) is 30 milliseconds (ms) or less, the ear will perceive this as one event (coming from the singer). If the gap between the first arrival and second arrival time is over 30 ms, the ear will perceive this as being two events, as if that second source (the sound system) was a repeat or an echo. This is also referred to as the *precedence effect*.

309

Hook   a central concept that motivates or is drawn upon to evolve ideas for a design or composition.

Hookup   a text document that defines everything in the schematic block diagram and exactly how it's hooked up. It includes every cable, connector, length, mult, processor, mixer, amplifier, loudspeaker, sound source, DI, RF, and in some cases, power connects.

Hotspot   an instance when shifting a control knob on a piece of sound equipment from, for example, 2 to 3 produces a greater effect than does moving the same knob from 1 to 2 or 3 to 4, making setting levels difficult.

Indicated cue   a particular piece of music or a specific sound effect that the playwright has called for in the script.

Jump drive   a small, portable storage device, typically a USB memory drive. Also referred to as a thumb drive, because its size is about the same size as a thumb. Convenient for storing and transferring documents, photos, and sound files.

Layering   a technique in which a number of discrete sounds are mixed together to produce a new sound or ambiance.

Loop   a repeated section of sound or music. Traditionally made from tape (the ends of the tape are spliced together), loops are now made digitally with the use of samplers or digital audio workstations.

Lossless   a form of data compression used on audio files. The sound file is compressed into a smaller size, which allows for less storage space and faster download times. Lossless uses complex algorithms for compressing data that result in no loss in sound quality.

Lossy   a form of data compression used on audio files. Data compression makes the audio file smaller, allowing for less storage space and faster download times. Lossy compression compromises the quality of the audio in the sound file.

Magic sheet   a simple but handy diagram that shows your sound system layout. It's a helpful reference to have during technical rehearsals.

MIDI   Musical Instrument Digital Interface, a technology by which electronic instruments (synthesizers and samplers), computers, and some signal-processing gear can communicate with each other. With MIDI, one keyboard can play other instruments, computers can store sequences of notes that can be accessed by a keyboard, or a reverb unit can be adjusted quickly and consistently.

Mix   the balance of volume between simultaneously playing tracks.

Mixing board, mixing console, or mixing desk   a piece of audio equipment that processes audio signals. The audio signal comes in through the board's inputs, and the signal's levels, tonality, and pan position are controlled by the board's controls. The audio signal is then routed out to the loudspeakers or other signal processing gear. All these terms are used synonymously.

Monitor loudspeaker   a loudspeaker used is to transmit the sound of another performer or the sound in the performance space.

310

MP3   an abbreviation for MPEG-1 audio layer 3, a compressed audio file format. MP3s, because they use compression technology to reduce file size, do not sound as good as uncompressed audio file types such as AIFF.

Mult   an area on a patch panel that allows you to multiply the number of instances of a connection. For example, if you wanted to send the output of a mic preamplifier to two different devices, you would patch the preamplifier into the mult, and then patch the inputs of the two devices into the same mult. Also a large cable, consisting of many conductors that connects signals from one section of a sound system to another. This is also known as a snake.

Musicality   the human quality of being sensitive to the rhythm, phrasing, concept, and interpretation of music.

Noise-based sounds   nonpitched sounds with irregular (sometimes random) wave shapes. They are observed in ambiant sounds like wind, rain, ocean waves, fire, electric fans, and even in the sound of frying foods. This differs from the kind of noise that describes an unwanted or annoying sound.

Outboard gear   sound-processing equipment, such as a reverb or equalizer, that isn't built into a mixing board.

Pan pot   a control knob on a mixing board that allows for moving a sound from one output to another.

Paper tech   a meeting for the director, stage manager, lighting designer, and sound designer to discuss where light and sound cues will happen in the show. This is when the stage manager puts the cueing information into the script. Paper tech usually takes place just before technical rehearsals.

PDA   an abbreviation for personal digital assistant. A PDA is a portable, versatile, hand-held computer. It's a very convenient device for storing contact information, taking notes, doing calculations, keeping a calendar, and playing music.

Plan view   See *Ground plan*.

Practical   a working device that produces sound onstage just as it would in real life, such as a telephone, doorbell, TV set, or radio.

Production sound mixer   the person responsible for mixing the sound reinforcement of a performance. They are typically found working on musical productions, but can be found whenever there is live miking of performers or musicians.

Quiet time   the designated time in the load-in process when the sound department can work in the performance space without other departments making noise. Typically, quiet time is used for balancing the sound system or setting preliminary sound cue levels.

Required music   a particular piece of music indicated at a certain moment in the script that is played as part of the action onstage or offstage.

Reverberation   multiple blended sounds caused by reflections from hard surfaces. It naturally occurs when sound bounces off of floors, walls, and ceilings. It can also be created using processing equipment. Reverberation differs from *echo*, which is a repeat of a sound, not a blend.

SBD   an abbreviation for a schematic block diagram, or full system line drawing.

Show-control   a technology used to link together multiple production elements such as lighting, sound, video, and special effects. For example, show-control allows for synchronization between a lighting console and a computer-assisted playback system.

Soloing   listening to a specific track by using the solo function on a mixing board. The act of soloing a track mutes all other tracks.

Soundscape   sounds that create the experience of a realistic or imagined acoustic environment.

Soundscore   a musical composition that uses realistic and/or nonrealistic sounds.

Specific cue   a cue that is primarily informational in purpose, supplying of-the-moment information to the audience, and supporting the play's development. Specific cues include required music, spot effects, ambiance, and a progression of effects.

Spot effect   a sound effect that occurs at a specific point in the play's action, as opposed to ambiance.

SRC   an abbreviation for the word *source*, typically used in sound plots.

Subwoofer   a speaker designed specifically to reproduce low-frequency sounds.

Surrounds loudspeakers   loudspeakers placed in the side and rear of the performance space.

Sweeteners   See *Aural identifiers*.

System balance   the part of the installation procedure when the output levels of individual loudspeakers are adjusted to create the desired balance between all of the loudspeakers.

Themed entertainment   productions set in specific locations such as theme parks, casinos, and museums.

Timbre   the tone color that distinguishes the quality/voice of one instrument or singer from another (e.g., flute from clarinet, lyric soprano from mezzo-soprano).

Unbalanced connection   an audio connection that uses two conductors to transmit the audio signal. This type of connection is more susceptible to audio interference. RCA or tip/sleeve ¼" audio connectors are examples of unbalanced connectors.

WAV   an abbreviation for waveform audio format, a high-quality sound file format commonly used with PCs.

Please visit our Facebook group: Sound and Music for the Theatre

Index

A

Abstract form, 21–22
Abstraction, 19
Acoustic weapons, 16–17
Acoustics, overview of, 104–105
Actors
  scripts and, 41
  voice processing for, 180
Aliasing, 169–170
Ambiance
  "establish and fade" technique of,
    31–32
  overview of, 27, 28
  removing, 32
  softening of, 32
  spot effects and, 28–29
  volume of, 31
American Conservatory Theatre, 8
American Society of Composers, Authors
  and Publishers (ASCAP), 60
American Theatre Wing, 81–82
Amplification, 104
Announcements, preshow, 25
Apple, Max, *The Propheteers*, 2
Appropriateness
  of musical instruments, 18
  of sounds, 18
  of timing, 43
Archiving, of sound effects, 58
Art, 2
Artifacts, 169–170
Artistic directors, 85–86
ASCAP. *See American Society of Composers,*
  Authors and Publishers
Assessing cue parameters,
  102–107
Audio industry, 2
Audio masters, 2
Audio show control system, 160f
Audio tools, 9
Aural identifiers, 105
Aural illusions, 34
Aural statement, 13
Aural vision, 12, 13
Auralizing, 13
Ayckbourn, Alan, *Sisterly Feelings*, 41

B

Backing up your work, 116
Balance, of sound cues, 34–35
Bandshells, 37
Barton, Todd
  background of, 223
  feedback from, 237–238, 243, 252,
    260, 271, 272, 287
Baryshnikov, Mikhail, 10
Berkeley Repertory Theatre, 16
Beyond Therapy, 46
Blending
  of live and prerecorded sounds,
    182–183
  of pitches, 176–177
Blocking, 3, 118
Blue Suede Shoes, 175–176
Blueberry Hill, 23
BMI. *See Broadcast Music Incorporated*
Brancato, Joe
  background of, 186–187
  feedback from, 191, 192, 194, 197,
    198, 199, 201, 203, 206, 209
Brecht, Bertolt, 7
Broadcast Music Incorporated (BMI), 60
Bronze Age, 4
Budgets
  for equipment, 49–50
  limitations of, 92–93
  margin for error in, 50
  overview of, 107–108
  for sound design, 48, 49–50
Budries, David
  background of, 231
  feedback from, 227–228, 234–235,
    245, 250–251, 254–255, 261–262,
    272–273, 278–281
Building the show, 112–113

C

Cables, for microphones, 101–102
Cart machines, 114–115
Cassette decks, 10
Casting directors, 86
Changes, in sound design,
  136–137

Characters
  hidden clues and, 43–44
  musical instruments and, 52–53
  unseen, 14–15
Checking, of equipment, 145–148
Chekhov, Anton, *The Seagull*, 5–6
Cherokee County, 20
A Christmas Carol (Dickens), 40–41
Cinematic design
  cinematic form and, 19–20
  preshows and, 20
Clark, Tom
  background of, 288–289
  feedback from, 290, 291, 292, 293,
    295, 297, 298, 299, 301, 302,
    302–303, 304
Collection list, 98f
A Comedy of Errors (Shakespeare), 40
Comic effect, 19
Commedia dell'arte, 4, 40
Commentary sounds, 24
Communication systems, multichannel,
    132–133, 147
Compact discs (CDs)
  disc format, 9–10, 10, 56–57
  players for, 113–114
Company managers, 87
Complex sound sequences, 172–173
Composers
  American Society of Composers,
    Authors and Publishers, 60
  design process and, 3, 224–225
  duties of, 2
  equipment and, 9
  research and, 52–53
  sound designers and, 11
Compressing underscoring, 178
Computer-assisted playback systems
  overview of, 115–116
  sound booth and, 132
  sound cues and, 112, 158–163
  sound design and, 8–9, 9–10
  sound plots and, 120f
Conceptual development, in design
    process, 40
Conference of the Birds, 22
Consistency, 19–20
Consumer audio products, 9
Contacts, 59–60
Contracts, 82
Contrast, 16–18
Copyright issues, 60, 60–61

Costume designers, 13
Costume designs, 45
Coward, Noel, 46
  Tonight at 8:30, 26
Crash box, 34, 37, 116
Creative audio tools, 9
Crediting, of sound designers, 8, 12, 13
Crossfading, of sound cues, 73, 121, 174
Crowd scenes, 35
Cueing
  language chart for, 159f
  overview of, 30–34
  rate of execution of, 31–33
  volume and, 31
Cues. *See Sound cues*
Cue-to-cue rehearsals, 135
Curtain calls, 22–23

D

Danforth, Roger T.
  background of, 187
  feedback from, 191, 192, 195, 197–
    198, 199, 200, 202, 204, 209–210
DATs, 9–10
DAW. *See Digital audio workstations*
Deans, Jonathan
  background of, 289
  feedback from, 290, 292, 293, 294,
    295, 296, 298, 299, 300, 302, 303,
    304–305, 305
Delorio, Victoria (toy)
  background of, 224
  feedback from, 228, 230–231, 240–
    241, 242–243, 243, 246, 248–249,
    254, 256–257, 263, 268–269,
    274–275, 276–277, 282–283, 286
Design process
  approaches to, 3
  composers and, 3, 224–225
  conceptual development, 40
  directors and, 1, 2, 11
  sound cues and, 14, 95
  sound designers and, 1, 3, 4, 224–225
  sound plots and, 98f, 97
Dialogue, and transitional music, 26–27
DiBucci, Michelle
  background of, 224
  feedback from, 233–234, 241, 245,
    258–259, 262–263, 270–271,
    273–274, 276, 283, 286
Dickens, Charles, *A Christmas Carol*,
    40–41

314

Digital audio workstations (DAW)
    overview of, 114
    sound design and, 8–9, 9–10, 49, 113
Dimmers, 124
Directors
    artistic, 85–86
    casting, 86
    design process and, 1, 2, 11
    duties of, 86
    hidden clues and, 44
    managing, 86
    meetings with, 47–48, 48
    scripts and, 44, 48
    sound cues and, 49
    sound design and, 15, 46
    sound designers and, 13, 14, 47–49
    technical, 89–90
Distribution area, for loudspeakers, 78f,
        127–128, 182
Domino, Fats, 23
Door slams, 107–108, 184
Doppler, Christian Johann, 174
Doppler effect, 174–176
Dramaturges, 52
Dress tech rehearsals, 138
Drum machines, 9
Dry tech rehearsals, 137–138
Du Boff, Jill BC
    background of, 224
    feedback from, 228–230,
        238–239, 245–246, 253, 257–258,
        263–264, 266–267, 274, 280–281,
        283–284, 287
Dugan, Dan, 8
Dumb show, 4

E

Electrical power, 124–125
Elizabethan theatre, 4, 53
Emergencies, 165–166
Emotion, 16–18, 44–45, 185
English Renaissance, 4
Entr'actes, 22–23, 25
Environmental sounds, 6
EQ. See Equalization
Equalization (EQ), 35, 35–36
Equipment
    budgets for, 49–50
    checking of, 145–148
    composers and, 9
    costs of, 10
    development of, 9

layout of, 122
rental of, 92–93, 106–107
sound delivery systems, 96, 103,
        127–131, 128f, 129f, 144–145
sound designers and, 8–9, 9–10
striking when show closes, 166
"Establish and fade" technique, of
        ambiance, 31–32
Expressionism, 6

F

Fading
    crossfading, of sound cues, 73, 121,
        174
    of lighting effects, 33
    of sound cues, 32, 66, 178
Fees
    schedules for, 82–84
    for sound designers, 49–50
Field recordings
    microphones for, 100–101
    overview of, 177
Final rehearsals, 139–140
Final tableau, 33
First tech rehearsal, 134–136
Fish Head Soup (Gotanda), 100
Focus, 30
Framing cues, 22–23, 24–25
Fugard, Athol
    background of, 187
    feedback from, 191, 193, 195, 198,
        201, 202–203, 204, 207
Function and intent, of sounds, 14–15

G

Gardner, Lewis, 1
Gas lighting, 5
Glass, Philip, 3
The Gospel According to St. Mark, 8
Gotanda, Philip Kan
    background of, 188–189
    feedback from, 212–213, 214, 216,
        217–218, 219, 220, 222
    Fish Head Soup, 100
Graces, Michael John
    background of, 188
    feedback from, 211, 213, 216, 219,
        221, 222
Gray, Amlin
    background of, 188
    feedback from, 212, 214–215, 217,
        218–219, 220, 221–222

315

Grounding effect, 30
Gutierrez, Gerald
    background of, 187
    feedback from, 193–194, 194, 197,
        199, 201, 201–202, 203–204,
        206, 209

H

Hair, 8
Hallas, Brian
    background of, 224
    feedback from, 226, 232–233, 241,
        242, 245, 246, 252, 254, 261, 265,
        269, 274, 278, 282, 286
Hamlet (Shakespeare), 53
Hard disk playback, 114
Harris, Jed, 6
The Haunting of Hill House,
    17–18
Heartbeat:mg, 10
Henry V (Shakespeare), 10
The Heron, 37–38
Hidden clues
    characters and, 43–44
    directors and, 44
    overview of, 43–44
High-frequency tones, 33
The Honeymooners, 23
    Hooker, Michael K
    background of, 224
    feedback from, 226, 236, 242, 248,
        249, 252–253, 260,
        264–265, 270, 275, 277,
        282, 286
Human reaction, to sounds,
    16–17
Hurt, William, 47–48
Hylenski, Peter
    background of, 289
    feedback from, 291, 292, 293, 294,
        296, 297–298, 299, 300, 300–301,
        301, 302, 303, 304

I

Identification system, for loudspeakers,
    71–72
Identifiers, 29
Identifiers, aural, 105
Incidental music. *See Underscoring*
Installation, of sound system, 127–131
Insurance, 82–84

Intellectual property rights, 82–84
Interconnectivity, 106
Internet, 54, 55, 57
Interpretation, of scripts, 44
Isolation, of sound booth, 123
Italian Renaissance, 4

J

Jacob, Abe, 8
Janney, Christopher, 10
Jesus Christ Superstar, 8
Journey into the Whirlwind, 20–21
Julius Caesar (Shakespeare), 53

K

Kanin, Garson, 7–8
    A Small War on Murray Hill, 7
Kernan, Bob, 8
Kesselman, Wendy
    background of, 189
    feedback from, 213, 214, 215–216,
        218, 219, 221
The King and I, 136

L

Lan, David, *Sgt. Ola and His Followers*,
    14–15
Language chart, for sound cueing, 159f
Lawrence, W. J., 4
Lawson, David
    background of, 224–225
    feedback from, 231, 239, 240, 260,
        261, 267, 268, 285–286, 286–287
Layering, 112
Layout, of equipment, 122
Lee, Phil
    background of, 225
    feedback from, 228, 231, 242,
        243–244, 246, 249, 255, 258, 263,
        267, 273, 278, 283, 286
Legal issues
    copyright, 60–61
    intellectual property rights, 82–84
    union rules, 93–94, 127
Lennon, John, 3
Levels, of volume, 31, 133–134, 165
Libraries
    public, 54–55, 55
    of sound effects, 57–58
Licensing, of sound effects, 60–61
Lighting boards, 9

316

Lighting design, 1, 45
Lighting designers, 13, 33, 45, 158
Lighting dimmers, 124
Lighting effects, 6, 31, 33
Lighting, in sound booth, 125–126
Limitations, budgetary, 92–93
Lincoln Center, 6–7
Line indications, and sound design, 43
Liszt, Franz, 3
Live effects, 34, 37, 42–43, 116–117, 183–185
Location
    movement and, 34
    of sounds, 33–34
The Lone Ranger Theme, 24
Loudspeakers
    distribution area for, 78f, 127–128, 182
    identification system for, 71–72
    overview of, 104
    plots for, 76f, 77–79
    as practicals, 184–185
    for production monitor, 123
Love's Labour's Lost (Shakespeare), 99
Low-frequency tones, 16–17, 169
LPs, 57
Lucas, Craig
    background of, 189
    feedback from, 213–214, 215, 218, 221

M

Macbeth (Shakespeare), 17, 18, 33, 53, 184
Madame Butterfly, 27
Making Whoopee, 8
The Man Who Came to Dinner, 46
Managing directors, 86
Manually operated playback, 152–158, 153f
Mardikes, Tom
    background of, 225
    feedback from, 227, 235, 236, 239, 243, 244, 246–247, 255, 259, 265, 275, 278, 283, 286
Margin for error, in budgets, 50
McAnuff, Des
    background of, 187
    feedback from, 189–190, 193, 194–195, 197, 199, 200, 202, 204, 205, 206–207, 211
Measure for Measure (Shakespeare), 66
Medieval drama, 4

Meetings
    with directors, 47–48, 48
    with production staff, 92
Melodramatic effect, 26–27
Meola, Tony
    background of, 289
    feedback from, 291, 293, 294, 295, 296, 298–299, 299, 300, 301, 303, 304, 305
The Merchant of Venice (Shakespeare), 27
The Merry Wives of Windsor (Shakespeare), 53
Microphones
    cables for, 101–102
    for field recordings, 100–101
    overview of, 106
    stands for, 102
MIDI. *See Musical Instrument Digital Interface*
A Midsummer Night's Dream (Shakespeare), 53
MiniDiscs, 9–10, 113–114, 121
Misalliance (Shaw), 51
Miss Saigon, 10
Mixing
    production sound mixers, 2, 91–92
    of sound cues, 38
    of sound effects, 38–39, 111
    systems for, 105–106
Modifying music, 176–177
Moscow Art Theatre, 5–6
Movement
    location and, 34
    of sounds, 33–34
Mozart, Wolfgang Amadeus, 3
    Ein Musikalischer Spass, 41
    Piano Sonata in D Major (K. 284), 61f
MP3s, 56–57, 100–101
Much Ado About Nothing (Shakespeare), 63–64
Multichannel communication systems, 132–133, 147
Munderloh, Otts, 21
    background of, 289–290
    feedback from, 291, 293, 295, 296, 298, 299, 300, 301, 303, 304
Music
    conventions of, 22–30
    modifying, 176–177
    from practical sources, 19
    required, 27
    research on, 44, 52, 54

317

Music (*continued*)
resources for, 54–57
segmentable, 61–63
styles of, 52
thematic, 26
timelines for, 53–54
transitional, 22–23, 23, 26–27
underscoring with, 22–23, 25–26, 178
volume of, 31, 145
Musical effects
choosing, 44–45
emotional characteristics of, 44–45
Musical indications, by playwrights, 42, 44
Musical Instrument Digital Interface (MIDI), 9, 180–181
Musical instruments
appropriateness of, 18
characters and, 52–53
Musical Instrument Digital Interface (MIDI), 9, 180–181
pitch range of, 39
Musicians, 5, 37–38
Ein Musikalischer Spass (Mozart), 41
My Heart's in the Highlands, 142–143

N

National Shakespeare Company, 40
Naturalism, 5–6
Nemirovich-Danchenko, Vladimir, 5–6
Neoclassical period of theatre, 5
Networking, 59–60
The Night of the Iguana (Williams), 29, 34
Noises off, 5
The Normal Heart, 180

O

O'Brien, Jack
background of, 187–188
feedback from, 191, 192–193, 196, 199, 200, 203, 205, 207, 210
Offstage sounds, 5, 6, 14
Onstage action
sound cues and, 15–16
sound design and, 15–16
sound effects and, 38–39
Operator cue sheets, 65
Orton, Joe, *What the Butler Saw*, 22
Othello (Shakespeare), 45
Our Country's Good, 172
Our Town (Wilder), 6–7, 21

Outboard gear, 106
Outside contacts, 59–60
Overdesigning, 3
Overmyer, Eric
background of, 189
feedback from, 213, 214, 215, 217, 218, 222

P

Panning, as sound effect, 103, 158–161, 174–176
Pantomime, 4
Paper tech rehearsals, 133
Paperwork, 126
Peaslee, Richard
background of, 225
feedback from, 226, 232, 239, 242, 243, 250, 254, 259, 266, 269, 274, 281–282, 287
Penn, Arthur, 7–8
People's Art Theatre, 5–6
Phantom images, 34
Phrase, 61
Piano Sonata in D Major (K. 284) (Mozart), 61f
Piscator. Erwin, 7
Pitch range, of musical instruments, 39
Pitches, blending, 176–177
Playback
compact discs players and, 113–114
computer-assisted systems, 8–9, 9–10, 112, 115–116, 120f, 132, 158–163
devices for, 72–73, 103
of hard disk, 114
manually operated, 152–158, 153f
systems, 113–116
Playwrights
intent of, 14
musical indications by, 42, 44
musicians and, 5
Plots, sound. *See Sound plots*
Positional specificity, lack of, 34
Positions, in theatre companies, 85–92
Post-show shutdown, 150–152
Practicals
loudspeakers as, 184–185
music from practical sources, 19
overview of, 34, 116–117
realism of, 35, 147
volume of, 37
Preliminary sound plots, 48, 65–67, 66f

318

Prerecorded items
    blending of, 182–183
    sound cues, 14–15, 35, 110–111
    sound effects, 7, 42–43, 57
Preshows
    announcements and, 25
    cinematic design and, 20
    conventions of, 22–23
    overview of, 24–25
Presley, Elvis, 175–176
Preview rehearsals, 138–139
The Private Ear, 16, 30
Producers, 86
Production managers, 80, 86–87
Production meetings, 92
Production monitor loudspeakers, 123
Production sound mixers, 2, 91–92
Production stage managers,
    87–88
Progression of effects, 27
The Propheteers (Apple), 2
Public libraries, 54–55, 55

Q
QLab, 112–113, 161, 253, 280–281,
    283–284

R
Rasputin, 7
Rate of execution, of sound cueing,
    31–33
Realism
    of practical effects, 35, 147
    theatrical, 5–6, 6
Realistic approach
    sound design and, 19–21
    v. stylistic approach, 19
Recording engineers, 2
Reel-to-reel tape decks, 9–10
Reference books, 55
Rehearsals
    cue-to-cue, 135
    dress tech, 138
    dry tech, 137–138
    final, 139–140
    first tech, 134–136
    overview of, 118
    paper tech, 133
    previews, 138–139
    sound design and, 118–119
    technical, 8, 49, 121–127
Relative distance, of sound effects, 182

Removing, of an ambiance, 32
Renaissance, 4
Rental, of equipment, 92–93, 106–107
Representational form, 20–21
Required music, 27
Research
    composers and, 52–53
    on music, 44, 52, 54
Resources
    for music, 54–57
    for sound effects, 57–59
Restoration period of theatre, 5
Ritualistic gatherings, 4
Romantic period of theatre, 5
Ronan, Brian
    background of, 290
    feedback from, 290, 291, 292–293,
        294, 295, 295–296, 296–297, 298,
        299, 300, 301, 302, 303, 304, 305
Rosencrantz and Guildenstern Are Dead,
    68f
Rudner, Sara, 10
Rumble effects, 16
Running crew, 108–109

S
Safety, 130, 127
Samplers, 9–10, 114–115, 169–170
Savages, 33
Schubert, Franz, 26
Scripts
    actors and, 41
    directors and, 48, 44
    interpretation of, 44
    sound design and, 41–44
    sound designers and, 41–42, 51–52
The Seagull (Chekhov), 5–6
*The Search for Signs of Intelligent Life in
    the Universe*, 21
Segmentable music, 61–63
Segue, 27
Set designers, 13, 37–38
Set designs, 45
78s, 57
Sgt. Ola and His Followers (Lan), 14–15
Shakespeare, William
    A Comedy of Errors, 40
    Hamlet, 53
    Henry V, 10
    Julius Caesar, 53
    Love's Labour's Lost, 99
    Macbeth, 17, 18, 33, 53, 184

Shakespeare, William (*continued*)
   Measure for Measure, 66
   The Merchant of Venice, 27
   The Merry Wives of Windsor, 53
   A Midsummer Night's Dream, 53
   Much Ado About Nothing, 63–64
   Othello, 45
   plays of, 4, 12
   The Tempest, 167
   Twelfth Night, 53
Shaw, George Bernard, *Misalliance*, 51
Shutdown, post-show, 150–152
Sisterly Feelings (Ayckbourn), 41
A Small War on Murray Hill (Kanin), 7
Softening, of ambiance, 32
Sound booths
   computer-assisted playback systems
      and, 132
   isolation of, 123
   lighting in, 125–126
   windows of, 122–123
Sound cues
   assessing parameters of, 102–107
   balance of, 34–35
   characteristics of, 34–39
   computer-assisted playback systems
      and, 112, 158–163
   crossfading of, 73, 121, 174
   design process and, 14, 95
   development of, 7–8
   directors and, 49
   fading of, 32, 66, 178
   language chart for, 159f
   mixing of, 38
   numbers/letters for, 74f, 73–77
   onstage action and, 15–16
   overview of, 30–34
   prerecorded, 14–15, 35, 110–111
   rate of executing of, 31–33
   sheets for, 152–163, 153f, 157f
   stage managers and, 88–89
   summaries of, 68f, 74f, 76f, 77, 162f
   timings of, 178–180, 179f
   tone quality of, 34–35
   volume of, 31, 34
Sound delivery systems
   diagrams of, 128f, 129–130, 129f
   installation of, 127–131
   overview of, 96, 103, 144–145
Sound design
   budgets for, 48, 49–50
   changes in, 136–137

computer-assisted playback systems
   and, 8–9, 9–10
development of, 4–11
digital audio workstations and, 8–9,
   9–10, 49, 113
directors and, 15, 46
evolution of, 1
foundation of, 12
line indications and, 43
onstage action and, 15–16
realistic approach to, 19–21
rehearsals and, 118–119
scripts and, 41–44
stage directions and, 5, 42–43
stage managers and, 15, 67, 139–140
stylistic approach to, 21–22
stylistic v. realistic approaches to, 19
theatrical forms/styles of, 19–22
Sound designers
   composers and, 11
   crediting of, 8, 12, 13
   design process and, 1, 3, 4, 224–225
   directors and, 13, 14, 47–49
   duties of, 2
   equipment and, 8–9, 9–10
   fees for, 49–50
   scope of job of, 50
   scripts and, 41–42, 51–52
   sound operators and, 141–142, 152
Sound effects, 6, 11
   archiving of, 58
   choosing, 44–45
   conventions of, 22–30
   informative characteristics of, 44–45
   length of, 29–30
   libraries of, 57–58
   licensing of, 60–61
   live, 34, 42–43
   mixing of, 38–39
   onstage action and, 38–39
   panning, 158–161, 174–176
   prerecorded, 7, 42–43, 57
   recording your own, 99–102
   relative distance of, 182
   resources for, 57–59
   stylized, 169–171
   unidentifiable, 171–172
   volume of, 38
Sound engineers
   assistants, 90
   duties of, 2, 90
Sound images, 13

320

Sound operators
  duties of, 2, 9, 91
  sound designers and, 141–142, 152
  training of, 163–164
Sound plots
  computer-assisted playback systems and, 120f
  design process and, 97, 98f
  for loudspeakers, 76f, 77–79
  overview of, 74f, 95
  preliminary, 48, 65–67, 66f
  subsequent, 67–72, 70f
  working, 48, 72–73
Sound reinforcement, 288
Sound sequences, complex, 172–173
Sound sources, 72–73
Sound supervisors, 2, 90
Sound technicians, 2
Soundchecks, 80–81, 91, 143–148
Sounds
  appropriateness of, 18
  blending, live and prerecorded, 182–183
  characteristics of, 13, 16
  commentary, 24
  environmental, 4
  function and intent of, 14–15
  human reaction to, 16–17
  location of, 33–34
  movement of, 33–34
  offstage, 5, 6, 14
  subliminal, 4, 171
  transitional, 22–23, 23, 26–27
Special effects, 80
Specific cues, 22–23, 23, 27–30
Splitting tracks, 112
Spot effects
  ambient effects and, 28–29
  overview of, 27, 28, 29
Stage directions, and sound design, 5, 42–43
Stage managers
  duties of, 7, 88–89
  sound cues and, 88–89
  sound design and, 15, 67, 139–140
Stands, for microphones, 102
Stanislavsky, Constantin, 5–6
Storage space, 126
Striking the show, 166
Styles, of music, 52
Stylistic approach

v. realistic approach, 19
to sound design, 21–22
Stylized sound effects, 169–171
Stylized theatrical form, 21
Subliminal sounds, 4, 171
Subwoofers, 16
Supplies, for writing, 126
Swados, Elizabeth
  background of, 225
  feedback from, 226–227, 233, 239, 242, 245, 250, 256, 259, 266, 269–270, 276, 277, 287
Sweeteners, 29
Synthesizers, 9, 22

T

Tableau, final, 33
Tape recorders, 7
Tartuffe, 44
The Tavern, 28
Tech position, 131–133
Technical directors, 89–90
Technical rehearsals, 8, 49, 121–127
The Tempest (Shakespeare), 167
Theatre companies, positions in, 85–92
Theatrical design, 1–2
Theatrical forms/styles, of sound design, 19–22
Theatrical realism, 5–6, 6
Thematic music, 26
Thompson, Tazewell
  background of, 188
  feedback from, 190, 191–192, 195, 196–197, 198, 199, 202, 204, 207–209, 210–211
Thunder runs, 5
Timbre, 35–36
Timelines, for music, 53–54
Timings
  appropriateness of, 43
  final, 49
  of sound cues, 178–180, 179f
Tomlin, Lily, 21
Tone quality, and sound cues, 34–35
Tonight at 8:30 (Coward), 26
Tony Awards, 81–82
Top-of-show preset, 148–150, 149f, 151f
A Touch of the Poet, 20, 29, 35–36
Touring considerations, 93–94, 164–165
Tracks, 73
Training, of sound operator, 163–164

321

Transitional sounds/music
  conventions of, 22–23, 23
  dialogue and, 26–27
  overview of, 26–27
Turntables, 7
Twelfth Night (Shakespeare), 53
Two-channel panning, 175

U

U. S. A. (stage play), 16
Underscoring
  compressing, 178
  conventions of, 22–23
  overview of, 25–26
Unidentifiable sound effects,
    171–172
Union rules, 93–94, 127
United Scenic Artists, 82
Unseen characters, 14–15

V

Van Bergan, Jim
  background of, 225–226
  feedback from, 236–237, 241, 244,
    247, 250, 256, 266, 270, 275–276,
    278, 284–285, 287
Very low frequency (VLF), 16–17, 169
Victory at Sea, 44–45
Vision, 12
Visual artists, 13

VLF. *See Very low frequency*
Voice processing, for actors, 180
Voiceovers, 24, 27, 30, 180
Volume
  ambiance and, 31
  cueing and, 31
  levels of, 31, 133–134, 165
  of music, 31, 145
  of practicals, 37
  of sound cues, 31, 34
  of sound effects, 38

W

WAVs, 100–101
What the Butler Saw (Orton), 22
Who's Afraid of Virginia Woolf, 181
Wikipedia, 54
Wilder, Thornton, *Our Town*, 6–7, 21
The William Tell Overture, 24
Williams, Tennessee, *The Night of the
    Iguana*, 29, 34
Windows, of sound booth, 122–123
Working effects.. *See Practicals*
Working sound plots, 48, 72–73
Writing supplies, 126

Z

Zaks, Jerry
  background of, 188
  feedback from, 191, 194, 196, 198, 199,
    201, 205

322